PHILOSOPHICAL PSYCHOLOGY IN ARABIC THOUGHT AND THE LATIN ARISTOTELIANISM OF THE 13 TH CENTURY

DERNIÈRES PARUTIONS
DANS LA MÊME COLLECTION

A CATALOGUE OF 13TH-CENTURY SOPHISMATA. Part I : Introduction and Indices ; Part II : Catalogue, by Sten EBBESEN and Frédéric GOUHIER, 2010.

ABÉLARD Pierre, *De l'unité et de la trinité divines (Theologia summi boni)*. Introduction, traduction et notes par Jean JOLIVET, 2001.

ALBERT LE GRAND, *Métaphysique. Livre XII, Traités II et III*. Texte (latin et français en vis-à-vis), introduit, traduit et annoté par Isabelle MOULIN, 2009, 480 pages.

AVERROÈS, *La béatitude de l'âme*. Édition, traduction annotée, études doctrinales et historiques d'un traité d' "Averroès" par Marc GEOFFROY et Carlos STEEL, 2001.

– *Commentaire moyen sur le* De interpretatione. Introduction, traduction et notes par Ali BENMAKHLOUF et Stéphane DIEBLER, 2000.

– *Grand Commentaire (Tafsîr) de la* Métaphysique. *Livre Bêta*. Présentation et traduction de Laurence BAULOYE précédé de *Averroès et les apories de la* Métaphysique *d'Aristote*, 2002.

BRENET Jean-Baptiste, *Transferts du sujet. La noétique selon Jean de Jandun*, 2003.

CESALLI Laurent, *Le réalisme propositionnel. Sémantique et ontologie des propositions chez Jean Duns Scot, Gauthier Burley, Richard Brinkley et Jean Wyclif*, 2007.

DEMANGE Dominique, *Jean Duns Scot. La théorie du savoir*, 2007.

GUIRAL OT, *La vision de Dieu aux multiples formes*. Quolibet tenu à Paris en décembre 1333. Édition, traduction et introduction par Christian TROTTMANN, 2001.

IBN KAMMUNA, *Examen de la critique des trois religions monothéistes*. Avant-propos et traduction par Simon BELLAHSEN, précédé de *La vie, l'œuvre et la pensée philosophique d'Ibn Kammuna*, par Réza Pourjavady et Sabine Schmidtke, 2012, 206 pages.

LA *SOPHISTRIA* DE ROBERTUS ANGLICUS. Étude et édition critique par A. GRONDEUX et I. ROSIER-CATACH, 2006.

LE PROBLÈME DES UNIVERSAUX À LA FACULTÉ DES ARTS DE PARIS ENTRE 1230 ET 1260. Édition critique sélective, traduction française, analyses structurelle et formelle et étude historico-philosophique par David PICHÉ, 2005.

MAÏMONIDE, *Les brouillons autographes du* Dalâlat al-Hâ'irîn *(Guide des égarés)*. Édition par C. SIRAT et S. DI DONATO, 2012.

NICOLAS D'AUTRÉCOURT, *Correspondance, Articles condamnés*. Édition critique par L. M. de RIJK, introduction, traduction et notes par Ch. GRELLARD, 2001.

PERINI-SANTOS Ernesto, *La théorie ockhamienne de la connaissance évidente*, 2006.

SIRAT Colette et GEOFFROY Marc, *L'original arabe du* Grand commentaire *d'Averroès au* De anima *d'Aristote. Prémices de l'édition*, 2005.

TISSERANT Axel, *Pars theologica. Logique et théologique chez Boèce*, 2008.

VALENTE Luisa, *Logique et théologie. Les écoles parisiennes entre 1150 et 1220*, 2008.

SIC ET NON

Directeur : Alain de LIBERA

PHILOSOPHICAL PSYCHOLOGY IN ARABIC THOUGHT AND THE LATIN ARISTOTELIANISM OF THE 13 TH CENTURY

Edited by

Luis Xavier LÓPEZ-FARJEAT

Jörg Alejandro TELLKAMP

PARIS
LIBRAIRIE PHILOSOPHIQUE J. VRIN
6, place de la Sorbonne, Ve

2013

Imprimé en France

ISSN 1248-7279
ISBN 978-2-7116-2461-4

www.vrin.fr

CONTENTS

ACKNOWLEDGEMENTS

The papers gathered in this volume were initially presented at the conference "Philosophical Psychology in Arabic and Latin Aristotelianism" in Mexico City, May 29th and 30th of 2008, held at the Universidad Panamericana. Despite the surrounding chaos and noise in a city of 20 million inhabitants, we could find a place of peace and quite in which to discuss the papers in a constructive and friendly atmosphere. We, the organizers of the conference, were especially happy that many renowned scholars followed our invitation to discuss topics on perception, intellect and soul in Medieval Arabic and Latin traditions.

The conference would have been impossible without funding from the Mexican Council for Science and Technology (Conacyt, J49596-H). The Faculty of Philosophy of the Universidad Panamericana provided support, the venue and much-needed coffee. Thanks are also due to a group of graduate and undergraduate students of the Faculty, especially to María del Carmen Elvira. Daniel Vázquez's help was greatly appreciated, since he prepared the manuscript, and proofread and formatted the articles.

INTRODUCTION

There seems to be little doubt that in the first half of the 13 th century, the reception of Aristotle's *De anima* was in fact more of a reception of Avicenna's *De anima* and Averroes's *Long Commentary on the De anima* [1]. Albert the Great acknowledged this much when he thought that the definition of soul based on the *translatio arabica*, i.e. Averroes's *Long Commentary*, is more coherent than the one stated in the *translatio graeca*, which is really Jacob of Venice's *translatio vetus* [2]. Albert's marginal note is, however, significant, because it highlights the fact that Arabic models of explanation of the soul were considered to be superior to what was thought

1. See H. Daiber, "Lateinische Übersetzungen arabischer Texte zur Philosophie und ihre Bedeutung für die Scholastik des Mittelalters", in Hamesse, J. and Fattori, M. (eds.), *Rencontres des Cultures dans la philosophie médiévale,* Louvain-la-Neuve/Cassino 1990, 203-250; Puig, J., "The Transmission and Reception of Arabic Philosophy in Christian Spain (until 1200)", in Butterworth, Ch. and Kessel, B. (eds.), *The Introduction of Arabic Philosophy into Europe*, Leiden 1994, 7-30.

2. ALBERTUS MAGNUS, *De anima* I, 1, 4 (ed. Colon. 7, 1), 8, 59-80: "Quod autem haec vera sint, quae dicta sunt, testatur Aristotelis translatio Arabica, quae sic dicit: *Et debemus praeservare nos, ne ignoremus, utrum diffinitio eius sit eadem ut diffinitio vivi aut sit alia in quolibet, verbi gratia diffinitio equi et canis et hominis et dei; vivum autem universale aut nihil est aut est postremum.* Et hoc exponit Averroes, sicut hic dictum est. Graeca autem translatio discordat ab hac et, ut puto, est mendosa. Habet enim sic: *Videndum autem, quatenus non lateat, utrum una ratio ipsius sit an sicut animalis est secundum unumquodque altera.* Et si deberet concordare cum Arabica, sic deberet habere: 'utrum una ratio ipsius sit sicut animalis an sit secundum unumquodque altera'; tunc enim plana esset. Sed quia in multis invenimus Graecas emendatiores quam Arabicas translationes, ideo et hoc sustinentes dicimus, quod animalis est una ratio ut generis. Si autem animal secundum esse sumitur in unoquoque, tunc variatur esse eius differentiis specierum sibi adiunctis, et tunc sic variatum habet alteram et alteram secundum hoc esse diffinitionem. Et licet hoc sit verum, tamen primum magis conveniens ad propositum est".

to be the plain Aristotelian text, obviously before William Moerbeke provided a new translation of the *De anima*.

Evidence for the predominant presence of Arabic thought in 13th century accounts of the soul, perception and intellect is abundant. At least from John Blund's *De anima* onwards do we know that Avicenna exerted a fundamental influence, which in some sense competed with the reception of Averroes's *Long Commentary on the De anima*, which started in the 1220s.

There has recently been a number of outstanding publications on the reception and development of the *De anima*, focusing on issues like intentionality, perception, representation, the soul, etc.[3]. What those publications have in common is that they take strong diachronic stance, since the articles they contain analyze the concepts at stake from Antiquity to Early Modern thought. Having this in mind, and from a historical point of view, the focus of this volume is purposely narrower, in the sense that there are only two identifiable periods of philosophy present: Arabic thought, mainly Avicenna's and Averroes's, and the Latin thought of the 13th century, including John Duns Scotus's *Quaestiones super secundum et tertium De anima*, which was probably written in the early 1290s[4].

The aim of this volume is to draw attention to the "first critical encounter" (Taylor) of Latin philosophers with Arabic conceptions of the soul and their powers. Thematically there are two topics that form the backbone of this volume: perception and intellect. Both show that Avicenna's and Averroes's reading of Aristotle is original insofar as they interpret the *De anima* based upon theoretical presuppositions handed down by commentators and philosophers with a strong Neoplatonic and Peripatetic influence. The Latin reception of the Arabic understanding of the *De anima* yields an amalgamated stance toward Aristotle. On the one hand it becomes clear that important portions of Arabic thought were assimilated in an affirmative fashion, sign of which is the use of theories of intentionality, intellection and inner senses, among others. On the other hand it is equally obvious that criticism arose due to basic tenets of the

3. D. PERLER (ed.), *Ancient and Medieval Theories of Intentionality*, Leiden 2001 and Vivarium 2008; Lagerlund, H. (ed.), *Forming the Mind. Essays on the Internal Senses and the Mind/Body Problem from Avicenna to the Medical Enlightment*, Dordrecht 2007; S. KNUUTILLA (ed.), *Theories of Perception in Medieval and Early Modern Philosophy*, Dordrecht 2008.

4. See "Introduction", in John DUNS SCOTUS, *Quaestiones super secundum et tertium de anima*, eds. B. C. Bazán et al., Opera philosophica vol. 5, Washington D.C./St. Bonaventure 2006, 143*.

Christian faith, which can best be seen in Aquinas's discussion of the unity of the intellect and the ontological status of the human soul. Thus, it becomes apparent that philosophical approaches, which are rooted in different theological traditions, are nourished by the same source: Aristotle.

In his article "From Arabic into Latin into Hebrew: Aristotelian Psychology and its Contribution to the Rationalisation of Theological Traditions", Alexander Fidora analyzes the prologues of Avendauth/Gundissalinus' translation of Avicenna's *De anima* and on Archdeacon of Cuéllar's *Tractatus de anima*, both significant examples of the reception of the Aristotelian psychology and its impact on the Latin-Christian and Jewish philosophical contexts of the 13th and 14th centuries. Fidora shows how the Aristotelian psychology became the basis for a philosophical reformulation of some central doctrines within different theological traditions, for example the incorporality of the soul.

The next three articles focus on Avicenna. In "New Light on Avicenna: Optics and its Role in Avicennan Theories of Vision, Cognition and Emanation", Jon McGinnis advances an interpretation of one of the most obscure passages in Aristotle's *De anima.* In III, 5, 430a10-17 Aristotle sustains that the active intellect functions as light. According to McGinnis the different interpretations of this passage depend on different theories of light and the various roles that light plays in the theories of vision. Following the optical advances of his time, Avicenna formulated an un-Aristotelian theory of light and vision that provides an innovative and better model for understanding the similarities between the active intellect and light. In "Rational Imagination: Avicenna on the Cogitative Power", Deborah Black gives a detailed account of the cogitative faculty and its peculiar status among the internal sense powers. Black argues that Avicenna offers a hybrid characterization of the cogitative that reflects his dualist and emanationist position. Finally, Luis Xavier López-Farjeat develops an Avicennan theory of musical perception. In his paper he explores the way in which musical creation and musical appreciation are tied to the activity of the internal sense powers such as imagination and the estimative.

The aim of Jean-Baptiste Brenet's paper, "Acquisition de la pensée et acquisition de l'acte chez Averroès. Une lecture croisée du *Grand Commentaire* au *De anima* et du *Kitāb al-Kašf'an manāhij al-adilla*" is to shed light on two theses found in Averroes's work. First he examines the notion of acquisition and attribution in the *Long Commentary on the De anima* and secondly he contrasts it with the theological conception of acquisition in *Kašf 'an manāhiğ al-adilla*. In doing so, he argues that Averroes's understanding of acquisition in the *Long Commentary* has to be read in light of the *Kašf*.

Richard C. Taylor puts forward an analysis of Aquinas's understanding of the intellect in his *Scriptum super Sententiis* (1252-1257) in book 2, d. 17, q. 2, a. 1, emphasizing the critical dialogue with philosophers of the Arabic/Islamic (Avicenna, Avempace, Averroes) and Greek traditions (Theophrastus, Alexander of Aphrodisias, Themistius). Taylor argues that Aquinas drew primarily on two philosophical sources, Averroes's *Long Commentary on the De anima* and the Latin translation of Avicenna's *De anima*. His analysis focuses on the use Aquinas makes of Averroes by calling attention to the positive influences, the critical rejections but also to important limitations and misunderstandings of Aquinas's comprehension of his main Arabic source. "Aquinas and the Arabs: Aquinas's First Critical Encounter with the Doctrines of Avicenna and Averroes on the Intellect, *In 2 Sent.* d. 17, q. 2, a. 1" includes an Appendix with the English translation of *In 2 Sent*. d. 17, q. 2, a. 1 basedon the provisional Latin text preparedby the late P.-M. Gils, O. P.

In "Avicenna's *Metaphysics* and Duns Scotus' *Quaestiones super secundum et tertium De anima*", Thérèse-Anne Druart examines the influence of Avicenna in Duns Scotus's conception of metaphysics and in his notion of the univocity of being. In a recent paper, Jan A. Aertsen has intended to show how the *Avicenna Latinus* influenced medieval philosophers, including Duns Scotus. However, as Druart observes, Aertsen omits the *Quaestiones super secundum et tertium De anima*. Thus, she focuses on this last work, mainly on *quaestio* 21 and *quaestio* 16, discussing the way in which Duns Scotus understands Avicenna's doctrine of the primary metaphysical notions to ground his own univocity of being.

"Albert the Great on Perception and Non-conceptual Content" by Jörg Alejandro Tellkamp stresses the interest Albert the Great had in establishing an account of how animals, including human beings, arrive at a complex, intentional perceptual grasp of the external world. Building on Avicenna's theory of intentionality, Albert thinks that animal perception does not require the active use of concepts, despite the fact that the content of perception can be said to be true or false, i.e. adequate or inadequate in a predominantly practical sense. The cases Albert examines in his *De animalibus* point not only at perceptual intentionality, they also indicate that some higher animals, e.g. primates, display quasi-rational activities, that reach from some kind of deliberation regarding actions to the use of incomplete syllogisms.

Jerry Hackett in "Bacon on Animal Cognition and his Reception of Avicenna" considers that Roger Bacon expounds in the *Perspectiva* a view that explains how common sense and scientific knowledge comes from knowing *per experientiam*. Bacon follows Augustine in emphasizing vision as the primary sense, but he also recurs to the teachings of the experts on *Perspectiva,* Natural Philosophy, the Philosophy of Mind (Aristotle, Avicenna, Averroes) and the Medical Thinkers (Constantine, Avicenna). Thus, he offers a synthesis of the teachings on vision and perception, which is based on a model of vision to such an extent that even sensory activities such as hearing must ultimately be verified on the basis of vision. Animal knowledge has to be seen in the context of a theory of vision, and hence as prior to rational knowledge.

Finally, Bernardo Carlos Bazán in "A Body for the Human Soul" discusses Aquinas's doctrine of the human body contrasting his theological understanding of the soul with his naturalistic conception of the body. Examining various passages from the *Corpus Thomisticum*, Bazán singles out several contradictions and philosophical inconsistencies that obscure Aquinas's purpose of unifying the body and the soul.

FROM ARABIC INTO LATIN INTO HEBREW: ARISTOTELIAN PSYCHOLOGY AND ITS CONTRIBUTION TO THE RATIONALISATION OF THEOLOGICAL TRADITIONS *

Alexander FIDORA
(ICREA – Universitat Autònoma de Barcelona)

Toledo, reconquered in 1085 by Alphonse VI from Muslim domination, was beyond any doubt the gateway through which Graeco-Arabic Aristotelian psychology first reached the Latin West.

Among the impressive number of philosophical texts that were translated in the 12th century at the so-called Toledan School of Translators from Arabic into Latin there are several treatises explicitly concerned with the theory of the intellect and the soul. In particular, Dominicus Gundissalinus (1110-1190), Archdeacon of Cuéllar, translated, along with many other works, al-Kindī's and al-Fārābī's respective tracts on the intellect as well as Avicenna's *De anima* from the *Kitāb aš-šifā*. This latter was translated by Gundissalinus together with a certain Avendauth (i.e. Ibn Daūd), who should be identified with the famous Jewish philosopher Abraham Ibn Daūd [1].

*. This paper was written within the framework of the research project "Latin Philosophy into Hebrew: Intercultural Networks in 13th and 14th Century Europe" (200403), at the Autonomous University of Barcelona, with the financial support of the European Research Council under the European Community's Seventh Framework Programme. – I am grateful for the assistance of Henryk Anzulewicz (Bonn), John N. Crossley (Melbourne) and Yossef Schwartz (Barcelona/Tel Aviv).

1. This identification was first advanced by D'ALVERNY (1954-1956), 19-43. Ibn Daūd's chief work, the *Book of the Exalted Faith* (*Emunah ramah*), being strongly influenced by Avicenna, d'Alverny's suggestion has generally been accepted by Ibn Daūd scholars; see, e.g., G. D. Cohen in his introduction to ABRAHAM IBN DAŪD, *A Critical Edition with a Translation and Notes of the Book of Tradition*, XXVII-XXVIII, and FONTAINE (1990), 262-263.

Apart from these translations, Gundissalinus also wrote important works on his own [2], namely *De unitate et uno*, *De processione mundi*, *De divisione philosophiae*, and a treatise *De immortalitate animae*, as well as a *Tractatus de anima*, the latter revealing his paramount interest in psychology. Relying on Arabic as well as Latin sources, Gundissalinus's works represent original, and often pioneering, contributions to the history of philosophy. This is true not only with regard to ontology and metaphysics (with the introduction of the term *metaphysica* to the Latin West) [3], as well as epistemology (giving up the traditional *ordo scientiarum*, i.e. the scheme of the liberal arts, in favour of an Aristotelian division of the sciences) [4], but also in the domain of psychology: thus Gundissalinus's *Tractatus de anima* has to be considered the first instance of a Latin reception of Avicenna's psychology as laid out in the latter's *De anima*, also known as *Sextus de naturalibus*.

Not only is Gundissalinus therefore the translator, or rather co-translator, of Avicenna's *De anima*, but he is also the first interpreter of this translation. In fact, Gundissalinus's interpretation of Avicenna's psychology has given rise, over the last eighty years, to a lengthy and polemical discussion, ever since Étienne Gilson suggested reading the *Tractatus* as an expression of what he called the "Augustinisme avicennisant" [5]. In Gilson's eyes, the most distinctive trace of Gundissalinus's reading of Avicenna was his identification of the agent intellect with God, an identification that would have combined genuinely Avicennian ideas, namely the role of the agent intellect within the process of human knowledge, with an Augustinian perspective locating the seminal ideas in the mind of God. As is well known, the French philosopher's interpretation on this point was immediately contested by Roland de Vaux, who suggested the alternative

On the other hand R. Lemay's criticism appears confused and pointless: *cf.* LEMAY (1987), 408-427.

2. For a detailed study of the Toledan Archdeacon and his thought FIDORA (2003).

3. *Cf.* FIDORA (2004).

4. See the introduction to and edition of DOMINICUS GUNDISSALINUS, *Über die Einteilung der Philosophie / De divisione philosophiae*, ed. Fidora / Werner.

5. *Cf.* GILSON (1929-1930), especially p. 85: "En réalité, il suffit de le suivre [sc. Gundissalinus] jusqu'au bout pour constater que, dans sa pensée, l'illumination de l'âme par l'Intelligence agente d'Avicenne fait place à l'illumination de l'âme par Dieu. C'est pourquoi, conservant jusqu'à la lettre même de son modèle, il n'a pas un seul instant l'impression de s'engager dans une voie scabreuse, et c'est avec une étrange inconscience qu'il devient l'initiateur de l'augustinisme avicennisant".

denomination of an "Avicennisme latin"[6]. It is not our intention to enter into this debate in the present paper; nor does it seem necessary, since the question has recently been revisited in a very convincing paper by Steven Marrone, who argues that this identification need not be accounted for with recourse to Augustine, for similar identifications are already present in Arabic texts, namely in al-Ġazālī's *Maqāṣid al-falāsifa*, which was translated by Gundissalinus himself[7].

Rather than taking up this somewhat tedious question, we shall focus on a completely different aspect of Gundissalinus's translation of Avicenna's *De anima* and his interpretation of this very text, namely the philosophical motivations for the Archdeacon's interest in Graeco-Arabic Aristotelian psychology, and its consequences. For this purpose we would like to draw attention to the respective prologues of Avendauth/Gundissalinus's translation of Avicenna's *De anima*, as well as that of the Archdeacon's own *Tractatus de anima*. In the dedicatory prologue that accompanies the translation of Avicenna's *De anima*, addressed to Archbishop John of Toledo, Avendauth and Gundissalinus set out by drawing a gloomy picture of their times, in which men trusted their senses alone and were no longer able to perceive their souls and themselves, and were thus incapable of loving God. So it happens, they write, that:

> men, who have abandoned themselves to the senses, either believe that the soul is nothing or, when they guess its existence from the movement of the body, most hold what it is by faith, and only very few do so by reason. [...] Therefore, Lord, I have taken care of your demand to translate this book on the soul by the philosopher Avicenna, in order that, through your generosity and my work, the Latins may attain certainty about that which until now was not known to them, namely proving by true reasons that the soul exists and what and how it is according to itself and to its effects[8].

6. *Cf.* DE VAUX (1934), with a partial edition of Gundissalinus's *Tractatus de anima*. De Vaux's suggestion was also subject to criticism, see BERTOLA (1971).

7. See MARRONE (2006). For a similar strand of argument *cf.* TEICHER (1934), 252-258.

8. AVICENNA, *Liber de anima seu Sextus de naturalibus*, ed. van Riet, vol. 1, 3-4: "Unde homines sensibus dediti, aut animam nihil esse credunt, aut si forte ex motum corporis eam esse coniiciunt, quid vel qualis sit plerique fide tenent, sed pauci ratione convincunt. [...] Quapropter iussum vestrum, Domine, de transferendo libro Avicennae philosophi de anima, effectui mancipare curavi, ut vestro munere et meo labore, Latinis fieret certum, quod hactenus existit incognitum, scilicet an sit anima, et quid et qualis sit secundum essentiam et effectum, rationibus verissimis comprobatum".

These words of the two translators, which can be read as a philosophical declaration of intention, are echoed by Gundissalinus in his *Tractatus de anima*, where the Archdeacon again emphasises the necessity of a rational examination of the contents of faith, in particular the existence of the soul and its nature. So, at the very beginning of this treatise, we read:

> While all men are composed equally by soul and body, nevertheless not all of them have as much certainty concerning their soul as they have concerning their body. This is so because the latter is an object of the senses, while the soul can be reached only through the intellect. Therefore men who have abandoned themselves completely to the senses, either believe that the soul is nothing or, if perhaps they guess its existence from the movement of the body in whatever manner, many hold what it is or how it is by faith only, but very few know this by reason. [...] This being so, I have found reasoned argument among philosophers, and have taken care to collect this in one single treatise. Thus this work, which was ignored by the Latins up to now, being concealed in Greek and Arabic archives, is given to the Latins so that believers, who work so hard for their souls, get to know about the soul not only by faith but also through reason [9].

This passage literally coincides with Avendauth and Gundissalinus's prologue to their translation of Avicenna's *De anima*. Yet its phrasing is even more radical: the contents of faith shall not only be believed in, but they need to be grounded on philosophical reasoning: "non iam fide tantum, sed etiam ratione comprehendant".

There can be no doubt that both prologues formulate a decidedly philosophical programme, namely incorporating the contribution of Graeco-Arabic Aristotelian psychology into the formation of a rational theology which should be based on a philosophical reflection upon its central tenets. This being the translators' and the author's ambitious programme, one can of course ask whether it had any impact on, or consequences for, the history of both philosophy and theology.

9. DOMINICUS GUNDISSALINUS, *Tractatus de anima*, ed. Alonso del Real / Soto Bruna, 64-66: "Cum omnes homines aeque constent ex anima et corpore, non tamen omnes sic certi sunt de anima sicut de corpore; quippe cum hoc sensui subiaceat, ad animam vero non nisi solus intellectus attingat. Unde homines solis sensibus dediti aut animam nihil esse credunt, aut, si forte ex motu corporis eam utcumque esse coniciunt, quod sit vel quomodo se habeat plerique fide tenent, sed paucissimi ratione convincunt [...]. Quapropter quicquid de anima apud philosophos rationabiliter dictum inveni, simul in unum colligere curavi. Opus siquidem latinis hactenus incognitum utpote in archivis [MSS C, P: arcanis] graecae et arabicae tantum linguae reconditum [...] ad notitiam latinorum est deductum ut fideles, qui pro anima tam studiose laborant, quid de ipsa sentire debeant, non iam fide tantum, sed etiam ratione comprehendant".

ALBERT THE GREAT'S PHILOSOPHICAL TRANSFORMATION OF THE THEOLOGICAL DISCOURSE ON THE SOUL

To answer this question in general would of course far surpass the scope of this paper; especially with regard to Avicenna. His role for later medieval philosophy has been dealt with in several monographs published in recent years, such as the excellent survey by Dag Nikolaus Hasse: *Avicenna's 'De anima' in the Latin West* [10]. The focus in this paper will be more modest: we will present two early – and in our eyes highly significant – examples of the reception of the psychological texts translated and produced in Toledo: one concerning their impact on the Latin-Christian tradition, and the other revealing their strong influence in the Jewish philosophical circles of the 13 th and 14 th centuries.

We shall start with the Latin-Christian case, since it is first chronologically. In fact, the Latin reception of Gundissalinus's translations and his own psychological doctrine can be traced back to the end of the 12 th or the beginning of the 13 th century, when John Blund wrote his *Tractatus de anima*, which draws strongly on both Avicenna's *De anima* and Gundissalinus's *Tractatus de anima* [11]. Yet the first explicit reference to Gundissalinus's treatise is to be found in the anonymous treatise *De anima et potentiis eius* (ca. 1225), edited by René-Antoine Gauthier, where we read: *Toletanum autem translator utrumque intelligit esse ponendum in definitione animae* [i.e., that it is a potency of an organic body, A.F.] [12].

Most important among the Latin recipients of Gundissalinus's psychological translations and works is Albert the Great. Although the 19 th-century Paris edition of his works disguised the presence of our philosopher by misreading the Latin "Toletanus" consistently as "Collectanus", it is nevertheless not at all difficult to identify large portions from both Gundissalinus's translation of Avicenna and his *Tractatus de anima* among Albert's very early writings, namely in his *De homine* [13].

10. HASSE (2000).

11. A comprehensive study of this work and its place in the history of philosophical psychology can be found in D. Werner's edition: JOHN BLUND, *Tractatus de anima*, ed. Werner, see her introduction p. 9-93.

12. GAUTHIER (1982), 29.

13. As H. Anzulewicz and J. R. Söder have done in their recent critical edition of the text published within the *Editio Coloniensis* of Albert's works. Parts of *De homine* have also been published in a Latin-German selection of texts: ALBERTUS MAGNUS, *Über den Menschen*, ed. Anzulewicz / Söder.

This work is the second part of Albert's *Summa de creaturis*, which is preceded by *De IV coaequaevis*, and was written before Albert started his studies in theology in Paris, viz. in the early 1240s, either in Paris or still in Cologne.

As such, the *Summa de creaturis* is a work that is theological in substance, dealing in its first part with the creation of prime matter, the heavens, time and the angels, and then turning, in its second part, to human beings and their psychological constitution. Through its form and contents the *Summa de creaturis* has to be seen in continuity with Albert's earlier works: *De sacramentis*, *De incarnatione* and *De resurrectione*. This is also true for the second part of the work, which we shall focus on, that is *De homine*, where Albert's approach is clearly oriented towards the analysis of the pre-lapsarian constitution of man. Nevertheless, and this is of great importance for our discussion, from the very first pages onwards, Albert introduces into this theological treatise on man a markedly philosophical perspective.

We shall illustrate this by a short glance at the fundamental question that Albert tackles right at the beginning of *De homine*: namely whether the soul is a substance or not. This is, as Albert says, a question that concerns its definition; and in order to solve this question he sets out by distinguishing two kinds of definitions of the soul: *Ponantur primo definitiones sanctorum et postea philosophorum*[14], in other words, he distinguishes theological and philosophical definitions. Accordingly, in what follows, Albert lists different definitions by the saints, i.e. Christian theologians, such as Augustine, St Bernard and others, who maintain that the soul is a substance. Subsequently these opinions are contrasted with opposing views, taken from the secular tradition. Now, before giving his own solution to the question, which will consist of a differentiation of a logical, a physical and a metaphysical approach to the soul and its definition, Albert turns explicitly to the arguments of the philosophers, which he promised at the beginning of this article, saying: *Sed in contrarium arguunt philosophi sic*; the philosophers are thus invoked to invalidate the opposing arguments to the saints' views and to prepare Albert's own reply.

Now, who are these "philosophers"? One of the arguments Albert produces under this title stems from Avicenna and his *Sextus de naturalibus* claiming that the proper subject of the soul can only be what it is through the soul itself and that therefore it must be a substance. In addition, he also quotes a certain Constabulus, i.e. Qusṭā Ibn Lūqā and his

14. ALBERTUS MAGNUS, *De homine* (Ed. Colon. 27, 2), 8.

De differentia spiritus et animae, a work that may have been translated with the participation of Gundissalinus. Gundissalinus included some of its arguments in his *Tractatus de anima*, among which is the argument referred to in this place by Albert. According to this argument whatever receives opposite influences and remains one and the same, is a substance, and since the soul is subject to opposite virtues and vices it must therefore be a substance. Next, we also find an explicit reference to Gundissalinus himself among the philosophical arguments listed by Albert. Thus we read:

> So says the Toledan: Whatever exists is either a substance or an accident. But nothing which through its presence constitutes a species of a substance and when it withdraws destroys it, is an accident. Yet, the different species of the soul through their presence constitute the species of the plant, of the animal and of man, and when they withdraw, they destroy it. Therefore each species of the soul is a substance [15].

There remain three further philosophical arguments in favour of the soul's being a substance, but they are not attributed to any philosopher in particular.

Thus, from the six philosophical arguments given, the three that Albert singles out by a clear attribution can be traced back to Gundissalinus and his translations and writings, which makes the Toledan philosopher an important point of reference for Albert's explicitly philosophical approach to anthropological and psychological questions. The extraordinary role that Gundissalinus plays for Albert's *De homine* is clearly confirmed by the further development of his treatise in which references to the Toledan philosopher, together with his psychological translations and writings, abound.

Thus, at another place, Albert, using the very same procedure of confronting theological and philosophical claims, poses the question of the soul's incorporality. Quoting once more Augustine and St Bernard, he states that the soul must be corporeal, one argument being that the angels seem to possess a body. To refute this position, Albert again quotes Qusṭā

15. ALBERTUS MAGNUS, *De homine* (Ed. Colon. 27, 2), 10: "Item Toletanus: Quicquid est, aut est substantia aut accidens. Nihil autem quod adveniens constituit speciem substantiae et recedens destruit eandem, est accidens; quaelibet species animae adveniens constituit speciem plantae, animalis et hominis, et recedens destruit eandem; ergo quaelibet species animae est substantia". *Cf.* DOMINICUS GUNDISSALINUS, *Tractatus de anima*, ed. Alonso del Real / Soto Bruna, 84: "Item quicquid est, aut est substantia aut accidens. Sed anima non est accidens. Nihil enim quod adveniens constituit et recedens destruit, accidens est; sed anima adveniens constituit animal et recedens destruit; ergo anima non est accidens; est igitur substantia".

Ibn Lūqā, listing five arguments from his *De differentia spiritus et animae* in favour of the soul's incorporality. At the end of this series of arguments, he remarks: "These are Ibn Lūqā's reasons. And some of them can also be found in the Toledan author, and he added one to them, which is taken from Avicenna, and which concerns the rational soul as such". According to this additional argument the intellectual species cannot be in the intellect as in a body[16]. Now, in his own solution to the question, Albert clearly sides with the philosophers, reinterpreting the authoritative statements of the saints, as he calls them, in a way that allows him to reconcile their position with the incorporality of the soul.

This discussion of the soul's incorporality not only gives us a taste of the complex argumentative balance Albert establishes between theological and philosophical approaches in *De homine*. Moreover, the text we have just quoted reveals Albert's awareness of the intricate connections between the different Toledan texts he is handling: on the one hand the influence of Qusṭā Ibn Lūqā's *De differentia spiritus et animae* on Gundissalinus's *Tractatus de anima*, which does indeed draw strongly on this text, and, on the other hand, Gundissalinus's close relation to Avicenna. This intertextual awareness, as we may call it, is a clear indicator of Albert's very good knowledge of these texts, which he must have been comparing systematically; a fact that is also confirmed by other references to Gundissalinus, in which Albert mentions him along with Avicenna and Qusṭā Ibn Lūqā [17]. He even makes a connection between Gundissalinus and al-Ġazālī, saying that both are following the tracks of Avicenna [18].

16. ALBERTUS MAGNUS, *De homine* (Ed. Colon. 27, 2), 13: "Istae sunt rationes Constabuli. Et quasdam etiam istarum ponit Toletanus, et addit unam quae sumpta est ab Avicenna, quae est de anima rationali specialiter, hanc scilicet: Species intelligibiles quae sunt in intellectu, aut sunt in eo ut in corpore vel habente esse per corpus, sicut potentia quae operatur in organo, habet esse per corpus; aut sunt in eo sicut in incorporeo. Si primo modo, aut illae formae sunt divisibiles, aut indivisibiles [...]". *Cf.* DOMINICUS GUNDISSALINUS, *Tractatus de anima*, ed. Alonso del Real / Soto Bruna, 86: "Id ergo quod est subiectum intelligibilium vel est corpus vel aliquid habens esse per corpus vel non. Si autem subiectum intelligibilium est corpus vel aliquid habens esse per corpus, tunc intellecta forma subsistit per se vel in aliquo eius divisibili vel in aliquo eius non divisibili [...]".

17. *Cf.* ALBERTUS MAGNUS, *De homine* (Ed. Colon. 27, 2), 58: "Sed contra hoc sunt multae rationes Toletani et Avicennae", and 70: "In contrarium sunt rationes Avicennae, quas ponit etiam Toletanus".

18. See ALBERTUS MAGNUS, *De homine* (Ed. Colon. 27, 2), 410: "In hac etiam sententia expresse est Avicenna in VI de *Naturalibus* et duo sequentes vestigia eius, scilicet Algazel et Toletanus".

Further, in the succeeding questions of *De homine*, Gundissalinus and his translations and writings remain an inescapable point of reference for the philosophical dimension of Albert's argumentation. Thus, when dealing with the soul's motion, Albert repeatedly refers to Gundissalinus. We cannot analyze his arguments here; suffice it to say that in his solution to the problem of whether the soul is subject to motion or not, Albert comes to the conclusion that "it has to be said that the soul is not moved by any species of motion, as is proved by the philosophers, namely Aristotle and Avicenna, Averroes, Qusṭā Ibn Lūqā, al-Fārābī and the Toledan" [19]. Gundissalinus and the authors he translated are invoked here as part of a venerable philosophical tradition: the last representative of which is the Toledan Archdeacon himself.

Yet, despite Albert's general sympathy for, and his familiarity with, Gundissalinus and the psychological tradition he represents, his attitude is not one of unconditional assent. In fact Albert criticises him severely for his doctrine of a *creatio mediante intelligentia*, i.e. the creation of the rational soul through the mediation of angels, operating in God's service. This is a doctrine that Gundissalinus expounds not only in his *Tractatus de anima* but also in his *De processione mundi* [20], and which one can trace to the *Liber de causis* [21]. It is also found in the works of the Jewish philosopher and co-translator of Gundissalinus: Abraham Ibn Daūd [22]. In the *Tractatus de anima* Gundissalinus puts forward a long list of arguments for his position, introducing them as the "philosophers' proofs" [23].

Albert picks up only three of these proofs, which he says are the Toledan philosophers' strongest arguments [24], namely that a) the cause of the soul must be in some way subject to change, since every soul is created anew in a specific moment in time – but God, of course, cannot be subject

19. ALBERTUS MAGNUS, *De homine* (Ed. Colon. 27, 2), 25: "Dicendum, quod anima non movetur aliqua specie motus, ut probant philosophi Aristoteles, et Avicenna, Averroes, Constabulus, Alpharabius et Toletanus".

20. DOMINICUS GUNDISSALINUS, *De processione mundi*, ed. Soto Bruna / Alonso del Real, 211, 214 and 220.

21. See FIDORA/NIEDERBERGER (2001), especially proposition 3, 8-9 and 18 and the editors' commentaries on these propositions.

22. *Cf.* ABRAHAM IBN DAŪD, *The Exalted Faith*, ed. Samuelson/Weiss, 173.

23. *Cf.* DOMINICUS GUNDISSALINUS, *Tractatus de anima*, ed. Alonso del Real / Soto Bruna, 128-136.

24. ALBERTUS MAGNUS, *De homine* (Ed. Colon. 27, 2), 75: "Istae sunt rationes Toletani fortiores, et quasdam alias ponit debiles, quas subticemus".

to change[25]; b) that if man's soul were created directly by God there would be no difference between the dignity of the human soul and that of an angel, and therefore God cannot have created man's soul directly[26]; and c) that God's act being infinite, the human soul's existence and essence would necessarily be infinite too if God created man's soul directly, but this is not the case, so God is not the creator of the human soul, but it is created by mediation of the angels[27]. Albert then goes on to quote further arguments for the *creatio mediante intelligentia*, e.g. the third proposition of the *Liber de causis*, and a passage from Isaac al-Israeli's *Liber de definitionibus*, another text translated by Gundissalinus[28].

Yet, this time, Albert's own solution is in line with the saints, namely Augustine and John of Damascus, and opposed to the philosophers' views.

25. ALBERTUS MAGNUS, *De homine* (Ed. Colon. 27, 2), 75: "Obiecit ergo Toletanus sic: Causa nunc agens et non prius necesse est quod agat per aliquam dispositionem novam sibi advenientem; causa animae humanae, quae modo fit, est causa nunc agens et non prius; ergo necesse est quod agat per dispositionem novam sibi advenientem. Primae causae sive deo nulla nova dispositio advenit; ergo non erit causa immediate creans hanc animam". *Cf.* DOMINICUS GUNDISSALINUS, *Tractatus de anima*, ed. Alonso del Real / Soto Bruna, 128-130: "Cum aliquis fit agens qui fuit non agens, necesse est hoc fieri propter novitatem alicuius rei quae contingit, scilicet vel conditionis vel naturae [...]. Deo autem nihil novi advenit, tunc enim variabilis esset, quod est impossibile. Igitur ab ipso non creatur anima".

26. ALBERTUS MAGNUS, *De homine* (Ed. Colon. 27, 2), 75: "Immediate recipere ab optimo nobilius est quam recipere per medium ab illo; si ergo anima recipit immediate esse a deo, recipit ipsum nobilissimo modo. Sed ad nobilissimum modum recipiendi sequitur nobilissimum esse receptum; ergo videtur quod anima deberet secundum hoc habere nobilissimum esse; hoc autem est esse intelligentiae angelicae; ergo anima deberet esse angelus, quod non est verum; ergo nec recipit immediate esse a deo, sed ab angelis". *Cf.* DOMINICUS GUNDISSALINUS, *Tractatus de anima*, ed. Alonso del Real / Soto Bruna, 132: "Item ad recipiendum aliquid ab aliquo, nihil est dignius eo quod illud recipit nullo mediante. Si igitur anima recipit esse a primo factore nullo mediante, tunc nihil est dignius ea ad recipiendum illud ab illo; sed substantia intelligentiae dignior est ad hoc; ergo anima non recipit esse a primo factore nullo mediante".

27. ALBERTUS MAGNUS, *De homine* (Ed. Colon. 27, 2), 75: "Ab infinito agente secundum potentiam agendi actus est infinitus; sed deus est infinitum agens; ergo actus eius immediatus erit infinitus; anima vero habet finitum esse; ergo non erit a deo immediate, sed mediantibus angelis". *Cf.* DOMINICUS GUNDISSALINUS, *Tractatus de anima*, ed. Alonso del Real / Soto Bruna, 134: "Quicquid movet animam non potest esse infinitum quoniam quicquid movet aliud aut movet per se aut per accidens. Si autem id quod infinitum est movet aliud per se, necesse est ut motus, qui ab eo fit, sit infinitus; sed motus animae finitus est; igitur non fit ab infinito [...]".

28. In later years (*ca.* 1264-1267), Albert wrote a commentary on the *Liber de causis*, in which the discussion of the *creatio mediante intelligentia* should play an important role. For the *Liber de causis* and its influence on Albert and others, see FIDORA/NIEDERBERGER (2001), 205ff.

For even though, as Albert says, Gundissalinus tried to ease the open contradiction between the philosophers' doctrine which he expounded and the saints' teachings, his position is still untenable. Rather, one has to maintain that the angels were not involved in the creation of human soul at all. As Albert says:

> The Toledan author tried to justify himself with respect to the saints, saying that although he wished to maintain that the angels created the souls, he was not claiming that the angels were creators. For the creator is he who by his own authority and power makes something from nothing. But the angels do this as ministers of God and by his authority. Yet even so, on the grounds of unquestionable faith, one has to maintain that the angels do not even create as God's ministers, since the honour of the creator is singular [...] and must not be transferred [29].

This very same discussion reappears in a later work of Albert's, his *Summa theologiae*. In its second part (written in the 1270s), Albert again deals with Gundissalinus's arguments concerning the *creatio mediante intelligentia*, which are now attributed to a certain "Johannes Toletanus" [30], an attribution which was used by Manuel Alonso for arguing that the *Tractatus de anima* was not written by Gundissalinus but that the work should be ascribed to his collaborator, the Jewish philosopher Avendauth [31]. Yet this later reference to the *Tractatus de anima* in Albert's work is of scant value, since the second part of the *Summa theologiae* seems to have been put together by his disciple Godefredus de Dusborch, drawing on material from Albert's early works, which he rearranged in a

29. ALBERTUS MAGNUS, *De homine* (Ed. Colon. 27, 2), 76: "Toletanus excusat se et a dictis sanctorum dicens quod licet consentiat animas creari ab angelis, non tamen dicit angelos esse creatores; quia creator est ille, qui propria auctoritate et virtute aliquid de nihilo facit; sed angeli faciunt hoc ministrantes deo et auctoritate dei. Sed indubitata fide tenendum est, quod angeli non creant etiam ministerio; honor enim creatoris singularis est [...] et ideo non debit transponi". *Cf.* DOMINICUS GUNDISSALINUS, *Tractatus de anima*, ed. Alonso del Real / Soto Bruna, 134-136: "Hoc autem quod philosophi probant, animas non a deo sed ab angeli creari, sane quidem potest intelligi, scilicet non dei ministerio, sed angelorum. [...] Et ideo anima creatura angeli non dicitur, sed dei, cuius auctoritate creatur". Gundissalinus here seems to be paraphrasing a passage from Peter Lombard (*IV Sent.*, lib. IV, d. V, 3, *cf.* PL 192, col. 852).

30. ALBERTUS MAGNUS, *Summa theologiae* (Ed. Colon. 34, 1), 52: "Proceditur ex rationibus quas ponit Johannes Toletanus Archiepiscopus in libro suo *De anima*".

31. See ALONSO (1948), 77 (Alonso maintained the identity of Ibn Daūd and John of Spain).

sometimes hasty and not very reliable manner[32]. Thus, the *Summa*'s arguments in favour of and against the *creatio mediante intelligentia* reproduce in a rather confused way the text from *De homine* we have just discussed[33].

At any rate, our concern here is not with internal textual criticism of Albert's works. What we have tried to outline and characterise in the course of the preceding remarks is Albert's use of Gundissalinus's translations and works on psychology. From the examples we have given, to which many other implicit and explicit references of Albert to Gundissalinus could be added[34], it is indubitably evident that the young Albert was very familiar with these Toledan texts on Graeco-Arabic Aristotelian psychology and that he introduced them into his discussion with a clear and well-defined objective: these texts were to serve as philosophical points of reference, which would ensure that the theological sources, whose authors Albert addresses as the saints, were read against a philosophical background.

Ludger Honnefelder has pointed out that *De homine*, which enjoyed a wide diffusion in the Middle Ages, is one of the very first instances of Albert's attempt to integrate philosophical reflection into the theological discourse of his time by applying the philosophical standards to theological discussions and thus transforming theology into a science[35]. As we have seen, this transformation is doubtless dependent on the Toledan Graeco-Arabic tradition of Aristotelian psychology, since Albert draws directly on these sources, and his intention is very much in line with that of Gundissalinus: *non iam fide tantum, sed etiam ratione*, that is how the discussions of the soul were to proceed according to the Spanish Archdeacon. With Albert the Great this ambitious philosophical programme would be implemented in the theological discourse of 13th-century Christian Europe while reaching, at the same time, its first culminating point.

32. See the introduction by D. Siedler and P. Simon to the edition of ALBERTUS MAGNUS, *Summa theologiae* (Ed. Colon. 34, 1), IX-XVI.

33. A. SCHNEIDER (1906), 436-439 discusses Albert's response to Gundissalinus.

34. A first list of references was produced by CALLUS (1939), 339, n. 4. It was completed by HASSE (2000), 13, n. 3. The editors of *De homine* have identified an impressive number of explicit citations from Gundissalinus, referring to the pages 10, 13, 21, 25, 58, 61, 65, 70, 71, 75, 76, 91, 92, 409 and 410 of their edition.

35. *Cf.* L. Honnefelder in his preface to ALBERTUS MAGNUS, *Über den Menschen*, ed. Anzulewicz/Söder, VIII-IX.

HILLEL OF VERONA AND PHILOSOPHICAL DISCOURSE ON THE SOUL IN THE JEWISH TRADITION

Not only can we identify the influence of Gundissalinus's psychology at the very origin of the transformations and shifts that would determine Latin philosophy during the 13th century, his influence was also decisive in medieval Jewish philosophy. The *Tractatus de anima* was the very first Latin philosophical text to be translated into Hebrew, giving rise to a long series of Hebrew translations of scholastic texts.

Gundissalinus's treatise on the soul was put into Hebrew in the 12th or the early 13th century[36] and is preserved in a single Cambridge manuscript together with fragments of a translation of Aristotle's *De anima*. After a few pages from Aristotle's text, the anonymous translator confesses:

> So far I have translated the text of the book written by Aristotle himself; but it was hard and difficult, and so I have given up translating it and have taken another book, one written by the philosopher of Toledo who expounded the subject of Aristotle's work. It begins with the words "All men" – the prologue of the book extending to the words "It is proper", which form the beginning of the book itself[37].

Obviously, the translator was primarily interested in Aristotle and his book, but faced with its difficulty, he preferred to translate Gundissalinus's treatise. The situation is, by the way, not very different from that of Hermann the German, a 13th-century Toledan translator who gave up his translation of Aristotle's *Poetics* because of its difficulty and instead translated Averroes's *Commentary* on the same work.

Most important for us is the fact that Gundissalinus's treatise was evidently known to, and used by, Jewish scholars in the 13th century. This is demonstrated, for instance, by Rabbi Gershom ben Shlomo of Arles in his encyclopaedic work called *The Gate of the Heavens*, which dates from the end of the 13th century[38]. In the prologue to this work Rabbi Gershom explains his intention and his method:

36. J. Teicher dates the translation to the first half of the 12th century. M. Zonta, however, believes it to be from the 13th century. *Cf.* TEICHER (1954-1956), 409, and ZONTA (1996), 195. The first half of the 12th century is certainly too early with regard to Gundissalinus's own dates; I would rather suggest the end of the 12th or the beginning of the 13th century.

37. MS Cambridge, University Library, Add. 1858, fol. 191a. Y. Schwartz has prepared an edition of the Hebrew translation of the *Tractatus de anima* which will appear in FIDORA/HAMES/SCHWARTZ (2013).

38. *Cf.* ZONTA (1996), 213.

> My spirit turned to the enquiry and study of the subtle and high science, asking for instruction; but this science is far away from me and hidden from my eyes. Now, I had at my disposal only a few books of wise philosophers translated from their languages into Hebrew, but with these books I gave light again to my eyes. And I turned to those big books and the arguments laid out in them, one here, the other there, and I collected these arguments in one place, abbreviating and gathering them with my hands. And I learned a lot from the mouths of Hebrews and non-Hebrews and I quoted everyone at his place [39].

Already the principle of composition of this encyclopaedia and Gershom's appraisal of the non-Hebrew authors remind us of Avendauth's, and especially of Gundissalinus's, attitudes. But there are further similarities, for in the 11th chapter, which Gershom devotes to the soul and its powers, he says:

> Aristotle writes in the beginning of his book *De anima* that all men are equal in body and soul, but not all are conscious of the reality of the soul (in the same degree) as they are aware of the reality of their body. This is not astonishing, since the body is perceived by the senses, while the soul is conceived only by reason. Accordingly, people who perceive only concrete things do not believe in the existence of a soul, or they assume that the soul extends over all the parts [40] of the body on the ground that this one moves. But they know of the essence and the properties of the soul by way of tradition. Only a few perceive this with reason. [...] Therefore we now have established by reasoning whether there exists a soul or not [...] [41].

These are, of course, Gundissalinus's words from the prologue to his *Tractatus de anima*, which we have quoted above. The parallelism continues and has been analysed by Jacob Teicher and, in more detail, by Juliane Lay [42]. The fact that Rabbi Gershom attributes his quotation to Aristotle should not surprise us, for he clearly depends on the afore-said Hebrew translation where, as we have said, Gundissalinus's text replaced the missing parts of the translation of Aristotle's *De anima*.

39. *Apud* TEICHER (1933), 8.

40. Gershom's Hebrew text, which follows the translation we have mentioned above, reproduces the reading of the Latin MS M (ed. Alonso del Real / Soto Bruna), which is corrupt here misreading 'ubicumque' for 'utcumque'.

41. GERSHOM BEN SHLOMOH, *The Gate of Heaven (Shaar ha-Shamayim)*, ed. and trans. Bodenheimer, 320-321.

42. *Cf.* her unpublished Mémoire de Maîtrise, Paris 1978: *L'astronomie et la métaphysique de Rabbi Gershom ben Salomon d'Arles*, especially p. 165-189.

The most interesting and prominent Jewish follower of Gundissalinus, however, is Rabbi Hillel of Verona, who was active in the second half of the 13th century in Northern Italy. Hillel, who may have studied in Barcelona, where he could have become acquainted with the Hispanic philosophical tradition, is the author of a book called the *Retributions of the Soul*, which dates from between 1287 and 1291 and was written in Forlì, close to Bologna. In this work, we again find a Rabbi having recourse to Gundissalinus's *Tractatus de anima* along with other texts by Latin authors, such as Thomas Aquinas.

Hillel draws strongly on Gundissalinus's treatise, which he is rendering directly from the Latin, viz. independently of the existing Hebrew translation. Already the opening remarks of the work betray the author's Toledan source materials, reproducing, as did Gershom, Gundissalinus's own words:

> I endeavoured to gather the sayings of the philosophers which are spread here and there in big and voluminous books, and I arranged them in an order and explained them, so that they be not difficult to grasp for those who long for wisdom, and that they be not refused. In this I pursued a single purpose, which is to understand the truth. [...] For, the soul being what makes a man be a man and thus constitutes human existence, it is not appropriate to forget that which has caused our own essence [43].

Hillel's treatise itself is divided into two parts, which may seem, at a first glance, rather loosely connected: the first half is dedicated to the soul's existence, its essence and its relation to the active intellect, while the second half turns to eschatological questions concerning the retributions of the soul after death [44]. It is in the first half of this philosophico-theological work that Hillel makes abundant use of Gundissalinus's *Tractatus de anima*. Surprisingly enough, he does not only quote extensive passages from the *Tractatus* but he also read and used Avendauth/Gundissalinus's Latin translation of Avicenna's *Liber sextus de naturalibus*.

As far as Gundissalinus's *Tractatus de anima* is concerned, there are three fields of particular interest where Hillel introduces this text's arguments: namely with regard to the existence of the soul, the question as to whether the soul is a substance or an accident, and the problem concerning the soul's motion. The passages he quotes within these contexts show a striking parallelism with regard to Albert's reading of the

43. HILLEL OF VERONA, *Über die Vollendung der Seele*, ed. and German trans. Schwartz, 50-52.

44. For a more detailed interpretation of Hillel's work see SCHWARTZ (2004).

Spanish Archdeacon. Thus, to prove the soul is a substance, Hillel sets out by saying:

> We have to assume that the soul is either a substance or an accident, for in these two all of reality is contained. Yet, it cannot possibly be an accident, since according to Aristotle this is something that exists only as a possibility but is not a necessary part of the definition [of a thing]. It [i.e the accident] is therefore corruptible, while its subject persists, that is to say, the existence of its subject does not depend on its presence; for its going does not affect its subject [45].

Even though Hillel gives it an Aristotelian colouring, this argument is clearly reminiscent of Gundissalinus, in particular of a passage which we have also come across in Albert. This becomes even clearer as Hillel's argument proceeds:

> [...] there can be no doubt that the soul is a substance that is joined with an accident, since apart from substance and accident there is nothing other than a substance joined with an accident. Furthermore, according to Plato's views on substance, whatever is one in number while capable of receiving various alterations, is called a substance. Likewise, whatever operates something while it exists, and once it ceases to be, its operation ceases too, is a substance. Now, with regard to the soul, both are true. [...] Therefore it is a substance [46].

In this quotation Hillel fuses two arguments from the *Tractatus de anima*, the Latin text of which reads:

> Plato animam sic definit dicens: anima est substantia incorporea corpus movens. Quod autem anima sit substantia sic probatur; quicquid recipit contraria, cum sit unum et idem numero, substantia est. Sed anima, manens una et eadem numero, recipit contraria quae sunt virtutes et vitia [...]. Ergo anima substantia est.
>
> Item quicquid est, aut est substantia aut accidens. Sed anima non est accidens. Nihil enim quod adveniens constituit et recedens destruit, accidens est; sed anima adveniens constituit animal et recedens destruit; ergo anima non est accidens; est igitur substantia [47].

45. HILLEL OF VERONA, *Über die Vollendung der Seele*, ed. and German trans. Schwartz, 70.

46. HILLEL OF VERONA, *Über die Vollendung der Seele*, ed. and German trans. Schwartz, 74.

47. DOMINICUS GUNDISSALINUS, *Tractatus de anima*, Alonso del Real / Soto Bruna, 84.

As a matter of fact, Gundissalinus's argument, which points to Plato, can be traced back to Qusṭā Ibn Lūqā's *De differentia spiritus et animae*, and it is under the latter's name that we have already encountered it in Albert's *De homine*. Thus, both arguments to prove the soul is a substance, which Hillel takes over from Gundissalinus, can be identified in Albert, one being attributed to Qusṭā Ibn Lūqā, the other to the "Toletanus":

> Constabulus in libro *De differentia spiritus et animae*: Quicquid recipit opposita, cum unum sit numero et immutabile in sua essentia, substantia est; sed anima rationalis recipit virtutes et vitia, cum sit una numero; ergo recipit opposita; est igitur substantia [...]. Item Toletanus: Quicquid est, aut est substantia aut accidens. Nihil autem quod adveniens constituit speciem substantiae et recedens destruit eandem, est accidens; quaelibet species animae adveniens constituit speciem plantae, animalis et hominis, et recedens destruit eandem; ergo quaelibet species animae est substantia[48].

It is very significant that Hillel and Albert use the same arguments in order to prove the soul is a substance; yet, while Albert attributes them to different authors, being well aware of Gundissalinus's sources, Hillel in presenting them *en bloc* seems to have taken them as he found them in Gundissalinus.

Further, also with regard to whether the soul is in motion or not, one can detect interesting parallels between Albert's and Hillel's approaches to Gundissalinus. Albert, as was said above, sided with Gundissalinus and other philosophers, such as Aristotle and Averroes, in maintaining that the soul was unmoved. Hillel also subscribes to the Toledan philosopher's position on this issue, reproducing literally many arguments concerning the discussion on the soul's motion as he found them in the *Tractatus de anima*[49].

Now, even though the similarities one can observe in the use both Albert and Hillel are making of Gundissalinus's text are striking, it seems that they cannot be explained in terms of a direct dependence of the latter on the former. The fact that Hillel quotes several passages that are not in Albert forbids us from establishing any direct textual relation between *De homine* and *The Retributions of the Soul*. It is true that Hillel of Verona was very familiar with 13th-century Latin scholasticism, quoting passages from Thomas Aquinas and others, as we have said before, but he does not seem to have used Albert's works for writing his *Retributions*.

48. ALBERTUS MAGNUS, *De homine* (Ed. Colon. 27, 2), 10.

49. *Cf.* HILLEL OF VERONA, *Über die Vollendung der Seele*, ed. and German trans. Schwartz, 86ff.

In the absence of an historical explanation, the similarities between Albert and Hillel with regard to their recourse to Gundissalinus have to be accounted for in a different way. Thus they have to be considered the expression of their common systematic interest in certain issues of Gundissalinus's psychology, namely its genuinely philosophical outlook, for which the discussion of the soul's being a substance, its incorporality and the problem of its motion are indeed paradigmatical.

As we have said before, Hillel's treatise, like Albert's, had a theological motivation, namely the eschatological perspective concerning the soul's retributions in the afterlife. For Hillel one of the greatest errors of some of his fellow Jews consisted in imagining these retributions as corporeal pleasure or suffering [50]. This is, as he states in the prologue to his work, the reason why he wishes to embark on a philosophical discussion of the soul and its incorporeal nature, before dealing with the rewards and chastisements of the soul in the context of Biblical and Talmudic tradition. Hillel's intention is obviously with theology, but his method of choice to establish the soul as an incorporeal substance is that of philosophy. This becomes very clear from the last sentences of the first half of the book, immediately before Hillel switches to the theological discussion concerning the soul's afterlife. Referring to the disposition of his work, he apologizes for dealing with the philosophers and their schools first, instead of starting off directly with the Holy Scripture and the wise Jews. However, he says it was convenient to do so, because the philosophers yield "irrefuatable demonstrations" [51], offering a solid basis for the theological discussion which is to follow.

What may have appeared to some of his interpreters as a loose juxtaposition of different treatises – a philosophical tract on the soul and its nature first, and a theological reflection in the second place – is therefore, quite the contrary, a well-tempered attempt to arrive at a synthesis of philosophical reasoning and theological wisdom. By the way, Hillel is well aware of the fact that the philosophical reasons he pieces together from different sources are not original in themselves, but – and this is what matters to him – the outcome of this synthesis is definitely innovative. Thus, with some pride, he tells his readers that he called this book *The Retributions of the Soul*, because in the Jewish tradition there existed no

50. *Cf.* HILLEL OF VERONA, *Über die Vollendung der Seele*, ed. and German trans. Schwartz, 52-54.

51. *Cf.* HILLEL OF VERONA, *Über die Vollendung der Seele*, ed. and German trans. Schwartz, 278.

other book under this title [52]. This should of course not be misunderstood as a merely bibliographical piece of information; rather, what is at stake here is Hillel's philosophico-theological programme, which is new. And indeed modern scholarship has confirmed that Hillel's book is the very first philosophico-theological or – to speak with Yossef Schwartz – "systematic" theological treatise on the soul. And as such, it seems to be unprecedented in the Jewish tradition placing Hillel clearly within the Latin-Christian context and its rationalisation of theology [53].

This process within Jewish philosophy does not end with Hillel; in the same way as Albert embodies both the implementation of a new approach and a first but not the last culminating point of this perspective, so too Hillel has to be considered as establishing an enduring tradition within Jewish philosophy. Thus from the 13th to 15th century, one can observe a rise of a very strong interest among Italian Jews in Christian philosophico-theological discussions. One of the protagonists of this movement, which has been described as "Hebrew scholasticism", is Yehudah Romano, who translated several Latin works into Hebrew during the first half of the 14th century. Among his translations we find Gundissalinus's tract *De unitate et uno* [54], as well as numerous works by Albert the Great, Thomas Aquinas and Giles of Rome. In both his translations and his own philosophical writings, Yehudah shows a particular concern with psychology, especially with the theory of the intellect. This topic becomes a *leitmotif* for his writings up to the point that, as Josef Sermoneta has stressed, the doctrine of the intellect turns into Yehudah's "fede filosofica", his philosophical creed [55].

In the light of this, it is no exaggeration to say that Graeco-Arabic psychology, as it was transmitted first through the texts written and translated in Toledo and later on in other parts of Christian Europe with the reception of Averroes, became a constitutive element of philosophico-theological endeavours not only in the Latin-Christian tradition, but was likewise decisive for the evolution of Jewish philosophy. This strictly parallel interest is eventually confirmed by the fact that among the translations done by Yehudah we also find parts of Albert's *De homine*

52. *Cf.* HILLEL OF VERONA, *Über die Vollendung der Seele*, ed. and German trans. Schwartz, 56.

53. See SCHWARTZ (2003).

54. A critical edition of this Hebrew translation has been prepared by Y. Schwartz and will appear in FIDORA/HAMES/SCHWARTZ (2013).

55. *Cf.* SERMONETA (1965).

– the "wise Teutonicus"[56], as Yehudah calls him –, a work which, as we have seen, was of paramount importance for the rationalisation of the Christian discourse on man and his soul[57].

CONCLUSIONS

We are now at the point where we can go back to the issue raised at the beginning of this chapter: namely, Avendauth's and Gundissalinus's programmatic interest in Graeco-Arabic Aristotelian psychology and its impact on, or consequences for, the history of both philosophy and theology. As we have said, with their translations and works, Avendauth and Gundissalinus suggested a philosophical programme that was directed at the rationalisation of Christian faith. Christians, they claimed, should not only believe in the soul's existence and its nature, but they should also be provided with rational, that is to say philosophical, arguments to prove their tenets. After what has been said, there can be no doubt that not only did 13th- and 14th-century authors, such as Albert and Hillel, use the translations and works on psychology by these Toledan authors, and closely follow their arguments, but in doing so they also stuck faithfully to the philosophical intentions expressed by Avendauth and Gundissalinus, incorporating, as those authors did, philosophical standards into their theological writings on the soul.

What is more, the programme outlined by the two Toledan scholars would not only shape the philosophico-theological discourse of the Latin-Christian world, but – far surpassing the scope of their explicit intentions – it became a crucial element for the rationalisation of the Jewish theological debates too. The translations of psychological texts from Arabic into Latin, as they were produced in 12th-century Toledo, are part of a much broader intellectual phenomenon, a pan-European project, if we may say so, in which the translation activity from Arabic into Latin gave way to an analogous translation process from Latin into Hebrew.

As we have stressed throughout this paper, it is hardly possible to account for this coincidence in purely historical terms. Rather, the strictly parallel evolution of the Latin and the Hebrew discussions on the soul has to be understood as a direct consequence of the inherent systematic potential of Graeco-Arabic Aristotelian psychology to become the basis

56. *Cf.* RIGO (1995), 154.
57. RIGO (1995), 151.

for a philosophical reformulation of some of the central tenets of the different theological traditions. It was on this basis that the different intellectual and religious communities around the Mediterranean started to revise their theological traditions and to work on a shared philosophical discourse that substantially contributed to the rationalisation of the different theological traditions across medieval Europe.

BIBLIOGRAPHY

Sources

ABRAHAM IBN DAŪD (1976), *A Critical Edition with a Translation and Notes of the Book of Tradition*, trans. G. D. Cohen (Judaica. Texts & Translations, 1st Series, Number 3), Philadelphia.

ABRAHAM IBN DAŪD (1986), *The Exalted Faith*, ed. and trans. N. M. Samuelson / G. Weiss, Cranbury, NJ.

ALBERTUS MAGNUS (1978), *Summa theologiae* I, 1, 1-50A, ed. P. Simon/ W. Kübel / H. G. Vogels (Ed. Colon. 34, 1), Münster i. W.

– (2004), *Über den Menschen*, ed. and German trans. H. Anzulewicz / J. R. Söder (Philosophische Bibliothek 531), Hamburg.

– (2008), *De homine*, ed. H. Anzulewicz / J. R. Söder (Ed. Colon. 27, 2), Münster i. W.

AVICENNA (1968-1972), *Liber de anima seu Sextus de naturalibus*, ed. S. van Riet, 2 vols. (Avicenna latinus), Louvain/Leiden.

DOMINICUS GUNDISSALINUS (1999), *De processione mundi*, ed. and Spanish trans. Mª. J. Soto Bruna / C. Alonso del Real (Colección de Pensamiento Medieval y Renacentista 7), Pamplona.

– (2007), *Über die Einteilung der Philosophie / De divisione philosophiae*, ed. and German trans. A. Fidora / D. Werner (Herders Bibliothek des Philosophie des Mittelalters 11), Freiburg i. Br.

– (2009), *Tractatus de anima*, ed. and Spanish trans. C. Alonso del Real / Mª. J. Soto Bruna (Colección de Pensamiento Medieval y Renacentista 107), Pamplona.

GERSHOM BEN SHLOMOH (1953), *The Gate of Heaven (Shaar ha-Shamayim)*, ed. and trans. F. S. Bodenheimer, Jerusalem.

HILLEL OF VERONA (2009), *Über die Vollendung der Seele*, ed. and German trans. Y. Schwartz / A. Fidora (Herders Bibliothek der Philosophie des Mittelalters 17), Freiburg i. Br.

JOHN BLUND (2005), *Tractatus de anima*, ed. and German trans. D. Werner (Herders Bibliothek des Philosophie des Mittelalters 6), Freiburg i. Br.

Studies

ALONSO, M. (1948), "Gundisalvo y el *Tractatus de anima*", in *Pensamiento* 4, 71-77.

D'ALVERNY, M.-Th. (1954-1956), "Avendauth?", in *Homenaje a Millás-Vallicrosa*, 2 vols., Barcelona, vol. 1, 19-43.

BERTOLA, E. (1971), "È esistito un Avicennismo latino nel Medioevo?", in *Sophia* 39, 318-334.

CALLUS, D. (1939), "Gundissalinus' *De anima* and the Problem of Substantial Form", in *The New Scholasticism* 13, 338-355.

FIDORA, A. (2003), *Die Wissenschaftstheorie des Dominicus Gundissalinus– Voraussetzungen und Konsequenzen des zweiten Anfangs der aristotelischen Philosophie im 12. Jahrhundert* (Wissenskultur und gesellschaftlicher Wandel 6), Berlin (revised Spanish edition: Pamplona 2009).

–(2004), "Zum Verhältnis von Metaphysik und Theologie bei Dominicus Gundissalinus", in M. Lutz-Bachmann / A. Fidora / A. Niederberger (eds.), *Metaphysics in the 12th Century – On the Relationship Among Philosophy, Science and Theology* (Textes et Études du Moyen Âge 19), Turnhout, 67-84.

FIDORA, A. / HAMES, H. / SCHWARTZ, Y. (eds) (2013), *Latin-into-Hebrew. Vol. 2: Texts in Contexts*, New York.

FIDORA, A. / NIEDERBERGER, A. (2001), *Von Bagdad nach Toledo. Das 'Buch der Ursachen' und seine Rezeption im Mittelalter.* Lateinisch-deutscher Text, Kommentar und Wirkungsgeschichte (excerpta classica 20), Mainz.

FONTAINE, T. A. M. (1990), *In Defence of Judaism. Abraham Ibn Daūd. Sources and Structures of 'ha-Emunah ha-Ramah'* (Studia Semitica Neerlandica 26), Assen, 262-263.

GAUTHIER, R.-A. (1982), "Le traité *De anima et potenciis eius* d'un Maître ès Arts (vers 1225)", in *Revue des sciences philosophiques et théologiques* 66, 3-55.

GILSON, É. (1929-1930), "Les sources gréco-arabes de l'augustinisme avicennisant", in *Archives d'histoire doctrinale et littéraire du Moyen Âge* 4, 4-149.

HASSE, D. N. (2000), *Avicenna's 'De anima' in the Latin West. The Formation of a Peripatetic Philosophy of the Soul 1160-1300* (Warburg Institute Studies and Texts 1), London/Turin.

LAY, J. (1978), *L'astronomie et la métaphysique de Rabbi Gershom ben Salomon d'Arles*, unpublished Mémoire de Maîtrise, Paris.

LEMAY, R. (1987), "De la scolastique à l'histoire par le truchement de la philologie : itinéraire d'un médiéviste entre Europe et Islam", in B. Scarcia Amoretti (ed.), *La diffusione delle scienze islamiche nel medio evo europeo. Convegno internazionale, Roma, 2-4 ott. 1984*, Rome, 399-535.

MARRONE, S. P. (2006), "From Gundisalvus to Bonaventure: Intellect and Intelligences in the Late Twelfth and Early Thirteenth Centuries", in M. C. Pacheco / J. F. Meirinhos (eds.), *Intellect et imagination dans la philosophie médiévale. Actes du XIe Congrès International de Philosophie Médiévale de la Société Internationale pour l'Étude de la Philosophie*

Médiévale (SIEPM), Porto, du 26 au 31 août 2002, 3 vols. (Rencontres en philosophie médiévale 11, 1-3), Turnhout, vol. 2, 1071-1081.

RIGO, C. (1995), "Yehudah ben Mosheh Romano, traduttore degli scolastici latini", in *Henoch* 17, 141-170.

SCHNEIDER, A. (1906), *Die Psychologie Alberts des Großen nach den Quellen dargestellt* (BGPhMA IV, 6), Münster i. W.

SCHWARTZ, Y. (2003), "Hillel ben Shmuel ben Elazar (bzw. Eliezer) aus Verona", in A. B. Kilcher / O. Fraisse / Y. Schwartz (eds.), *Metzler Lexikon jüdischer Philosophen. Philosophisches Denken des Judentums von der Antike bis zur Gegenwart*, Stuttgart/Weimar, 74-76.

– (2004), "Die Seelenlehre des Hillel aus Verona: Aristotelische Psychologie zwischen Maimonismus und Thomismus", in M. Lutz-Bachmann / A. Fidora / P. Antolic (eds.), *Erkenntnis und Wissenschaft – Probleme der Epistemologie in der Philosophie des Mittelalters / Knowledge and Science – Problems of Epistemology in Medieval Philosophy* (Wissenskultur und gesellschaftlicher Wandel 10), Berlin, 253-264.

SERMONETA, J. (1965), "La dottrina dell'intelletto e la 'fede filosofica' di Jehudàh e Immanuel Romano", in *Studi medievali*, Serie terza, 6/2, 3-78.

TEICHER, J. (1933), "Gershon ben Shelomoh e Gundissalino", in *Accademia Nazionale dei Lincei* 9, 5-25.

– (1934), "Gundissalino e l'agostinismo avicennizzante", in *Rivista di filosofia neo-scolastica* 26, 252-258.

– (1954-1956), "The Latin-Hebrew School of Translators in Spain in the Twelfth Century", in *Homenaje a Millás-Vallicrosa*, 2 vols., Barcelona, vol. 2, 401-443.

DE VAUX, R. (1934), *Notes et textes sur l'avicennisme aux confins des XIIe-XIIIe siècles*, Paris.

ZONTA, M. (1996), *La filosofia antica nel Medioevo ebraico. Le traduzioni ebraiche medievali dei testi filosofici antichi* (Philosophica. Testi e studi 2), Brescia 1996.

NEW LIGHT ON AVICENNA: OPTICS AND ITS ROLE IN AVICENNAN THEORIES OF VISION, COGNITION AND EMANATION

Jon McGinnis
(University of Missouri, Saint Louis)

At *De anima* III 5 (430a10-17), Aristotle in a notoriously short and obscure passage writes:

> Since in all of nature there is something that is the matter for each kind, which is potentially all of those things, and another that is the cause and maker that makes all of them [...] these differences must also belong to the soul. On the one hand, there is an intellect such as to become all things and, on the other hand, there is one that makes all things, like a certain disposition as, for instance, light (for light also in a certain way makes what is potentially colored to be actually colored).

It is not because Aristotle presents a philosophically technical argument here that I say that this passage is obscure. In outline the position is quite straightforward. In nature there are two classes of things: those that are potentially something *x* and those that in virtue of actually being *x* bring the first class to the state of likewise actually being *x*. These two classes are similarly found with respect to the soul, namely, that intellect, which later commentators would call the "potential or material intellect", and another intellect, later dubbed the "agent or active intellect". The role of the active intellect in understanding is, Aristotle concludes, like that played by light. To this extent there is relative agreement among Aristotle's interpreters. What makes the passage difficult is understanding how the active intellect functions like light; for there can be as many different interpretations of this passage as there are different theories of light. This number is increased even further when we note that Aristotle models his theory of intellection or understanding (*nous*) on that of vision, and so there will be as many interpretations of this passage again as there are different roles that light plays in one's theory of vision.

In this study, I begin by briefly considering Aristotle's own account of light's role in vision, which I claim does not provide a very illuminating example of how the active intellect is related to the potential intellect. After this brief foray into the thought of Aristotle, I turn to the medieval Arabic-speaking philosopher Avicenna (980-1037) and his theory of light and vision. I shall argue that while in general Avicenna's theory can be labeled "Aristotelian" in nature, certain elements in it, specifically concerning the nature of light and light's role in vision, are decidedly un-Aristotelian. While advances in optical theory, both in the Hellenistic and Islamic milieus, were undoubtedly one reason that Avicenna adopted these non-Aristotelian elements, I shall suggest that there was the additional benefit that these new features also provided Avicenna with a better model for explaining his own unique accounts of the active intellect as well as how to understand the very act of the intellect itself[1]. To this end, then, I shall consider Avicenna's "new" theory of light, and the role light plays in Avicenna's thought first with respect to the transparent, then color, and finally vision. Thereafter I shall turn to his theory of intellection: where I shall focus on the parallels in Avicenna's thought between light and the emanation issuing from the active intellect as they appear in his theories of vision and intellection.

Aristotle on perception and light

Let me begin with Aristotle's account of light and vision, but before doing that I want to outline in a very sketchy way his general theory of perception (Grk. *aisthēsis*; Arb. *idrāk*), since in general Avicenna will adopt much of this aspect of Aristotle's theory of vision[2]. Perception for Aristotle, as opposed to understanding (Grk. *nous*; Arb. *ʿaql*), involves a type of alteration of a given potentiality or faculty (Grk. *dunamis*; Arb.

1. In fact, Avicenna uses his "new" account of light as an explanatory model not only in his psychology, but also in physics proper (*Kitāb aṭ-Ṭabīʿī*, III 6), the special physical science treating heavenly phenomena (*Kitāb as-Samāʾ wa-l-ʿālam*, 5), and metaphysics (*Kitāb al-Ilāhīyāt*, II 4).

2. Aristotle's general account of perception is found at *De anima* II 5. For in-depth studies of Aristotle's theory see EVERSON (1997) and JOHANSEN (1997).

qūwa) that belongs to an animal, where the actuality of that potentiality is perception. This potentiality is harbored in a suitably disposed sense organ. In other words, the sense organ is potentially like what the perceived object is actually, that is, the organ is such that it can be acted upon or actualized by the sensible form belonging to the object of perception. It is this actuality of the potential (namely, a type of motion) that is perception. So, for example, in the act of seeing, the form or species of color in some object impresses itself on the eye such that the eye takes on this color-form and consequently is altered by it, and so thereby color is seen.

For Aristotle every case of sensory perception requires the presence of a medium, which the various sensible forms of the perceptible objects set into motion, and then through the intermediacy of the medium's motion the sensible forms set the corresponding sense organ into motion. In the case of vision (Grk. *horāsis*; Arb. *baṣar* or *ibṣār*)[3], the medium is either air or water (or ether in the case of the perception of supra-lunar objects). Strictly speaking, however, air and water are only potential media of vision and are only truly acted upon by the visible form or species when these media are made actually transparent by fire or the Sun[4]. According to Aristotle, light (Grk. *phōs*; Arb *ḍaw'*)[5] is this actualized state of the medium, whether air, water or ether, such that that medium is actually transparent. In other words, light is the actualization of a medium such that the medium is properly disposed so as to allow the species of colors in the object to act and so move the medium through which the animal's visual system is in turn acted upon. In contrast darkness (Grk. *skotos*; Arb. *ẓulma*) is the absence of light, and thus Themistius commenting Aristotle says of it:

> Darkness is in the [bodies] in which there is potentially light; for darkness is nothing but the transparent in potency, whereas light is an actuality and perfection of what is transparent *qua* transparent, for it is not [transparent] *qua* air, or *qua*, water[6].

Finally, in the *De anima* Aristotle describes color (Grk. *chroma*; Arb. *lawn*) as that which by its very nature sets the actually transparent medium

3. ARISTOTLE, *De anima* II 7 and *De sensu et sensibilia* 2-3.

4. For a discussion of Aristotle's theory of the transparent (*diaphanēs*) and the suggestion that it is a response to Plato's cosmology see VASILIU (1997).

5. This is the preferred translation of *phōs* in the only extant Arabic translation of the *De anima*, *Fī nafs*, ed. 'Abd al-Raḥmān Badawī. Concerning the translations of Aristotle's *De anima* in the Arabic-speaking world, see FRANK (1958-9).

6. Themistius, *De anima paraphrasis*, ed. Richard Heinze, 59, 31-34; Aristotle himself suggests much the same position at *De anima* II 7, 418b18-20.

into motion so as to act on the eye such that there is vision of the visible object[7]. This account of color, however, is relational in that it describes color by how it acts upon another. In *De sensu et sensibilia*, Aristotle attempts to define what color is in itself, saying color is "the extremity of the transparent (*diaphanēs*) in the delimited body"[8]. While here I have retained the translation "transparent" for *diaphanēs* in order to make clear the relation of this definition of color with the earlier one, it is an unhappy one in this context. So for the moment let me speak of the "diaphanous" in order to explain what Aristotle means by this definition of color. For Aristotle all natural bodies must be either indeterminate, such as air and water, in which case we may loosely say that they have no fixed extremities or limits, or the bodies are determinate, such as a stone, tree or human, and so have fixed limits in the form of some determinate shape. Moreover according to Aristotle all natural bodies are to some degree diaphanous: with respect to delimited bodies, again bodies having a determinate surface and definite shape, those that are white are diaphanous to the highest degree, while those that are black are at the lowest degree, with the intermediate colors corresponding with intermediary degrees to which these bodies are diaphanous. As for indeterminate bodies that have no natural limits, such as air and water, they are diaphanous to an unlimited degree and so appear, as we would say, truly transparent[9].

Having seen Aristotle's theory of light and vision, we find ourselves still in the dark when it comes to understanding the role of the active intellect. Indeed, the active intellect is supposed to function in understanding analogously to the way that light functions in vision, and yet it is not at all clear how to make sense of the analogy. Recall that for Aristotle light is the actuality of the transparent medium that stands between the object of vision and the eye. In the act of understanding, however, there does not seem to be anything that is analogous to the transparent medium that functions as the tool of the intelligible object. If light is the actuality of the medium, and yet there is no obvious medium in understanding, how could the active intellect function like light? Perhaps Aristotle simply means that the active intellect makes the potentially intelligible actually

7. ARISTOTLE, *De anima* II 7, 418a31-b2 and 419a6-11; at *De sensu et sensiblia* 3, 439b11-12, Aristotle defines color strictly speaking as the limit of the transparent in a delimited body.

8. ARISTOTLE, *De sensu et sensibilia* 3, 439b11-12.

9. For this interpretation of Aristotle definition of *chroma* see ALEXANDER OF APHRODISIAS, *De anima*, ed. Ivo Bruns, 46, 6-19; English translation in ALEXANDER OF APHRODISIAS (1979), trans. Athanasios Fotinis, 62.

intelligible in the way that light makes the potentially visible actually visible. While Aristotle might have this understanding in mind, he would certainly be using "light" in a non-technical way that is at odds with his explicit account of light and color. That is because the visible object as such is always actually colored for Aristotle, insofar as the delimited diaphanous body actually has some extremity. So strictly speaking light does not make what is potentially colored actually colored; rather, again, light is the alteration of the medium such that the already actualized color can act upon that medium, which in its turn acts upon the eye. So again if Aristotle intends by his light analogy that the active intellect makes the potentially intelligible actually intelligible, it is not a very illuminating example.

AVICENNA ON LIGHT AND VISION

Dag Hasse has brought our attention to the fact, that Avicenna's theory of light as it appears in his mature works such as his philosophical encyclopedia, the *Šifā'*, is not the standard Aristotelian account that we have just considered, where again light is understood merely as an affection of the medium [10]. In fact, as we shall see, Avicenna's theory of light is considerably more complex than that of Aristotle's and in many salient ways at odds with Aristotle's account.

Avicenna begins his account of vision, which takes up all of book III of his work on psychology from the *Šifā'*,with an entire chapter dedicated to the vocabulary of light. He first notes that as a matter of linguistic convention the Arabic terms *ḍaw*, *nūr* and *šu'ā'* are often used without distinction, all corresponding with what we would roughly call "light" [11]. For the purposes of discussing vision, however, he wants to assign each term a technical meaning. In the present context Avicenna says that he is not particularly concerned with *šu'ā'*, a term that we can safely translate as "ray", and which we shall discuss more thoroughly below. Instead, in this chapter he focuses on *ḍaw'* and *nūr*. The first, *ḍaw'*, I shall over-translate as "luminous light". Luminous light is that which is observed when one considers things like the Sun or fire without taking into account colors such yellow, white or red; it is something belonging in itself (*li-ḏātihi*) to a thing of this sort by which that thing can be seen. He next defines *nūr* as "the

10. See HASSE (2000), 108-119.

11. AVICENNA, *Avicenna's* De anima *(Arabic Text), being the psychological part of* Kitāb al-Shifā', ed. Fazlur Rahman, III.1, 91; henceforth *Kitāb an-nafs*.

thing that radiates (*yasṭa'u*) from [the body having luminous light], and is then imagined to fall upon bodies, in which case [this type of light] will appear white, black or green" [12]. For our purposes we can term this kind of light "radiant light" [13].

Having provided general descriptions of luminous light and radiant light he now approaches them from a different angle, namely, the bodies to which they belong. He notes that there are two classes of bodies: on the one hand, there are those that when positioned between a would-be-perceiver and a luminous body, such as fire, these intervening bodies hinder the perceiver from seeing the luminous body behind them. On the other hand, there are also those bodies that do not hinder one from seeing what is behind them. Those bodies that do not hinder one's seeing a luminous body behind them are like air and water. They are what we would most generally call "transparent" (*šaffāf*). Those bodies that hinder one's seeing what is behind them are again of two kinds: those bodies that are themselves luminous and those that are not. So, for example, a wall of fire, which is a luminous body, can just as effectively prevent one from seeing some light on the opposite side of it as a brick wall. The class of bodies that are self-luminous can be seen of themselves and need nothing further to be seen except that the body between them and the perceiver be transparent, whereas the latter sort of bodies cannot be seen merely given a transparent medium, but need something else. Avicenna identifies these latter bodies with "colored objects", which, if they are to be seen need in addition to a transparent medium the radiant light of a luminous body.

Up to this point most of what Avicenna has had to say about light, while certainly going beyond Aristotle, is not at odds with what Aristotle and latter Hellenistic Aristotelian commentators had to say about light. Where Avicenna's position is clearly at odds with the Aristotelian theory concerns the states of potentiality and actuality of transparent and colored objects. Recall that on the traditional Aristotelian theory color is in a sense always

12. AVICENNA, *Kitāb an-nafs*, III.1, 91

13. It is certainly worth noting that Ibn al-Hayṯam (965-1039), an immediate contemporary of Avicenna who lived in Cairo, also distinguished two types of light nearly corresponding with Avicenna's division here: light that radiate from self-luminous bodies and accidental light that is acquired by bodies that are not self-luminous; see IBN AL-HAYṮAM, *Kitāb al-Manāẓir*, ed. A. I. Sabra, Book I, chap. 3, esp. sections 21 and 87-88; for an English translation see IBN AL-HAYṮAM (1989), trans. A. I. Sabra. The similarities become even greater when compared with Avicenna's subsequent comments about rays radiating from the illuminated object so as to form a visual cone that falls upon the eye and projects a sensible image of the visible object to the visual system of the perceiver.

actual. It is only the medium that is sometimes potentially transparent and so actually dark, while at other times actually transparent and so light (for again light in Aristotle's technical sense is the state of the actually transparent medium as such). Thus for Aristotle a colored object fails to produce sight in a properly situated perceiver, not because there is no actual color in the object, but because the tool by which color acts upon the perceiver, namely, the medium, is not in a proper state, that is to say, the medium is not at that time actually transparent. In other words, the potentially transparent, that is, the dark, acts as an obstacle that prevents vision. In short, on the traditional Aristotelian model, color is always actual, while the medium can be either potentially or actually transparent.

In contrast, for Avicenna media such as air and water are strictly speaking always actually transparent, whereas it is color that might either be in a state of potentiality or actuality. Thus he writes:

> Do not suppose that white, red and the like actually exist in the bodies in the way that they are seen, but that the dark air prevents the vision of it, for the air itself is not dark. What is dark is only that which itself receives the radiant light, whereas the air itself (even if there is nothing having light in it) does not hinder the perception of that which receives the radiant light nor does it conceal the color when it exists in something [14].

He continues that in the absence of luminous or radiant light we simply imagine that the air is dark. The fact is, however, because there is no light there is nothing stimulating one's visual system. Thus it is not that one is "seeing" darkness, but rather one is simply not seeing at all. Avicenna likens this case to either being blind or having one's eyelids closed. Now while Avicenna will follow the Aristotelian tradition and occasionally speak of the "potentially transparent", he is also clear that its becoming actually transparent does not involve any alteration in the medium itself; rather, it involves an alteration or motion in another, either by the motion of some luminous body into a given place or a radiant light's falling onto a colored object.

In contrast with the strict reading of Aristotle sketched above where colors are always actualized, Avicenna believe that the color of a given body can be either in potentiality or in actuality. The term "color" (*lawn*) in its proper sense, he continues, refers to the phenomenal colors, white, red, green, etc., namely, the colors as they are seen. One is simply using the term "color" equivocally, says Avicenna, if "color" is meant to refer to

14. AVICENNA, *Kitāb an-nafs*, III 1, 93.

"various dispositions that are in the bodies, which when they receive luminous light, one of them comes to be something that we see as white and another as red" [15]. Now in those bodies that are not luminous, and so not visible in themselves, a radiant light that comes from a luminous body must fall upon the body and blend or mix with the potential color in the body. The result of this mingling of radiant light and potential color is then actual color [16].

Sometimes Avicenna speaks of actual color, that is, the combination of radiant light and potential color together emanating from the illuminated body as itself "luminous light" (*ḍaw'*), but since he almost as frequently uses the term "ray" (*šu'ā'*), I shall use this latter term in order to avoid possible confusion. Thus at III 7, he says that a ray is that which connects (*ittiṣāl*) the visible form or species in the perceived object, that is to say, actual color, with the visual system of some perceiver in order that the object "might project its sensible image (*šabaḥ*) into the [perceiver]" [17]. Also at III 1, where Avicenna initially discussed light terms he there quickly defined "ray" as "the thing that is imagined, as it were, to well-up [from colored bodies], cloak their color and then emanate (*yufīḍu*) from them" [18]. Avicenna more frequently expresses this sense of a ray's welling up and emanating from the body by saying that the light is simply reflected (*in'ikās*) from the body [19].

Avicenna additionally claims that when one sees some visible object, this ray or rays, which convey an object's sensible image, form a cone (*maḫrūṭ*), whose base is at the sensible object and whose vertex is at the back of the crystalline humor forming part of the eye. The sensible image projecting from the visible object affects the eye at the surface of the crystalline humor, rather than at the back of it where the vertex of the visual cone has fallen. Consequently, the sensible image affects the eye at a section of this visual cone. He next asserts that, "if the angle [at which the sensible image falls upon the surface of the crystalline humor] is larger

15. AVICENNA, *Kitāb an-nafs*, III 1, 94.

16. AVICENNA, *Kitāb an-nafs*, III 3, 103.

17. AVICENNA, *Kitāb an-nafs*, III 7, 142.

18. AVICENNA, *Kitāb an-nafs*, III 1, 91.

19. Dag Hasse criticizes John Blund's interpretation of Avicenna on the grounds that Blund makes Avicenna's rays "somehow participate in the formation of an image in the eye by traveling themselves" (HASSE [2000], 124). According to Hasse the sensible images "are transmitted instantaneously by the translucent medium" (*ibid.*). To me it seems that Hasse is forcing an Aristotelian understanding onto Avicenna, and in fact Blund's understanding is the correct one.

because the thing is nearer, the section is greater and the sensible image in it is greater, whereas if the angle is smaller because the thing is farther away, the section and sensible image that is in it are smaller"[20]. Avicenna's appeal to a visual cone and his explanation of the apparent size of a visible object in terms of the angular separation between the visual rays coming from the object's extremes is interesting (see figure 1); for this is the very account that geometrically inclined optical theorists, such as Euclid, Ptolemy and al-Kindī, had given to explain differences in apparent size[21].

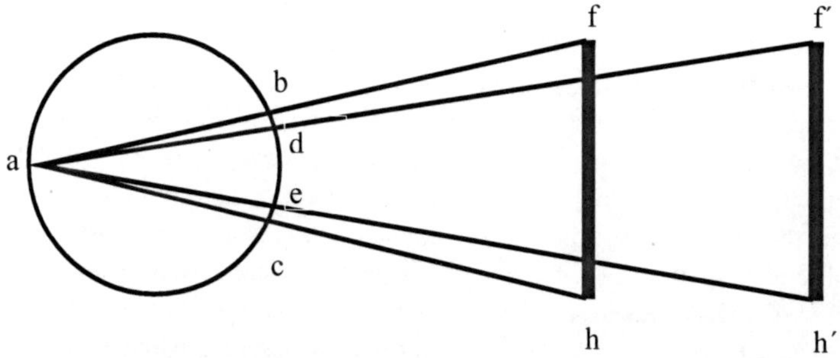

Figure 1

Where Avicenna's analysis differs from theirs is that while he thought that the rays must emanate from the visible objects itself, and then impinge upon the visual system, they thought that the rays emanate from the eyes of the perceiver. Avicenna rejects this extramission theory of vision on the grounds that it in fact cannot take advantage of the very geometrical analysis, which was thought to be its primary strength. Avicenna argues thus: if vision involves a ray that purportedly emanates from the eyes and its coming into contact with a visible object, and the perception of that object results from the contact of that ray, then when that ray extends to where the visible object is, it should in fact perceive the visible object according to how big the object actually is, since it is in actual contact with the whole of the object according to its actual size. So, for instance, when

20. AVICENNA, *Kitāb an-nafs*, III 5, 124.

21. See LINDBERG (1976), chapters 1 and 2, for discussions of these thinkers and their extramission theories of vision.

there are similarly sized objects, which are at different distances, the perceiver should not see them as appearing either smaller or larger just as he would not feel them as either smaller or larger[22]. In contrast, claims Avicenna, if something comes back down the visual ray such that the vision takes place in the visual system of the perceiver, then the emanation of rays from the eyes is redundant, since one needs merely posit, as Avicenna himself does, that rays emanate from the visible object, either owing to the object itself in the case of a luminous body, or when radiant light falls upon the object and mixes with the potential colors in the object, and then is reflected from it, in the case of a colored object.

Finally, given his account of why rays are needed in order for there to be vision (for again it is by means of rays that the sensible image is able to reach the perceiver from the visible object), Avicenna can explain why vision always requires a medium, or to be more exact, why some distance between the visible object and the eye is always needed for vision[23]. Recall that for Aristotle the transparent medium is necessary in order that the actual color in a visible object can use the medium as a tool by which to affect the perceiver. In contrast, Avicenna maintains that the reason why a visible object cannot be seen when it is placed in immediate contact with the eye is that in this case the visible object cannot emanate the requisite rays, which form the visual cone that impresses the sensible image upon the surface of the crystalline humor when there is vision. So it is not the absence of a medium *per se* that explains why there is no vision in this scenario; rather, it is the absence of a requisite emanation that explains the lack of seeing.

Now to finish up Avicenna's theory of vision, let us briefly talk about his account of the physiology of vision[24]. We have already seen that for Avicenna vision requires that the sensible image of a visible object be conveyed through a transparent medium via rays emanating from the visible object. These rays, which apparently emanate in all directions, form a cone relative to a properly functioning visual system that is facing the visible object, where the vertex of that cone falls at the back of the crystalline humor, which makes up part of the eye. Once this sensible image impinges upon the eye it stimulates or impresses itself on the crystalline humor; however, there is not vision at this point, since if there

22. For a more thorough presentation of Avicenna's refutation of not only mathematically inspired extramission theories of vision, but also the Galenic extramission theory see LINDBERG (1976), 43-52.

23. See AVICENNA, *Kitāb an-nafs*, III 7, 141-142.

24. See AVICENNA, *Kitāb an-nafs*, III 8, 151-154.

were, there would be two distinct sensible images in the two eyes and the single visible object would be seen as two. Instead, the sensible image is transferred via a conveying pneuma (*rūḥ*) along the optical nerves, (literally "hollow nerves") to the optic chiasma (*ṣalīb*), at which there is then vision. The sensible image is then conveyed to the anterior ventricle of the brain where it is impressed upon the common sense at which point there is what Avicenna terms "the perfection of vision".

Let us now take one step beyond the process of seeing, which will be of use shortly when we discuss Avicenna's vision of the act of the intellect. After appearing in the common sense, the sensible image passes onto the retentive imagination (*ḫayāl*), also called the form-bearing faculty (*qūwa muṣawwira*), which is arrayed behind the anterior ventricle of the brain where the image is stored until it is called up by the estimative faculty. At the time that the image is needed,

> [the estimative faculty] opens up the *cerebellar vermis* (*dūda*) by removing what is between the two porous appendages (which [just] are the *cerebellar vermis*) and [the form that is in the retentive imagination] conjoins with the pneuma harboring the estimative faculty by means of the pneuma harboring the imaginative faculty (which in humans is called the cogitative [faculty] (*qūwa mufakkira*)). The form that is in the retentive imagination is then imprinted onto the pneuma of the estimative faculty, and the imaginative faculty, which serves the estimative faculty, conveys what is in the retentive imagination to it [25].

Professor Black's paper provides the details as to what occurs at and after this stage, particularly as it relates to human cognition, and so I direct the reader to her discussion to fill in those finer points [26].

Let me quickly sum up the most salient points of Avicenna's optical theory in order that we may better appreciate the role it plays in his theory of intellectual understanding. Light is of two types. There is luminous light, which belongs to certain bodies like the Sun and fire, and by which these bodies are visible in themselves. Additionally, there is radiant light, which radiates from luminous bodies and mixes with the potential colors of certain other types of bodies. What is potentially colored but not actually colored only becomes actually colored through a certain motion or alteration; however, the alteration or motion does not take place in the transparent medium, which is always actually transparent for Avicenna, but by some motion that brings the potentially colored object into the

25. AVICENNA, *Kitāb an-nafs*, III 8, 153.
26. See BLACK (2012).

presence of a radiant light. Thereafter the mixture of radiant light and potential color form a ray, which when it is connected with a perceiver that is facing the visible object, that visible object projects a sensible image of itself that is seen as actual color.

It is certainly worth mentioning here that virtually all of the new features appearing in Avicenna's optics find their counterparts in the more fully developed optics of Ibn al-Hayṯam, the Alhazen of Latin fame, (965-1039), a near contemporary of Avicenna who lived in Cairo, whose works on optics were probably some of the most significant in both the Muslim East and Christian West until the seventeenth century[27]. I shall not speculate whether what Avicenna presented here in mere outline, Ibn al-Hayṯam would pick up and expand upon, or whether Avicenna derived his optical model from the works of Ibn al-Hayṯam, or if even in fact both men were drawing upon some incipient mathematical model of the intromission theory current at the time. Still the similarities between their theories of vision suggest that the position Avicenna lays out here represented the cutting edge of optical theory at his time, and thus is not merely some *ad hoc* account that he concocted so that he could explain the relation between the potential and active intellects, the topic to which I now turn.

AVICENNA ON COGNITION AND EMANATION

I began this paper with a quotation from Aristotle's *De anima* concerning the role of the active intellect and its similarity with light. Let me now give the corresponding account of the active intellect and its relation to light as it appears in Avicenna's *Kitāb an-Nafs*:

> Since [the active intellect] is the cause providing the intellectualizing forms (*ṣuwar ʿaqlīya*), it is nothing but an actual intellect in whom the principles of the intelligible forms are separate, and whose relation to our souls is the relation of the Sun to our vision. Just as the Sun is actually visible in itself (*bi-ḏātihi*) and through its radiant light (*nūr*) it makes actually visible what is not actually visible, so likewise is the state of this intellect vis-à-vis our souls; for when the intellectual faculty reviews the particulars that are in the retentive imagination and the aforementioned active intellect radiates its

27. For an overview see LINDBERG's chapter (1976), "Alhazen and the New Intromission Theory of Vision" and the translation and commentary of Ibn al- Hayṯam's *Optics* in IBN AL-HAYṮAM (1989). The Latin translation of Ibn al- Hayṯam's *Kitāb al-Manāẓir*, *De aspectibus*, is in places markedly different from the Arabic; for a translation and commentary of the Latin see IBN AL-HAYṮAM (2001), trans. A. Mark Smith.

> light into us [and] upon them, the things separated from matter and its concomitants are altered and impressed upon the rational soul [...] in the sense that reviewing them prepares the soul in order that the thing separate from matter [coming] from the active intellect [i.e., the intellectualizing forms] emanates upon them; for discursive thought and selective attention are certain motions that prepares the soul to receive the emanation [...] So when a certain relation to this form falls to the rational soul by means of the active intellect's radiant activity, then, from [the relation], there comes to be in [the rational soul] something that in one way is of the genus of [the form] and in another way is not. Just like when luminous light falls on colored objects, it produces from them an impression on the visual system that is not in every way [reduced] to their sum, so likewise the images that are potentially intelligible become actually intelligible – not themselves but what is acquired from them. In fact, just as the impression of the sensible forms conveyed by means of luminous light [or we would prefer, "rays"] is not itself those forms, but rather something related to them that is engendered by means of the luminous light in the recipient facing [the light], so likewise when the rational soul reviews those forms in the retentive imagination and the radiant light of the active intellect comes into a type of contact (*ittiṣāl*) with them, then they are prepared so that from the luminous light of the active intellect they come to be the abstract version of those forms free from [material] taints within [the rational soul] [28].

Unlike Aristotle's account of the active intellect and his comparison of it with light, we see that virtually every feature in Avicenna's account of intellectual understanding has its analogue in his optics.

So to begin with the most obvious point of similarity: first, the active intellect is likened to the Sun, and just as the Sun is both luminous in itself as well as being a source of radiant light, so the active intellect as one of the immaterial substances is intelligible in itself as well as a source of intelligibility in the sub-lunar world [29].

28. AVICENNA, *Kitāb an-nafs,* V 5, 234-236.

29. It was a standard position among most medieval philosophers (at least those working within the *falsafa* tradition) that since matter is what prevents intelligibility, anything immaterial must be intelligible in itself. Thus at *Kitāb al-Burhān*, III 5, Avicenna writes: "Exiting things are divided into two classes: essences intelligible in existence and essence perceptible in existence. Essences intelligible in existence are those that have neither matter nor any consequential accidents of matter. They are intelligible in themselves precisely because no operation is needed to make them intelligible, and because they cannot be an object of sensation in any way" (AVICENNA, *Kitāb al-Burhān*, ed. 'A. Badawī, 160). Hence the fact that the active intellect is completely separate from matter guarantees that it is intelligible in itself.

Second, as with the Sun, there radiates from the active intellect an analogue of radiant light in the form of "intellectualizing forms" (*ṣuwar ʿaqlīya*). In an earlier work, I had argued that the active intellect's emanation of these intellectualizing forms should not be identified simply with intelligible forms or species themselves, that is, with fully actualized and specific intelligibles, such as the intelligible species of human, horse or oak tree, as such intelligibles exist in the intellect as something actually understood [30]. Instead, I claimed that this emanation, that is, these intellectualizing forms, should be viewed as the intelligible accidents mentioned by Avicenna in his *Madḫal* (*Introduction*) [31], which particularize an essence considered in itself such that that essence exists as an object of conceptualization. Examples that Avicenna gives of such intelligible accidents are universality or particularity in predication, and essentiality or accidentality in predication. As such the intellectualizing forms have to mix with the potentially but not actually intelligible object stored in the retentive imagination; the combination of the intellectualizing forms and potential intelligible is the actual intelligible. In my earlier work, I argued for this thesis on the basis of an analysis of Avicenna's doctrine of essences considered in themselves, those essences considered in concrete particulars and considered in conceptualization. We now see that this thesis is further borne out by the comparison between the functions of the Sun's radiant light and the active intellect's emanation; for it is only by a radiant light's mixing with potential color that there comes to be actual color, just as it is only by actualizing forms mixing with the potentially intelligible in the retentive imagination that there comes to be something actually intelligible in the potential or material intellect.

A third point of comparison is the need for a certain type of alteration and preparatory motion in both cognition and vision. To understand the comparison we must note that sensible forms stored in the retentive imagination are potentially intelligible in the way that certain bodies in the absence of a luminous source are potentially colored. In the case of the potentially colored object the required motion is locomotion, either moving some light to where the object is or moving the object to where the light is. In its cognitive counterpart, the motion involves the rational intellect's taking control of the compositive imagination (*mutaḫayyila*), and thereby transforming it into the cogitative faculty (*qūwa*

30. See McGINNIS (2007), 169-183.

31. AVICENNA, *Madḫal*, ed. G. Anawātī, M. al-Ḫuḍayrī and F. al-Ahwanī, I 2, 15.

mutafakkira)[32]. The cogitative faculty, then, combines and divides the forms in the retentive imagination – literally a kind of motion – either as those forms manifest themselves as images or the linguistic counterparts thereof. The result from this motion of the cogitative faculty is a new image or proposition.

This leads to a fourth point of comparison. Given the presence of this new image or proposition, that is, something potentially intelligible in itself, the rational soul can then focus on what the image is essentially of, ignoring the sensible aspects of it that are concomitants of matter, such as a particular color, shape, location and the like. The intellect's turning towards and focusing on what the image is essentially about is, I have argued elsewhere[33], what Avicenna intends when he speaks of the process of abstraction (*tajrīd*)[34]. It has its visual analogue in the requirement that the perceiver must turn and face the actually colored object in order that that object may project a sensible image of itself onto the eye of the perceiver.

Here we now have the fifth and I believe final point of comparison. Once the rational soul has abstracted away the concomitants of matter, the emanation from the active intellect, that is, its intellectualizing forms, radiates upon and mixes with the potentially intelligible object making it actually intelligible, analogous to the way that radiant light mixes with potential color to make it actual color and form rays. The now actually intelligible object then impresses itself upon the potential intellect, and there is understanding in the way that the sensible image impresses itself on the eye when there is vision. What comes to exist in the potential intellect, while being of the same genus as the form in the retentive imagination, cannot simply be reduced to that form any more than what comes to exist in the eye, namely, the sensible image conveying a body's color can be reduced to that body's various dispositions that are identified with potential color. The intelligible species is only efficacious when there is a mixture of the potentially intelligible and the actualizing accidents emanated from the active intellect, just as color is only efficacious when there is a mixture of potential color and the radiant light of a luminous body.

32. See BLACK (2012), especially sections 3 "The Hybrid Character of the Cogitative Faculty" and 5 "Cogitation and Conceptualization".

33. See MCGINNIS (2007), 174-175.

34. My own understanding of Avicennan abstraction has been much influenced by HASSE's superb study of that subject (2001).

To conclude, unlike Aristotle's opaque reference to the similarities between the active intellect and light, Avicenna's comparison between the active intellect and the Sun seem to me to be quite illuminating.

BIBLIOGRAPHY

Sources

ALEXANDER OF APHRODISIAS (1887), *De anima*, ed. Ivo Bruns, *Supplementum Aristotelicum* vol. 2.1, Berlin.

– (1979), *The De anima of Alexander of Aphrodisias*, a Translation and Commentary, trans. Athanasios Fotinis, Washington, DC.

ARISTOTLE (1831), *De anima*, ed. Immanuel Bekker, vol. 1, Berlin.

– (1954), *Fī nafs*, ed. 'Abd al-Raḥmān Badawī, Cairo.

– (1831), *De sensu et sensibilia*, ed. Immanuel Bekker, vol. 1, Berlin.

AVICENNA (1952), *Madḫal*, ed. G. Anawātī, M. al-Ḫuḍayrī and F. al-Ahwanī, Cairo.

– (1959), *Kitāb an-Nafs, Avicenna's* De anima *(Arabic Text), being the psychological part of* KITĀB AL-SHIFĀ', ed. Fazlur Rahman, London.

– (1966), *Kitāb al-Burhān*, ed. 'A. Badawī, Cairo.

– (1969), *As-Samā' wa-l-'ālam*, ed. M. Qāsim, Cairo.

– (1996), *As-Samā' aṭ-ṭabī'ī*, ed. J. Āl Yāsīn, Beirut.

– (2005), *Ilāhīyāt*, ed. and trans. Michael E. Marmura, Middle East Text Initiative, Provo, UT.

IBN AL-HAYṮAM (1983), *Kitāb al-Manāẓir*, ed. A. I. Sabra, Kuwait.

– (1989), *Optics*, trans. A. I. Sabra. Studies of the Warburg Institute, vol. 40, i, London.

– (2001), *De aspectibus*, trans. A. Mark Smith, 2. vols., Philadelphia, PA.

THEMISTIUS (1899), *De anima paraphrasis*, ed. Richard Heinze, *Commentaria in Aristotelem Graeca* vol. 5.3, Berlin.

Studies

BLACK, Deborah (2012), "Rational Imagination: Avicenna on the Cogitative Power", in the present volume.

EVERSON, Stephen (1997), *Aristotle on Perception*, New York.

FRANK, Richard (1958-9), "Some Fragments of Isḥāq's Translation of the *De anima*", in *Cahiers de Byrsa* 8, 215-229.

HASSE, Dag Nikolaus (2000), *Avicenna's* De Anima *in the Latin West: the Formation of a Peripatetic Philosophy of the soul, 1160-1300*, Warburg Institute Studies and Texts vol. 1, London and Turin.

– (2001), "Avicenna on Abstraction", in *Aspects of Avicenna*, ed. Robert Wisnovsky, Princeton, NJ.

JOHANSEN, T. K. (1997), *Aristotle on the Sense Organs*, Cambridge, UK.

LINDBERG, David C. (1976), *Theories of Vision, From al-Kindi to Kepler*, Chicago.

MCGINNIS, Jon (2007), "Making Abstraction Less Abstract: The Logical, Psychological, and Metaphysical Dimensions of Avicenna's Theory of Abstraction", in *Proceedings of the American Catholic Philosophical Association* 80, 169-183.

VASILIU, Anca (1997), *Du Diaphane : image, milieu, lumière dans la pensée antique et médiévale*, Études de Philosophie Médiévale, vol. 76, Paris.

RATIONAL IMAGINATION: AVICENNA ON THE COGITATIVE POWER

Deborah BLACK
(University of Toronto)

Discussions of the cluster of powers known collectively as the "internal senses" (*al-ḥawāss al-bāṭinah*) often focus on the various functions and activities of the individual faculties themselves, in isolation from their broader contribution to human knowledge as a whole. Unfortunately this tends to marginalize the role of the internal senses in medieval cognitive psychology, and to obscure the fact that medieval philosophers, like their modern counterparts, tended to attribute the majority of both human and animal cognitive functions to faculties localized in the brain. While the intellect may be accorded pride of place as the highest and most distinctively human of the soul's faculties, it is the internal senses that perform most of our everyday cognitive tasks.

Indeed, most medieval philosophers agree that the internal senses must play an integral role even in the operations of rational thinking. This holds true for one of the most rationalist and dualist of medieval philosophers and the founder of the internal sense tradition itself, namely, Ibn Sīnā (Avicenna). In his standard classification of the internal senses, the power that is commonly referred to as the "cogitative faculty" (*al-quwwah al-mufakkirah*) after its Latin translation as the *vis cogitativa,* is posited for the express purpose of accounting for the interaction between the intellect and the internal senses in human cognitive acts. My aim here is to offer a detailed analysis of Avicenna's account of the cogitative faculty in order to provide a more accurate picture of how the Persian philosopher understands the nature of human thinking in the light of his soul-body dualism. I argue that the crucial point for a proper understanding of Avicenna's account of the cogitative faculty is its peculiar status among the internal sense powers. As Avicenna defines it, the cogitative faculty is simply the label given to the uniquely human manifestation of the compositive imagination (*al-mutaḫayyilah*) when it is at the service of and controlled by the intellect. It is not a full-fledged faculty with an independent organ, operation, or object of its own [1]. On the basis of this hybrid characterization of the cogitative faculty, I contend, it is possible to account for all of Avicenna's references to "thinking" or "cogitation" (*fikr, fikrah, tafakkur*) within a single, unified theory in which the internal senses play a leading role.

I. Imagination and cogitation among the internal senses

The fundamentals of Avicenna's account of the internal senses in general, and of the cogitative power in particular, are most fully spelled out in the *De anima* of the *Ŝifā* or *Healing*, and these fundamentals in my view remain quite consistent throughout the rest of Avicenna's mature writings [2]. So I will begin with a brief overview of the Avicennian schema of internal senses, focusing on those features that are of special importance to understanding the function of the cogitative faculty.

Avicenna sees the internal senses as a cluster of five different faculties localized in the various ventricles of the brain. These five powers are in

1. It is interesting to note that in this respect the Avicennian cogitative faculty reflects the view of Aristotelian *phantasia* as functionally incomplete, advanced in WEDIN (1988), 45ff.

2. Earlier treatments of the internal senses display some minor variations from the standard *Ŝifā* account. Perhaps the most interesting is found in the *Maqālah fī an-nafs (Compendium on the Soul)*. In chap. 6 of this treatise, Avicenna differentiates the compositive imagination (*al-mutaḫayyilah*), of which the cogitative faculty is the rational manifestation, from the retentive or formative imagination (*al-muṣawwirah*) by claiming that the latter only contains forms first impressed on the common sense (i.e., forms that were not first perceived by the external senses), whereas the former contains "nothing but true forms bestowed by sensation". In his later discussions of the differences between these two faculties, Avicenna allows the formative faculty to preserve any fictional creations that the compositive imagination has concocted, even if they are not true.

With respect to later texts, few offer any discussion of the internal senses that are as detailed as that provided in the *Healing*. But there are several allusions to cogitation (*fikr*) in Avicenna's discussions of human cognition as a whole, in particular as a foil against which to compare intuition (*ḥads*). GUTAS (2001) argues for a development in Avicenna's account of intuition that is also reflected in his later accounts of thinking. By contrast, I believe that the hybrid character of the cogitative faculty which is present in all of Avicenna's writings is sufficient to explain those features of the *fikr-ḥads* contrast that Gutas argues are later (i.e., post-*Ŝifā*) developments.

turn organized into two pairs of faculties, and each of these pairs contains one receptive and one retentive capacity. Between these two pairs the fifth faculty, which I will call the "compositive imagination" (*al-mutaḫayyilah*) to differentiate it from retentive imagination (*al-ḫayāl*, also known as the *formative* faculty, *al-muṣawwirah*), completes the entourage. This intermediate power is physically identical with the cogitative faculty, though functionally and definitionally distinct from it.

It is important to emphasize that Avicenna arrives at this division of the internal senses by deducing it from a set of principles of faculty differentiation[3]. The list is neither arbitrary nor simply derived from tradition. The basic split into two receptive-retentive pairs derives from the principle that the same faculty cannot both receive and retain its perceptual objects. This principle ultimately reflects the fact that the internal senses are physiological powers with instruments in the brain; and since different physical matters display different degrees of malleability and stability when affected by other bodies, different physical organs will be appropriate for reception, which requires a fluid substratum that is easily impressed, and retention, which requires denser matter to preserve the impressions once received.

A different principle is invoked by Avicenna to explain why two pairs of receptive and retentive powers are required. In this case the principle is a familiar one within the Aristotelian tradition, namely, that different cognitive objects must be perceived by distinct faculties. Avicenna's application of this principle is novel, however, because of his well-known differentiation between forms (*ṣuwar,* singular *ṣūrah*) and intentions (*ma'ānin*, singular *ma'nan*)*,* the former of which are perceived by the external and common senses and retained in the formative faculty, and the latter of which are perceived by the estimative faculty (*wahm*) and stored in the faculty of memory (*ḏikr*).

Avicenna's claim that forms and intentions constitute distinct perceptual objects is relevant to his accounts of compositive imagination and cogitation, since these powers are in some fashion constituted by their intermediate position between the formative and memorative faculties, i.e., the retentive capacities for forms and intentions respectively. A full consideration of Avicenna's complex and still controversial notion of estimative intentions is not necessary for our present purposes. Rather, it is sufficient to note that Avicenna defines intentions broadly as properties that are not in themselves material, although they can also exist as

3. For the principles see AVICENNA, *De anima* I 5, 43-44; *Avicenna's Psychology*, 30.

properties of things in the physical world that accompany their sensible qualities. Because they are not intrinsically material, however, these intentions have a different nature from the proper and common sensibles (which are what Avicenna means here by "forms"), and thus intentions cannot be perceived by faculties which are specifically designed to grasp material forms. Nonetheless, since intentions are on Avicenna's view part of the make-up of the physical world, and since there is evidence that many non-rational animals are able to perceive them, there must be a corporeal faculty for which they constitute the proper object – hence the need to posit a distinct faculty of estimation. While the range of properties included under the rubric of estimative intentions appears to be quite broad, the most vivid and well-known examples that Avicenna gives are of affective qualities, such as the sheep's grasp of the fact that the wolf is her natural enemy, and her recognition of her offspring as an object of affection.

Avicenna's final principle of faculty differentiation is the one which accounts for his claim that the retentive and compositive (or creative) functions of imagination must fall under the scope of two distinct faculties. According to this principle, one must differentiate between passive faculties which simply perceive their objects as they present themselves to the percipient, and faculties which have the capacity to perform further actions on the objects that they have perceived[4]. To act upon images in this context means to have the capacity to combine and divide them at will, and this, Avicenna holds, requires a separate faculty, namely, the compositive imagination with which we are here concerned:

> The distinction between perception accompanied by action (*al-idrāk ma'a al-fi'l*) and perception which is not accompanied by action is that one of the acts of a certain internal faculty is to compose some of the perceived forms and intentions with others and to divide some from others, so that it would have had both to perceive and to act upon what it perceived. As for perception without action, it is for the form or the intention to be merely impressed in the thing without it having any independent action (*taṣarrufan*) over it at all[5].

In this passage, Avicenna clearly maintains that the capacity to manipulate images and intentions freely necessarily includes the ability to perceive the ingredients being combined. While this may be a reasonable position to hold, it does call into question Avicenna's claim that distinct

4. AVICENNA, *De anima* I 5, 43-4; IV 1, 165; *Naǧāh*, 201; *Avicenna's Psychology*, 31.
5. AVICENNA, *De anima* I 5, 43. (Except where otherwise stated, translations are my own).

faculties are required to explain perception and action. Parsimony would seem to favour the positing of a single faculty, given that the capacities involved do not seem to be mutually exclusive [6]. Now, while Avicenna does not explicitly provide the rationale for his position, it emerges readily enough from his description of the compositive capacity of the imagination. Central amongst its functions is the ability to concoct fictional compositions which do not conform to anything that has been or can be perceived in the real world, without any regard whatsoever to their veridicality (and perhaps even their possibility) [7]:

> Next, we know certainly that it is in our nature to compose some sensibles with others, and separate them from one another, not according to that form which we found in them externally, and not accompanied by assent to the existence of any of them nor to their non-existence. So it is necessary for there to be a faculty in us by which we do this, and this is the faculty which is called cogitative (*mufakkirah*) when the intellect employs it, and imaginative (*mutaḫayyilah*) when the animal faculty uses it [8].

Avicenna's worry, then, is that if the same faculty were assigned both the fundamental perceptual task of grasping and preserving forms and intentions from the external world, and the further freedom to manipulate these images creatively, there would be no mechanism to ensure the veridical character of retained perceptions [9]. The distinction between

6. Avicenna's later critic and commentator, Faḫr al-Dīn al-Rāzī, argued that this view is both inconsistent and uneconomical. He suggested that the estimative faculty was sufficient to account for the animal soul's compositive abilities, and therefore the compositive imagination is superfluous. In attempting to answer this charge on Avicenna's behalf, al-Ṭūsī countered that the compositive imagination does not in fact perceive the items that it acts upon, despite Avicenna's explicit declaration to the contrary. For this point see BLACK (1993), 251 n. 41.

7. This latter qualification is rather tricky, given Avicenna's remarks on the nature of fictional or vain forms and his attempt to classify them as impossible. For a consideration of Avicenna's views on the status of fictional forms, see BLACK (1997).

8. AVICENNA, *De anima* IV 1, 165-66. The earlier overview of the internal senses in *De anima* I 5, 45, gives a similar though more cursory description, including brain localization: "Next is the faculty called 'imaginative' in relation to the animal soul, and 'cogitative' in relation to the human soul. It is a faculty set up in the middle ventricle of the brain at the vermiform [tissue] whose function is to combine [things] in the imagination and to separate them from each other as it wills". For the distinction between retentive and compositive imagination based on the latter's capacity for creating fictions, see also the text from *Qanūn* quoted in n. 14 below.

9. This is one of the ways in which the proliferation of internal senses can be seen as a correction of the underlying Aristotelian psychology of imagination, and not a decadent multiplication of principles. Aristotle's own grouping of both "voluntary" or creative and

perception *simpliciter*, and perception accompanied by action, is thus meant to ensure the reliability of the internal senses in providing accurate information concerning the physical states of the extramental world [10].

To summarize, the basic picture of the imaginative faculty that emerges from Avicenna's deduction of the number of internal sense faculties is as follows. The distinction between the formative faculty or retentive imagination and the compositive imagination is the result of parcelling out two distinct functions of Aristotelian *phantasia* to two distinct internal sense faculties [11]. The compositive imagination is posited to account for the capacity to combine and divide sensible forms and images with estimative intentions without reference to the actual configuration of things in the external world, that is, without any stipulation that the external senses have previously been affected by such combinations. This basic compositive capacity of the imagination in turn admits of two distinct applications, one of which is common to all animal souls, and the other of which is unique to the human soul. In its mere animal manifestations, the combinatory activities of the imagination are controlled by the estimative faculty which, in addition to being the primary percipient of intentions, is viewed by Avicenna as the primary judgmental and controlling power within the animal soul. When it is controlled instead by the intellect, the imagination

passive or perceptual tasks under the rubric of *phantasia* in *De anima* III 3 makes it difficult to give a unified account of the Aristotelian concept. By parcelling out the competing operations on *phantasmata* to distinct faculties, Avicenna is able to eliminate some of the tensions within the Aristotelian account.

10. JANSSENS (2004), 54 n. 22, suggests that there is a puzzle in the fact that the imaginative/cogitative faculty "deals with both forms *and* intentions, [...] hence using data derived from both imagination *and* estimation". That is, if distinct faculties are required to explain the perception of forms and intentions, it seems puzzling that the imaginative faculty is able to perceive both types of objects. Presumably the solution to this lies in the basic empirical facts that sensible qualities *are* distinct from intentional properties, i.e., colour is not hostility; and that there are cases where animals perceive sensible qualities that are *not* accompanied by any intentions. Hence, the perception of intentions indicates the presence of a percipient other than the percipients of sensible qualities, i.e., the external and common senses. This does not of itself preclude the possibility that a faculty might be found that is capable of perceiving both forms and intentions – something that the estimative faculty itself must do in its role as the central judgemental faculty in the animal soul.

11. For *phantasia* as retentive see ARISTOTLE, *De anima* III 3, 428b30-29a9; also pertinent is the link between *phantasia* and memory at *De memoria* 1, 450a22-25; and the so-called "decaying sense" account in *Rhetoric* I 13, 1370a28-30; see NUSSBAUM (1978), 222-23 for this terminology. For fictive *phantasia*, see *De anima* III 3, 427b18-24.

is transformed into the cogitative faculty [12]. It is of crucial importance to Avicenna's account of the internal senses to note that the cogitative faculty is not, properly speaking, the human imagination, that is, it is incorrect to say that for Avicenna (in contrast to many Latin authors), imagination is replaced by cogitation in humans [13]. Human beings have estimative faculties as well as intellects on Avicenna's view, and so they may continue to indulge in purely animal exercises of their compositive imagination free from any influence of the intellect. Avicenna may be a rationalist but he is also a dualist, and the possibility of conflicts between the animal and purely human aspects of human nature are very real in his view.

II. IMAGINATION WITHOUT REASON: AVICENNA'S ACCOUNT OF THE COMPOSITIVE IMAGINATION

In light of the dependence of cogitation upon the imaginative faculty, it is impossible to understand the function that the cogitative faculty plays in Avicenna's account of knowledge-acquisition without first understanding the underlying compositive capacities of the imagination itself, since the cogitative power is constituted by the intellect's manipulation of those capacities. The central feature that emerges in Avicenna's theory of the compositive imagination is its restlessness or randomness. Indeed, while Avicenna's general accounts of the imagination in his enumeration of the internal senses suggest that the faculty has two principal manifestations, one of which is in the service of estimation and the soul's animal

12. The same description is found in works ranging from the early *Maqālah fī an-nafs* through to the *Išārāt*. See *Maqālah*, chap. 6, 359-60 (though note that DAVIDSON (1992), 81 n. 30, expresses some scepticism regarding the authenticity of this text.) For other texts see *Mabdā'*, 3.3, 93-4; *'Uyūn*, chap. 14, 38-9; *Išārāt*, 125. The stipulation that the estimative faculty is the controller of the animal manifestations of the compositive imagination is explicit in all of these passages save the first. And while the passage from the *Healing* cited at n. 8 above does not make explicit reference to the estimative faculty, its controlling function is a theme that is repeated in all of Avicenna's accounts of the internal senses, including the remaining chapters of *De anima* Bk. 4, each of which discusses one or two of the internal sense powers in depth.

13. Avicenna is generally quite careful not to refer to the cogitative faculty as the human imagination, and to emphasize that humans have both capacities. The only exception to this that I have found is the following brief remark, which occurs in passing in an explanation of how seeing double occurs: "Then [the form] conjoins with the spirit that bears the estimative faculty through the mediation of the spirit that bears the imaginative faculty (*li-l-quwwah al-mutaḫayyilah*), which in people is called cogitative (*mufakkirah*)" (AVICENNA, *De anima* III 8, 153).

operations, and the other of which is in the service of the intellect and its rational operations, it would be more precise to say that the compositive imagination has three basic types of activity, the most fundamental of which is free from subordination to any other controlling faculty, be it rational or animal. It is when its activity is in this pure and uncontrolled state that the imagination produces phenomena such as dreams and hallucinations, but it is essentially the same type of activity which, when harnessed by the intellect, produces cogitative thought.

In its absolute and uncontrolled state, then, the compositive imagination is characterized by incessant activity. That is, by its very nature imagination composes and divides images and intentions continually and, as we would now say, subconsciously. Avicenna often refers to the activity of the compositive imagination as a *taṣarruf*–a term that implies that the act in question is independent and under the control of the agent or power who exercises it. In accordance with this conception, the unharnessed imagination is depicted as having free reign to play with whatever images and intentions the soul has stored up in the retentive imagination and memory [14]. It is clear that Avicenna believes that this free play of the imagination can never be shut off, even though it may often take place beneath the level of conscious awareness. So while there is an element of the voluntary in imagination–to the extent that (1) it is not constrained by what is actually encountered through the senses; and (2) its activity is able to be directed by the intellect or the estimation–there is no "on-off switch" for this faculty [15]:

> Part of the nature of this imaginative faculty is to be continually preoccupied with the two storehouses of the formative and memorative

14. AVICENNA, *Qanūn*, 96-7: "[...] This faculty acts independently on what has been stored in the retentive imagination (*al-ḫayāl*) in such a way that it composes and divides. So it can make present (*tastaḥḍiru*) a form in accordance with the way in which it has been conveyed from the sense, as well as a form different from it, like a man who flies and a mountain of emerald. And as for the retentive imagination, nothing is present in it except on account of the reception from sensation".

15. It may seem that this claim conflicts with Avicenna's general position that the soul can only perform one activity at a time, a position that is based upon what might be called Avicenna's "unity principle", i.e., the view that the soul is one thing with multiple capacities. (For texts asserting this principle, see n. 30 below). But the unity principle is meant to apply to conscious activities to which the soul is actively attending. Avicenna does not deny that things may be going on in the soul of which we are not aware; but he does deny that we can attend to all of them simultaneously. In fact, in *De anima* IV 2, 169-71, Avicenna explicitly draws on the unity principle to explain how the imaginative faculty can do its own thing, so to speak, while the subject's attention is diverted to other tasks.

> [faculties], and to be always inspecting the forms, beginning from a sensed or remembered form, and transferring from it to a contrary or a similar [form], or to something which comes from it through a cause – for this is its nature [16].

This free play of the imagination is, as I've already noted, at the root of the identification of activities such as dreaming and divination as functions of the compositive imagination, and more fundamentally, it is the reason why the imaginative faculty is associated with the production of fictional images, such as "flying men" (not the kinds that are self-aware!), individuals half-human and half-tree, and emerald mountains, to name some of Avicenna's examples [17]. When there are no controls on the imagination, it randomly follows its innate rules of association – similarity, contrariety, and causality – wherever they may lead, and the results are as likely to be fictional as veridical.

Now while there are some perspectives from which this picture of the imagination would be considered a positive one – with its link to creativity and free association – it is problematic within a philosophical system in which the attainment of truth and demonstrative knowledge is the primary goal. For our present concerns, however, the randomness and freedom of the compositive imagination are especially problematic for Avicenna's account of thinking, since truth is the end at which the intellect aims. So Avicenna's account of the compositive imagination brings with it many of the problems that also arise in the Aristotelian association of *phantasia* with error [18]. When the compositive imagination is left to its own devices, then, Avicenna recognizes that it may in fact impede the intellect and cause the mind to wander and lose focus:

> Know that rational thinking (*al-fikr al-nuṭqīy*) is afflicted by this faculty, for it is preoccupied by the delusiveness of this power. For whenever it uses [this power] concerning some form, in a manner directed toward some end, it is quickly led to some other thing which is not related to [that end], and from it to a third thing, so that it makes the soul forget the first thing from which it began, until it makes it necessary for the soul to recollect, by taking

16. AVICENNA, *De anima* IV 2, 174-75.

17. For these examples see AVICENNA, *Mabdā'* 3.3, 94: "And the difference between [the compositive imagination] and the [retentive] imagination is that there is nothing in the latter except what it has taken from sensation, whereas the compositive imagination may compose and divide and create forms which have not and cannot be sensed at all. For example, a flying human being, and an individual half human and half tree". See also *Qanūn* 96-7, quoted in n. 14 above.

18. ARISTOTLE, *De anima* III 3, 427b1-18.

refuge in analysis by conversion (*al-taḥlīl bi-al-'aks*), in order to return to its starting point [19].

Now it may appear from this passage that I have backed myself into a corner, since my argument is that all references to *fikr* in Avicenna should *prima facie* be read as evoking the operations of the cogitative faculty, and so by definition all forms of thinking involve the compositive imagination. But here one could justifiably take Avicenna to be differentiating "rational thinking" or "cogitation" (*al-fikr al-nuṭqīy*) from the compositive imagination, since it is hard to see how something could be afflicted by itself. But this, I maintain, is exactly what Avicenna is claiming in this passage: because of its hybrid nature human thinking is indeed internally conflicted, as we might say. Avicenna's notion of the cogitative power is designed precisely to account for the vagaries that inflict embodied intellects, in a way that preserves the purity and infallibility of the intellect while at the same time doing justice to the empirical fact that much of human thinking is a product of interaction with the imagination, as Aristotle had asserted [20]. And there are escape routes, as the foregoing passage makes clear. When daydreaming and the other pleasant distractions provided by the imagination overtake the thinker, she will have to take control again by directing the imagination back to its starting point. This process of redirection is one that Avicenna here identifies with Aristotelian recollection, which Aristotle himself described as a "sort of syllogism", and which Avicenna more specifically identifies as a form of analysis whereby one traces a conclusion back to its principles [21]. So the inspiration for the cogitative faculty is in many ways vintage Aristotle, though as we shall see, the Avicennian realization of these Aristotelian themes has a unique flavour of its own.

III. The hybrid character of the cogitative faculty

As I have already indicated, the most important feature of Avicenna's cogitative faculty is its hybrid status. This hybrid nature is nicely captured by the description that Avicenna provides in his treatise *On the Proof of Prophecies:* "The cogitative power, in the absolute sense, is not one of the

19. AVICENNA, *De anima* IV 2, 175.

20. ARISTOTLE, *De anima* III 7, 431a16-17; 431b2; III 8, 432a3-10.

21. ARISTOTLE, *De memoria* 2, 453a13. Avicenna's account of recollection, which he identifies as a form of "inference" (*al-istidlāl*), can be found in his *De anima* IV 3, 185-87.

pure rational powers where light emanates without restriction [...] Nor is it one of the animal powers where light is utterly lost"[22]. On the one hand, as a manifestation of the compositive imagination, the cogitative power is a bodily faculty whose proper objects are sensible images and the estimative intentions associated with them. As an internal sense power, its distinguishing characteristics are its combinatory capacity and its incessant exercise of that capacity. On the other hand, the cogitative faculty is also rational by definition, and as such it has some sort of access to the universal intelligibles that are the proper objects of an immaterial intellect. For this reason, as soon as Avicenna employs the "cogitative" label, he is no longer speaking of a mere sense faculty. Rather, references to cogitation necessarily invoke the controlling function of the intellect, and thus imply a rationally-directed, voluntary activity. While Avicenna will occasionally add the adjectives "rational" or "intellectual" to his descriptions of cogitation in order to be precise (as in the passage I just cited from the *Healing*)[23], these characteristics are already built into his theory of the cogitative faculty. For this reason, it is legitimate for *fikr* and its cognates, used as technical Avicennian terms, to be rendered by their more natural English equivalents of "thinking" and "thought". For thinking is simply the interplay of the innate motion of imagination with the motionless grasp of abstract universals by the intellect, and this is what Avicenna says the cogitative faculty does. On Avicenna's account, then, thinking – in the sense of rational, discursive reflection – just is cogitation.

It is this annexation of the operations of the cogitative faculty to the realm of rational thought that explains the relative paucity of attention paid to the cogitative faculty's operations in *De anima* IV 2, the chapter that is purportedly devoted to an in-depth consideration of the formative and imaginative/cogitative powers. Since cogitation is a rational activity directed by the intellect, its operations are more properly studied as part of the account of knowledge-acquisition found Book V of the *De anima* of the *Healing,* in the epistemological parts of its logic, and in parallel passages in Avicenna's other major writings.

That is not to say that Avicenna entirely ignores the cogitative, ratiocinative operations of the compositive imagination in Book IV of his *De anima*. Near the beginning of *Psychology* IV 2, for example, Avicenna describes forms stored in the retentive imagination as the subjects not only of the compositive imagination's creative activity, but also of the

22. AVICENNA, *Iṯbāt al-nubūwāt,* 127; trans. Marmura, 117.
23. At n. 19 above.

cogitative faculty's rational operations of analysis and synthesis: "For the cogitative power may freely manipulate (*tataṣarrafu*) the forms which are in the formative faculty, through synthesis and analysis, because they are its subjects"[24]. Avicenna then proceeds to contrast the purposive and controlled character of cogitation with the randomness and restlessness of the compositive imagination when left to its own devices:

> The imaginative faculty is one which the soul may divert from its special operations in two ways. [...] The [second of these ways] is when the soul sometimes uses [the imagination] in those of its actions which are conjoined to it by way of discrimination (*al-tamyīz*) and cogitation (*al-fikrah*), something which also happens in two ways. One of them is for [the soul] to have mastery over the imaginative faculty and make use of it, along with the common sense, in composing and analyzing forms in their singularity (*bi-'ayni-hā*), in a way in which a correct aim would occur to the soul. And for this reason the imagination does not have control over the exercise (*al-taṣarruf*) of that which belongs to it by nature to exercise independently. Instead, it is in some way driven by the rational soul's control over it[25].

In this passage, Avicenna clearly assigns the standard operations of discursive thinking – analysis and synthesis – to the compositive imagination when it is under the control of the rational soul. Yet it is no accident that Avicenna says little more here regarding the operations of the cogitative faculty. As I have just suggested, Avicenna considers the various manifestations of cogitation to be of relevance primarily to the study of the operations of the rational soul which controls it. While the cogitative faculty, considered psycho-physically, is nothing but the compositive imagination seated in the brain, the activity of cogitation itself is not primarily one of imagining, but of thinking. So it is necessary to turn now to Avicenna's account of the role of cogitation in the operations of the intellect itself.

24. AVICENNA, *De anima* IV 2, 169. I take it Avicenna does not mean to exclude estimative intentions here; he simply omits to mention them for the sake of brevity, and because his main topic in this chapter is the relations between the formative and compositive imaginations.

25. AVICENNA, *De anima* IV 2, 172.

IV. Two types of thinking?

In a recent article Dimitri Gutas claims that Avicenna recognizes two different types of thinking (*fikrah*) in his late (i.e., post-*Healing*) works, especially the *Investigations (Al-Mubāḥaṯāt)*. According to Gutas, while one type of thinking is indeed a function of the internal sense faculty of cogitation, there is another type of thinking which is proper to the intellect alone[26]. Gutas also takes issue with both me and Herbert Davidson, suggesting that we fall into the trap of assuming that *fikr* in Avicenna always pertains to the realm of the internal senses[27]. Gutas's rejection of this claim is based on the fact that in the course of a discussion of *fikr* in his *Investigations*, Avicenna denies that a bodily faculty can combine and divide universals. This, Gutas alleges, indicates that any act of thinking which involves universals cannot be attributed to the cogitative faculty. Gutas's alternative is to posit two distinct but simultaneous activities of thinking concurring in the soul:

> So what Avicenna is necessarily doing here [...] is *setting up two parallel processes of thinking,* one in the rational soul and the other in the animal. The function of the former is to combine universal propositions. [...] The function of the second process in the animal soul, that of the Cogitative faculty, is to combine conceptual images of particulars *in imitation of* [...] the process in the intellect for the purpose of aiding it[28].

As may be obvious from my argument thus far, I am not convinced by Gutas's account, since I believe that the concern he raises is easily explained by the hybrid character of the cogitative faculty that I have been highlighting. It is a truism not only for Avicenna, but for the entire Aristotelian tradition, that insofar as thinking involves universals it cannot be the function any body or bodily power. So I agree with Gutas that imagination alone, as a bodily power, cannot compose and divide

26. Gutas (2001), 18ff. It should be noted that Gutas is not distinguishing here between discursive thinking and non-discursive understanding or contemplation, which would roughly parallel the Aristotelian distinction between *dianoia* and *noēsis*. Such a distinction is in my view unproblematic, and in fact it is crucial to the understanding of Avicennian cogitation. In Avicennian terms, I would take Aristotelian *noēsis* to be equivalent to "simple knowledge" in the terminology of *De anima* V 6; the cogitative knowledge with which it is contrasted would be an Avicennian interpretation of *dianoia*. For a consideration of this distinction see section VI below.

27. Gutas (2001), 36-37 n. 45. The works in question are Black (1997), 448, and Davidson (1992), 95ff.

28. Gutas (2001), 22.

universals. But there are important issues of explanatory economy and duplication at stake here. Gutas's interpretation of the interplay between intellectual and cogitative thought ignores the fact that the intellect is by definition already involved in the operations of the cogitative power[29]. Thus, on his view the intellect must not only be engaging in the composition of universal propositions and deductive syllogisms, but at the same time directing the imagination's combination of the images which imitate them, as Avicenna's account of the cogitative power explicitly requires. But since Avicenna holds that the soul cannot turn its conscious, rational attention to two disparate activities at once, this seems problematic: "It is not in the capacity of our souls to understand [many] things together in a single instant"[30], as Avicenna famously declares, and it is hard to see how Gutas's thesis would not constitute a violation of this dictum.

Perhaps most importantly, however, on Avicennian principles the imagination's role within cogitation is required to explain the intellect's own capacity to engage in discursive thinking – a crucial point that Gutas's account overlooks. For, as Avicenna makes clear, the activities of even a human intellect, inasmuch as it is an intellect, cannot involve motion, temporality, or divisibility, all of which are essential elements in discursive ratiocination. Strictly speaking, then, for Avicenna there is no real composition and division of universals except incidentally, in virtue of the concomitant activity of the imagination. To that extent, composition and division are the discursive parallels to abstraction. Thinking, a cognitive activity peculiar to human intellects, can therefore only be accounted for by the intellect-body interaction which defines the cogitative power unique to human knowers. And this too is a point that I believe Avicenna upholds not only in the *Healing*, but also in his later writings.

29. It is telling that Gutas refers to the thinking going on in the Cogitative/imagining faculty as something that is "*in the animal soul*" (*ibid.*, 18). This seems to overlook the distinction between cogitation – a distinctively human manifestation of the imagination – and simple compositive imagination. The latter alone, properly speaking, is an activity in the animal soul.

30. AVICENNA, *De anima* V 6, 241. In *De anima* V 2, 220, Avicenna also asserts the more general principal that the rational soul cannot attend simultaneously to the operations of the body and to its own purely intellectual operations: "The substance of the soul has two acts: an act belonging to it in relation to the body, namely, governing; and an act belonging to it in relation to itself and to its principle, namely, intellectual apprehension (*al-idrāk bi-al-'aql*). These two [acts] are mutually opposed and contradictory. For if [the soul] occupies itself with one of the two, it turns away from the other, for it is difficult for it to combine the two". The full discussion of this point extends from 219-221; for the corresponding discussion in the *Naǧāh*, see *Avicenna's Psychology*, chap. 10, 53-54.

V. COGITATION AND CONCEPTUALIZATION

While I have already noted that Avicenna says comparatively little about cogitation in Bk. 4 of the *De anima* of the *Healing*, which contains his most sustained account of the internal sense powers, cogitation figures prominently throughout the discussion of how the human intellect acquires knowledge in chapters 5 and 6 of *De anima* Bk. 5. In the opening passage of chapter 5, cogitation is included in Avicenna's brief sketch of his thesis that all new intelligibles must ultimately be explained with reference to a direct emanation from the Agent Intellect[31]. Here cogitation, like all activities involving images, is presented as a necessary pre-condition for emanation to occur, even though it is not itself sufficient to provide a full causal explanation of how a new intelligible is produced. In this context cogitation or thinking is described as a motion in virtue of its association with the combination and division of simple terms which results in propositions, an activity that is parallel in function to the role of the middle term in producing knowledge of a syllogistic conclusion[32]:

> For cogitations and reflections (*al-afkār wa-al-ta'ammulāt*) are motions which prepare the soul for the reception of the emanation, just as middle terms [of syllogisms] are a preparation, in a way more intense, for the reception of the conclusion, although the first occurs in one way, and the second in another way, as you shall learn[33].

The role of cogitation in all human knowledge is asserted even more strongly in *De anima* 5.6, which includes Avicenna's notorious views on the true nature of intellectual memory, as well as his account of rational prophecy as a function of intellectual intuition (*ḥads*). Central to all of these topics is a basic distinction, elaborated in the middle of this chapter, between simple and cogitative knowledge (*al-'ilm al-basīṭ; al-'ilm al-*

31. It should be noted that Gutas links his views on cogitation to his acceptance of the theory advanced in HASSE (2001), that Avicenna is indeed an abstractionist. While I agree with both Hasse and Gutas that Avicenna does have an account of what the philosophical tradition usually refers to as "abstraction", I am not convinced that the traditional emanationist account of knowledge-acquisition attributed to Avicenna is incorrect, and indeed, it seems to me to make the best sense both textually and in terms of its coherence with Avicenna's philosophical views as a whole.

32. In the *Healing* Avicenna remains silent on any role that cogitation might have in relation to middle terms. The passage from the *Investigations* that I cite at n. 44 below, however, links cogitation both to propositional knowledge and to syllogistic knowledge via middle terms.

33. AVICENNA, *De anima* V 5, 235.

fikrīy)[34]. The distinction between these two types of knowledge is itself part of a broader division of the modes of conceptualization (*taṣawwur*) into three types: (1) actual conceptualization; (2) intellectual "memory"; and (3) a phenomenon for which Avicenna has no technical term, but which, for reasons that will become clear below, I have chosen to call "spontaneous" conceptualization.

Actual conceptualization for Avicenna is the basic act of entertaining a complex proposition as a single, unified thought. Avicenna describes it as "conceptualization which is in the soul in actuality, distinguished and ordered" and he offers as an example the proposition, "Every human is an animal"[35]. Avicenna affirms that the parts that are ordered here are "universal meanings", so they must have something incorporeal as their subject. He adds that there may also be a concomitant arrangement of parts in the imagination (*al-ḫayāl*) when the proposition is expressed linguistically[36]. This linguistic, imagined counterpart may also admit of different but equivalent formulations. For example, one could say instead, "Animal is said of every human", but in such cases, Avicenna claims, "their pure intelligible is one" nonetheless.

Actual conceptualization, then, is the end product of the intellect's normal cogitative operations, which issue in universal intelligibles that are structured unities. The linguistic expressions of our conceptualizations (which Avicenna believes are merely an incidental by-product of our embodied nature)[37] are the remnants of those cogitative operations on images, whose goal is to produce the "ordering and arrangement" of universals. But how can cogitation, an operation that involves the combining and dividing of images, be the source of ordered universal propositions?

34. AVICENNA, *De anima* V 6, 243. For a discussion of some of the same texts I consider here, see ADAMSON (2004), 90-93. Adamson translates *fikrīy* in this context as "discursive", which allows him to bracket the question of whether the term constitutes a technical reference to the internal sense power. But Adamson does endorse Gutas's claim that there are in fact two forms of *fikr*, one taking place in the intellect, and another occurring in the cogitative power of the brain (91-92 n. 10).

35. AVICENNA, *De anima* V 6, 241. Notice that Avicenna uses propositional examples here, even though the act of understanding in question is one of "conceptualization", *taṣawwur*.

36. Note that Avicenna uses the term for retentive imagination here. I don't think this is especially problematic; Avicenna is sometimes sloppy in his use of terminology when the distinction between the two imaginative faculties is not of central concern. And it is possible that he is assuming here that the result of cogitative thinking issues in a new imaginative composition that itself becomes stored as a sense memory within the formative faculty.

37. On this see BLACK (1992), 54-56.

What becomes clear from Avicenna's ensuing account of the other modes of conceptualization in this chapter is that cogitation is in fact the only process that can introduce multiplicity into the intellect, something it is able to do in virtue of the underlying images it employs. The entire thrust of Avicenna's theory of conceptualization in *De anima* V 6 is to uphold the simplicity of the intellect on the one hand, and the unity of the intelligible on the other. Cogitation allows Avicenna to account for the apparent manipulation of universals that our linguistic and inferential operations imply, without thereby violating the maxim that "the pure intelligible is one".

That the discursive character of thinking is not intrinsic to the intellect's own operations, but rather reflects its cogitative interactions with the imagination, is nowhere more evident than in Avicenna's remarks on the curious phenomenon that I am calling "spontaneous conceptualization". This is an act of understanding that occurs when someone immediately recognizes the answer to some problem which she has not previously considered, and only after acquiring this knowledge does she resort to cogitative sorting in order to articulate what she has discovered:

> Another type of conceptualization is like what happens to you when a question is asked of you about what you know or what you are close to knowing, and the answer presents itself to you in an instant. For you would be certain that you are answering it with something that you know, without there being any distinguishing there at all. Rather, you only begin to distinguish and compose in your soul when you begin the answer which proceeds from your certitude that you know it, before distinguishing and composing [38].

There are, of course, all sorts of puzzling issues that arise from Avicenna's account of this unusual, if recognizable, phenomenon, but pursuing those issues is beyond the scope of my present concerns. What is crucial in the present context are the claims that Avicenna makes here about the role of composing and distinguishing the contents of one's thoughts in episodes of spontaneous conceptualization, as compared to the paradigm case of actually conceptualizing a proposition such as "A human being is an animal". Avicenna tends to minimize the differences between these two scenarios, reducing them more or less to the temporal relations that hold between the cogitative sorting and the ultimate emanation of the universal intelligible. Thus he declares, "The third [spontaneous conceptualization] differs from the first [actual conceptualization] in that it is not

38. AVICENNA, *De anima* V 6, 241-2.

something arranged in cogitation (*al-fikr*) at all, but rather it is like a principle for this when conjoined with certitude"[39]. Avicenna is insistent that what we have here is an example of actual knowledge, which is, after all, the ultimate aim of cogitative thought. Yet with spontaneous conceptualization, one begins to "think" or cogitate only after one already knows the answer. This, needless to say, seems counterintuitive. But Avicenna does not believe that such cogitation is superfluous. We need cogitation in this case as a form of articulation for the purpose of teaching not only others, but even ourselves, something of which we already have certain knowledge:

> And it is something wonderful that when this respondent begins to teach someone else some distinction which occurred in himself all at once (*da'fatan*), he learns knowledge of the second type [i.e., intellectual memory] along with what he is teaching the other person, so that this form is arranged in him along with the arrangement of its verbal expressions [40].

VI. SIMPLE VERSUS COGITATIVE KNOWLEDGE

Now Avicenna is aware that some readers might be sceptical of his claim that the person who enjoys spontaneous conceptualization has actual knowledge of any intelligible prior to articulating it linguistically. To counter such scepticism, Avicenna argues that such a person is still lacking the sort of knowledge that we normally associate with human minds, though she does in fact possess the higher sort of knowledge that is proper to human minds not *qua* human, but *qua* intellect. The former sort of knowledge which is lacking in this case is in fact cogitative knowledge; the latter – in keeping with Avicenna's emphasis on the unity of actual intellection – is more properly called "simple" knowledge:

39. AVICENNA, *De anima* V 6, 242. Avicenna also notes that spontaneous conceptualization differs from intellectual memory as follows: "It differs from the second by not being turned away from it, but rather, it is actually considering it in some way". In spontaneous conceptualization, the knower is not recalling something she previously learned in order to answer a question, but rather, she is discovering for the first time that she already knows the answer to a new question being posed to her.

40. AVICENNA, *De anima* V 6, 243. The reference to learning knowledge of the second variety in this passage seems to suggest that the cogitative process and its linguistic unfolding perform a mnemonic function: until I sort out my insights, I will be unable to call them "mine" and thereby develop the necessary habit for reconnecting with their corresponding intelligibles in the Agent Intellect.

> But one of these two [types of knowledge] is cogitative knowledge, in which ultimate perfection is only reached when it is ordered and composed. The second is the simple knowledge whose nature is not to have in itself one form after another form, but instead it is one and from it forms emanate into the receiver of forms. For this knowledge is the agent (*al-fāʿil*) of what we have called cogitative knowledge, and its principle (*mabdāʾ la-hu*). This [simple knowledge] belongs to the absolute intellectual faculty (*li-l-quwwah al-ʿaqlīyah al-muṭlaqah*) of the soul which resembles the agent intellects. As for the act of distinguishing (*al-tafṣīl*), it belongs to the soul *qua* soul, for what does not have this does not have psychological knowledge [*ʿilm nafsānīyah,* i.e., knowledge that is characteristic of souls][41].

Human beings do, then, possess some glimmer of simple knowledge, as is manifested in their acts of spontaneous conceptualization (and of intuition as well). It is only a glimmer, however, to which we have access precisely to the degree to which we do indeed possess intellects, and thus share the core of our true natures with the separate, agent intellects. *Qua* human, however, we are more properly characterized as psychological beings, not intellectual ones, and our mode of knowing is dependent upon the body which acts as an instrument to our soul. Hence the mode of knowledge most proper to us is cogitative knowledge, wherein the intellect uses our imaginative faculties to sort through the complex unities to which our participation in simple knowledge gives us access. Throughout the course of *De anima* V 6 Avicenna repeats the theme that composition and division are characteristic of the mode of knowing proper to human minds or souls: "For the soul which belongs to the knower inasmuch as it is a soul has the sort of conceptualization which composes and divides, and for this reason it is not simple in every respect"[42]. By the same token, Avicenna

41. AVICENNA, *De anima* V 6, 243.

42. AVICENNA, *De anima* V 6, 243-44. The full passage is as follows: "Know that, of the two, in the pure intellects there is nothing at all which involves multiplicity, nor is there any ordering of one form after another, but rather, [the pure intellect] is the principle for every form which emanates from it into the soul. [...] For the soul which belongs to the knower inasmuch as it is soul has the sort of conceptualization which composes and divides, and for this reason it is not simple in every respect. And every intellectual act of apprehension (*idrāk ʿaqlīy*) is a sort of relation (*nisbah mā*) to a form separate from matter and its material accidents in the aforementioned way. But this belongs to the soul insofar as it is a substance which receives what is impressed on it, whereas it belongs to the intellect insofar as it is substance [which is] an agent, creative principle. Thus what is characteristic of the essence [of the intellect] in virtue of its being a principle for [the forms] is its intellectuality in act (*ʿaqlīyatu-hu bi-al-fiʿl*), whereas what is characteristic of the soul in virtue of its conceptualizing through them and its reception from them is its intellectuality in act".

later reiterates that the act of differentiating or unpacking what the intellect receives as a simple unity is fundamentally a cogitative act: "Learning is the search for the perfect disposition (*isti'dād*) for conjunction with [the Agent Intellect], until the understanding which is simple comes from it. Then the forms differentiated (*munfaṣalah*) by means of cogitation emanate from it into the soul"[43].

The *Healing*'s distinction between simple and cogitative knowledge seems to be reflected as well in Avicenna's scattered allusions to cogitation in late works such the *Investigations*:

> Cogitation (*al-fikr*) requires conjunction with the principles in the procurement of definitions and their conceptualization, and in the procurement of the middle [term]. As for combination, this belongs to [cogitation], which it sometimes does well, and sometimes poorly[44].

Avicenna's claim in the *Healing* that cogitative knowledge has its roots in an act of simple knowledge that is ultimately traceable to an emanation from the Agent Intellect is parallel to the claim in this text that cogitation requires conjunction with the principles of knowledge, i.e., the separate intellects. By the same token, all compositional activity required for the acquisition of knowledge is once again assigned to cogitation itself. There is no more reason here than in the *Healing* to see this form of cogitation as a function of anything other than the internal sense power of compositive imagination, which is elevated to the level of a rational faculty – the cogitative power – through the controlling influence of the intellect and its contribution to an intellectual end. Even more noteworthy, however, are the echoes of the hybrid character of the internal sense power of cogitation in the following answer to the query of one of his followers reported elsewhere in the *Investigations*:

> And if by the cogitative faculty (*al-quwwah al-fikrīyah*) one means [the faculty] which is seeking, it belongs to the rational soul and it is of the species of the habitual intellect, especially when it adds a perfection by way of surpassing the habit. And if one means by it the moving faculty which presents the forms, it is the imaginative faculty insofar as it is moved with the desire of the rational faculty[45].

43. AVICENNA, *De anima* V 6, 247; the context here is Avicenna's account of the nature of intellectual memory.

44. AVICENNA, *Mubāḥaṯāt*, ed. Badawi, §359, 199; ed. Bidarfar, §595, 198.

45. *Ibid.*, ed. Badawi §468, 232; ed. Bidarfar, §255, 111. GUTAS (2001), 36-37 n. 45, expresses puzzlement that I should take this passage as an allusion to the internal sense faculty of cogitation. I am in turn puzzled as to why this passage would be considered evidence that

The question to which Avicenna is replying here is whether any faculty other than the intellect employs the cogitative power (*al-mufakkirah*). Just before the passage that I cite, Avicenna notes that except in rare cases where an intelligible is emanated immediately through intuition (*ḥads*), the intellect will have no choice but to "take refuge in the motions of other faculties whose role is to prepare it for the reception of the emanation". And he adds that these other faculties are able to play such a preparatory role because what is impressed on them has "a likeness or a resemblance" to the forms that are in the Agent Intellect. Avicenna then proceeds to reiterate in this passage the dual aspects of the cogitative faculty as both rational and imaginative that have characterized his account of this power in all of his previous philosophical writings. Against the background of his standard account of the cogitative faculty as an internal sense power, then, Avicenna's meaning here is unambiguous. He is reminding the questioner of the hybrid character of the cogitative faculty, a point on which the questioner himself seems confused. To ask whether another faculty than the intellect can use the cogitative power is to forget that every exercise of cogitative power involves both the rational faculty, which is directing or controlling the search for knowledge, and the compositive imagination, which is doing the seeking. The cogitative faculty can thus be viewed as a complex power composed of an unmoved mover – the intellect – and a moved mover – the imagination [46]. Avicenna is not asserting here that there are twotypes of cogitation, one rational and one imaginative: he is reminding us that cogitation is always and by its very nature an activity of both faculties.

VII. Conclusion

For Avicenna the cogitative faculty represents an adaptation, suitable to his own dualist and emanationist framework, of the basic Aristotelian dictum that the soul never thinks without an image. Like many of the characteristic theses of Avicenna's philosophy, his theory of the cogitative

there is a second type of thinking taking place within the intellectual soul, since this overlooks the fact that the internal sense power of cogitation has an intellectual or rational element built into it. I do, however, accept Gutas's suggestion that the adjective "moving" probably modifies "faculty" rather than "forms", though both readings remain possible.

46. The reference to the habitual intellect also serves to evoke the more elaborate account of intellectual memory in *De anima* V 6, 245-48, which Avicenna reinterprets as a facility for conjoining at will with the Agent Intellect, rather than as a form of storage.

faculty is a compromise that allows him to assert the fundamentally intellectual and immaterial character of human minds, while at the same time taking due account of the obviously sensible and empirical basis of human knowledge. The cogitative faculty, as simultaneously both intellect and imagination, allows Avicenna to uphold his conviction that the human soul is essentially a subsistent intellect, whose sojourn in the body nonetheless circumscribes the methods by which it is able to gain access to the intelligible realm.

BIBLIOGRAPHY

Sources

ARISTOTLE (1984), *The Complete Works of Aristotle: The Revised Oxford Translation*, ed. Jonathan Barnes, Princeton.

AVICENNA (1875), *Maqālah fī al-nafs 'alā sunnah al-iḫtiṣār (Compendium on the Soul)*, ed. S. Landauer, in "Die Psychologie des Ibn Sīnā", Zeitschrift der Deutschen Morgenländischen Gesellschaft 29, 335-418.

– (1892), *Al-Išārāt wa-al-tanbīhāt (Le livre des théorèmes et des avertissements)*, ed. Jacques Forget, Leiden.

– (1947), *Al-Mubāḥaṯāt* (Investigations), ed. A. R. Badawi, in *Arisṭū 'inda al-'Arab*, Cairo, 118-239.

– (1952), *Avicenna's Psychology*, trans. F. Rahman, London.

– (1959), *Avicenna's De anima, Being the Psychological Part of Kitāb al-Shifā'*, ed. F. Rahman, London.

– (1963), *On the Proof of Prophecies,* trans. M. E. Marmura, in *Medieval Political Philosophy: A Sourcebook,* ed. M. Mahdi and R. Lerner, Ithaca, New York, 112-121.

– (1968), *Iṯbāt al-nubūwāt (The Proof of Prophecies),* ed. M. E. Marmura, Beirut. [English translation in (1963)].

– (1980), *'Uyūn al-ḥikmah (Sources of Wisdom)*, ed. A. R. Badawi, Beirut.

– (1984), *Kitāb al-mabdā' wa-al-ma'ad (Genesis and Return),* ed. A. Nurani, Montreal.

– (1985), *Kitāb al-nağāh,* ed. M. Fakhry, Beirut. [English translation in (1952)].

– (1987), *Qanūn fī al-ṭibb (Canon of Medicine),* ed. A. Zi'ur and E. Al-Qashsh, Beirut.

– (1992), *Al-Mubāḥaṯāt (Investigations),* ed. M. Bidarfar, Qum.

Studies

ADAMSON, P. (2004), "Non-Discursive Thought in Avicenna's Commentary on the *Theology of Aristotle*", in J. McGinnis and D. Reisman (eds.) *Interpreting Avicenna: Science and Philosophy in Medieval Islam,* Leiden, 86-111.

BLACK, D. L. (1992), "Aristotle's *Peri hermeneias* in Medieval Latin and Arabic Philosophy: Logic and the Linguistic Arts", in *Aristotle and His Medieval Interpreters,* R. Bosley and M. Tweedale (eds.), *Canadian Journal of Philosophy* suppl. vol. 17, 25-83.

– (1993), "Estimation in Avicenna: The Logical and Psychological Dimensions", in *Dialogue* 32, 219-58.

– (1997), "Avicenna on the Ontological and Epistemic Status of Fictional Beings", in *Documenti e studi sulla tradizione filosofica medievale* 8, 425-453.

DAVIDSON, H. A. (1992), *Alfarabi, Avicenna, and Averroes on Intellect. Their Cosmologies, Theories of the Active Intellect, and Theories of Human Intellect,* Oxford.

GUTAS, D. (2001), "Intuition and Thinking: The Evolving Structure of Avicenna's Epistemology", in R. Wisnovsky (ed.), *Aspects of Avicenna*, Princeton, 1-38.

HASSE, DAG (2001), "Avicenna on Abstraction", in R. Wisnovsky (ed.), *Aspects of Avicenna*, Princeton, 39-72.

JANSSENS, J. L. (2004), "'Experience' (*tağriba*) in Classical Arabic Philosophy (al-Fārābī-Avicenna)", in *Quaestio* 4, 45-62.

NUSSBAUM, MARTHA C. (1978), *Aristotle's* De motu animalium, *Text with Translation, Commentary, and Interpretive Essays*, Princeton.

WEDIN, MICHAEL V. (1988), *Mind and Imagination in Aristotle,* New Haven and London.

AVICENNA ON MUSICAL PERCEPTION

Luis Xavier LÓPEZ-FARJEAT
(Universidad Panamericana, Mexico)

Most of the studies dealing with inner senses in Arabic psychology are dedicated to the commentaries or paraphrases on Aristotle's *De anima*. Almost all of them exclude musical treatises. The contributions of al-Kindī, al-Fārābī and Avicenna to the philosophy of music have been left out of the conversation. By this, I mean not only their musical theories (understanding of harmony, rhythm and melody) or their innovating observations on composition [1], but also their theories of musical perception. In this paper, I focus on Avicenna's philosophy of music and relate it to his psychology. The Persian philosopher gives a functionalist [2] account of the origin of meaningful sounds, i.e. voices (music among them), as well as some references to the interaction between hearing and internal perception. Avicenna shows that animals can articulate meaningful sounds, even though they cannot compose music.

First of all, I explain the relation between sound and hearing. Their relations, as well as their distinctions, establish that there are some sounds in which meaning goes beyond mere hearing, i.e. voices and music, which

1. In this regard, the work of Henry George Farmer is an essential reference. Farmer explored the influence of Arabic musical theories in the shaping of Western music, its contribution to the creation and refinement of musical instruments as the lute (*'ūd*), the *rabāb*, the guitar (*qitār*) (see FARMER [1925], 61-80), and even the influence of al-Fārābī and some other writers in the development of Western music. See FARMER (1932), 561-592; (1959-61), 37-47. RANDEL has also studied the presence of al-Fārābī in Latin musical theories (1976), 173-188.

2. By 'functionalism', I mean that some functions, in this case, the articulation of language, appear for teleological reasons. I am not referring, hence, to a strictly psycho-physical functionalism as stated by contemporary philosophers such as Putnam.

constitute a subclass of sounds. Following this line of argument, I examine what distinguishes music from articulated voices, the latter being present in some animals too. I will try to clarify the role played by imagination (*mutaḫayyilah*) in the configuration of language and music. Throughout these first two sections, I will point out some insufficiencies of the functionalist account of the origins of music and I will defend its imitative origin. Finally, in the last section, I will explain how these sounds relate to internal perceptive faculties (*ḥawāss al-bāṭinah*): musical creation and musical appreciation are mental acts tied to imagination (*mutaḫayyilah*) and to the estimative power (*wahm*). Musical appreciation, as presented by Avicenna, is not reduced to mere hearing or to proper conceptual knowledge. As we shall see, in musical appreciation the internal perceptive faculties interact with our thinking capacity (*fikrah*)[3].

The estimative power is a leading faculty in musical appreciation since we understand intentions (*ma'nī*), i.e. *non-material* properties that exist accidentally in matter, and, therefore, are perceived conjointly with the sensible[4]. Furthermore, those 'musical meanings' are associated, as is every intention, to an emotion. If the latter can be a satisfactory explanation of musical perception, it prompts relevant philosophical questions: Can animals with an estimative power produce meaningful sounds too? If they can, are they capable of producing music? If they are not, why are they unfitted to do so, given that their cognitive faculties are so similar to ours? Can animals understand the intentional meanings present in melodies?

3. By 'thinking capacity', I mean discursive thinking and not the intellect's activity when it deals with universals. GUTAS (2001) holds that we can recognize two kinds of thoughts in Avicenna's epistemology: on the one hand, thinking as a function of the cogitative power (which is what I am referring to here); and on the other hand, thinking as an activity concerning only the intellect (thinking of universals would not be, in this case, something proper of the cogitative power but something belonging exclusively to the intellect). I agree with Gutas on the existence of two different activities. I do not believe, however, that the knowledge of universals involves the intellect exclusively. I think that the operations of the cogitative power are necessary for the intellective activity to take place and, of course, imagination is required as well. Despite this, I find Gutas' interpretation quite interesting, even though I accept the interpretations of DAVIDSON (1992), 99-102, and BLACK (1997), 425-453, which have been criticized by Gutas in note 45 of the referred article for not considering 'thinking' as an exclusive activity of the intellect independent of the internal senses.

4. Dag Hasse insists that Avicenna conceives intentions as non-material although merged (*muḫāliṭa*) with objects, and for this purpose, he refers to *De anima* IV.3. This, as Hasse claims, would be the key aspect for distinguishing Avicenna's doctrine from some contemporary theories of intentionality in which intentions are not in the world but only in perceptions or in the mind. See Dag HASSE (2000), 130.

Perhaps musical appreciation implies some intellection and, in this sense, the intervention of the cogitative power (*fikr*)?

I. SOUND AND HEARING

Avicenna dedicated a part of his most important work, the *Kitāb al-Šifā* (*The Book of Healing*), to music [5]. He treats of it in the third section of the book in which he deals with mathematics. Just like al-Kindī, Avicenna is greatly indebted to the general principles of the Pythagorean conception of music and consequently accepts that music has a mathematical structure [6]. Nevertheless, in his exposition he does not completely agree with Pythagoreanism [7], and he follows some Peripatetic remarks from Aristoxenus [8]

5. The edition I use is IBN SĪNĀ, *al-Šifā*, ed. Zakariyya Yousef. All the translations of the quoted passages are mine. The French version of ERLANGER (2001) has been very helpful; this is a valuable translation, although it does not grasp some of the subtleties of the philosophical terminology.

6. AL-KINDĪ, al-*Musawwitāt al-watariyyah*, *Mu'allafāt al-Kindī*, ed. Zakariyyah Yousef, 18.

7. As it is well known, among Pythagoreans there was a cosmological doctrine based on the notions of order and harmony. As stated by AETIUS in *Aetii Placita*, the Pythagoreans were the first to use the term *kosmos* to refer to the set of all things that compose the world and, in addition, they maintained that a mathematical structure underlies the universal order. Furthermore, according to the Pythagorean cosmology and metaphysics, harmony rules everything in the *kosmos* and it is specifically reflected in the harmonic proportions of the universe. That is why music works as an explanation of the *kosmos*. Also for this reason Aristotle says in his *Metaphysics* (1090a, 20-25) that Pythagoreans: "[...] saw many attributes of numbers belonging to sensible bodies, supposed real things to be numbers – not separable numbers, however, but numbers of which real things consist. But why? Because the attributes of numbers are present in a musical scale and in the heavens and in many other things". This thesis of musical harmony in the *kosmos* is the same as the one found in Plato's *Timaeus*. There, another Pythagorean idea is also present: cosmic harmony is proportional to the harmony of the soul. The analogy between cosmic proportion and *psychic* or *animic* proportion explains why we listen to music with pleasure: at the moment of musical appreciation, the soul and the world are tuned. Now, in the *Fihrist* al-Nadīm mentions the work of the Pythagorean Nicomacus of Gerasa. He is the author, as it appears in the catalogue of the tenth century, of a treatise called *On Arithmetic* and another called *On Music* (see IBN AL-NADĪM, *Fihrist*, trans. B. Dodge, 643). The work of Nicomacus of Gerasa influenced al-Kindī who, among others works, he wrote seven musical treatises. FARMER (1930, 325-333) is an essential source for the Greek influences on Arab theories of music.

8. In the *Fihrist* al-Nadīm mentions the Peripatetic philosopher Aristoxenus, one of the most prestigious authorities on music. He wrote, according to the *Fihrist*, the treatises *On Rhythm* and *On Harmony* (AL-NADĪM, *Fihrist*, trans. B. Dodge, 644). Aristoxenus was Aristotle's disciple and argued for a wider understanding of musical appreciation, going

and, of course, from al-Fārābī[9]. The Peripatetic influence on Avicenna is important since it is most probably the point of departure for his theory of musical perception.

beyond the definition of harmony and postulating a theory of auditory perception. Aristoxenus is extremely Aristotelian when privileging a theory of hearing (in *De anima* Aristotle dedicates vast passages to visual perception and Aristoxenus does the same but with regards to the ear). He is practically a modern, almost an empiricist critic of the Pythagorean mathematical-intellectualist conception of music. This does not mean that harmony is not mathematical. Rather, harmony is not grasped without rhythm, metre and composition. The ear grasps intervals and rhythms and without that sensorial experience it is not possible to recognize the essence of music, i.e. harmony. For more details on Aristoxenus's musical theory see WINNINGTON-INGRAM (1932), 195-208.

9. Al-Fārābī wrote *The Great Book of Music* (*Kitāb al- Musiqa al-kahīr*), a treatise *On Melody* (*Fi'l Īqā'*) and the *Transition to Melody* (*al-Nuqlah ilā'l-Īqā'*). In his *Enumeration of the Sciences* (*Ihsā' al-'ulūm*), known in the Latin West as *De scientiis*, there is a section where the theoretical and practical dimensions of music are explained. Some biographers attribute to him the invention of a musical instrument called the qanun. Others simply mention that he was an excellent laud player. We find in al-Fārābī's writings the most novel conception of music within the Arabic-Muslim world. In his writings, he is interested in defining what the principles of the musical science are and, following a typically Aristotelian methodology, he deals with the previous claims and mistakes of previous conceptions of music. Obviously, the Pythagorean conception of music appears in his historical inventory and he considers it incomeplete and deficient in some regards. In some way, al-Fārābī places himself within the Peripatetic tradition so that even if he finds an evident relation between music and mathematics – just as Pythagoreans did – he thinks, nonetheless, that the essence of music is not number but melody. The pleasure and displeasure we experience in presence of a musical piece comes only from melody and that pleasure has nothing to do with heavenly spheres, as the Pythagoreans thought. In fact, according to al-Fārābī, music is almost synonymous with melody (*alhān*), and melody must be understood as a set of audible tones combined in a particular way, namely, intervallically and rhythmically. The musical theory of al-Fārābī resembles his poetic theory. He relates to musical appreciation a definitely novel element: imagination. Melody can be twofold: internal or imaginative (and by this al-Fārābī refers to the fact that we imagine melodies, and can actually execute them with the hands, such as percussions and strings, or with the mouth, as happens with wind instruments). The most interesting part is the association between melody and imagination. As far as I know, no musicologist of Antiquity noticed the importance of imagination for the creation of melodies. Imagination is capable of evoking absent objects, of recreating them, of making them present. Within Arabic aesthetics imagination plays a definitive role and al-Fārābī is a good example. In some of his writings devoted to poetical discourse, the philosopher insists on the importance of images for persuading, even for fixing convictions. When words are needed, as in the case of poetry, imagination takes mainly a visual role. In fact, many theoreticians of imagination, not only of Antiquity but also of the seventeenth and eighteenth centuries and even some contemporaries, erroneously reduce imagination to a mere visual faculty. Strange as it may seem, we can also imagine aromas and even sounds, as al-Fārābī suggests. In a way, al-Fārābī postulates an "auditory imagination". The 'objects' that this faculty produces are melodies. The drafter and the sculptor imagine beautiful and attractive forms; the musician

As Shehadi (1995, 67) has pointed out, the third section of the *Šifā* or *Healing* presents rudiments of an aesthetical analysis of music and a psychobiological account of aesthetic appreciation. In my opinion, such rudiments are important in order to recognize the role of the internal senses in musical appreciation. Throughout Avicenna's discourse, some Aristotelian accounts of the *De anima* are present along with references to some other Aristotelian biological works such as the treatises on animals [10].

After a short allusion to what others have understood by musical science [11], Avicenna explains what ought to be understood by "sound" (*ṣawt*) and immediately starts speaking of the perception of delightful (*la̲di̲d̲*) and hateful (*takariha*) sounds:

imagines agreeable melodies. This, however obvious or strange, is in fact revealing: al-Fārābī would argue that the eyes serve not only to see and the ears not only to listen, but also to delight us. For all this, one thing is the simple sensorial stimulus (see any object or listen to any sound) and another thing is the pleasure attached to the stimulus. Al-Fārābī to some extent anticipates one of the richest empiricist theories of imagination of the eighteenth century, namely, that of Joseph Addison in *Pleasures of Imagination*. In this work a similar thesis is found but is applied to visual imagination: the eye sees, but the imagination recreates and makes pleasant the visual stimulus. Something similar would happen with auditory imagination in al-Fārābī's case: the musician reinvents brute sounds transforming them, thanks to imagination, into something pleasant. For a thorough exposition of music in al-FĀRĀBĪ see *Grand traité de la musique*, trans. Erlanger, 1-101; FARMER (1932), 561-92; and RANDEL (1976) 173-88.

10. As it is well known, the Arabs gathered the Aristotelian works on animals in a single book entitled *The Book of Animals* (*Kitāb al-ḥayāwān*). The Syriac and Arabic versions integrated nineteen books distributed as follows: ten books of *Historia animalium* (the tenth spurious book was included), five books of *De generatione animalium* and four books of *De partibus animalium*. The Latin translation of Michael SCOTUS, *De animalibus*, ed. Van Oppenraaij, Part III, XV-XIX *Generation of animals* and Part II, XI-XIV *Parts of animals*, is well known, and it served as the basis for Albert the Great's *Quaestiones super libros de animalibus* and *Reportatio de animalibus*. It was also Michael Scotus who translated the eighth section of the philosophy of nature of the *Šifā'* dedicated, precisely, to animals: *Compendium Avicennae de animalibus*. The Syriac, Arab and Latin reception of the works on animals is detailed in the known work of PETERS (1968), 47-8. Regarding the translation of Michael Scotus see WINGATE (1931), 72-85.

11. Shehadi pays attention to this introduction, because Avicenna refers there to the necessity of going beyond the Pythagorean conception of music and even presents some critiques against Neopythagorean ideas. In fact, as CRUZ HERNANDEZ (1981), 31-2, points out: "The sources of the rejected Neopythagorean ideas seem to be the second book of the *Republic* and book A of *Metaphysics*. Instead, the origin of Ibn Sīnā's theory is mainly in the second book of *De anima* and in *De sensu et sensato*; secondarily, in *Peri hermeneias*, *Historia animalium* and, maybe, in *Problemata*. The texts of *Politeia* must be rejected. Ibn Sīnā and beside him all the Islamic thinkers were ignorant of this work of Aristotle".

> Therefore, I say that sound is one of the exterior manifestations that our senses perceive [with] the feeling that it can be pleasant for us. I refer here to the sound quality that makes it pleasant or unpleasant to the ear, and not to the negative effects resulting from an excess that may be abnormal. Sound is, indeed, like all the other sensibles. Thus, a smell may be disgusting because of its nature, as it happens with different things, even if it is low and hidden, or by its excesses, [as it is the case of,] for example, the pleasant smell of the musk: if it is too strong, it will be unpleasant, just as we suffer a painful sensation with the sun's rays excesses when they are normally beneficial [if they are moderate].

The sound sensation cannot be pleasant or unpleasant itself; our ear suffers only when it is too violent. A musical instrument, played too loudly, produces a disagreeable sound that we instinctively reject. In a different way, however, a sound can be pleasant or unpleasant, not qua sensation, but in its relation to our ability to understand, which considers the idea that the sound reminds us of the role that it plays in a composition. We have also clearly explained the function of the faculty of understanding possessed by humans and animals, so we do not say anything here [12].

This description of sound is fundamentally psychological. Avicenna clearly states he is referring to certain qualities of sounds, which will contribute to the pleasantness or hatefulness of auditory perception. He seems to leave aside the problems related to the excess of sensory stimulus excesses (the excess of light damages the eye or an extremely loud sound will affect the ear and both experiences turn out to be unpleasant). However, besides discussing why a sensory stimulus would be unpleasant, a reason for the opposite effect should be found, namely, why some stimuli are pleasant. Perception of something unpleasant, at least as it is described in these passages, implies a violent action upon the external senses and, as such, it seems to be a physiological explanation. What Avicenna tries to explain surpasses the mere physiological comprehension of sensation. It is, I insist, a psychological approach that tries to explain why certain sensible qualities please us and even why others displease us without it being necessary for us to experience the excesses of a sensory stimulus.

If a purely physiological understanding of sensation suffices, an approach to musical perception would be impossible. In order to achieve it, it does not suffice for us to explain in which way vibrations affect our ears. We have to explain what makes musical sounds agreeable. In order to do this, it is necessary to begin with a physiological account and later move on

12. AVICENNA, *al-Ŝifā, Jawāmi' 'ilm el-mūsiqā*, I, 1: 4, 15-5, 5.

to a psychological explanation. In canonical treatises like the *Šifā* and the *Kitāb an-Najāt* (*The Book of Salvation*) the physical descriptions of hearing that can be found are, in my opinion, implicit in the Avicennan conception of music. For example, in *Šifā, an-Nafs,* 2.5, 82ss we find a detailed study of hearing (*samā'*) and, before, in *Šifā, an-Nafs* 1.5.41-42, when Avicenna talks of perception in general, there are already descriptions like the following:

> The faculty of perception has two divisions: that of external perception and that of internal perception. The faculty of external perception comprises the five, or eight, senses. These include sight, which is a faculty arrayed in the concave nerve that perceives the form of what is imprinted on the vitreous humor, that is, the images of the bodies possessing color that are transmitted through the actually transparent bodies to the surfaces of smooth bodies. Another sense is hearing, which is a faculty arrayed in the nerve dispersed on the surface of the ear canal that perceives the form of what is transmitted to it from the oscillation of the air that is compressed between what causes the disturbance [of the air] and what, with resistance, receives the disturbance, the air being compressed by a disruption that produces a sound. In this case, the oscillation of the air is transmitted to the still air enclosed in the chamber of the ear canal, and makes it move in the pattern of its motion, and the vibrations of that motion touch the nerve, and one hears [13].

In this description, Avicenna is clearly distinguishing between sound and hearing (see also *De anima* II 8; *Šifā, an-Nafs,* 2.5.85-86). Sound is a physical phenomenon, while hearing is a biological phenomenon and, as I have already showed, a psychological one too. Sound precedes hearing and does not presuppose it since it actually gives rise to it. Hearing is posterior and presupposes sound, which is its proper object. Avicenna, like Aristotle, considers the physiological structure of the ear because it is what

13. AVICENNA, *Šifā, an-Nafs* 1.5.41-42, 180. Avicenna writes in *an-Najāt,* trans. F. Rahman, 26: "The perceptive faculty can be divided into two parts, the external sense and the internal sense. The external senses are the five or eight senses. One of them is sight, which is a faculty located in the concave nerve; it perceives the image of the forms of colored bodies imprinted on the vitreous humor. These forms are transmitted through actually transparent media to polished surfaces. The second is the sense of hearing, which is a faculty located in the nerves distributed over the surface of the ear-hole; it perceives the form of what is transmitted to it by the vibration of the air which is compressed between two objects, one striking and the other being struck, the latter offering it resistance so as to set up vibrations in the air which produce the sound. This vibration of the air outside reaches the air which lies motionless and compressed in the cavity of the ear, moving it in a way similar to that in which it is itself moved. Its waves touch that nerve, and so it is heard".

makes hearing possible. Now, sound, just as Aristotle remarks, is produced when two solid bodies hit each other: "the sound actually produced is of something striking against something else in a medium"[14]. So it is explained by Avicenna:

> The sense of hearing, which is a faculty located in the nerves distributed over the surface of the ear-hole; it perceives the form of what is transmitted to it by the vibration of the air which is compressed between two objects, one striking and the other being struck, the latter offering it resistance so as to set up vibrations in the air which produce the sound[15].

In order for sound to take place it is necessary that two objects hit each other, but besides, those objects need to be hard, plain, hollow and the striking must start in a continuous medium, such as air or water. In this way, just as it is described in *De sensu* 6, 446b30ff. and in *De audibilibus* 800a1ff., the movement of the medium is transmitted to the ear. Avicenna, following Aristotle, holds that air works as a medium of transmission of sound, but also, as can be inferred from the previous passage, he claims that the principal agent of sound is not exactly air, rather it is the vibrations produced when two hard objects strike each other and against the air[16]. Aristotle believes that the main agent of hearing is vacuum[17]. Air is not sonorous because it is easily disaggregated, but if it is restrained, its movement becomes sound. An object is sonorous if it is capable to set a continuous mass of air in motion up to the ear[18]. It is because of this that wool or sponges cannot produce any sound despite being hit, while bronze can. Following Aristotle, Avicenna affirms that the movement of the stars cannot produce sound either (see *De caelo* II, 9; *Šifā, Jawāmi' 'ilm el-mūsiqā* I, 1: 4, 5). Now then, the ear is naturally adapted to air because it is immersed in air and, when the outer air moves, the inner air moves too[19].

The sonorous variations oscillate between the high and low tones, so the ear is a kind of middle term (*mesótes*) between one and another extreme. This description coincides, as can be seen, with the one made by Aristotle of the other external senses. In short, the ear can grasp a wide

14. ARISTOTLE, *De anima* II 8, 419b9.
15. AVICENNA, *an-Najāt*, trans. F. Rahman, 26.
16. ARISTOTLE, *De anima* II, 8, 419b20.
17. ARISTOTLE, *De anima* II, 8, 419b34.
18. ARISTOTLE, *De anima* 420a ss.
19. ARISTOTLE, *De anima* II, 8, 420a5-10.

range of sonorous variations that oscillate between high and low tones [20]. Both Aristotle and Avicenna agree that without sound there is no hearing and that, even though they are different things, in the act of auditory perception they become one and the same thing [21].

After the analysis of hearing, Aristotle deals with a related subject, namely, voice. Dealing with voice is pertinent because it is the kind of sound that living things emit, and because of it, it is clear that voice adds perfection to sound. Avicenna takes up again this issue in the introduction of the section dedicated to music [22]. Living things grasp but also emit sounds full of meaning. This is precisely the functionalist explanation I referred to in the first lines: the meaningful sounds, i.e. voice, are basic for animal communication.

In regard to the last issue, Avicenna appeals to a series of biological considerations that, undoubtedly, takes into account Aristotle's writings concerning animals. Avicenna explains that, since nature is a manifestation of God, He decided to regulate the functions of living creatures in order to preserve the species and, for this reason, animals reproduce. Reproduction urges animals to unite and, for it, nature has endowed them with a certain capacity to communicate their presence to other members of their species through certain communicative capacities:

> The imperative need for the reproduction of the species encourages the animals to come together, to couple after being separated [sic]. Nature gave them the skill to call, to report their presence, and they also use this ability in other circumstances, such as to report an unseen danger. These are obvious things that are confirmed by experience, so we have no doubt that the Creator takes care of his creation. God's Providence attends to the needs of his creatures and provides them with things that are necessary and useful [23].

Animals have certain communicative capacities that enable them to associate, to mate, and as can be read in the passage, to report some experiences like danger. The grasp of danger is possible due to the estimative faculty, which makes animals both capable of understanding

20. In this respect, Aristotle offers a physiological account in *De anima* 420a28-420b1: "But the differences in things which sound are shown in sound actually realized; for just as colors cannot be seen without light, so sharp and heavy noises cannot be distinguished without sound. These terms are used by analogy from the sense of touch. The sharp sensation excites to a great extent in a short time, the heavy to a slight extent in a long time".

21. AVICENNA, *Šifā, an-Nafs*, 2.5.85-86.

22. AVICENNA, *Šifā, Jawāmi' 'ilm el-mūsiqā*, I, 1: 5, 15.

23. AVICENNA, *Šifā, Jawāmi' 'ilm el-mūsiqā*, I, 1: 5, 15.

hostility and friendship and of making the other members of their species aware of a given state of affairs. Now, if animals are able to communicate amongst themselves, this means that they are able to emit meaningful sounds, i.e. voices. Avicenna holds that animals emit sounds that are either a call of danger or an expression of pleasure and pain. In my opinion, animals can emit voices with meaning because of two main reasons: a) their physiological constitution and b) their cognitive faculties.

In *Šifā, Jawāmi' 'ilm el-mūsiqā*, I, 1, Avicenna does not treat animals' physiological dispositions in sufficient detail to explain why some of them have voices. He only mentions that Nature has endowed some animals with an organ that enables the emission of useful sounds so that they can understand each other. That would work as a preamble to demonstrate that in animals – including human beings – there is a natural disposition to sound, that the latter is necessary to survive and that, among animals, human beings are the only ones able to give harmony to sound. The introduction of harmony, i.e. music, in Avicenna's argument is somewhat abrupt. The difference between sound and music would be, up to this point, harmony. But there is more to the definition than this: if some animals can emit meaningful sounds, their physiological structure should be disposed for it. Avicenna presupposes that animals that emit voices are precisely those that have both external and internal perception. We can infer that in his studies on music Avicenna gives a definitive relevance to sensation: animals have certain perceptions of the world and Avicenna claims that animals report such sensitive experiences (danger or pleasure) through sounds directed toward the world. If animals did not have the support of relevant organs, they could not emit sounds with meaning. Even the internal senses do have a location in the brain. This physiological disposition of the cognitive faculties enables the sensitive soul to link perception with the world. The internal faculties play a relevant role in this process, especially, imagination and the estimative power. But before examining this point more closely, it is convenient to recall a passage where Aristotle insists on the relation between the physiological disposition and the capacity of emitting voices:

> Voice is the sound produced by a creature possessing a soul; for inanimate things never have a voice; they can only metaphorically be said to give voice, e.g., a flute or a lyre, and all other inanimate things which have a musical compass, and tune, and modulation. The metaphor is due to the fact that the voice also has these, but many animals – e.g., those which are bloodless, and of animals which have blood, fish – have no voice. And this is quite reasonable, since sound is a kind of movement of the air. The fish, such as those in the Achelous, which are said to have a voice, only make a

> sound with their gills, or with some other such part. Voice, then, is a sound made by a living animal, and that not with any part of it indiscriminately. But, since sound only occurs when something strikes something else in a certain medium, and this medium is the air, it is natural that only those things should have voice which admit the air. As air is breathed in Nature makes use of it for two functions: just as she uses the tongue both for taste and for articulation, of which taste is an essential to life (and consequently belongs to more species), and articulate speech is an aid to living well; so in the same way she employs breath both to conserve internal heat, as something essential (why it is so will be explained in another treatise), and also for the voice, that life may be of good standard [24].

Which animals emit meaningful voices? In *Historia Animalium* IV, 9, 535b3ss. bees, cicadas and crickets are excluded. Instead, in *Historia Animalium* IV, 9, 535b32-536b23 animals with the right physiological apparatus are included, namely, those with lungs, trachea, and larynx: mammals (human beings included), four-legged oviparous animals, and birds. Almost all fish lack voice. Almost all water creatures in fact lack voice, with the exception of perhaps the most studied sea mammal within contemporary cognitive sciences: dolphins. Dolphins, unlike fish, have lungs and trachea and therefore are able to emit voice. The same happens with other sea mammals like whales, sea lions, or seals.

Avicenna does not pay a lot of attention to physiological details like the ones I have described. Nevertheless, it is easy for him to tell the importance of the internal faculties for musical perception. And this is so because besides physiological constitution, voice-emitting animals require specific cognitive faculties. They need at least one internal sense, namely, imagination. Aristotle affirms that:

> For, as we have said, not every sound made by a living creature is a voice (for one can make a sound even with the tongue, or as in coughing), but that which even causes the impact, must have a soul, and use some imagination (*phantasía*); for the voice is a sound which means (*semantikós*) something, and is not merely indicative of air inhaled, as a cough is [25].

This text is relevant because coughs and sneezes are not voices because they are not associated to any representation (*metá phantasías tinós*). Vocal sound being associated with an act of imagination implies that this vocal sound has meaning (*psófos semantikós*). Now, if it has meaning, it cannot be an operation explained through a merely mechanic action, it is

24. ARISTOTLE, *De anima* II, 8, 420b5-23.
25. ARISTOTLE, *De anima* II, 8, 420b29-421a1.

rather explained because there is a sensitive soul, and because of it, the animal emits a sound semantically linked to imagination.

II. SOUND AND MUSIC

As we have just seen, voice is a sound associated with a representation, and this sound constitutes the most basic form of language. Both Aristotle and Avicenna accept that animals have a form of language, since nature has provided them with what is physiologically and cognitively necessary for it. It is relevant to clarify that even though voice is a form of sound (*ṣawt*) [26], the latter is not yet a form of language. However, we should ask if meaningful sounds, i.e. voice, also explain the origin of music (*mūsīqā*). Avicenna abruptly introduces music when he is giving his functionalist account of language. There is, indeed, a thematic gap. Avicenna is explaining why animals manifest a natural disposition to sound and how it is useful for communicating amongst themselves, when suddenly he mentions that human beings are the only ones capable of organizing sound harmonically.

Shehadi also points out this gap in the argument. Until it occurs, Avicenna acts as a biologist in order to show how articulated language enables communication. However, one should ask if this functionalist approach tells us something about the origin of music. Music could be considered an articulated language, though this would be an unsatisfactory definition since not every articulated language is music. Shehadi (1995, 70) denies that a functionalist account of music's origin can be found in Avicenna, just as it is present in Darwin or Spencer. I share Shehadi's interpretation since if we were partisans of this type of functionalism: a) we would not have consistent reasons for explaining how articulated language becomes musical language, and b) we could hardly entertain an aesthetic account of music. In other words, functionalism would not give an answer to aspects related with the kind of musical perception we are here interested in: imagination and its creative capacity to structure sounds in a harmonic fashion and the pleasure or displeasure those sounds generate in us.

It is true that Avicenna introduces music abruptly, but it is also true that the characterization of musical composition offered there goes beyond the merely functional:

26. See AVICENNA, *Šifā, Jawāmi' 'ilm el-mūsiqā*, I, 1.

> Man uses his voice's inflection and, conventionally, each of his inflections corresponds with an idea. The natural effects of sound have been enriched by those conventional effects thanks to human art. A voice, for example, if it murmurs at a certain time, and it starts over again after pausing, expresses weakness and impotence and pleads for clemency. If, on the contrary, a voice is high and brusque it will be threatening and it will seem strong and firm and will lead to obedience and, gradually, to absolute resignation [27].

However, I believe that the Avicennan characterization surpasses a sheer communicative conception of music and allows us to understand it from an aesthetic stance as well. To arrive at this point, it is necessary to refer to some observations from the section of the *Šifā* dedicated to *Poetics*. In this way, we can notice that just as animals have a natural disposition to sound, human beings seem to be naturally inclined to imitate. Avicenna clearly states that among living creatures, human beings are the only ones who are delighted with imitation [28]. When he deals with music he seems to refer to a human natural disposition to discern well-combined sounds and to link them with Nature and with our characters:

> Especially those things that make him remember other things do entice man; he therefore represents and imitates them. Some musical notes have the property of reminding us of some quality, and those notes provoke in us the impression that we possess that quality, the attributes of that quality, and its necessary consequences. This is why sonorous combinations seduce us. Our discerning ability, which has a different role from our faculty of hearing, recognizes in musical composition certain order and obtains from it different suggestions: that is what makes us find music agreeable.

27. AVICENNA, *Šifā, Jawāmi' 'ilm el-mūsiqā*, I, 1: 8, 5.

28. In AVICENNA, *Šifā, Kitāb al-shi'r* IV, 1 is read: "There are two causes that make the human mind create Poetry. One is the pleasure of imitating and the use of imitation from childhood. In this [men] differ from the speechless animals in that man is more capable of imitating than all other animals. Some of them are incapable of imitating at all, and some are capable of insignificant imitation, such as the parrot, by means of voice, and the monkeys, by gestures". Further on AVICENNA, *Šifā, Kitāb al-shi'r* IV, 3: "An evidence that imitation is delightful is that men are pleased by contemplating the portrayed forms of hateful and disgusting animals which they would avoid if seen in actuality. What is delightful is not that form itself nor what is portrayed but its being a precise imitation of something else. For this reason, learning is pleasant not to philosophers alone but to common people due to the imitation that is in it, and because learning consists of a certain representation of a thing in the 'seat' of the soul. Men, therefore, find a great delight in portrayed forms if they can well relate these to the originals".

> A special quality of composition (harmony) that is strange to all genres of composition is for us another cause of enticement. It consists in the following: the first of two notes produces upon our souls an agreeable impression, as any unexpected and desirable thing. This sensation will be followed by another similar to it that provokes in us the sudden disappearance of a beloved thing of ephemeral duration. This recollection that followed pleasure disappears when the second note arrives. This will be for us nothing but the return of the first one under another form and the latter will be with the former as in a relation that corresponds to our ear. It is known, however, that among the causes of pleasure the main cause is the surprise we experience in the presence of a harmonic sensation after the return of some other previously erased. The unexpected sensation of sound, its sudden disappearance, and afterwards its return, as well as the seduction of the composition (harmony), yield the greatest and sweetest pleasure to the soul. This is why the ordered combination of sounds – its composition – deeply entices us, just as does the ordered and regular combination of rhythmic percussions. Both of these make us imagine sounds and approach them for their nature [29].

In musical perception the first things that fascinate us are the sensible qualities of sound and, more specifically, harmony. In the section dedicated to poetics in the *Šifā*, Avicenna affirms that, besides the natural inclination for imitation, we also naturally tend to harmony. In fact, in *Šifā, Kitāb al-shi'r*, IV, 4, when Avicenna announces the causes of human imitation, we read: "The second cause is men's natural love of harmonious combination and melodies. The measures were found to be analogous to melodies; and consequently, the soul became favorably disposed to and thus [learned to] create them". This inclination to harmony yields us pleasure, while the shared necessity with animals to communicate is not necessarily pleasant. There are reasons to privilege, say, a mimetic-natural origin of music instead of a functionalist one. In the passage just quoted, Avicenna refers to our capacity to enjoy music, which is not to be confused, as he explains, with the mere act of listening, since it rather appeals to our cognitive faculties. The passage suggests that only animals with certain cognitive faculties can appreciate music. I will insist on this in the next section. For now, it seems appropriate to explain the role of such cognitive faculties in the *Jawāmi' 'ilm el-mūsiqā*. I will defend the importance of imagination both in musical creation and in its perception. This takes us back once more to the origin of music: there is music because there is voice, even though not all voices are music.

29. AVICENNA, *al-Šifā, Jawāmi' 'ilm el-mūsiqā*, I, 1: 8, 10.

It is true that there is no meaningful voice without imagination. How is it possible that certain articulated voices do not limit themselves to communicative action, but also generate pleasure thanks to their harmonic structure, their tonality, their intervals (*ab'ād*), their rhythm (*'īqā'*), and their melody (*laḥn*)? To answer this question it is necessary to distinguish some capacities of the imaginative faculty. In fact, imagination is a faculty we share with animals. However, imagination is capable of interacting with other cognitive faculties that animals lack. In *Kitāb an-Najāt,* Avicenna distinguishes between rational imagination (*mufakkirah*) and sensitive or compositive imagination (*mutaḫayyilah*)[30]. A basic and useful difference between humans and animals, despite all the similarities, is rational imagination. Imagination under the domain of the estimative power (*wahm*) is proper to animals; on the other hand, imagination under reason's domain is proper to human beings. In the latter case, Avicenna uses the term *mufakkirah*, translated into Latin word as *cogitatio*[31]. Nevertheless, Avicenna insists that the cogitative power replaces neither imagination nor the estimative power in rational animals. Human beings actually have estimative power too. This clarification is relevant: only human beings have a cogitative power, whereas the estimative power is common to animals and humans. The latter is important in order to explain affective qualities (hostility, friendship, etc.), incidental perception, some of our ethical beliefs and creativity[32].

My claim is that the distinction between *mutaḫayyilah* and *mufakkirah* is relevant to understanding how meaningful voices are articulated. I also think that the cognitive functions of those two faculties suggest how human beings are capable of articulating "conceptual language" and a subclass of it, namely, music. As I have said before, in order to emit voices with meaning a specific physiological apparatus (lungs and trachea) and a cognitive one (imagination) are required. I think that language is possible because *mutaḫayyilah* enables some kind of link or association between

30. AVICENNA, *Kitāb an-Najāt,* trans. F. Rahman, 31.

31. AVICENNA, *Šifā, an-Nafs,* 1.5.45, 182: "Next is the faculty called the imaginative faculty in relation to the animal soul and the cogitative faculty in relation to the human soul. It is a faculty arrayed in the medial ventricle of the brain at the *cerebellar vermis*, whose function is to combine and divide at will any [forms] in the imagery. Thereafter, there is the estimative faculty, being arrayed at the back of the medial ventricle. It perceives the connotational attributes not perceptible to the senses but that are nonetheless in particular sensible objects, like the faculty in the sheep that judges that this wolf is something to flee and that this lamb is something to love. It would seem to operate also on objects of the imagination by combining and dividing them".

32. BLACK (1993), 219-58.

voice and content. This would explain why some animals articulate meaningful sounds, indeed, for social convenience (functionalism). Animals do attain the articulation of certain sounds with meaning [33] that are associated with an emotion. It is clear that Avicenna admits that animal perception is directed toward the world and animals recognize meanings or connotational attributes (also called intentions).

I have already argued that humans have estimative power too – this explains the directionality of our knowledge toward non-material properties perceived through sensible – but the interaction of this faculty with other internal senses makes human knowledge superior to that of animals. It is clear that, following Aristotle, Avicenna is correct in that we cannot form concepts without images. This means that the intervention of imagination in knowledge is inevitable. Now, the interaction between *mutaḫayyilah*, *wahm* and *mufakkirah* in our rational operations is extremely relevant for Avicenna. In fact, although it is true that the intellect plays a privileged role in his epistemology, the internal senses actually play the leading role in knowledge. The internal senses make the intellective operation possible and perform the functions of retention and reception of forms and intentions. In this way, the perceptive contents coming from the external senses are *received* by common sense (*ḥiss al-mushtarak*) and retained by the retentive imagination (*khayāl/muṣawwarah*); the estimative power (*wham*) receives intentions retained by the memory (*dhikr*); the compositive imagination (*mutaḫayyilah*) is a permanently active faculty which composes and divides both forms and intentions [34]. This latter faculty can be dominated by the estimative power or by reason, as I have already said, and in the last case we would be dealing with *mufakkirah*, i.e. images controlled by reason.

This sketch of the internal senses mainly found in the second book of *Kitāb an-Najāt* and in the fourth book of *De anima* of the *Šifā* and even in the eight lesson of the *Canon of Medicine* (*al-Qānūn fi'l-tibb*), helps us understand: a) how we can articulate a more complex language than animals and, b) how we can create different forms of language, either figurative, poetic or musical, which are not related to communicative needs but to the creation of pleasure. I think we could claim that the difference

33. As Aristotle explains, some physiological factors such as an adequate tongue (wide and mobile) also intervene (ARISTOTLE, *Part. Anim.* II, 17, 660a25-27). The intervention of teeth and lips is evident in human beings.

34. A detailed account of the role of the internal senses in Avicenna and its reformulation in other philosophers such as Averroes, Albert the Great and Thomas Aquinas, can be found in BLACK (2000), 59-75.

between animal and human cognitive faculties is as follows: in animals there is a link between voice and intentions that allows for the creation of knowledge and a kind of articulation similar to language. But in human beings the interaction of our internal perceptive faculties with the intellect enables us to articulate a highly complex language alien to animals, since they lack a linguistic-conceptual apparatus.

In my view, with respect to (a), it is necessary to go deeply into the structure of human language. While some contemporary philosophers give priority to language over mental states, I hold that human language presupposes thought. In other words, humans have a conceptual apparatus that enables us to articulate language. In fact, when Avicenna conceives that *mufakkirah* is the anteroom of the judicative faculty, he is telling us that thanks to it we can have propositional attitudes towards the world. In fact, a propositional mental structure implies the possession of complex language. This last issue is an assumption of some of Avicenna's commentaries on works of logic like *The Book of Syllogism* (*Kitāb al-Qiyās*), *Remarks and Admonitions on Logic* (*Ishārāt wa-al-tanbīhāt*), *Isagoge* (*al-Madkhal*), and *Peri Hermeneias* (*al-ibarah*). It should be kept in mind that the main interest of Avicenna in epistemology is the levels of abstraction and, in logic an essential topic for him is concepts (*tasawwir*). Hence, even though language – understood as a set of particular rules conventionally established – plays no essential role, we cannot say the same of the kind of language that I have called "conceptual language", namely, the kind of language that enables us to establish a link between voice and concept. It must be kept in mind then that humans can articulate voices directed towards the sensible world and, in addition, voices directed toward mental concepts. Avicenna might concede that not all of our knowledge is propositional (for example, the connotational attributes that we recognize thanks to the estimative power), although he might argue that our nobler and higher way to know is conceptual knowledge.

Regarding (b), i.e. the creation of forms of figurative or musical language, it must be said that Avicenna gives a relevant place to imagination and, in fact, without it we could not even think universals; it is not strange then that images also enable us to compose figurative language. The compositive imagination would be interacting with the estimative power. The compositive imagination is capable of combining and dividing images, even involuntarily. The estimative power, then, enables humans to compose voluntarily figurative language and imaginative discourse [35]. It is precisely in his commentary to *Poetics* where Avicenna defines poetry as an imaginative discourse composed of expressions with measure, rhythm and, among Arabs, with rhyme. The opening passage of the *Kitāb al-shi'r* is relevant to our purpose:

> We first say that poetry is imaginative speech, composed of utterances that are measured, commensurate and, in Arabic, rhymed. The meaning of being measured is that they have rhythmical quantity; the meaning of being commensurate is that each utterance, which is rhythmical, has a temporal duration equal to that of the others; and the meaning of been rhymed is that the letters that terminate each utterance are the same. The logician considers [poetry] only in so far as it is imaginative speech. Otherwise, the measure is the [proper] concern of the musicologist (in terms of investigation and general practice) and the prosodist (in terms of scansion and according to the practice of each nation). The rhymist considers rhyme [36].

The poetic discourse is imaginative because imagination is able to combine images. This capacity is indispensable for our mental acts, from the mere act of thinking to acts of recalling and even dreaming. Poets combine images voluntarily thanks to the compositive imagination; thanks to the estimative power, those images can be loaded with "emotive meanings" [37]. The capacity of imagination to "bring to mind" images

35. This would be a especial capacity of the estimative power in human beings, since animals are not capable of composing figurative language even though they also have imagination and estimative power. It seems then that the creation of figurative language involves in some way certain intellective capacities. In this sense, the creation of figurative language or the creation of metaphors are part of a logical process, even a syllogistic one. This is why Avicenna had conceived a poetic or imaginative syllogism; see KEMAL, (1991) and (2003); BLACK, (1990). Commenting *Poetics* 21, Avicenna refers to metaphors as the transfer of a name based on resemblance, and writes in AVICENNA, *Al- Šifā, Kitāb al-shi'r* VII, 3: "The transfer is applying to a name with a given sense the sense of another, but not to the extent that the one becomes the name of the other and the distinction is lost between the first and the second. The transfer is sometimes from genus to species, or from species to genus, or from species to species, or the analogous of a thing is transferred from its like in relation to a fourth, as when old age is called the evening of life or the autumn of life". Apparently, Avicenna holds a tensional view of metaphors, quite close to the Aristotelian, but also quite close to the metaphoric interactionism of contemporary thinkers such as Max Black or Paul Ricoeur. Avicenna speaks of transfer of terms, but not of substitution of meaning. Making metaphors is an act that cannot put our reasoning capacity aside.

36. AVICENNA, *Šifā, Kitāb al-shi'r*, I, 1.

37. In this emotive element lies the persuasive force of poetry, see AVICENNA, *Al- Šifā, Kitāb al-shi'r*, I, 3: "If the imitation (*muhākā*) of a thing which is untrue moves the soul, then it is no surprise that the depiction of a true thing as such moves the soul, too. The latter is even

loaded with meanings beyond sensible objects translated into intentions (or emotions), allows Avicenna to conclude that the estimative power is decisively linked with our thought and our judgments. And thanks to it, both assent and conviction can be caused by means of imagination:

> Both imaginative assent and conviction are [kinds of] compliance. Imaginative assent, however, is a compliance due to the wonder and the pleasure caused by the utterance itself, while conviction is a compliance due to the realization that the thing is what it is said to be. Imaginative assent results from the utterance itself, conviction from what is spoken of, i.e., the focus is on the matter being conveyed [38].

The preceding passage implies that we can be convinced of something because it has been presented to us through agreeable images and, therefore, we can accept or reject something without considering, reasoning or choosing. Hence, the logician knows that in the poetic discourse demonstrative syllogisms should not be used, since the soul is more inclined to an object through imaginative representations. Avicenna mentions that although the logician is concerned with this logic-discursive dimension of poetry, the musicologist is concerned with measure. That is why we have the definition of music presented by Avicenna in his *Jawāmi' 'ilm el-mūsiqā*:

> Music is a mathematical science the aim of which is the study of musical notes; it examines its consonance and dissonance, as well as its duration and thus, how is it that the rules of musical composition are set. Music, then, comprises two branches: the first, which refers to the notes, is denominated "sciences of melodic composition;" the second concerns the time that separates the notes of a melody and is denominated "rhythmic". At the base of these two sciences are found the principles obtained from sciences not related to music. Some of them are arithmetical, others are physical taken from the Natural Sciences, and some others are, so to say, geometrical. The existence of physical principles in music is due to the physical contents of this art. [However,] if we are to explain precisely and through strong principles the affairs related with music, we cannot do so by just recurring to physical principles. The mathematical principles that formally [compose] music are too material to understand this art, just as it has been seen in *The Book of Demonstration*. In this way, in fact, music

more necessary. But human beings are more amenable to imaginative (*tajyīl*) representation than to conviction; and many of them, when hearing the demonstrable truths, respond with aversion and dissociation. Imitation has an element of wonder (*ta'ŷīb*) that truth lacks".

38. AVICENNA, *Šifā, Kitāb al-shi'r*, I, 4.

> receives the numerical relations through which it appears as harmonic or as being out of tune [39].

Music has principles, rules and objective forms of composition that guarantee the objectivity of harmony. I will not treat these, since it would demand an extremely technical approach to the forms of musical composition, which, by the way, can actually be found in Avicenna's treatise. What I want to point out is that in the last passage, Avicenna has clearly expressed that music has a numerical structure; and this structure is grasped, precisely, thanks to the estimative power. (It is not necessary to make a conversion from musical notes to numerical signs to appreciate music). But it is not only numerical relations that we grasp in it. In that combination and succession of notes we find something pleasant that we can associate with an emotion. The next passage turns out to be especially important, since Avicenna suggests in it that all our internal faculties are involved in musical perception, particularly, imagination. The latter is what allows us to discern succession and combination from sound:

> The considered law is that melody and rhythm are perceptible. This perceptibility depends on the way in which the melodies and rhythms impress the imagination and the way in which the overall composition is presented to it. A composition is agreeable when its elements constitute a whole. Such unity could not exist in sensation (*ḥasn*), since one could not feel at the same time two consecutive notes; but its impressions persist in imagination, and there they group together; it is then that, first, everything takes unity in the imagination and, afterwards, beauty is searched in that unity. If a second note or a second percussion took place when the imprint of the first one has been already erased, there could be no unity and any impression of the composition would have been eliminated. Therefore, something new must be perceived when the imprint of the other is still in the imagination, so it seems that they were perceived at the same time. This happens at the end of the rhythm of the percussions that are separated by too much time, but imagination retains the memory when it proceeds as we have pointed out. Thus, the rhythmic percussion of drums accompanies the final stages of many melodies. But here we do not talk of the tempi that separate the percussions of this genre, but of the tempo preserved in imagination when it is summed, after the imprint of the first percussion, a second lacking any intermediate percussion or any other reminder of it [40].

39. AVICENNA, *Jawāmi' 'ilm el-mūsiqā* I, 2: 9, 10.
40. AVICENNA, *Jawāmi' 'ilm el-mūsiqā* V, 1: 90, 10.

III. MUSICAL PERCEPTION AND MUSICAL THINKING

The differences between sound and hearing and between sound and music described above, lead to an explanation of how sounds are related through the internal perceptive faculties. Avicenna affirms that sound is one of those qualities that we can perceive through our senses. The ear can listen to sounds, but cannot perceive them as something delectable or detestable. In this regard, there is an important difference between Aristotle and Avicenna. In *De anima* III 7, 431a8-14 Aristotle affirms that external senses perceive what is agreeable and disagreeable in sensations and, therefore, that 'information' is already conveyed by them to common sense and the imagination. Avicenna, instead, understands that the only things external senses are able to grasp are proper and common sensibles, but not experiences of pleasure and displeasure. That is why the intervention of the estimative power is required.

Avicenna's stance allows us to construct a theory of aesthetic perception: the pleasure and displeasure we experience towards a color, an aroma or a sound would not come from external sensation but from the internal perceptive faculties. In this way, even when there are external objective properties that trigger our aesthetic experiences, the mind has an extremely active role. In this sense, the role of the internal senses is essential to explain the overall aesthetic experience and, obviously, musical perception. Within aesthetic perception, the estimative power plays a fundamental role. At the same time, the role of the estimative power must be understood according to the levels of abstraction that Avicenna sets forth in his epistemology as well as in his metaphysics.

According to the explanation in Avicenna, *Kitāb an-Najāt*, 38-40, Avicenna places the most basic degree of abstraction (*taŷrīd*) within sensible perception. In fact, when we perceive the form of an object (*ṣūrat al-mudrak*), we perceive a sensorial stimulus which is yet corporeal and, therefore, limited. But in a second moment, the retentive imagination (*al-jayāl/al- mutaṣawwira*) manages to make those forms remain so that the compositive imagination (*mutaḫayyilah*) composes and recombines the retained images. We could certainly situate artistic creation in this level (in our case, musical creation). Avicenna describes a series of mental processes or operations that enables the production of new forms and images and, in our case, of combinations and successions of sounds from which we can compose harmonic melodies. However, in this level, Avicenna would not be referring to some kind of 'intuitive capacity', but to a particular capacity that can take place because there are certain mental operations, though they are not yet conceptual. For this reason, at the level of musical creation, the mind is capable of ordering a series of 'imaginary' sounds regulated from the superior intellective faculties [41].

A third degree of abstraction, namely that which is possible thanks to the estimative power, explains how musical perception can take place. In fact, the estimative power, as I have already suggested, enables us to recognize connotational attributes not grasped by the senses, but ungraspable if not present in a material medium:

> The faculty of estimation goes a little farther than this [i.e., the representation degree] in abstraction, for it receives the intentions which in themselves are non-material, although they accidentally happen to be in matter. This is because shape, color, position, etc., are attributes which cannot be found except in bodily matters, but good and evil, agreeable and disagreeable, etc., are in themselves non-material entities and their presence in matter is accidental. The proof of their being non-material is this: If it were of their essence to be material, then good and evil, agreeable and disagreeable would be inconceivable as accidents in a physical body. Nevertheless, sometimes they are conceived in themselves apart from matter. It is clear that in themselves they are non-material and their being in matter is entirely by accident. It is such entities which the faculty of estimation perceives; and thus it perceives non-material objects which it abstracts from matter [42].

The pleasure caused by the agreement (*muwāfiq*) of musical sounds, i.e. harmony, would be then a connotational attribute. We can recognize it and delight in it. This is why the estimative power plays a leading role in musical perception and even in every aesthetic experience. Artistic beauty would be, in this sense, a non-reducible experience to the first degree of abstraction, i.e. the external sensible perception. But now another problem

41. This means that there are some cognitive acts in which the internal senses interact with intellective faculties. I think that in musical creation, where even imagination and the estimative power play a relevant role, the cogitative power intervenes too. For this reason, Avicenna does not have a mere sensitive conception of music and he is also aware of music's precise formal structure that easily surpasses mere 'auditory imagination'. Hence, within his *Jawāmi' 'ilm el-mūsiqā* we can find extremely technical musical aspects: the numeric ratio of consonance, the explanation of intervals and its mathematical justification; remarks on the musical semi-phrase, rhythmic and melodic structures and many other technical terms. It is clear that in order to appreciate music it is not necessary to know all these aspects. The composer, however, does require them: musical composition requires imagination, but also a faculty closely related to the intellect, i.e. the cogitative power.

42. AVICENNA, *Kitāb an-Najāt*, 39-40.

arises: If the estimative power is the highest faculty of animals, can they recognize musical intentions?

Animals cannot create music since, as I have said, they cannot order sound, because they lack the interaction of the imagination with other intellective faculties. Nevertheless, it seems that animals actually grasp consonance, harmony, and rhythm. Music, in this sense, is agreeable to animals. Avicenna, like al-Kindī before him, even admits that melodies can generate emotional effects in animated beings[43]. However, the fact that animals can perceive music does not imply that they can reach an aesthetic experience resembling that of humans. Animals might recognize harmony, but they cannot associate it with beauty. In order to do that, according to Avicenna, they would require another degree of abstraction, one that surpasses sensible perception, imagination and the estimative power, namely, intellection. Avicenna says:

> All convenient beauty and all good perceived is loved and desired, being the principle of its perception in the senses (*ḥiss*), the imagination (*jayāl*), the estimative power (*wahm*), opinion (*ẓann*) and the intellect (*'aql*)[44].

It is necessary to distinguish between the aesthetic perception found within the scope of external and internal perception from the appreciation of beauty. We share the former with animals because it is a purely sensorial perception. In this sense, it is relevant to emphasize the material conditions of this kind of perception. In fact, aesthetic perception, as any other sensorial perception, necessarily requires corporeal organs:

43. In fact, just as SHEHADI reminds us (1995, 27-31), in al-Kindī's *Musawwitāt* there are some observations that allow us to verify how the philosopher was convinced of the effects of music in the animal kingdom. Al-Kindī says, for example, that the sound of flutes attracts dolphins and whales; that fishes like the notes of the laud; and that before string instruments peacocks spread their tails. Al-Kindī mentions how according to their races, some persons reject some instruments: Persians reject the organ and the gong; Hindus and Romans reject the sound of the long-necked laud of Kuhrāsān. From these typologies, al-Kindī composes his "musical therapy". There are different kinds of melodies and each one induces different emotional effects (whether positive, like it might happen with melodies that put us in a good mood, or negative, like it might happen with those melodies that annoy us). The philosopher of music would be then in suitable condition to give musical therapy. Just as there are different eating habits according to races and nationalities, and the physician can heal certain conditions by applying dietetics, the philosopher – or the musicologist – could make of music a remedy for some diseases. Avicenna, actually, resorted to music in his medical practices and even managed to establish certain relations between music and pulse. AVICENNA, *Qānūn*, 12.3.9, §111, 291-292.

44. AVICENNA, *Kitāb an-Najāt*, 282, the translation is mine.

> All perception of the particular is through a bodily organ. As for the faculty which perceives individual forms, for instance, the external senses which perceive them in a way not completely divested of or abstracted from matter and not at all divorced from material attachments, the question of such a faculty is quite easy and clear. This is because these forms are perceptible only so long as their matter is present and a body can be present only to another body; it cannot be present to what is incorporeal. It has no relation whatever of presence and absence to an immaterial faculty, for a thing in space cannot have a relation of presence and absence to anything non-spatial. [...]
>
> And as for the faculty which perceives the individual forms as completely abstracted from matter but not at all abstracted from material attachments, like representation, it also needs a physical organ. For the faculty of representation cannot perceive without the represented forms being imprinted on a body in such a way that both it and the body share the same imprint [45].

The internal senses are, in fact, situated in the brain. In Avicenna's opinion, the *sensus communis* is located in the forepart of the front ventricle of the brain; the retentive imagination is located in the rear part of the front ventricle of the brain; the compositive imagination is located in the middle ventricle of the brain; the estimative is located in the far end of the middle ventricle of the brain; and memory is located in the rear ventricle of the brain [46]. The organic dependence both of external and internal senses makes it impossible for universal concepts to be grasped through them [47]. In fact, the knowledge we have at the perceptive level, both external and internal, is precisely non-conceptual knowledge.

Naturally, only the rational soul is capable of reaching the highest degree of abstraction, the universal degree. But it cannot make it without the assistance of animal faculties. It is clear that the appearance of the functions of the soul, according to Aristotle and Avicenna, is gradual. In this sense, the animal soul, characterized by motion and perception, also includes the functions of the vegetative soul, while the rational soul supposes the vegetative and animal functions. This gradation found in the Aristotelian psychology, is useful for distinguishing between the properly aesthetic perception (in our case, the pleasure produced by musical harmony), and the appreciation of beauty that, in Avicenna's case, would require a higher function than the perceptive one. It becomes clear that in

45. AVICENNA, *Kitāb an-Najāt*, 41.
46. AVICENNA, *Kitāb an-Najāt*, 31.
47. AVICENNA, *Kitāb an-Najāt*, 41.

the passage quoted above[48], where Avicenna talks of beauty appreciation, he integrates the senses, the imagination, the estimative power, opinion[49] and the intellect.

The appreciation of beauty is possible only for the rational soul (*al-nafs al-nāṭiqa*). The rational soul possesses two faculties, a theoretical (*naẓariyya*) and a practical (*'amaliyya*) one. The practical faculty guides ethics and all the practical arts and, in this sense, it would be responsible for artistic creation, since in the latter all our different faculties interact with the intelligence and with the purpose of creating. On the other hand, the perception of beauty is guided by the theoretical part of the rational soul. A passage of the *Kitāb an-Najāt* informs us of Avicenna's conception of the metaphysics of beauty:

> In the Necessary Being we find the highest degree of beauty (*ŷamāl*), of perfection and splendor. He understands His own essence in the highest degree of splendor and beauty. In His intellection, there is achieved a unity of the one who understands and what He understands[50].

It is beyond the parameters of this study to go deeply into Avicenna's conception of metaphysical beauty. It is enough to point out that it is not accessed by means of sensible perception. Avicenna is thinking of the highest degree of separation. That ascending way would lead to the metaphysics of the *Šifā*, to the *Ilāhiyyāt*. This would require another study, one with a focus on beauty rather than on musical perception.

CONCLUSION

I think that in his work dedicated to music, Avicenna offers a series of observations that are relevant for the theory of perception. We have seen how his disquisitions presuppose a physical description of hearing. Although the proper object of hearing is sound, music is a kind of meaningful sound characterized by harmony, intervals, and rhythm. The conjunction of those elements accounts for the pleasure humans find in melodies. In fact, Avicenna explains that the pleasure derived from the

48. AVICENNA, *Kitāb an-Najāt*, 282.

49. Opinion (*ẓann*) would be listed here, perhaps, because it would intervene in the process of judging what is pleasant and unpleasant and in the reactions of attraction and rejection of what is presented to us in an attractive or reprehensible way; see AVICENNA, *an-Najāt*, trans. F. Rahman, 26.

50. AVICENNA, *Kitāb an-Najāt*, 252, the translation is mine.

consonances surpasses the scope of purely sensorial hearing and does force us to understand the phenomenon of musical creation and its appreciation on the basis of the activity of our internal faculties. I have described the leading role of the compositive imagination and the estimative power. In this sense, I believe it is clear that musical perception demonstrates that our internal perceptive faculties play a fundamental role in cognitive acts. The case of music seems exemplary to me since in it our perceptive faculties are able to interact and recognize numerical harmonies, affective qualities, consonances and dissonances that are in fact connotational attributes. In my view, musical appreciation cannot be explained based on mere sensation. But it is not explained by intellection either: musical perception is not conceptual. In it, the imagination and the estimative power lay a bridge between sensation and intellection of beauty.

Musical acts allow us to establish resemblances and differences between animal and human perception. Since we share our perceptive faculties with animals, they can grasp musical harmony too. Actually, certain melodies would please animals too and would engender in them certain emotions. However, although animals can perceive music, they cannot compose nor appreciate it. Musical composition demands certain intellective capacities that enable humans to articulate harmonic sounds voluntarily. Animals, on the other hand, can recognize the intentions that accompany music, but according to Avicenna, they cannot appreciate music as something beautiful. The perception of beauty is possible only at the highest level of abstraction and in this sense it is a metaphysical experience.

BIBLIOGRAPHY

Sources

AL-FĀRĀBĪ (2001), *Grand traité de la musique*, trad. R. Erlanger, *La Musique Arabe*, t. 2, Société Nouvelle Librairie Orientaliste Paul Geuthner (reproduction de l'édition de 1935), Paris.

AL-KINDĪ (1962), *al-Musawwitāt al-watariyyah*, *Mu'allafāt al-Kindī*, ed. Zakariyyah Yousef, Bagdad.

AL-NADĪM, ibn (1998), *The Fihrist*, trans. B. Dodge, Columbia University Press, New York.

ARISTOTLE (2000), *On the Soul*, trans. W. S. Hett, Loeb Classical Library, London.

– (1995), *The Complete Works of Aristotle (On the Heavens, History of animals, Parts of animals, On Things Heard)*, ed. Jonathan Barnes, vol. 1, Princeton University Press, Princeton.

– (1995), *The Complete Works of Aristotle* (*Metaphysics*), Jonathan Barnes (ed.), vol. 2, Princeton University Press, Princeton.

AVICENNA (1952), *Avicenna's Psychology*, trans. F. Rahman, Oxford University Press, London.

– (1956), al-*Šifā'* (Mathématiques. 3. Musique (*Jawāmi' 'ilm el-mūsiqā*), ed. Zakariyya Yousef, Imprimerie Nationale, Cairo.

– (1959), *Avicenna's De anima, being the Psychological Part of Kitāb al-Shifā'*, ed. F. Rahman, Oxford University Press, London.

– (1974), *Commentary on the Poetics of Aristotle*, trans. Ismail M. Dahiyat, Brill, Leiden.

– (1985), *Kitāb al-Najāt*, ed. Majid Fakhry, Dar al-'Afaq al-Jadidah, Beirut.

– (1999), *The Canon of Medicine* (*al-Qānūn fi'l-ṭibb*), adapted by Laleh Bakhtiar, O. Cameron Gruner and Mazar H. Shah (trans.), Great Books of the Islamic World Inc., Chicago.

– (2001), *Mathématiques, Kitābu' š-šifā'*, trad. R. Erlanger, *La Musique Arabe*, t. 2, Société Nouvelle Librairie Orientaliste Paul Geuthner (reproduction de l'édition de 1935), Paris.

– (2007), "Sections on Psychology from *The Cure*", in McGinnis, J., Resiman, D. (trans., eds.), *Classical Arabic Philosophy. An Anthology of Sources*, Hackett Publishing Company Inc., Indianapolis/Cambridge.

MICHAEL SCOTUS (1992), *De animalibus: Michael Scot's Arabic-Latin translation. Part three, books XV-XIX Generation of animals*, ed. Van Oppenraaij, Brill, Leiden.

– (1998), *De animalibus: Michael Scot's Arabic-Latin translation. Part two, books XI-XIV: parts of animals*, ed. Van Oppenraaij, Brill, Leiden.

Studies

BLACK, Deborah (1990), *Logic and Aristotle's Rhetoric and Poetics in Medieval Arabic philosophy*, Brill, Leiden.

– (1993), "Estimation (Wahm) in Avicenna: The Logical and Psychological Dimensions", in *Dialogue* XXXII, 212-258.

– (1997), "Avicenna on the Ontological and Epistemic Status of Fictional Beings" in *Documenti e Studi sulla Tradizione Filosofica Medievale* 8, 425-453.

– (2000), "Imagination and Estimation: Arabic Paradigms and Western Transformations", in *Topoi* 19, 59-75 (Kluwer Academic Publishers: Printed in the Netherlands).

CRUZ HERNÁNDEZ, Miguel (1981), "La teoría musical de Ibn Sina en el *Kitāb al-Shifā'*", en *Milenario de Avicena*, Instituto Hispano-Árabe de Cultura, Madrid, 26-36.

DAVIDSON, Herbert (1992), *Alfarabi, Avicenna and Averroes on Intellect*, Oxford.

FARMER, Henry G. A. (1925), "Clues for the Arabian Influence on European Music", in *Journal of the Royal Asiatic Society,* 61-80.

–(1930), "Greek Theorists in Arabic Translations", in *Isis*, vol. 13, núm. 2, 325-333.

–(1931), "Music", *The Legacy of Islam*, Oxford University Press, London

–(1932), "The Influence of al-Fārābī's "Ihsa al-'Ulum" (*De scientiis*) on the Writers on Music in Western Europe", in *Journal for Royal Asiatic Studies,* 561-592.

–(1959-61), "Tenth-Century Arabic Books on Music", in *The Annual of Leeds Universal Oriental Society* II, 37-47.

GUTAS, Dimitri (2001), "Intuition and Thinking: The Evolving Structure of Avicenna's Epistemology", in *Aspects of Avicenna*, ed. Robert Wisnovsky, Princeton, 1-38.

HASSE, Dag Nikolaus (2000), *Avicenna's De anima in the Latin West*, London/Turin.

KEMAL, Salim (1991), *The poetics of Alfarabi and Avicenna*, Brill, Leiden.

–(2003), *The Philosophical Poetics of Alfarabi, Avicenna and Averroës*, Routledge Curzon, London.

PETERS, F. E. (1968), *Aristoteles Arabus*, Brill, Leiden.

RANDEL, Don M. (1976), "al-Fārābī and the Role of Arabic Music Theory in the Latin Middle Ages", in *Journal of American Musicological Society* 2, 173-188.

SHEHADI, F. (1995), *Philosophies of Music in Medieval Islam*, Brill, Leiden.

WINGATE, S. D. (1931), *The Mediaeval Latin Versions of the Aristotelian Scientific Corpus, with Special Reference to the Biological Works*, The Courier Press, London.

WINNINGTON-INGRAM, R. P. (1932), "Aristoxenus and the Intervals of Greek Music", in *The Classical Quarterly*, Vol. 26, N. 3/4, 195-208.

ACQUISITION DE LA PENSÉE ET ACQUISITION DE L'ACTE CHEZ AVERROÈS. UNE LECTURE CROISÉE DU *GRAND COMMENTAIRE* AU *DE ANIMA* ET DU *KITĀB AL-KAŠF 'AN MANĀHIĞ AL-ADILLA*

Jean-Baptiste BRENET
(Université de Paris I – Panthéon - Sorbonne)

On propose de connecter ici deux thèses d'Averroès. Il s'agit premièrement de dégager de son *Grand Commentaire* au traité *De l'âme* d'Aristote une doctrine précise relative à l'« acquisition » et à l'« attribution » de la pensée pour dans un second temps la relier aux développements du *Kašf 'an manāhij al-adilla* roulant sur la doctrine théologique de l'« acquisition » (*kasb* ou *iktisāb*). L'idée, plus exactement, est de lire la thèse du *Grand Commentaire* à la lumière de la conception de l'*iktisāb* qu'Averroès défend dans le *Kašf.* Ce faisant, on tâche d'envisager la proposition : « je pense », non plus simplement comme un problème noétique, mais comme un *cas* – fût-il le plus compliqué – de cette tâche conceptuelle plus ample qu'est la justification de la proposition : « je fais ».

Dans son *Grand Commentaire* du traité *De l'âme*, Averroès, comme on sait, pointe lui-même les problèmes qu'entraîne sa conception de l'intellect matériel substantiellement séparé et unique pour toute l'espèce humaine. Il en repère explicitement trois : celui de l'adventicité de l'intelligible (si les intellects agent et matériel sont des substances éternelles, comment pourrait-il proprement y avoir une production de l'intelligible ?) ; celui de son individuation (si l'intellect matériel, perfection première de l'homme, est unique, comment pourrait-il y avoir une diversification de sa perfection seconde, c'est-à-dire de la pensée ?) ; enfin, celui du genre d'être de l'intellect matériel (quelle peut être la nature du substrat des pensées s'il faut à la fois qu'il n'ait aucune forme et qu'il soit « un certain étant » ?)[1]. Le deuxième problème est présenté comme « le plus difficile » mais reçoit pour l'essentiel la même solution que le premier. Il existe « deux sujets » (*duo subiecta*) pour la pensée humaine : l'intellect matériel, d'un côté, unique support des intelligibles en acte, et l'image individuelle, de l'autre, moteur nécessaire dans le processus abstractif d'engendrement de ces intelligibles. De même donc que les intelligibles théoriques sont produits parce qu'on ne pense pas sans images, et que les images sont fluctuantes, ces intelligibles « sont multipliés par le nombre des hommes individuels »[2] dans la mesure où les images fluctuantes sont elles-mêmes individuelles et qu'elles permettent à chacun, en tant qu'elles constituent la détermination formelle des intentions intelligées, de se joindre singulièrement au principe universel de la pensée[3].

Si cette thèse liée au problème expressément formulé de la multiplication de la pensée humaine est connue, elle ne rend pas compte de l'entière position d'Averroès. À la question de l'individuation relative des intelligibles, en effet, paraît devoir être ajoutée celle, moins visible, mais peut-être plus fondamentale, de leur *acquisition* et de leur *attribution*. En insistant sur la dimension empirique de notre pensée, Averroès n'entend pas seulement présenter ce qui en quelque façon singularise le rapport qui unit tel individu à l'universel, mais aussi ce qui explique que ce soit bien *lui* qui pense et pas un autre, c'est-à-dire, précisément, que c'est bien à lui, en tant qu'il en est l' « acquéreur », que la pensée « s'attribue », et non pas à un autre. Il ne suffit donc pas d'expliquer que les pensées de l'homme adviennent, sont effectivement produites, et qu'elles se multiplient en raison de la diversité des images singulières qui les conditionnent, il faut encore établir ce qui fait de l'intelligible ainsi produit, subjecté dans l'intellect matériel séparé et unique, la pensée de cet homme-ci ou de cet homme-là. L'idée, seule, d'une *continuatio* ou d'une *copulatio* (avec l'intelligible en acte) n'y suffisant pas, c'est ce que viendraient étayer les notions techniques d' « acquisition » et d' « attribution ».

Le repérage de cette double thématique au sein du *Grand Commentaire* se justifie d'un point de vue à la fois lexical et conceptuel. Commençons par relever certains éléments relatifs à l'acquisition. Lorsqu'il présente les

1. Pour la présentation des trois problèmes, voir AVERROES, *Comm. Mag. De anima*, III, 5, éd. Crawford, 399 (244-361) ; cf. *L'intelligence et la pensée*, éd. de Libera, 68-69.

2. AVERROES, *L'intelligence et la pensée*, 71 ; cf. *Comm. Mag. De anima*, III, 5, éd. Crawford, 401 (427-428).

3. Sur les « deux sujets » de la pensée chez Averroès, voir notamment BRENET (2003), 311-328 ; *id.* (2005), 53-86.

difficultés induites par l'unicité de l'intellect matériel, perfection première de l'humanité, Averroès écrit ceci (où a*cquirere* traduit probablement l'arabe *istafāda*) :

> si la perfection est une et la même pour tous les hommes et n'est pas multipliée par leur nombre, il faudra que quand *j'acquiers (acquirerem)* un certain intelligible, tu *acquières (acquireres)* exactement le même, et que quand j'oublie un certain intelligible, tu l'oublies également [4].

S'il n'y avait qu'un seul intellect pour toute l'humanité, l'homme semblerait donc incapable d'« acquérir » de manière singulière un intelligible. D'un intellect unique sortirait une pensée nécessairement mondiale, reçue par tous à l'identique et dans le même rythme ; ce qui est absurde. Cette menace de l'indifférenciation de la perfection seconde est reprise plus bas dans les mêmes termes :

> Si nous posons que cet intellect n'est pas nombré par les individus, il en résultera que son rapport à tous les individus existant selon sa perfection première dans la génération sera le même, d'où il sera nécessaire, si l'un de ces individus *acquiert (acquisierit)* une certaine chose intelligible, que celle-ci soit *acquise (acquiratur)* par la totalité de ces individus [5].

Le problème est le suivant : si penser consiste à se joindre à l'intelligible en acte, comment cette jonction peut-elle s'établir pour chaque homme pensant de manière chaque fois diverse ? Le modèle de la sensation paraît conduire à une impasse, dans lequel l'appropriation de l'acte second découle de la possession de la faculté qui, à titre de principe premier, l'opère [6]. En effet, note encore Averroès :

> si la jonction de ces individus [avec la chose intelligible en acte] a pour cause la jonction de l'intellect matériel avec eux, de même que la jonction de l'homme avec l'intention sensible a pour cause la jonction de la perfection première du sens avec lui qui reçoit l'intention sensible [...], il sera nécessaire que quand tu *acquiers (acquisieris)* un certain intelligible, moi aussi j'*acquière (acquiram)* cet intelligible : ce qui est impossible [7].

4. AVERROES, *L'intelligence et la pensée*, 63 ; cf. *Comm. Mag. De anima* III, 5, éd. Crawford, 393 (177-181).

5. AVERROES, *L'intelligence et la pensée*, 71 ; cf. *Comm. Mag. De anima* III, 5, éd. Crawford, 402 (449-454).

6. Voir BRENET (2005), 79 *sq*.

7. AVERROES, *L'intelligence et la pensée*, 71-72 ; cf. *Comm. Mag. De anima* III, 5, éd. Crawford, 402 (454)-403 (465).

Plus bas, dans le commentaire 36, Averroès détaille le processus d'élaboration de la pensée humaine. Tout commence par les « premières propositions » (*prime propositiones*), dont l'individu dispose quasiment d'emblée, à la suite sans doute d'expériences immédiates et incontrôlées [8]; puis adviennent les intelligibles qui résultent proprement d'une intervention individuelle décidée sur la base de ces premières propositions. Usant à nouveau du vocabulaire de l'acquisition, Averroès explique ce qui suit :

> les intelligibles adviennent de deux manières en nous – soit naturellement (et ce sont les premières propositions, dont nous ne savons ni quand elles nous sont venues ni d'où ni comment), soit volontairement (et ce sont les intelligibles *acquis (acquisita)* à partir des premières propositions) [9].

Ce qu'il répète quelques lignes plus loin, en soulignant que « nous ne pouvons ni dire que ces propositions ne sont pour rien dans l'existence des intelligibles *acquis (acquisitorum)* ni dire qu'elles sont leurs seuls causes agentes » [10]; ou pour rappeler « le discours affirmant que quand les conclusions sont *acquises (acquiruntur)* par nous à partir de l'intellect agent et des premières propositions… » [11].

Enfin, héritier des complexifications propres au péripatétisme gréco-arabe, Averroès recourt évidemment au lexique de l'acquisition quand il est question de l'intellect dit « acquis » (dont il ne fait, au vrai, pas si grand cas) [12]. Lorsqu'il paraît reprendre la notion à son propre compte (sans doute pour désigner un simple synonyme de la *continuatio* ou *copulatio*, *ittiṣāl*, de l'intellect avec l'individu pensant), il écrit :

8. Voir Black (1999), 172, n. 31 ; et Geoffroy (2007), 92, n. 51.

9. Averroes, *L'intelligence et la pensée*, 163-164 ; cf. *Comm. Mag. De anima*, III, 36, éd. Crawford, 496 (490-493).

10. Averroes, *L'intelligence et la pensée*, 164 ; cf. *Comm. Mag. De anima*, III, 36, éd. Crawford, 496 (496-501).

11. Averroes, *L'intelligence et la pensée*, 165 ; cf. *Comm. Mag. De anima*, III, 36, éd. Crawford, 498 (539-540).

12. Pour quelques développements récents montrant comment Averroès relance cependant le concept alexandrino-farabien, voir Geoffroy (2007), 85-96. Sur cette notion, plus largement, voir les développements de Davidson (1992) ; sur Alfarabi en particulier, voir Jolivet (1977).

> Et quand l'intellect matériel est uni [à l'intellect agent] en tant qu'il est parfait par l'intellect agent, alors nous sommes unis avec l'intellect agent; et cet état est appelé *acquisition (adeptio)* et *intellect acquis* [13].

Le français « acquisition » traduit ici le latin *adeptio*, tiré du verbe *adipisci*, et non plus *acquirere*, pour désigner ce qui devait être en arabe *iktisāb*, *i.e.* l'état du *'aql muktasab* et non pas – ce qui, en revanche, devait apparaître dans le contexte polémique de discussion des thèses d'Alfarabi et d'Alexandre – celui du *'aql mustafād* [14].

Considérons à présent l'« attribution ». Averroès écrit par exemple qu'« il est nécessaire d'*attribuer* (*attribuere*; ar. *nasaba [15]) ces deux actions à l'âme [qui est] en nous – recevoir l'intelligible et le produire –, bien que l'agent et le récepteur soient des substances éternelles » [16]; puis, plus bas, qu'« il est apparu nécessaire de nous *attribuer (attribuere)* ces deux facultés de l'intellect » [17]; ou encore – parlant cette fois de l'attribution de l'intellect plutôt que de l'intelliger – que

> l'intellect existant en nous a deux activités en tant qu'il nous est *attribué (attribuitur)*, dont l'une est du genre de la passion (et c'est concevoir), tandis que l'autre est du genre de l'action (et c'est extraire les formes et les dépouiller de toute matière, ce qui n'est rien d'autre que de les rendre [intelligibles] en acte après l'avoir été en puissance) [18].

Sans doute les occurrences qu'on a relevées ne sont-elles pas à mettre toutes sur le même plan [19]. Il reste qu'Averroès suggère lui-même qu'on doit prolonger la question de l'individuation de la pensée par celle de

13. AVERROES, *L'intelligence et la pensée*, 80; cf. *Comm. Mag. De anima,* III, 5, éd. Crawford, 411 (703-706).

14. Pour les textes polémiques, voir AVERROES, *L'intelligence et la pensée*, 114; 150-154; cf. *Comm. Mag. De anima,* III, 20, éd. Crawford, 445 (55 *sq.*); et III, 36, 481 (48), 486 (190). Par ailleurs, pour l'importante déformation du *'aql mustafād min ḫāriǧ* de l'Alexandre arabe (à laquelle, *via* Alfarabi, Averroès est confronté), voir l'article de GEOFFROY (2002), 191-231; et *id.* (2007), 77-110.

15. *Cf.* par exemple AVERROES, *Middle Commentary on Aristotle's* De anima, éd. Ivry, 6, 14; 29, 3; 51, 3 et 4.

16. AVERROES, *L'intelligence et la pensée*, 108; cf. *Comm. Mag. De anima,* III, 18, éd. Crawford, 439 (71-74).

17. AVERROES, *L'intelligence et la pensée*, 10; cf. *Comm. Mag. De anima,* III, 18, éd. Crawford, 440 (85).

18. AVERROES, *L'intelligence et la pensée*, 163; cf. *Comm. Mag. De anima,* III, 36, éd. Crawford, 495 (462-468).

19. Parler d'« acquisition » de la science pour désigner l'apprentissage sur la base de propositions premières pourrait ainsi passer pour banal et n'être donc le signe d'aucune intervention conceptuelle particulière.

l'acquisition et de l'attribution de cette pensée individuée, dont l'efficacité motrice de l'image individuelle ne suffit pas à rendre raison. Que manque-t-il en effet qui fasse d'une pensée de quelque chose la pensée de quelqu'un ? L'intervention de la « volonté » *(voluntas*; ar. **'irāda)*. Si c'est bien moi qui pense, et non pas un autre, ce n'est pas seulement parce que mes images, à la base du processus, ont conditionné cette abstraction, mais plus originairement parce que j'en ai par ma « volonté » commandé l'exécution. *Je* pense, par conséquent, dans la mesure où je l'ai « voulu », c'est-à-dire dans la mesure où j'ai motivé moi-même l'action, fondée sur mes images, des principes éternels abstracteur et récepteur de l'intelligible. Dans la pensée, dans ma pensée, je ne suis pas offert passivement, comme à mon insu, à l'opération cosmique des intellects. Je n'y joue pas le rôle d'un simple support d'images, d'une fourniture, d'un objet. Le passage de l'imaginé au pensable puis au pensé se déclenche à mon gré; et c'est par cette initiative que telle ou telle pensée abstraite des formes individuelles inscrites dans mon corps me revient en propre.

La lecture *in extenso* des passages cités plus haut le confirme. Averroès écrit en effet ceci :

> *il est nécessaire d'attribuer ces deux actions à l'âme [qui est] en nous* – recevoir l'intelligible et le produire –, bien que l'agent et le récepteur soient des substances éternelles, *du fait que ces deux actions* – abstraire les intelligibles et les concevoir – *dépendent de notre volonté* [20].

Et, dans la même page :

> Comme il est constant que nous agissons par ces deux facultés *(virtutes)* de l'intellect quand nous le *voulons*, et puisque rien n'agit sinon par sa forme, il est apparu [également] nécessaire de nous *attribuer* ces deux facultés de l'intellect [21].

Enfin :

> Disons donc : puisque l'intellect existant en nous a deux activités en tant qu'il nous est *attribué*, dont l'une est du genre de la passion (et c'est

20. AVERROES, *L'intelligence et la pensée*, 108 (nous soulignons) ; cf. *Comm. Mag. De anima*, III, 18, éd. Crawford, 439 (72-76). Plus haut, dans le commentaire cinq, Averroès écrivait à propos de Théophraste et Thémistius : « comme ils voyaient que cette action, créer les intelligibles *(creare intellecta)* et les engendrer, *se réduisait à notre volonté (esse reversam ad nostram voluntatem)*... » (nous soulignons ; *cf.* AVERROES, *Comm. Mag. De anima*, III, 5, éd. Crawford, 390 (105-106)).

21. AVERROES, *L'intelligence et la pensée*, 108 ; cf. *Comm. Mag. De anima*, III, 18, éd. Crawford, 439 (83)- 440 (85).

> concevoir), tandis que l'autre est du genre de l'action (et c'est extraire les formes et les dépouiller de toute matière, ce qui n'est rien d'autre que de les rendre [intelligibles] en acte après l'avoir été en puissance), il est manifeste qu'il dépend de notre *volonté*, dès que nous possédons [un] intellect en habitus, de concevoir chaque intelligible que nous *voulons* et d'extraire chaque forme que nous *voulons*[22].

Que désigne cependant cette « volonté » ? En quoi commande-t-elle le processus discursif d'abstraction ? Un élément de réponse apparaît dans le commentaire 60 de *De an.* II, 5, 417b22-25. Aristote distingue dans ce passage les rapports qu'entretiennent la sensation et la science avec leurs objets respectifs. Il présente ainsi leur différence dans l'arabo-latine :

> *sensus in actu comprehendit particularia, scientia autem universalia, quasi essent in ipsa anima. Et ideo homo potest intelligere cum voluerit, sed non sentire, quia indiget sensato*[23].

La sensation a donc pour objets des choses individuelles tandis que la science porte sur des universels ; et dans la mesure où ceux-ci sont « en quelque sorte dans l'âme même », l'homme peut intelliger « quand il le veut », alors qu'il est, pour sentir, soumis à la présence extrinsèque et contingente des réalités mondaines. C'est le caractère intrinsèque des universels, par conséquent, qui fonde l'indépendance intellectuelle. L'homme pense quand il le veut parce que la pensée, dans son dernier mouvement, n'est jamais du dehors, et qu'il tient, sans aléas, l'intelligible à disposition. C'est ce que dit Averroès dans son texte :

> *Et ideo potest homo intelligere*, etc. Idest, et quia moventia virtutem rationalem sunt intra animam et habita a nobis semper in actu, ideo homo potest considerare in eis cum voluerit, et hoc dicitur formare ; et non potest

22. AVERROES, *L'intelligence et la pensée*, 163 ; cf. *Comm. Mag. De anima*, III, 36, éd. Crawford, 495 (462-471).

23. AVERROES, *Comm. Mag. De anima* II, 60, éd. Crawford, 219. Traduit du grec, *De an.* II, 5, 417b18-26 donne : « L'activité de sentir s'entend comme l'acte de spéculer, à la différence, toutefois, que, dans ce cas, les agents susceptibles de produire l'activité viennent de l'extérieur : ce sont le visible et l'audible, de même que le reste des sensibles. Et le motif en est que la sensation en acte porte sur les objets particuliers, alors que la science porte sur les objets universels. Or ces derniers résident en quelque sorte dans l'âme elle-même. C'est pourquoi l'on a le ressort d'exercer son intelligence toutes les fois que l'on veut, mais pas celui de sentir, car il faut nécessairement disposer du sensible » (ARISTOTE, *De l'âme*, éd. Bodéüs, 163-164).

> sentire cum voluerit, quia indiget necessario sensibilibus, que sunt extra animam[24].

Le Cordouan cependant ne manque pas de relever une nuance du texte. Aristote n'écrit pas des objets de l'intellect que « sunt in anima », mais plus exactement que « *quasi* sunt in anima ». Ce qui donne lieu à cette glose :

> Intellectus autem movetur ad ultimam perfectionem a rebus universalibus, et iste sunt in anima. Et dixit : *et iste quasi sunt in anima*, quia post declarabit quod ea que sunt de prima perfectione in intellectu quasi sensibilia de prima perfectione sensus, scilicet in hoc quod ambo movent, sunt intentiones ymaginabiles, et iste sunt universales potentia, licet non actu ; et ideo dixit : *et iste quasi sunt in anima*, et non dixit *sunt*, quia intentio universalis est alia ab intentione ymaginata[25].

Ainsi, les universels sont bien dans l'âme rationnelle; mais pour se conformer au texte, Averroès précise qu'Aristote parle ici de ces agents qui sont à la perfection première de l'intellect ce que les sensibles sont à la perfection première du sens, c'est-à-dire des moteurs; or ces objets-moteurs, ce sont les intentions imaginées, lesquelles ne sont intelligibles qu'en puissance, si bien qu'on doit dire d'elles, pour les distinguer des universels en acte qui seront reçus dans l'intellect dépouillés de toute espèce de matérialité, que « *quasi* sunt in anima ».

Le moteur « intrinsèque » qui permet à l'homme d'intelliger « quand il le veut » est donc l'image individuelle; et si l'homme pense à son gré, c'est que, dans une certaine limite, il contrôle ces images dont dépend l'effectuation de l'opération strictement intellectuelle[26]. Comme le confirmera le commentaire du troisième livre, il apparaît ainsi que la « volonté » dont parle Averroès ici est solidaire d'une puissance de l'imagination, et plus précisément de la faculté cogitative[27], puissance individuelle, inscrite dans le corps, et dont l'activité quasi rationnelle de distinction des intentions individuelles constitue le préalable nécessaire, voire l'amorce, de l'abstraction intellective : c'est elle, en effet, assurant une sorte d'interface

24. AVERROES, *Comm. Mag. De anima,* II, 60, éd. Crawford, 220 (24-29).

25. AVERROES, *Comm. Mag. De anima,* II, 60, éd. Crawford, 220 (15-24).

26. Sur le caractère volontaire de l'« imagination » qui, en un sens, la distingue aussi de l'*existimare* et de l'*intelligere*, *cf.* AVERROES, *Comm. Mag. De anima,* II, 153 (à propos de *De an.* 427b14-21), éd. Crawford, 363 (26-37).

27. Le rapport entre cogitative et *voluntas* chez Averroès a été en partie abordé ailleurs ; voir notamment TAYLOR (2000), 111-146 (surtout 138-142). De même, sur la nature de la cogitative et de ses activités, voir BLACK (1996), 161-187 ; TAYLOR (1999), 217-255 ; BRENET (2003), 195-275 ; *id.* (2006), 1179-1190 ; *id.* (2008).

entre ces deux autres facultés cérébrales que sont l'imaginative et la remémorative, qui prépare « la matière de l'art » (l'image) à recevoir « l'action de l'art » (l'illumination abstractrice)[28], c'est-à-dire qui permet que soit présentée à l'intellect agent la forme dégrossie, affinée, déjà partiellement abstraite, que cet intellect réclame pour effectuer son ultime dépouillement; dans cette mesure, la cogitative s'identifie à l'intellect *passible* (*De an.* III, 5, 430a24)[29], et sans son intervention sur les images, « l'intellect qu'on appelle matériel ne conçoit rien »[30].

Pour des raisons en partie accidentelles, liées à l'histoire des traductions et des transmissions des textes, cette « cogitative » et sa « cogitation » sont au centre des derniers développements du *De anima* arabe (et donc de son *Grand Commentaire*) sur l'intellect pratique et le principe moteur[31]. De fait, Averroès, expliquant *De an.* 433a19-26 (c. 50)[32], les introduit dans la distinction qu'il propose entre « volonté » et « désir » :

28. Voir AVERROES, *Comm. Mag. De anima*, III, 20, éd. Crawford, 450 (185-188) : « hee enim virtutes sunt quasi res que preparant materiam artificii ad recipiendum actionem artificii » ; *cf.* AVERROES, *L'intelligence et la pensée*, 118 : « ces facultés en effet sont comme les choses qui préparent la matière de l'art à recevoir l'action de l'art. »

29. Voir AVERROES, *Comm. Mag. De anima*, III, 20, éd. Crawford, 449 (173-175) : « Et intendebat hic per intellectum passibilem formas ymaginationis secundum quod in eas agit virtus cogitativa propria homini » ; *cf.* AVERROES, *L'intelligence et la pensée*, 118 : « Or [Aristote] entend ici par *intellect passible* les formes de l'imagination en tant qu'agit sur elles la faculté cogitative propre à l'homme. »

30. Voir AVERROES, *Comm. Mag. De anima*, III, 20, éd. Crawford, 450 (184-185) : « [...] et sine virtute ymaginativa et cogitatiua nichil intelligit intellectus qui dicitur materialis » ; voir aussi *Commentarium magnum in Aristotelis de anima libros* III, 20, 449 (175-182) : « Ista enim virtus [*i.e* la cogitative] est aliqua ratio, et actio eius nichil est aliud quam ponere intentionem forme ymaginationis cum suo individuo apud rememorationem, aut distinguere eam ab eo apud formationem et ymaginationem. Et manifestum est quod intellectus qui dicitur materialis recipit intentiones ymaginatas post hanc distinctionem. Iste igitur intellectus passibilis necessarius est in formatione » ; pour la fin, *cf.* AVERROES, *L'intelligence et la pensée*, 118 : « il est manifeste que l'intellect qu'on appelle matériel reçoit les entités imaginées après cette distinction. Par conséquent l'intellect passible est nécessaire à la conception [par l'intellect]. »

31. Voir sur ce point TAYLOR (1999). Sur la volonté, par ailleurs, outre le *Commentaire moyen* de l'*Ethique à Nicomaque*, *cf.* le troisième problème du *Tahāfut at-Tahāfut* (sur Dieu comme agent du monde) ainsi que *Averroes on Plato's* Republic, éd. Lerner, 1974, 92-94.

32. Notamment ces deux lignes du *textus* : « modo autem intellectus non uidetur mouere preter desiderium. Voluntas enim et desiderium quando mouentur in cogitatione, tunc uoluntas mouet » (*Comm. Mag. De anima*, III, 50, éd. Crawford, 518) ; *cf.* ARISTOTE, *De l'âme*, III, 10, 433a22-24, éd. Bodéüs, 245-246 : « l'intelligence, de son côté, ne déclenche manifestement pas de mouvement sans appétit, puisque le souhait (*boulésis*) est un appétit (*orexis*), et que, lorsque le mouvement se règle sur le raisonnement, il se règle aussi selon le souhait. »

> Et differentia inter voluntatem et desiderium est quia, quando voluntas et desiderium movent, tunc *voluntas movet secundum cogitationem*, desiderium autem movet non secundum cogitationem[33].

Plus bas, dans son commentaire 57 de *De an.* 434a5-15[34], il précise le déroulement du processus mené par la cogitative qui, sur la base des images issues des choses, conduit à un « consensus » et à l'« élection » dont dépendra l'action :

> Et ymaginatio existit in aliis animalibus, cogitatio autem in rationabilibus. *Eligere enim facere hoc ymaginatum et non hoc est de actione cogitationis*, non de actione ymaginationis. Iudicans enim quod hoc ymaginatum est magis amabile quam hoc debet esse eadem virtus de necessitate que numerat ymaginationes in quibus iudicat magis delectabilius. Et hoc intendebat cum dixit : *Et numerat ipsum unum de necessitate*.
>
> Idest, secundum quod reputo, et necesse est ut una virtus numeret illas ymaginationes donec comprehendat ex eis magis amatum, sicut unum numerat numeros inequales donec comprehendat magis maiorem ; similiter *cogitatio numerat ymaginationes et comparat inter eas donec possit pati ab ymaginatione alicuius earum*. Et hec est causa quare animal rationale habet existimationem ; *existimatio enim est consensus qui provenit a cogitatione*[35].

Mais cette intervention dans l'ordre pratique illustre ce qui vaut aussi dans l'ordre théorique, comme le montre, par exemple, le commentaire 33 de *De an.* III, 7 431b3-8 :

33. AVERROES, *Comm. Mag. De anima*, III, 50, éd. Crawford, 519 (32-35), nous soulignons.

34. Il commente en particulier le *textus*, *Comm. Mag. De anima libros* III, 57, 529 *sq.* (une fois de plus très éloigné de l'original grec) : « virtus autem cogitatiua est in rationalibus tantum. Eligere autem facere hoc aut hoc est de actione cogitatiua. Et numerat ipsum unum de necessitate ; mouetur enim erga maius, ita quod potest ex multis ymaginationibus ut agat. Et hec est causa existimationis ». *Cf.* ARISTOTE, *De l'âme*, III, 11, 434a6-12, éd. Bodéüs, 249-250 : « Donc, la représentation sensitive, comme on l'a dit, appartient également aux animaux privés de raison, tandis que la représentation délibérative (*bouleutikè*) appartient aux animaux doués de raison. En effet, décider entre cette action-ci ou celle-là, c'est déjà une opération qui relève du calcul et qui, nécessairement, implique toujours une unité de mesure, puisque, de deux choses, on poursuit celle qui offre le plus d'intérêt ; d'où la capacité de faire l'unité à partir de plusieurs représentations. Et le motif pourquoi un animal semble n'avoir pas d'opinion, c'est qu'il ne possède pas celle que fournit un raisonnement conclusif, alors que la représentation délibérative l'implique. »

35. AVERROES, *Comm. Mag. De anima*, III, 57, éd. Crawford, 529-530 (1-31), nous soulignons.

> Comme on l'a expliqué dans le livre *Du sens et du senti*, quand elle s'adjoint l'informative et la remémorative, la faculté cogitative est naturellement apte, à partir des images des choses, à rendre présente à l'assentiment et à la conception *(fide et informatione)* une chose qui n'a jamais été sentie, dans la disposition même qui serait la sienne si elle était sentie; et c'est alors que l'intellect juge ces images d'un jugement universel[36].

Revenons donc au déclenchement «volontaire» de l'intellection. Vouloir penser consiste par le biais d'un processus individuel d'évaluation, de discrimination et, si l'on peut dire, de «fiction», à mobiliser des images qui, à titre de pôle objectif conditionnant leur spécification formelle, serviront de pendant aux concepts reçus dans l'intellect matériel séparé[37]. L'exercice de cette «volonté» de penser, comme on l'a rapidement noté plus haut, requiert pour chacun un premier ensemble d'intelligibles qu'Averroès appelle «les premières propositions» et dont, note-t-il, «nous ne savons ni quand elles nous sont venus ni d'où ni comment»[38]. Mais sur cette base, dont l'homme bénéficie naturellement, tout dépend ensuite, au fil des expériences proprement

36. AVERROES, *L'intelligence et la pensée*, 144-145; cf. *Comm. Mag. De anima*, III, 33, éd Crawford, 476 (51-57).

37. Car «l'intellect qui est en nous ne voit quelque chose et ne le pense que s'il le pense joint à une image. En effet, les images sont les sensibles de l'intellect» (AVERROES, *L'intelligence et la pensée*, 172; cf. *Comm. Mag. De anima*, III, 39, éd. Crawford, 506 (33-37)). Sur ce point, le texte essentiel est le suivant: «Disons qu'il est manifeste que l'homme n'est doué d'intellection en acte qu'à cause de la jonction de l'intelligible en acte avec lui. Et il est aussi manifeste que la matière et la forme s'unissent l'une à l'autre d'une manière telle que l'agrégat qui en résulte ne fait qu'un. C'est par excellence le cas de l'intellect matériel et de l'intention intelligible en acte: ce qui se compose à partir d'eux n'est pas une troisième "chose" distincte d'eux, comme c'est le cas des autres composés de matière et de forme. Par conséquent, il est impossible que la jonction de [cet] intelligible avec l'homme ait lieu sans la jonction de l'une de ces deux parties avec lui [l'homme], que ce soit cette partie de lui (c'est-à-dire l'intelligible) qui est comme [sa] matière ou l' [autre}] partie qui est comme [sa] forme. Et puisqu'il est [maintenant] établi à partir des précédentes discussions qu'il est impossible que l'intelligible soit uni avec chacun des hommes et multiplié par leur nombre pour ce qui est de la partie de lui qui est comme [sa] matière, à savoir l'intellect matériel, il reste que la jonction des intelligibles avec nous autres hommes se fait par la jonction des intentions intelligibles avec nous, [plus précisément] de cette partie des [intentions intelligibles] qui est en nous d'une certaine manière comme [leur] forme –et ce sont les intentions imaginées» (AVERROES, *L'intelligence et la pensée*, 72-73; cf. *Comm. Mag. De anima*, III, 5, éd. Crawford, 404 (501)-405 (520)).

38. AVERROES, *L'intelligence et la pensée*, 163 ; cf. *Comm. Mag. De anima* III, 36, éd. Crawford, 496 (491-492).

dites, de la mise en œuvre individuelle correcte et répétée des puissances de l'imagination. On lit ceci :

> Tu dois savoir que l'usage et l'exercice sont cause de ce qu'apparaissent [en l'homme] la puissance de l'intellect agent, qui est en nous pour abstraire, et celle de l'intellect matériel, [qui est en nous] pour recevoir. [L'usage et l'exercice] sont cause, dis-je, [de ce qu'apparaissent en l'homme les puissances à abstraire et à recevoir] du fait de l'habitus existant, grâce à eux, dans l'intellect passible et corruptible, qu'Aristote [lui-même] appelle *passible* et dont il dit sans équivoque qu'il est sujet à la corruption[39].

Par conséquent, ainsi qu'Averroès l'écrira plus bas, si l'homme qui s'avance vers la philosophie, le savoir total, peut progressivement disposer d'un intellect en *habitus*, c'est-à-dire d'un intellect qui lui permet de tout concevoir « de lui-même et quand il le veut »[40], c'est en proportion de l'habitus qu'il aura su par ses cogitations entretenir dans son intellect passible, lesquelles cogitations lui permettent de solliciter l'intervention des intellects comme cause agente du produit de ses activités discursives. C'est en cela, comme on le disait, qu'il « acquiert » l'intelligible, et même l'intellect, et que la pensée lui est « attribuée ». Les intellects agent et matériel sont certes éternels, uniques, par essence inengendrés et incorruptibles, mais l'individu, tant qu'il se meut vers la jonction[41], a les moyens, en cogitant, sur la base d'un rapport plus ou moins direct au monde, de provoquer leur intervention ponctuelle, c'est-à-dire d'activer

39. AVERROES, *L'intelligence et la pensée*, 122; *Comm. Mag. De anima*, III, 20, éd. Crawford, 453 (301)-454 (306).

40. Voir AVERROES, *L'intelligence et la pensée*, 106: « il est nécessaire qu'il y ait en elle [la partie de l'âme qu'on appelle intellect] une partie qu'on appelle intellect en tant qu'[il] devient tout sur le mode de l'assimilation et de la réception, et qu'il y ait aussi en elle une deuxième partie qu'on appelle intellect en tant qu'[il] fait concevoir tout en acte à cet intellect qui est en puissance [...] Et il entend par cet [intellect] celui est [est] produit, lequel est en *habitus*. [...]. Et il faut ajouter au discours [d'Aristote]: *en tant qu'il lui permet de tout concevoir* "de lui-même et quand il le veut". Telle est en effet la définition de l'*habitus*: elle [pose] que celui qui possède [cet] *habitus* pense par lui ce qui lui est propre, de lui-même et quand il le veut, sans qu'il ait besoin pour ce faire de quelque chose d'extrinsèque »; *cf.* AVERROES, *Comm. Mag. De anima*, III, 18, éd. Crawford, 437 (9)-438 (29).

41. Voir AVERROES, *L'intelligence et la pensée*, 167 (cf. *Comm. Mag. De anima*, III, 36, éd. Crawford, 500 (605-606)). Lorsque ce mouvement est achevé, en effet, le type de causalité qu'exerce l'intellect agent change: la cause agente, qui nous restait extérieure, devient pleinement cause formelle. Sur cette double causalité, voir l'article cité plus haut de GEOFFROY (2007).

l'actualisation des images qu'il porte. Et dans cette mesure, c'est lui qui pense.

Cette question de l'attribution sera centrale dans l'anti-averroïsme latin et dénoncée comme le maillon faible de la noétique du *Grand Commentaire*, l'idée générale étant que dans un système averroïste, quelles que soient les nuances, la pensée qui advient sur la base des images ne peut qu'être la pensée de l'intellect séparé (une pensée extrinsèque, anonyme, en surplomb) et jamais proprement l'acte de cet homme-ci ou de cet homme-là [42]. Il ne s'agit pas d'étudier ici la pertinence de ces critiques, même si l'on peut mesurer combien Thomas d'Aquin manque sa cible lorsque, dans son *De unitate intellectus*, il reproche aux averroïstes de nous retirer « quod est in nobis », *i.e.* le volontaire, étant donné, dira Thomas au nom d'Aristote (III, 8, 432b5), que la volonté est dans l'intellect et que ce dernier, pour le Commentateur et ceux qui le suivent, est unique et substantiellement séparé [43] : ce qui précède, en effet, a montré qu'Averroès se soucie d'une forme de propriété de l'acte intellectif et que le volontaire désigne chez lui le désir associé au moteur *intrinsèque* qu'est l'image [44].

Outre l'idée courante des sciences « acquises » par apprentissage [45], Averroès avait sans doute plusieurs raisons d'aborder dans ce cadre les problèmes de l'acquisition et de l'attribution qu'on a relevés. Le texte même du traité *De l'âme* en est une, qui suggérait en divers endroits une question de l'*attributio* qui pouvait les recouper [46]. La notion d'intellect

42. À titre d'exemples, parmi des dizaines d'autres, voir THOMAS D'AQUIN, *L'unité de l'intellect contre les averroïstes*, éd. de Libera, 137 ; 139 ; 141 ; *cf.* THOMAS D'AQUIN, *De unitate intellectus*, éd. Léonine, 303, 93 et 95 ; 304, 125. Pour une lecture critique de ces interprétations, voir BLACK (1993) ; BRENET (2003), 299-340.

43. Voir THOMAS D'AQUIN, *L'unité de l'intellect*, 153 ; cf. *De unitate intellectus*, 306, 336 *sq.*

44. Même si les choses, évidemment, nous sont extrinsèques, et que, tant que nous cogitons, l'intellect agent vient en nous de l'extérieur. Notons du reste qu'Averroès, pour *De an.* III, 8, 432b5, lit un autre *textus* que Thomas. L'arabo-latine donne : « principale enim existit in parte cogitativa » ; et la traduction gréco-latine de Guillaume de Moerbecke : « in rationatiua enim uoluntas fit ».

45. À ce propos, voir GARDET (1967), 62.

46. À titre d'exemple, signalons qu'à quatre reprises au moins, en effet, Averroès recourt de manière nette à la notion d' « attribution » pour commenter Aristote. (a) Au livre I, 1, pour la séquence 403a3-10 (C12 ; *Comm. Mag. De anima*, I, 12, 16) et 403a10-16 (C13 ; *Comm. Mag. De anima*, I, 13, 18), qui porte sur les affections de l'âme, dont on se demande s'il en est une qui soit propre à l'âme ou si toutes sont communes à l'âme et au corps. (b) Au livre I, 4, pour la séquence 408b11-17 (C64 ; *Comm. Mag. De anima*, I, 64, 85) et 408b24-31 (C66 ; *Comm. Mag. De anima*, I, 66, 88-89), dans laquelle il s'agit d'abord de savoir si c'est l'âme qui « habet pietatem », « docet » ou « distinguit », ou si c'est l'homme qui le fait par son âme ; et

« acquis » en est une autre – on l'a brièvement rappelé –, qu'alimentait une tradition péripatéticienne gréco-arabe charriant ses difficultés propres[47]. Cela étant, nous proposons de relier ici ces thèses noétiques aux développements du *Kašf* concernant le *kasb* ou l'*iktisāb*[48].

Averroès en traite lorsqu'il aborde le thème classique en *'ilm al-kalām* du *qaḍā' wa-l-qadar*, c'est-à-dire, en un mot, du « décret » de Dieu (en son éternité comme en ses réalisations contingentes). Le problème général est celui de l'articulation entre la toute-puissance divine et la responsabilité humaine. La première implique une prédestination qui paraît interdire la seconde. Si Dieu crée et détermine tout, il semble que disparaisse ce libre choix dont on fait dépendre la dimension morale de l'acte humain. Averroès relève d'emblée que sur cette question religieuse fondamentale les arguments d'autorité aussi bien que les arguments rationnels se contredisent les uns les autres. Pour ce qui est de l'autorité, à commencer par le Livre, « il se trouve de nombreux versets affirmant de manière générale que toute chose [arrive] d'après un décret (*bi-qadar*) et que l'homme est contraint (*majbūr*) dans ses actes. Mais on y trouve aussi de nombreux versets indiquant (*tadullu*) que l'homme réalise une *acquisition* (*iktisāb*) par son acte et qu'il n'est point contraint à ses actes »[49]. D'un côté, donc, tout a lieu *nécessairement* (*al-umūr kullu-hā ḍarūriyya*) en vertu d'une détermination préalable de Dieu ; de l'autre, le Coran lui-même indique « qu'il y a pour les hommes une *acquisition* [des actes] en tant que les choses en elles-mêmes sont *possibles et non nécessaires* (*mumkina lā wājiba*) »[50]. Averroès estime que de ces contradictions sont issues trois

ensuite d'établir si l'« intelligere » puis la « distinctio », l'« amor » et l'« odium » sont des actes de l'intellect éternel ou d'autres facultés inférieures. (c) Au livre II, 2, pour la séquence 414a4-14 (C24 ; *Comm. Mag. De anima*, II, 24, 163), lorsqu'il convient d'expliquer que « ce par quoi » nous vivons et sentons, tout comme « ce par quoi » nous savons, peut s'entendre de deux manières, selon qu'on parle de ce qui joue le rôle de forme ou le rôle de matière. (d) Au livre II, 4, enfin, pour la séquence 416a13-18 (C41 ; *Comm. Mag. De anima,* II, 41, 193), dans laquelle Aristote soutient que c'est l'âme, plutôt que le feu, qui est responsable de la croissance et de la nutrition.

47. Pour une lecture concernant ce point, voir GEOFFROY (2007).

48. Sur cette notion, voir SCHWARZ (1972) ; WATT (1948) ; *id.* (1943) ; GARDET (1967) ; *id.*, articles « Kasb », « Al-qaḍā' wa-l-qadar », *Encyclopédie de l'Islam*²; GIMARET (1980) ; *id.* (1990) ; WOLFSON (1976), spécialement, 663-719.

49. AVERROES, *Dévoilement des méthodes de démonstration des dogmes de la religion musulmane*, trad. Geoffroy, 131 ; cf. *Al-Kašf 'an manāhiğ al-adilla*, éd. al-Jābirī, 186, § 285.

50. AVERROES, *Dévoilement des méthodes de démonstration*, trad. Geoffroy, 131-132 (nous soulignons) ; cf. *Al-Kašf 'an manāhiğ*, éd. al-Jābirī, 186, § 287. Le verbe *kasaba* et ses dérivés appartiennent d'abord, en effet, à la langue coranique ; voir sur ce point GARDET,

thèses théologiques différentes. Il l'explique dans une présentation critique très condensée :

> à cause de cela [*i.e.* de ces contradictions], les musulmans se partagèrent sur cette question en deux tendances : l'une croyant que l'acquisition par l'homme est la cause de la désobéissance et des bonnes œuvres, et que c'est pour cela que s'appliquent à lui le châtiment et la récompense, les mu'tazilites ; et l'autre croyant le contraire, à savoir que l'homme est contraint à ses actes, qu'il y est forcé, les jabrites. Quant aux ash 'arites, ils voulurent proposer une thèse intermédiaire entre ces deux, et ils dirent : l'homme *acquiert*, mais ce par quoi il y a acquisition *(al-muktasabu bi-hi)* et l'acquis *(al-muksab)* sont tous deux créés par Dieu – exalté soit-Il –, mais cela n'a pas de sens, car si à la fois l'acquisition *(al-iktisāb)* et ce qui est acquis *(al-muktasab)* sont œuvres de Dieu – loué soit-Il –, le serviteur est nécessairement contraint à son acquisition[51].

Les deux premières écoles s'opposent comme deux extrêmes. D'un côté, les mu'tazilites, auxquels Averroès prête l'idée d'une « acquisition » par l'homme qui le rend responsable et justifie les sanctions positives ou negatives[52] ; de l'autre, les jabrites, qui soutiennent au contraire que l'homme est « contraint » dans son acte[53] ; et au centre, portée par le désir

article « Kasb », *Encyclopédie de l'Islam*², IV, 720. En revanche, Belo juge que *ḍarūrī* et *wājib* « have aristotelian overtones » (voir BELO [2007], 210 n. 67).

51. AVERROES, *Dévoilement des méthodes de démonstration*, trad. Geoffroy, 132-133 ; cf. *Al-Kašf 'an manāhiǧ al-adilla*, éd. al-Jābirī, 187, § 291-292 ; et *Faith and Reason in Islam*, éd. Najjar, 107.

52. Averroès ne dit rien ici de la forme d'autonomie ou de liberté de l'agent que suppose l'« acquisition » qu'il évoque à propos des mu'tazilites. Ces derniers, comme on sait, soutiennent que l'acte humain volontaire échappe à la toute-puissance de Dieu et que l'homme, par conséquent, en est l'« agent » à proprement parler. Le terme « acquisition » est donc équivoque puisque, comme on va le rappeler, il est central, en un sens anti-mu'tazilite, dans la théologie aš'arite. « Pour les théologiens mu'tazilites », écrit D. Gimaret, « le seul sens concevable que l'on puisse donner au terme de *kasb* est celui d'un acte "grâce auquel on retire un avantage ou on écarte un dommage" » (GIMARET [1980], 299) ; et plus loin : « Ici le *kasb* ne représente pas l'acte lui-même, mais ce qu'on obtient grâce à l'acte. Ǧubbā'ī distinguait en effet entre l'action d'acquérir (*iktisāb*) et l'acquis (*muktasab*). Le fait d'acquérir de l'argent est autre chose que l'argent lui-même. Ce qui est *kasb* au sens propre (c'est-à-dire : *muktasab*), c'est l'argent et non l'acte grâce auquel on l'obtient » (*ibid.*, 299).

53. Les « jabrites » se réclament de Ǧahm ibn Ṣafwān (m. 128h./745) et défendent l'idée selon laquelle l'homme n'est rien d'autre que le réceptable d'actes produits en lui par Dieu. « Selon Ǧahm, écrit Gimaret, l'homme n'est pas agent (*fā'il*) au sens propre : seul Dieu est agent. C'est Lui qui crée en l'homme ses actes, comme Il crée les mouvements des corps inertes. Et si ces actes sont attribués à l'homme, c'est par métaphore, comme, par métaphore, on attribue aux corps inertes leurs mouvements. [...] Tout est acte contraint, au sens précis que les Ǧubbā'ītes donneront à ce terme, à savoir celui d'un acte opéré dans un sujet par un

de combiner les deux pôles, la doctrine aš'arite du *kasb* qui voudrait que Dieu crée tout et que, nonobstant, l'homme « acquière » ses actes. De fait, s'il considère que Dieu crée tout ce qui vient à l'être et que Lui seul, donc, mérite d'être qualifié de « créateur » (*ḫāliq*) ou d'« agent » (*fā'il*) au sens propre [54], l'aš'arisme prétend malgré tout faire droit au sentiment de liberté que peut éprouver l'individu et distinguer, par conséquent, entre les mouvements qui lui arrivent indépendamment de sa volonté (le frisson dû à la fièvre, le flux du sang dans les artères, etc.) et ceux qui se produisent ou cessent selon qu'il le veut (s'asseoir, se lever, avancer, reculer, etc.). Ce sont ces derniers, dont il ressent qu'ils se font à sa guise, que l'homme « acquiert ». Dieu, seul, en est proprement l'« agent », mais l'individu en est l'« acquéreur ».

Qu'entendre, cependant, par « acquérir » ? Un premier élément, on l'a vu, est fourni par la notion de volonté. Car, comme l'écrit D. Gimaret à propos d'al-Aš'arī,

> c'est bien cela, en fait, qui, dans notre expérience immédiate, comme l'explique A. en *Lm* § 92, caractérise essentiellement l'acte acquis ; nous reconnaissons qu'un acte est *notre* acte, notre « acquisition », au fait que, systématiquement, il se produit quand nous le voulons et cesse de se produire quand nous le voulons, alors qu'il en va tout au contraire de l'acte contraint. Cet acte acquis est tout autant créé en nous par Dieu que l'acte contraint, mais il a en propre que, systématiquement, *Dieu le crée quand nous le voulons*. Pourquoi donc alors ne pas définir précisément l'acte acquis comme celui que, de façon constante, Dieu crée en nous conformément à notre volonté [55] ?

Néanmoins cela ne suffit pas. Il faut ajouter que cet acte n'est « acquis » que dans la mesure où lui correspond chez l'acquéreur une « puissance » produite par Dieu. C'est ce que note al-Aš'arī, dans son *Kitab al-Luma'*: « l'acquéreur acquiert la chose parce qu'elle se produit par une puissance qu'il en a et qui est adventée (*waqa'a bi-qudrat*[in] *lahu 'alayhi muḥdaṯa*) » [56]. Et cette puissance, outre le fait d'être créée en l'homme par Dieu, présente deux caractéristiques majeures qu'al-Ašarī développe par ailleurs. Premièrement, elle n'est pas puissance de deux contraires mais est exclusivement puissance de l'acte effectif et apparaît dans le même

plus puissant que lui. L'homme n'a pas d'autre relation à son acte que le fait d'en être le réceptable, le "récipient" (*ẓarf*) » (GIMARET [1980], 64-65). Sur les ǧahmiyya, voir la notice de Watt dans *Encyclopédie de l'Islam*², II, 398-399.

54. Chez al-Aš'arī, *ḫalaqa* et *fa'ala* sont synonymes.

55. GIMARET (1990), 393 ; *cf.* AL-AŠ'ARĪ, *al-Luma'*, éd. McCarthy, 41 du texte arabe.

56. AL-AŠ'ARĪ, *al-Luma'*, éd. McCarthy, 40 (7-8) ; voir GIMARET (1980), 82.

instant[57]; elle est ainsi concomitante à l'acte, duquel elle ne se dissocie pas, si bien que, sans alternative, elle le nécessite autant qu'elle l'autorise[58]. Deuxièmement, puisque Dieu crée tout et qu'il n'y a ni *tawlīd* (une cause créée qui engendre) ni *tawallud* (un effet engendré par une cause créée)[59], elle ne fait pas être son effet. S'il faut, donc, donner un sens au *bi-* (par, du fait de…) qui suit *waqa'a* (se produire, arriver) dans notre citation, ce ne sera jamais pour reconnaître à la puissance l'efficacité causale d'un adventeur[60].

Il ne s'agit pas de débrouiller ici cette doctrine dont l'obscurité est légendaire. Historiquement, du reste, les positions sunnites qui se sont succédées ont apporté chacune sur tel ou tel point leurs variations. En l'occurrence, Averroès connaît sans doute celles de Juwaynī (m. 1085) et de Ġazālī (m. 1111)[61]. Dans l'*Iršād*, Juwaynī défend ce que Gimaret appelle un aš'arisme « strict » ou « radical »[62]. Contre les jabrites, sur la base du sentiment qu'on peut avoir d'une différence entre nos actes contraints et nos actes volontaires, il admet l'existence en l'homme d'une puissance; et à ces actes volontaires, qui relèvent de la puissance humaine, il donne le nom d'« acquisition » (*kasb*); mais il nie, lui aussi, toute efficience (*ta'ṯīr*) de cette puissance sur l'acte, puisque seul Dieu est créateur. De même que la science s'applique au connu sans avoir d'effet sur lui, la volonté de l'homme s'applique à l'acte qui lui correspond sans la moindre efficace: « il faut donc affirmer catégoriquement, écrit-il, que la puissance adventice n'a absolument aucun effet sur son possible (*lā*

57. Sur la puissance contemporaine de l'acte et en rapport, seulement, à l'acte effectivement réalisé, voir GIMARET (1990), Partie I, chapitre VI, 131-154.

58. La formule est de BRUNSCHVIG (1976), 193-194. L'auteur rapproche à raison cette querelle sur la puissance « contraignante » du « débat antique » entre les Mégariques et le Lycée ; voir *ibid.*, 185-186 et la n. 5, 185 évoquant Averroès.

59. Sur la négation de la thèse du *tawallud*, voir GIMARET (1990), Partie III, chapitre II, 401-409.

60. Sur la « qualification » que la puissance humaine détermine cependant dans son effet, voir GIMARET (1990), 391-393, où l'auteur analyse le sens de *bi-* qui fait suite à *waqa'a* dans la définition de l' « acquisition » comme « *mā waqa'a bi-qudrat*^{in} *muḥdaṯa* » (ce qui se produit du fait d'une puissance adventée). Nous reprenons ici les suggestions de traduction proposées par Gimaret pour rendre la racine *ḥadaṯa*, « venir à l'être », et ses dérivés. Il utilise généralement « adventer », « adventeur », « adventé » pour *aḥdaṯa*, *muḥdiṯ*, *muḥdaṯ* (voir GIMARET [1980], XII).

61. Nous verrons plus loin qu'Averroès cite d'ailleurs Ġazālī et la *Risālat an-niẓāmiyya* de Juwaynī.

62. *Cf.* GIMARET (1980), 121.

tu'attiru fī maqdūrihā aṣl[an]) »[63]. C'est ce qu'on retrouve dans l'*Iqtiṣād* de Ġazālī. Si l'on objecte qu'il est « inconcevable qu'une puissance s'applique au possible sans avoir d'effet sur lui et sans déterminer son existence », que « la relation entre le possible et le puissance ne peut être qu'une relation d'effet à cause (*nisbat al-musabbab ilā s-sabab*) », il répond que la connexion entre une puissance humaine et son objet n'est pas nécessairement causale, comme le prouve l'exemple de la science[64]. Les « déterministes » (*al-mujbira*) ont donc tort de ne distinguer en rien le mouvement spasmodique, purement contraint, du mouvement volontaire ; mais les mu'tazilites ont tort aussi lorsqu'ils prêtent à cette « volonté » et à cette « puissance », qu'il faut reconnaître en l'homme, une réelle efficacité créatrice. La puissance créée ne crée pas son objet, elle lui est concomittante, et le *kasb* désigne précisément cette relation paradoxale d'« endossement »[65] qui unit, sans pourtant qu'il l'advente, l'homme à *son* acte[66]. À l'objection qu'« une puissance par quoi ne se produit pas un possible équivaut à l'impuissance », Ġazālī peut ainsi répondre :

> Si vous voulez dire que l'état [psychique] perçu par l'homme quand cette puissance existe est semblable à celui qu'il perçoit lors de l'impuissance, dans un mouvement convulsif, vous niez l'évidence. Mais si vous voulez dire que la puissance équivaut à l'impuissance en tant que le possible ne se produit pas par elle, c'est vrai[67].

« Telle a été, à ma connaissance, soutient Gimaret, la position constante de Ġazzālī »[68]. De fait, si dans l'*Iḥyā'* Ġazālī soutient d'abord que l'acte libre de l'individu dépend d'une puissance, laquelle est mue par la volonté,

63. Cité par GIMARET (1980), 121 ; *cf.* AL-JUWAYNĪ, *al-Iršād ilā qawāṭi'al-adilla fī uṣūl al-i'tiqād*, éd. Luciani, 119, 14.

64. *Cf.* MARMURA (1994), 308-310.

65. « Endossement » est le terme utilisé par BRUNSCHVIG (1976).

66. *Cf.* MARMURA (1994), 307-308 : "the object of power is not through the power of the servant, even though it exists with him. For this reason he is named neither 'creator' not 'inventor'. It thus becomes incumbent to seek for this type of relation another different name. Hence the term 'acquisition' was sought for it auspiciously from the book of God, exalted be He" ; *cf.* la discussion XVII sur la causalité et les miracles dans le *Tahāfūt al-falāsifa* (voir AL-ĠAZĀLĪ, *The incoherence of the philosophers*, éd. MARMURA, 166-177). Cela dit, la nature exacte de la doctrine ghazalienne de la causalité est discutée. Outre les articles de Marmura (dont nous suivons, pour les grandes lignes, la position), voir, pour quelques références classiques, FRANK (1966) ; *id.* (1992) (*cf.* la recension de MARMURA [1995], surtout 93-97 sur le *kasb*) ; ABRAHAMOV (1988) ; GOODMAN (1978) ; ALON (1980) ; DUTTON (2001).

67. Cité par GIMARET (1980), 129 ; *cf.* AL-ĠAZĀLĪ, *al-Iqtiṣād fī l-i'tiqād*, Le Caire, 51 (*cf.* MARMURA [1994], 310-311).

68. GIMARET (1980), 129.

elle-même déclenchée par la connaissance, c'est pour conclure que l'homme est en réalité contraint dans son choix (*majbūr ʿalā l-iḫtiyār*) puisque, contrairement à ce que notre ignorance nous laisse croire, chacun des éléments de cette chaîne, sans aucun lien causal entre eux, est en fait directemement créé par Dieu[69]. Ainsi, « Dieu crée tout à la fois la puissance et le possible, le choix et le choisi »[70].

On n'est pas surpris, dans ces conditions, de lire la critique d'Averroès. Pour ménager à la fois la toute-puissance divine et le sentiment de liberté, les aš'arites, on l'a dit, soutiennent que « l'homme *acquiert*, mais [que] ce par quoi il y a acquisition *(al-muktasabu bi-hi)* et l'acquis *(al-muksab)* sont tous deux créés par Dieu – exalté soit-Il »; mais « cela n'a pas de sens, rétorque Averroès, car si à la fois l'acquisition *(al-iktisāb)* et ce qui est acquis *(al-muktasab)* sont œuvres de Dieu – loué soit-Il –, le serviteur est nécessairement contraint à son acquisition »[71]. Il le reprend à la fin du chapitre :

> Et on a montré de quelle manière existe pour nous une acquisition; et que celui qui a soutenu un des deux extrêmes à propos de cette question, comme les mu'tazilites et les jabrites, est dans l'erreur. Quant à la voie médiane grâce à laquelle les ash'arites voudraient être les tenants de la vérité, elle n'a aucune réalité. Car ils n'accordent à l'homme pour ce qui est du nom d'acquisition que la différence que réalise l'homme entre le mouvement de sa main à cause d'un frisson et le fait de bouger sa main par son propre choix. En effet il n'y a aucun sens à ce qu'ils admettent cette différence si c'est pour dire que les deux mouvements ne proviennent pas de nous; car s'ils ne proviennent pas de nous, nous n'avons pas la puissance de nous en abstenir, et nous y sommes contraints. Il y a égalité de sens entre le mouvement du frisson et le mouvement qu'ils appellent « acquis » (*kasbiyya*). Il n'y a de différence que dans les termes, et la divergence dans les termes n'implique pas un jugement (*ḥukm*) quant aux essences[72].

Ainsi, quoi qu'ils disent, les aš'arites sont en vérité des jabrites. Tout chez eux n'est que contrainte, et la distinction qu'ils prétendent sauver entre acte volontaire et acte involontaire est seulement verbale, et donc nulle, puisque rien, *a parte rei*, ne la fonde vraiment.

69. Sur ce point, *cf.* GIMARET (1980), 131-132; MARMURA (2002), 105-108.

70. AL-ĠAZĀLĪ, *Iḥyā' 'ulūm ad-dīn*, Le Caire, vol. I, 151 ; cité par GIMARET (1980), 132.

71. AVERROES, *Dévoilement des méthodes de démonstration*, trad. Geoffroy, 133 ; cf. *Al-Kašf 'an manāhiğ al-adilla*, éd. al-Jābirī, 187, § 291.

72. AVERROÈS, *Al-Kašf 'an manāhiğ al-adilla*, éd. al-Jābirī, 194, § 318; cf. *Faith and Reason in Islam*, éd. Najjar, 114-115.

Par conséquent, quelle est la solution ? La raison ne la livre pas plus vite que l'autorité. Averroès souligne en effet les contradictions qu'alimentent les arguments rationnels. D'un côté, si l'on pose que « l'humain donne l'être à ses actes et les crée, il y aura donc des actes qui ne se dérouleront pas en vertu du dessein *(mashī'a)* de Dieu – exalté soit-Il – et de son choix, et il y aura donc un créateur autre que Dieu », alors que « les musulmans s'accordent par consensus à considérer qu'il n'est d'autre créateur que Dieu – loué soit-Il »[73]. D'un autre côté, « si [...] on suppose que l'homme n'est point l'acquéreur de ses actes, il faut qu'il y soit contraint (car il n'y a pas de demi-mesure entre la contrainte et l'acquisition) »[74], ce qui est inconcevable pour au moins deux raisons : premièrement, parce que « si l'homme était contraint à ses actes, alors la charge de la responsabilité légale (*taklīf*) serait de l'ordre de l'inassumable » – et Ǧuwaynī lui-même, souligne Averroès, « a déclaré dans sa *'Aqīdat an-niẓāmiyya* que l'homme réalise l'acquisition de ses actes et qu'il a la puissance de les accomplir », car il serait impossible que l'homme fût chargé de ce qu'il ne peut assumer[75] ; deuxièmement, parce que

> s'il n'y avait point pour l'homme d'acquisition, un ordre [donné à quelqu'un] de se préparer [à faire face] à une catastrophe prévisible serait absolument dépourvu de sens. Et, de même, l'ordre [que l'on donnerait en vue] d'attirer un bienfait. Et tous les arts dont l'invention est d'attirer des bienfaits seraient aussi absolument vains, comme l'art de l'agriculture et les autres arts par lesquels on espère quelque bénéfice. Comme seraient vains les arts par lesquels on a l'intention de se sauvergarder, ou de

73. AVERROES, *Dévoilement des méthodes de démonstration*, trad. Geoffroy, 133 ; *Al-Kašf 'an manāhiǧ al-adilla*, éd. al-Jābirī, 190, § 305. Comme le remarque M. Geoffroy (n. 111, 113), Averroès rapatrie les mu'tazilites « au sein d'un consensus auquel pourtant eux-mêmes ne souscriraient pas », puisque selon eux l'homme est véritablement le créateur de ses actes. Du reste, les propos du Cordouan posent ici la question du statut de l'*iǧma'* dans l'argumentation rationnelle.

74. AVERROES, *Dévoilement des méthodes de démonstration*, trad. Geoffroy, 133-134 (nous modifions légèrement la ponctuation) ; *Al-Kašf 'an manāhiǧ al-adilla*, éd. al-Jābirī, 188, § 293.

75. AVERROES, *Dévoilement des méthodes de démonstration*, trad. Geoffroy, 134-135 ; *Al-Kašf 'an manāhiǧ al-adilla*, éd. al-Jābirī, 188, § 294 ; pour le texte de Ǧuwaynī, voir *al-'Aquidat an-niẓāmiyya*, éd. M. Zāhid al-Kawṯarī ; la référence à cette épître de Ǧuwaynī est particulièrement remarquable puisque, selon Gimaret, Ǧuwaynī y « renie totalement » les positions qu'il défendait, en aš'arite radical, dans l'*Iršād* (GIMARET [1980], 122 ; pour une présentation du texte, voir 122-126). Qui plus est, la thèse qu'il paraît soutenir (où s'articulent la liberté de choix de l'homme, sa qualité d'agent libre, et l'omniprésence déterminante de Dieu) pourrait sembler voisine sur plusieurs points de celle qu'adopte Averroès lui-même dans le *Kašf*. Cela demande une étude propre qu'il faut réserver pour plus tard.

repousser une nuisance, comme l'art de la guerre, l'art nautique, la médécine, etc. Or tout cela n'est guère concevable [76].

C'est donc une voie médiane qu'il faut choisir conciliant, autrement que chez les aš'arites, qui échouent, « acquisition » d'un côté, création et détermination divines de l'autre. Dans un premier temps, Averroès la présente ainsi :

> Nous disons : il apparaît bien que l'intention de la Révélation n'est pas de dissocier ces deux croyances, mais de les rassembler en une position médiane, qui constitue la vérité en la matière. En effet, il apparaît bien que Dieu – béni et exalté soit-Il – a créé pour nous des puissances pour que nous soyons capables d'acquérir des choses qui sont contraires. Mais, comme l'acquisition de ces choses ne s'accomplit pour nous que moyennant le concours des causes que Dieu nous procure *ab extrinseco*, et par la cessation de ce qui s'y oppose, les actes qui nous sont attribués s'accomplissent grâce à l'une et l'autre chose [*i.e.* les facultés inhérentes à l'homme et les causes extrinsèques]. Et, puisqu'il en est ainsi, même les actes qui nous sont attribués s'accomplissent en fait par notre volonté *et* en tant que des actes extrinsèques concordent avec celle-ci : ce sont eux qui sont désignés par l'expression « décret divin » [77].

Premièrement, donc : Dieu nous dote de « puissances », et de puissances antérieures à l'acte effectif capables de deux « contraires ». De ce point de vue, l'idée d'acquisition de l'acte et celle de son attribution sont valides. Récuser l'aš'arisme, autrement dit, ne revient pas à nier toute idée de *kasb*. Deuxièmement, cependant, cette puissance des contraires ne s'exerce pas à vide, sans motif, dans une indépendance qui la soustrairait à la causalité réglant le déroulement de l'univers. Si la puissance, et notamment la volonté, est en elle-même offerte à des alternatives, elle ne se détermine concrètement qu'avec le concours de causes « venues du dehors » (*min ḫāriǧ*) et providentiellement ordonnées par Dieu. C'est ce qu'Averroès précise dans un second temps lorsqu'il détaille le processus

76. AVERROES, *Dévoilement des méthodes de démonstration*, trad. Geoffroy, 135 ; *Al-Kašf 'an manāhiǧ al-adilla*, éd. al-Jābirī, 188, § 295. Cela renvoie à l'évidence à ARISTOTE, *De l'interprétation*, 9, notamment 18b26-19a22. *Cf.* AVERROES, *Commentaire moyen sur le* De interpretatione, éd. Benmakhlouf et Diebler, 106-107 ; voir aussi 63-64 de l'introduction, la comparaison faite, sur ce point, entre les lectures d'Averroès et de Farabi, qui fait allusion aux théologiens niant la possibilité pour ne sauver que l'omnipotence divine ; sur cela, voir VALLAT (2004), 245-249.

77. AVERROES, *Dévoilement des méthodes de démonstration*, trad. Geoffroy, 135-136 ; cf. *Al-Kašf 'an manāhiǧ al-adilla*, éd. al-Jābirī, 188, § 297 ; et *Faith and Reason in Islam*, éd. Najjar, 108.

qui conduit à l'acte volontaire [78]. Il insiste, jusqu'à parler de « nécessité » [79], sur la portée de cette influence extrinsèque qui l'insère dans le monde tenu par Dieu. En effet,

> ces causes qui sont procurées par Dieu *ab extrinseco*, ce ne sont pas seulement les [conditions adjuvantes] par lesquelles s'accomplit l'acte que nous projetons de faire, ou qui s'y opposent; c'est aussi la cause qui fait que nous voulons l'une ou l'autre de deux choses opposées. Car la volonté n'est rien d'autre qu'un désir qui survient en nous à cause d'un [acte d'] imagination, ou de notre assentiment à quelque chose. Or cet assentiment n'est pas le fait de notre volonté, il est quelque chose qui nous arrive à cause des choses extérieures : ainsi, lorsque se présente à nous, de l'extérieur, une chose désirable, nous désirons cette chose nécessairement, non par choix, et nous sommes mus vers elle. De même, lorsqu'il nous survient de l'extérieur quelque chose devant être fui, c'est nécessairement que nous éprouvons de la répulsion pour cette chose et que nous la fuyons. Et, puisqu'il en est ainsi, notre volonté est tenue par ces choses extrinsèques, et liée à elle [80].

La conclusion suit, qui demande d'associer les deux éléments :

> Si tout cela est conforme à ce que nous avons décrit, il t'a été montré de quelle manière nous avons une acquisition, et comment toutes nos acquisitions existent en vertu d'un décret et d'une prédétermination préétablis. Et cette combinaison est ce que la Loi a voulu dire par ses versets généraux et par les Traditions dont on a l'opinion qu'elles se contredisent, alors que si se particularise leur généralité dans le sens [donné plus haut] la contradiction est levée. Et par cela aussi tous les doutes qu'on a émis à ce propos sont dissipés; je veux dire par là: les preuves rationnelles contradictoires; je veux dire par là que les choses qui existent par notre volonté se réalisent par les deux choses à la fois, c'est-à-dire par notre volonté et par les causes qui sont *ab extrinseco*. Si les actes sont uniquement attribués à l'une de ces deux choses, les doutes précédents surgissent [81].

78. Dans des termes qui rappellent, notamment, les développements du traité *De l'âme* d'Aristote qu'on a évoqués plus haut sur l'intellect pratique (par exemple *De an.* III 7, 431a8-14; 431b2-12).

79. C'est ce qui fait dire à C. Belo, par exemple, que « we have in Averroes an analysis of *qadar* that is both deterministic and predestinarian » (voir BELO [2007], 221).

80. AVERROES, *Dévoilement des méthodes de démonstration*, trad. Geoffroy, 136; cf. *Al-Kašf 'an manāhiğ al-adilla*, éd. al-Jābirī, 189, § 298; et *Faith and Reason in Islam*, éd. Najjar, 108-109. Pour une lecture de ce passage, voir HOURANI (1962); *cf.* BELO (2007), 214-222, dont nous ne partageons pas la thèse.

81. AVERROÈS, *Al-Kašf 'an manāhiğ al-adilla*, éd. al-Jābirī, 190, § 304.

Ce n'est pourtant pas le dernier mot. Car cette thèse pose non seulement qu'existent des puissances (créées par Dieu) capables des contraires, mais elle soutient aussi que ces puissances, dont le fonctionnement est providentiellement conditionné par les choses extrinsèques, disposent sur l'acte d'une efficace réelle. Autrement dit, elle « est fondée sur l'idée qu'il y a des causes *agentes* produisant les effets causés (*'asbāb an fā'ila li-musabbabāt maf'ūlat*) »[82]. Or, rappelle Averroès, « les musulmans s'accordent à considérer qu'il n'y a d'autre agent (*fā'il*) que Dieu » [83]. En trois pages, qu'on ne peut exposer ici, il doit montrer pour finir en quels sens on peut l'entendre et comment s'accordent l'exclusivité créatrice de Dieu et l'existence dans le monde d'une causalité seconde [84].

Résumons ce qui nous importe. J'« acquiers » mon acte, il m'est « attribué », et cela, certes, en tant que je le « veux »; mais les aš'arites se méprennent, pour qui « ce par quoi il y a acquisition », « l'acquisition » elle-même et « l'acquis » sont œuvres de Dieu: vouloir l'acte consiste à exercer une causalité vraiment efficace par le biais d'une faculté inhérente capable des contraires, même si cette faculté est créée par Dieu, même si son exercice s'insère dans le déterminisme universel et même si, par elle, je ne « crée » jamais l'acte puisque, à proprement parler, il est exact qu'il n'y a de créateur que Dieu.

82. AVERROES, *Dévoilement des méthodes de démonstration*, trad. Geoffroy, 137; cf. *Al-Kašf 'an manāhiğ al-adilla*, éd. al-Jābirī, 190, § 305; nous soulignons.

83. AVERROES, *Dévoilement des méthodes de démonstration*, trad. M. Geoffroy, 137; cf. *Al-Kašf 'an manāhiğ al-adilla*, éd. al-Jābirī, 190, § 305.

84. Voir AVERROES, *Dévoilement des méthodes de démonstration*, trad. Geoffroy, 138-142; cf. *Al-Kašf 'an manāhiğ al-adilla*, éd. al-Jābirī, 190-193, § 305-314. Voici l'essentiel des deux solutions : (1) « Qu'il n'y a pas d'autre agent que Dieu – béni et exalté soit-Il – et que toutes les autres causes – hormis Lui-même – procurées par lui, ne sont appelées agentes que dans un sens figuré, parce que leur être n'est que par Son être, que c'est Lui qui les a fait être comme causes; bien plus, c'est Lui qui les maintient à l'être dans leur "être agents", et Lui qui maintient leurs effets après [que s'est exercé] leur acte, Lui qui crée les substances [des choses causées] lors de la mise en relation des causes avec eux, et encore Lui qui assure le maintien [de ces effets] pris en eux-mêmes » (AVERROES, *Dévoilement des méthodes de démonstration*, trad. Geoffroy, 138); (2) « en deuxième réponse, nous disons: parmi les êtres adventices, il y en a qui sont des substances et des êtres individuels, et d'autres qui sont des mouvements, de la chaleur, du froid, en somme des accidents. Quant aux substances et aux êtres individuels, leur création n'est imputable qu'au Créateur – loué soit-Il. Quant aux causes qui entrent en relation avec [ces êtres], elles n'influent jamais que sur les accidents affectant des êtres individuels, non sur leurs substances » (*ibid.*, 141). L'exposé de cette partie capitale nous porterait trop loin. Il est du reste difficile d'apprécier le statut exact des deux développements que propose Averroès (et les échos d'Alexandre d'Aphrodise comme d'Avicenne qu'ils font entendre), ainsi que leur rapport avec ce qu'on peut extraire par ailleurs du *Tahāfut at-tahāfut* ou du *Grand Commentaire à la* Métaphysique.

C'est cette position qu'il peut être éclairant de rapporter au *Grand Commentaire* sur le traité *De l'âme*, comme si Averroès, exposant l'idée d'une « acquisition » de la pensée, songeait en quelque manière à l' « acquisition » de l'acte qu'il aborde et défend dans le *Kašf*. En un sens, c'est la même question qui est traitée ici et là. Et c'est pour l'essentiel la même réponse. Comme on l'a vu, Averroès demande implicitement ceci dans le *Grand Commentaire* : à quelles conditions une pensée *créée par l'intellect* sur la base de mes images est-elle véritablement *ma* pensée ? Sa solution complète, c'est l'*acquisition* : une pensée est mienne *dans la mesure où je l'acquiers*, c'est-à-dire, comme on l'a noté, dans la mesure où, par le contrôle de mes images, au terme d'un processus qui me relie au monde, j'en *veux* le déclenchement. L'intellect « agent » (*agens* ; *fā'il*) [85] est séparé, éternel, unique, et il « crée » [86] la pensée ; mais j'interviens efficacement, à titre individuel, dans cet « engendrement » [87] de l'intelligible, si bien que j'endosse ce qui est « produit » [88] dans l'intellect matériel. C'est ce qu'on trouve dans le *Kašf*, mais dans un autre cadre, plus large, qui ne concerne plus seulement la pensée (avec tous ses problèmes spécifiques) mais l'acte humain en général. À quelles conditions, demande Averroès, un acte peut-il être l'acte d'un individu ? Étant donné, d'une part, que Dieu est d'une certaine manière le seul « agent », et qu'Il crée tout ce qui est, mais que, d'autre part, on ne peut raisonnablement admettre que l'homme soit absolument contraint, en quel sens ce dernier « agit »-il et dans quelle mesure l'action est-elle sienne ? La réponse fut, là aussi, une forme d' « acquisition », suspendue à l'exercice d'une volonté autonome quoique non autarcique. La noétique radicale du *Grand Commentaire* avait sans doute

85. C'est au niveau de l'intellect « agent » (s'il n'est pas Dieu), déjà, que surgit la question de la causalité seconde. De ce point de vue, comme on le redira, la noétique redouble le problème qu'aborde le *Kašf* en termes généraux.

86. *Cf.* par exemple AVERROES, *Comm. Mag. De anima*, III, 5, éd. Crawford, 390 (109-110) : « et iam fuit declaratum quod intellectus qui creat eg generat intelligibilia et intellecta est intelligentia agens » ; 408 (624-627), etc.

87. *Cf.* par exemple AVERROES, *Comm. Mag. De anima*, III, 5, éd. Crawford, 390 (110) ; 407 (587-589) ; 408 (626-627), etc. Notons ce passage du *Commentaire moyen* au *De anima* (où A. ELAMRANI-JAMAL (1997), 297, traduit *taḫliq* par « préformation ») : « il est évident que cet intellect est d'un côté agent et d'un autre côté forme pour nous, puisque l'engendrement (*tawlīd*) des intelligibles dépend de notre volonté. En effet, quand nous voulons penser une certaine chose, nous le faisons. Notre pensée de la chose n'est autre en premier que la préformation (*taḫlīq*) de l'intelligible, puis, en second sa réception » ; *cf.* AVERROES, *Middle Commentary on Aristotle's* De anima, éd. Ivry, 116 (14-18).

88. L'intellect théorétique est « factum » ; *cf.* par exemple AVERROES, *Comm. Mag. De anima*, III, 17, éd. Crawford, 436 (19).

fait ressortir l'urgence d'une réflexion sur l'appropriation intellectuelle («je pense»), qui croisait la justication théorique, au cœur du *Kašf*, de l'énoncé : «j'agis». La double question de l'acquisition et de l'attribution de la pensée pouvait ainsi apparaître comme un cas, certes aggravé par l'éternité, l'unicité et la séparation substantielle des intellects, de ce problème de l'agir humain dont le *Kašf*, accordant Révélation et raison, tentait de donner une solution générale. Les pensées abstraites des images qui adviennent comme pensées de quelque chose sont toujours aussi les pensées de quelqu'un. Nul homme ne les crée, *stricto sensu*; mais celui qui pense l'a voulu, en manifestant, au sein d'un univers ordonné par Dieu, l'efficience seconde de toutes ses facultés.

Une telle lecture relance la question de l'unité théorique du *corpus* d'Averroès, en qui l'on doit à l'évidence cesser de saisir, de manière exclusive, tantôt le commentateur philosophe, tantôt le juriste ou le théologien[89]. Elle enrichit également la réflexion concernant la manière qu'ont pu avoir les problématiques philosophiques et théologiques de se nourrir les unes les autres. En éclairant la noétique sous un autre jour, elle donne enfin de nouveaux éléments pour envisager chez Averroès la question de la responsabilité morale et intellectuelle de l'individu, et ce faisant pour continuer de réévaluer les critiques qu'en proposeront certains Latins. *Mutatis mutandis*, ces derniers feront du Commentateur une sorte de jabrite, instigateur d'un système où l'homme, littéralement dé-ment, n'est qu'un réceptacle d'images qu'on tâche vainement de joindre à une pensée extérieure. Averroès semble pourtant avoir forgé un *kasb* aristotélicien contre cette simple «mise en relation», sans réalité *ab intra*, cette pure «attribution extrinsèque» créé par Dieu dans le sujet humain[90] que fut pour lui le *kasb* aš'arite. Renan écrivait ceci: «la personnalité de la conscience ne s'est jamais bien clairement révélée aux Arabes»[91]. Et Jolivet, plus récemment: «Averroès médite sur le terme du chemin noétique où il n'y a plus que l'un»[92]. Rien n'est moins sûr.

89. Dans cette optique, voir CANOVA (2007).

90. C'est ainsi que Gardet comprend le kasb aš'arite ; cf. *Encyclopédie de l'Islam*², IV, 721.

91. RENAN (1997), 108.

92. JOLIVET (2006), 233.

Bibliographie

Sources

Aristote (1993), *De l'âme*, traduction inédite, présentation, notes et bibliographie par R. Bodéüs, Paris, GF-Flammarion.

Al-Aš'arī (1953), *al-Luma'*, éd. R. J. McCarthy, *The Theology of al-Ash'arī*, Beyrouth, Imprimerie Catholique.

Al-Ġazālī (1967-1968), *Iḥyā' 'ulūm ad-dīn*, 5 vol., Le Caire.

– (1971), *al-Iqtiṣād fī l-i'tiqād*, Le Caire.

– (2000), *The incoherence of the philosophers*, a parallel English-Arabic text translated, introduced, and annotated by M. E. Marmura, Provo, Utah, Brigham University Press.

Al-Juwaynī (1938), *al-Iršād ilā qawāṭi' al-adilla fī uṣūl al-i'tiqād*, éd. J. D. Luciani, Paris.

– (1948), *al-'Aqīdat an-niẓāmiyya*, éd. M. Zāhid al-Kawṯarī, Le Caire.

Averroes (1953), *Averrois Cordubensis commentarium magnum in Aristotelis de anima libros*, éd. F. S. Crawford, Cambridge (Mass.), The Medieval Academy of America.

– (1974), *Averroes on Plato's* Republic, translated, with an introduction and notes, by R. Lerner, Ithaca and London, Cornell University Press.

– (1998), *L'intelligence et la pensée. Grand Commentaire du* De anima. *Livre III (429a10-435b25)*, traduction, introduction et notes par A. de Libera, Paris, GF-Flammarion.

– (1998), *Al-Kašf 'an manāhiǧ al-adilla fī 'aqā'id al-milla*, éd. M. 'Ā. al-Jābirī, Beyrouth, Markaz dirāsāt al-waḥda al-'arabiyya.

– (2000), *Commentaire moyen sur le* De interpretatione, introduction, traduction et notes de A. Benmakhlouf et S. Diebler, Paris, Vrin.

– (2000), *Dévoilement des méthodes de démonstration des dogmes de la religion musulmane*, trad. M. Geoffroy, dans Averroès, *L'Islam et la raison. Anthologie de textes juridiques, théologiques et polémiques*, Paris, GF-Flammarion.

– (2001), *Faith and reason in Islam. Averroes' exposition of religious arguments*, éd. I. Y. Najjar, Oxford, Oneworld.

– (2002), *Middle Commentary on Aristotle's* De anima, éd. A. L. Ivry, Provo, Utah, Brigham Young University Press.

Thomas d'Aquin (1976), *De unitate intellectus. Contra Averroistas*, Rome, Editori di San Tommaso (*Sancti Thomae de Aquino Opera Omnia*, t. XLIII).

– (1994), *L'unité de l'intellect contre les averroïstes*, suivi des *Textes contre Averroès antérieurs à 1270*, texte latin, traduction, introduction, bibliographie, chronologie, notes et index par A. de Libera, Paris, GF-Flammarion.

Études

Belo, C. (2007), *Chance and determinism in Avicenna and Averroes*, Leiden-Boston, Brill.

BRENET, J.-B. (2003), *Transferts du sujet. La noétique d'Averroès selon Jean de Jandun*, Paris, Vrin.

DAVIDSON, H. A. (1992), *Alfarabi, Avicenna and Averroes, on intellect. Their cosmologies, theories of the active intellect, and theories of human intellect*, New York-Oxford, Oxford University Press.

GARDET, L. (1967), *Dieu et la destinée de l'homme*, Paris, Vrin.

GIMARET, D. (1980), *Théories de l'acte humain en théologie musulmane*, Paris, Vrin.

– (1990), *La doctrine d'al-Ash'arī*, Paris, Ed. du Cerf.

JOLIVET, J. (2006), *Perspectives médiévales et arabes*, Paris, Vrin.

RENAN, E. (1997), *Averroès et l'averroïsme*, Paris, Maisonneuve et Larose.

VALLAT, Ph. (2004), *Farabi et l'école d'Alexandrie. Des prémisses de la connaissance à la philosophie politique*, Paris, Vrin.

Articles

ABRAHAMOV, B. (1988), « Al-Ghazālī's theory of causality », *Studia Islamica*, 67, 75-88.

ALON, I. (1980), « Al-Ghazālī on causality », *Journal of the American Oriental Society*, 100, 397-405.

BLACK, D. (1996), « Memory, individuals, and the past in Averroes's Psychology », *Medieval Philosophy and Theology*, 5, 161-187.

– (1999), « Conjunction and the identity of knower and known in Averroes », *American Catholic Philosophical Quaterly*, 73, 161-184.

BRENET, J.-B. (2005), « Averroès a-t-il inventé une théorie des deux sujets de la pensée ? », *Tópicos. Revista de filosofía*, 29, 53-86.

– (2006), « Du phantasme à l'espèce intelligible : la ruine d'Averroès par l'averroïste Jean de Jandun », dans Maria Cândida Pacheco et José F. Meirinhos (éd.), *Intellect et imagination dans la Philosophie médiévale. Intellect and Imagination in Medieval Philosophy. Intellecto e imaginação na Filosofia Medieval. Actes du XIe Congrès International de Philosophie Médiévale de la Société Internationale pour l'Étude de la Philosophie Médiévale (S.I.E.P.M.), Porto, du 26 au 31 août 2002*, Turnhout, Brepols, vol. 2, 1179-1190.

– (2008), « *Habitus* de science et subjectité. Thomas d'Aquin, Averroès – I* », dans Ch. Erismann et A. Schniewind (éd.), *Compléments de substance. Études sur les propriétés accidentelles offertes à Alain de Libera*, Paris, Vrin, 325-344.

BRUNSCHVIG, R. (1976), « Devoir et pouvoir. Histoire d'un problème de théologie musulmane », dans *id.*, *Études d'islamologie*, Paris, Maisonneuve et Larose, vol. I, 179-220.

CANOVA, B. (2007), « Aristote et le Coran dans le *Kitāb al-Kašf 'an manāhiğ al-adilla* d'Averroès », dans J.-B. Brenet (éd.), *Averroès et les averroïsmes juif et latin. Actes du colloque international (Paris, 16-18 juin 2005),* Turnhout, Brepols.

DUTTON, B. D. (2001), « Al-Ghazālī on possibility and the critique of causality », *Medieval Philosophy and Theology*, 10, 23-46.

ELAMRANI-JAMAL, A. (1997), « Averroès : la doctrine de l'intellect matériel dans le *Commentaire moyen* au *De anima* d'Aristote. Présentation et traduction, suivie d'un lexique-index du chapitre 3, livre III : *De la faculté rationnelle* », dans A. de Libera, A. Elamrani-Jamal, A. Galonnier (éd.), *Langages et Philosophie. Hommage à Jean Jolivet*, Paris, Vrin, 281-307.

FRANK, R. M. (1966), « The structure of created causality according to al-Aš'arî. An analysis of the *Kitâb al-Luma'*, §§ 82-164 », *Studia Islamica*, 25, 13-75.

– (1992), *Creation and Cosmic System: al-Ghazālī and Avicenna*, Heidelberg, Carl Winter Universitätverlag.

GEOFFROY, M. (2002), « La tradition arabe du περὶ νοῦ d'Alexandre d'Aphrodise et les origines de la théorie farabienne des quatre degrés de l'intellect », dans *Aristotele e Alessandro di Afrodisia nella tradizione araba*, a cura di C. D'Ancona e Giuseppe Serra, Padova, Il Poligrafo, 191-231.

– (2007), « Averroès sur l'intellect comme cause agente et cause formelle, et la question de la "jonction" – I* », dans J.-B. Brenet (éd.), *Averroès et les averroïsmes juif et latin. Actes du colloque international (Paris, 16-18 juin 2005)*, Turnhout, Brepols, 77-110.

GOODMAN, L. E. (1978), « Did al-Ghazālī deny causality ? », *Studia Islamica*, 47, 83-120.

HOURANI, G. H. (1962), « Averroes on Good and Evil », *Studia islamica*, 16, 13-40.

JOLIVET, J. (1977), « L'intellect selon Al-Fârâbî. Quelques remarques », dans *Mélanges offerts à Henri Laoust*, Institut Français de Damas, *Bulletin d'Études Orientales*, XXIX, 251-259.

MARMURA, M. E. (1994), « Ghazālī's chapter on divine power in the *Iqtiṣād* », *Arabic Sciences and Philosophy*, 4, 279-315.

– (1995), « Ghazālian causes and intermediaries », *Journal of the American Oriental Society*, 115/1, 89-100.

– (2002), « Ghazālī and ash'arism revisited », *Arabic Sciences and Philosophy*, 12, 91-110.

SCHWARZ, M. (1972), « Acquisition (kasb) in Early Kalām », dans *Essays presented to Richard Walzer. Islamic Philosophy and the Classical Tradition*, Oxford, 355-387.

TAYLOR, R. C. (1999), « Remarks on cogitatio in Averroes' *Commentarium Magnum in Aristotelis De anima Libros* », dans G. Endress et J. A. Aertsen (éd.), *Averroes and the Aristotelian Tradition. Sources. Constitution and reception of the philosophy of Ibn Rushd (1126-1198). Proceedings of the fourth symposium averroicum (Cologne 1996)*, Leyde-Boston-Cologne, Brill, 217-255.

– (2000), « *Cogitatio*, *cogitativus* and *cogitare*: remarks on the cogitative power in Averroes », dans J. Hamesse et C. Steel (éd.), *L'élaboration du vocabulaire philosophique au Moyen Âge. Actes du Colloque international de Louvain-la-*

Neuve et Leuven 12-14 septembre 1998 organisé par la Société Internationale pour l'Étude de la Philosophie Médiévale, Turnhout, Brepols, 111-146.

WATT, W. M. (1943), « The Origin of the islamic doctrine of acquisition », *Journal of the Royal Society*, 234-247.

– (1948), *Free will and predestination in Early Islam*, Londres.

WOLFSON, H.-A. (1976), *The Philosophy of the Kalām*, Cambridge (Mass.) and London (England), Harvard University Press.

AQUINAS AND 'THE ARABS': AQUINAS'S FIRST CRITICAL ENCOUNTER WITH THE DOCTRINES OF AVICENNA AND AVERROES ON THE INTELLECT, *IN 2 SENT.* D. 17, Q. 2, A. 1 [1]

Richard C. TAYLOR
(Marquette University, Milwaukee)

Throughout his entire career as a theologian and philosophical thinker, Thomas Aquinas was deeply concerned with the interpretation of Aristotelian teachings on the nature of the human soul and intellect as provided by Averroes in the latter's *Long Commentary on the De Anima of Aristotle* [2]. As is well known, Aquinas engaged the reasoning of Latin followers of Averroes as well as that of Averroes himself in his polemical *De unitate intellectus contra averroistas* written in 1270 by drawing upon arguments already set forth in critical accounts in the *Summa contra gentiles* (1259-64), the *Compendium theologiae* (ca. 1265-67), the *Quaestiones disputatae de anima* (1265-68), the *Quaestio Disputata De Spiritualibus Creaturis* (1267-68), the *Commentary on the De Anima of Aristotle* (1267-1268), and the *Summa theologiae* (1267-1268). However, his first critical engagement with the doctrine of Averroes on the intellect is found in his *Scriptum super Sententiis* (1252-1257) at book 2, d. 17, q. 2, a. 1, entitled,

1. This study is a product of the *Aquinas and the Arabs Project*. For information, see www.AquinasAndTheArabs.org.

2. AVERROES, *Commentarium Magnum in Aristotelis De Anima Libros*, ed. Crawford. Hereafter this work will be cited as *LCDA* with page numbers in brackets { }. An English translation of this is now available. See TAYLOR-DRUART (2009). This translation will be cited in what follows as *LCDA*, Taylor, tr.

"Whether there is one soul or intellect for all human beings" [3]. Posed in this fashion, the question driving his analysis is seen by Aquinas to bear upon the teachings of Theophrastus, Alexander of Aphrodisias, Themistius, Avicenna, and Ibn Bajjah (Avempace), as well as Averroes [4], since, as Aquinas writes,

> nearly all the philosophers after Aristotle are in agreement that the agent intellect and the possible [intellect] differ in substance and that the agent intellect is a certain separate substance both last among the separate intelligences and related to the possible intellect as that by which we understand, as higher intelligences [are related] to the souls of the spheres [5].

In forming this view of post-Aristotelian philosophy Aquinas drew primarily upon two philosophical sources: (i) the *Long Commentary* by Averroes for all the teachings of the other philosophers mentioned above and for the doctrine and arguments of Averroes himself and (ii) the Latin translation of Avicenna's *De Anima* for the Persian philosopher's own teachings on the soul [6]. In the present article and the translation in the Appendix, my primarly focus is on the use of Averroes by Aquinas though the important role of Avicenna in the development of the thought of Aquinas on epistemology will also be addressed.

In the first section below I provide an analysis of Aquinas's accounts of his philosophical predecessors and of their reasoning for their positions

3. A provisional text of this article of Aquinas's *Commentary on the Sentences of Peter Lombard* was prepared by the late P.-M. Gils, O. P. My English translation is found in the Appendix at the end of this book. My thanks to Dr. Adriano Oliva, O. P., president of the *Commissio Leonina,* for providing the provisional Latin text used here. My thanks also to Prof. Isabelle Moulin for her helpful comments on a draft of my translation.

4. It is curious that Aquinas neglects to mention al-Fārābī in this context since the latter's *Letter on the Intellect* or *De intellectu* was available in Latin translation. Perhaps the reason for this was that this work was not easily at hand for Aquinas. Another reason may be that, while he made extensive use of the *Long Commentary on the De Anima of Aristotle* by Averroes as will be shown below, he did not fully understand the critical accounts of the teachings of al-Fārābī as set forth by Averroes. The Latin text of al-Fārābī's *De Intellectu* was edited and discussed by Etienne GILSON (1929), 4-149; see 115-126. For a discussion of the importance of the teachings of al-Fārābī to the development of the thought of Aquinas, see TAYLOR (2006), 151-168. For a general account of the thought of al-Fārābī, see DAVIDSON (1992), 44-73; and REISMAN (2005), 52-71.

5. AQUINAS, *In 2 Sent., d. 17, q. 2, a. 1, sol.* See Appendix, Solution, section [C].

6. Among the key texts in Averroes are *LCDA* Book 3, Texts and Comments 5, 18-20, and 36. For AVICENNA, the key text is *Kitāb al-Šifā', al-Nafs*, Part 5, ed. F. Rahman, 202-269; AVICENNA LATINUS, *Liber De Anima seu Sextus de Naturalibus I-II-III*, ed. S. Van Riet; *Liber De Anima seu Sextus de Naturalibus IV-V*, S. ed. Van Riet, vol. 2, 69-185.

together with his critical rejection of their views asserting in various ways that human intellect or intellective soul is one for all human beings. This will make clear his own impressive depth of understanding of his sources as well as his sophisticated critical insights into arguments relevant to the formation of his own quite distinct doctrine. I will also indicate important limitations of his understanding of the philosophical teachings of his chief source, Averroes, of which Aquinas was unaware. As we shall see, consideration of those teachings will go far toward saving Averroes from definitive refutation by Aquinas. In the second section I focus on Aquinas's exposition of his own teaching on the nature of the intellect or intellective soul and provide an analysis of the arguments and presuppositions underlying his novel account of the multiplicity of individual human intellects and of the multiplication of sets of intelligible species in individual intellects. I then conclude with a summary and some remarks about Aquinas's natural and supernatural epistemologies.

I. Aquinas on the unity of intellect in "nearly all the philosophers after Aristotle"

Thomas [A][7] begins his solution to the issue of whether there is one intellect or one intellective soul for all human beings by stipulating, first, that he will not consider here views that there exists just one intellect for all reality or that the intellect is nothing but the divine essence and, second, that his main concern will be the unity and diversity of the human rational soul. While he treats of this issue in Avicenna, Alexander, Theophrastus and Themistius, Ibn Bājja (Avempace), and Averroes, it is clear that his primary source is the *Long Commentary* by Averroes and that his chief concern is the challenge posed by the doctrine of intellect set forth in that work. This is evident [B] in his account of the terminology of intellect: possible intellect, agent intellect and intellect in a positive disposition (*intellectus in habitu*)[8] which is based on this work by Averroes. For his explanation that this is a state consequent upon the attainment of abstracted knowledge which enables the intellect to operate per se [9], Aquinas draws on Averroes who holds the intellect in a positive disposition

7. These bracketed references are to my divisions of the text found in the translation in the Appendix.

8. This is *al-ʿaql bi-l-malakah*. In my translations of the *LCDA*, I render *intellectus in habitu* as "intellect in a positive disposition".

9. AQUINAS, *In 2 Sent.* d. 17, q. 2, a. 1, sol.; section [B].

> to refer to the human being who is the one understanding. It is necessary to add in the account: insofar as it makes it understand everything in its own right and when it wishes. For this is the definition of a positive disposition, namely, that what has a positive disposition understands in virtue of it what is proper to itself in its own right and when it wishes, without it being the case that it needs something external in this [10].

In contrast, for the Latin Avicenna read by Aquinas, the intellect *in habitu* or intellect in a positive disposition instead is a disposition of the intellect in virtue of the possession of general principles of the understanding known per se such as that a thing cannot be and not be in the same respect at the same time [11]. A similar affinity for the phraseology found in Averroes can also be seen in the initial definitions used by Aquinas for the agent intellect and possible intellect [12], this latter called "material intellect" by both Avicenna and Averroes, a term bequeathed to the tradition by Alexander of Aphrodisias [13]. The description of Aquinas coincides broadly with the functions attributed to these intellects by both these thinkers, though Avicenna and Averroes have strongly contrasting differences in the details, as Aquinas will make clear. Here Aquinas describes the possible intellect as "what is in potency for receiving all understood forms" [14]. For Avicenna the material intellect is a "pure aptitude" (*aptitudo pura*) [15] for "universal intelligible intentions altogether separate from matter" [16]. For Averroes the material intellect is said to have "no nature according to this except the nature of the possibility for receiving intelligible material forms" [17] and to be defined as "that which is

10. AVERROES, *LCDA* {438} Taylor tr., 350: "[...] Referri ad hominem intelligentem. Et oportet addere in sermone: secundum quod facit ipsum intelligere omne ex se et quando voluerit. Hec enim est diffinitio habitus, scilicet ut habens habitum intelligat per ipsum illud quod est sibi proprium ex se et quando voluerit, absque eo quod indigeat in hoc aliquo extrinseco".

11. AVICENNA LATINUS, *De Anima* V 1, 81.78-82; Arabic, 209.

12. The term "possible intellect" is taken from ARISTOTLE, *De Anima* 429a21-24.

13. See ALEXANDER OF APHRODISIAS, *De Anima Liber Cum Mantissa*, ed. Ivo Bruns, 81.24.

14. AQUINAS, *In 2 Sent.* d. 17, q. 2, a. 1, sol. Averroes provides a precise definition of the material intellect: AVERROES, *LCDA*, {387}; Taylor tr., 304: "Idest, diffinitio igitur intellectus materialis est illud quod est in potentia omnes intentiones formarum materialium universalium, et non est in actu aliquod entium antequam intelligat ipsum".

15. AVICENNA, Latin, *De Anima* V 1, 81.77; Arabic, 209.

16. AVICENNA, Latin, *De Anima* V 1, 76.5-6; Arabic, 206.

17. AVERROES, *LCDA*, {387}; Taylor tr., 304: "Non habet naturam secundum hoc nisi naturam possibilitatis ad recipiendum formas intellectas materiales". Aquinas writes in AQUINAS, *In 2 Sent.* d. 17, q. 2, a. 1, sol.: "Et dicitur intellectus possibilis qui est in potentia ad

in potency all the intentions of universal material forms and is not any of the beings in act before it understands any of them" [18], functioning as "the subject of the theoretical intelligibles and of the agent intellect" [19]. Regarding the agent intellect, Aquinas writes that this term "names what makes intelligibles in potency to be [intelligibles] in act, as light which makes colors visible in potency to be visible in act" [20]. The agent intellect performs that function for both Avicenna and Averroes. However, for Avicenna it is more properly understood as "the intellect in act" which causes the human soul to go from potency to act by giving separate or abstract intelligible form to the soul by way of emanation [21]. For Averroes, the agent intellect "makes that intellect which is in potency to understand everything in act" [22] and "makes everything intelligible in potency to be intelligible in act after it was in potency" [23], not by emanation but by a genuine abstraction when an imagined intention "is transferred in its being from one order into another" [24]. With the clarification of the vocabulary of intellect complete, Aquinas states directly what motivates the discussion of the intellect in this his first theological work.

These two accounts of agent intellect and possible intellect differ in substance and must be rejected according to Aquinas [C] as entailing consequences deeply contrary to the Catholic faith. For while the philosophers hold that the conjoining of human beings to the agent intellect yields ultimate human perfection of knowing and thereby ultimate human happiness, such a view would mean that human salvation would be brought about by a separate intelligence or angel and not by God Himself. Noting that some Catholic teachers seek to correct and in part accept this view by

recipiendum omnes formas intellectas, sicut uisus est in potentia ad recipiendum omnes colores".

18. See note 14 for the text.

19. AVERROES, *LCDA* {499}; Taylor tr., 398: "Nos autem cum posuerimus intellectum materialem esse eternum et intellecta speculativa esse generabilia et corruptibilia eo modo quo diximus, et quod intellectus materialis intelligit utrunque, scilicet formas materiales et formas abstractas, manifestum est quod subiectum intellectorum speculativorum et intellectus agentis secundum hunc modum est idem et unum, scilicet materialis".

20. AQUINAS, *In 2 Sent.* d. 17, q. 2, a. 1, sol.; section [B].

21. AVICENNA, Latin, *De Anima* V 5, 126.28-127.47; Arabic, 234-35.

22. AVERROES, *LCDA* {437}; Taylor tr., 349: "[...] Facit intellectum qui est in potentia intelligere omnia in actu".

23. AVERROES, *LCDA* {438}; Taylor tr., 350: "Facit omnem rem intellectam in potentia intellectam in actu postquam erat in potentia".

24. AVERROES, *LCDA* {439}; Taylor tr., 351: "[...] Transferri in suo esse de ordine in ordinem". On the roots of this notion in al-Fārābī, see Taylor (2006).

identifying the agent intellect with God[25], since "by devotion to Him our soul is blessed, which they confirm in virtue of what is written at *John* 1, 9: *He was the true light which illumines all human beings coming into this world*", Aquinas here is content that their view has a certain reasonableness, though he himself rejects that view[26]. In the present context, then, his motivation is clearly and expressly theological, though, as we shall see, his engagement with the philosophical tradition will be on philosophical grounds.

Aquinas proceeds [D] to his critical analysis of the views of the philosophers on the unity of intellect by considering those of Alexander of Aphrodisias, Ibn Bājja (Avempace), Avicenna, Theophrastus and Themistius, and finally Averroes, dividing them into three groups. The first [E-G] is that of Alexander and Ibn Bājja (Avempace) who regard the possible intellect as corruptible with the body. The second [H] is that of Avicenna who holds the possible intellect to be multiplied and distinct in individual human beings, with its subject not the body or a bodily power but the essence of the rational soul itself, and to come into being with the human body but to persist in existence after the death of the body[27]. The third view [I-M] is that "the possible intellect is one for all [human beings], which Aquinas subdivides into two: [I] the view of Themistius and Theophrastus with [J] a refutation by Averroes and [K-M] the view of Averroes with [N] a refutation by Aquinas. Aquinas concludes the *Solutio* with his own views [O-P] which involve accepting principles from Avicenna and Averroes and incoporating them into his own understanding of agent intellect and possible intellect as powers belonging individually to particular human souls. However, with the exception of two sentences on the teaching of Avicenna [H], the sole source for Aquinas on these thinkers appears to be the *Long Commentary* by Averroes.

25. This may include William of Auvergne and Roger Bacon among others. See GILSON (1926-27), 5-127; in particular, 67-72.

26. Note that Aquinas rejects this view in all his works with the exception of a brief and troubling remark in his late *De unitate intellectus* where he mentions that the principle of intellectual light is a separate substance, "uel Deus secundum Catholicos, uel intelligentia ultima secundum Avicennam" ("either God according to Catholics or the last intelligence according to Avicenna"). See AQUINAS, *De unitate intellectus*, V, 368-70, 314. On this issue, see LIBERA (2004), 497-8.

27. This is an accurate account of the view of Avicenna available in Latin texts. See the brief account of Avicenna's view by WISNOVSKY (2005), 92-136, specifically 96-105. Also see WISNOVSKY (2003), Ch. 6 "Avicenna on Perfection and Soul. The Issue of Separability", 113-141. Also see DAVIDSON (1992).

Alexander of Aphrodisias and Ibn Bājjah

Following closely the *Long Commentary* by Averroes, Aquinas argues [E] that Alexander[28] held "that the possible intellect is nothing other than a disposition[29] which is in human nature for receiving the impressions of the agent intellect and that this is a bodily power consequent upon the human constitution"[30]. In the work of Averroes he found the following quotation from the Arabic version of the *De intellectu* of Alexander.

> Since, therefore, from this body, when it is mixed in a certain mixture, something will be generated from the whole mixture such that it is fit for being an instrument of that intellect which is in this mixed thing, since it exists in all the body, and that instrument is also a body, then it will be called the intellect in potency. It is a power made from a mixture which occurred in bodies, [a power] disposed to receive the intellect which is in act[31].

28. The *De intellectu* of Alexander was available in Latin translation from Arabic, but Aquinas makes no use of it here and instead relies completely on Averroes. R. A. Gauthier in his introduction to the Leonine edition of Aquinas's *Commentary on the De Anima* finds that Aquinas never directly read this treatise by Alexander. See AQUINAS, *Sententia de anima, Opera omnia* XLV, 1, ed. R. A. Gauthier, 230-31. Averroes himself had in Arabic translation both Alexander's the paraphrasing *De Anima* and his *De intellectu*. See AVERROES, *LCDA*, Taylor, tr., introduction, lxxxi-lxxxii; and DAVIDSON (1992), 259-60. The Latin translation of the *De intellectu* is edited by THÉRY (1926), 3-120; see 74-82.

29. *preparationem*. The corresponding Greek is *epitēdeiotēs*. See ALEXANDER OF APHRODISIAS, *De Anima Liber Cum Mantissa*, ed. Ivo Bruns, [Commentaria in Aristotelem Graeca, Suppl. II, pt. 1], 84.24-85.5.

30. AVERROES, *LCDA* {444}; Taylor, tr., 355: "Quidam enim dicunt intellectum possibilem nichil aliud esse quam preparationem que est in natura humana ad recipiendam impressionem intellectus agentis, et hanc esse uirtutem corporalem consequentem complexionem humanam". In lines 134-137 we find, "Potest enim intelligi secundum Alexandrum quod intendebat per intellectum in potentia preparationem existentem in complexione humana, scilicet quod potentia et preparatio que est in homine ad recipiendum intellectum in respectu uniuscuiusque individui est prior tempore intellectu agenti". In the text that immediately follows Averroes explains that this intelligible comes about when the immortal Agent Intellect is united to us as "form for us", *forma nobis*, according to Alexander.

31. AVERROES, *LCDA* {394}; Taylor tr., 310: "Cum igitur ex hoc corpore, quando fuerit mixtum aliqua mixtione, generabitur aliquid ex universo mixti ita quod sit aptum ut sit instrumentum istius intellectus qui est in hoc mixto, cum existit in omni corpore, et istud instrumentum est etiam corpus, tunc dicetur esse intellectus in potentia; et est virtus facta a mixtione que cecidit in corporibus, preparata ad recipiendum intellectum qui est in actu". For the Greek, see ALEXANDER OF APHRODISIAS, *De Anima Liber Cum Mantissa*, ed. Ivo Bruns, 112.11-16. On the unsatisfactory status of the editions of the Arabic of the *De Intellectu*, see DAVIDSON (1992), 7 n. 2.

For his criticism of Alexander that the possible intellect is intended by Aristotle to be itself receptive of intelligible species and that Aristotle refutes the notion that intelligible forms may be received into a body or a power in a body, Aquinas relies wholly on Averroes's refutation of Alexander in the *Long Commentary*[32]. Aquinas saw in Averroes himself a great disdain for the materialist view of Alexander where Averroes writes,

> A more unthinkable aspect of the opinion of Alexander is that he said that the first dispositions for the intelligibles and for the other later actualities of the soul are things produced from the mixture, not powers produced by an external mover as is well known of the opinion of Aristotle and all the Peripatetics. For that opinion regarding the apprehensive powers of the soul, if it is as we have understood it, is false. For from the substance and the nature of the elements there cannot come to be an apprehensive discerning power. For if it were possible that there come to be such powers from their nature and without an external mover, then it would be possible for the final actuality, which is the intelligibles, to be something produced from the substance of their elements, as color and taste come to be. This opinion is similar to the opinion of those who deny agent causes and those who allow only material causes: these are those who speak of chance. Alexander has greater nobility than to believe this, but the questions which were posed to him regarding the material intellect forced him to this [position][33].

32. AVERROES, *LCDA* {395-6}; Taylor, tr., 312: "Sed hoc quod dixit Alexander nichil est. Hoc enim vere dicitur de omni preparatione, scilicet quod neque est corpus neque forma hec in corpore. Quare igitur appropriavit Aristoteles hoc preparationi que est in intellectu inter alias preparationes, si non intendebat demonstrare nobis substantiam preparati sed substantiam preparationis? Sed impossibile est dicere quod preparatio est substantia, cum hoc quod dicimus quod subiectum istius preparationis neque est corpus neque virtus in corpore. Et est illud quod conclusit demonstratio Aristotelis alia intentio ab ea secundum quam dicitur quod preparatio neque est corpus neque virtus in corpore. Et hoc manifestum est ex demonstratione Aristotelis. Propositio enim dicens quod omne recipiens aliquid necesse est ut in eo non existat in actu aliquid ex natura recepti manifesta est ex eo quod substantia preparati et natura eius querit habere hoc predicatum secundum quod est preparatum. Preparatio enim non est recipiens, sed esse preparationis a recipiente est sicut accidentis proprii. Et ideo, cum fuerit receptio, non erit preparatio, et remanebit recipiens. Et hoc manifestum est et intellectum ab omnibus expositoribus ex demonstratione Aristotelis".

33. AVERROES, *LCDA* {397-8}; Taylor, tr., 314: "Et magis inopinabile de opinione Alexandri est hoc quod dixit quod prime preparationes ad intellecta et ad alias postremas perfectiones de anima sunt res facte a complexione, non virtutes facte a motore extrinseco ut est famosum ex opinione Aristotelis et omnium Peripateticorum. Ista enim opinio in virtutibus anime comprehensivis, si est secundum quod nos intelleximus, est falsa. A substantia enim elementorum et a natura eorum non potest fieri virtus distinguens comprehensiva; quoniam, si esset possibile ut a natura eorum et sine extrinseco motore fierent tales virtutes, tunc esset possibile ut postrema perfectio, que est intellecta, esset aliquod factum a

Here Averroes (i) attacks Alexander's notion of the receptive material intellect as "an apprehensive discerning power" which arises from a mixture of physical elements. Averroes later goes on to rail at length (ii) against what he characterizes as Alexander's impossible notion that somehow the disposition for receptivity called the material intellect might be a disposition somehow distinct from a subject such as a body or a power of a body, saying of Alexander's account, "I am ashamed of this account and of this fantastic exposition"[34]. Futhermore, according to Averroes, (iii) given that a disposition must be in a subject, one must reject "the impossible results [reached] by Alexander, namely, that the subject receiving the intelligible forms is a body made from the elements or a power in a body"[35]. It is precisely on these three points that Aquinas refutes the view of Alexander: (i) "no power caused by the commixture of elements is able to know"; (ii) "a disposition is not [itself] receptive but rather something which has been disposed [is receptive];" and (iii) "what is disposed by this disposition is a body or a power in a body, and in such a way that what receives intelligible forms would be a body or a power in a

substantia eorum elementorum ut color et sapor fiunt. Et ista opinio est similis opinioni negantium causas agentes et non concedentium nisi causas materiales; et sunt illi qui dicunt casum. Sed Alexander est maioris nobilitatis quam ut credat hoc; sed questiones que opponebantur ei in intellectu materiali coegerunt ipsum ad hoc".

34. AVERROES, *LCDA* {430-431}; Taylor, tr., 344: "Dicere autem quod intellectus materialis est similis preparationi que est in tabula, non tabule secundum quod est preparata, ut exponit Alexander hunc sermonem, falsum est. Preparatio enim est privatio aliqua, et nullam habet naturam propriam nisi propter naturam subiecti, et propter hoc fuit possibile ut preparationes diversentur in unoquoque ente. O Alexander, reputas Aristotelem intendere demonstrare nobis naturam preparationis tantum, non naturam preparati (et non est natura istius preparationis propria ei, si fuerit possibile sine cognitione nature preparati), sed naturam preparationis simpliciter, in quocunque sit? Ego autem verecundor ex hoc sermone et ex hac mirabili expositione. Si enim Aristoteles intendebat demonstrare naturam preparationis que est in intellectu per omnes sermones predictos in intellectu materiali, necesse est aut ut intendat demonstrare per eos naturam preparationis simpliciter, aut naturam preparationis proprie. Naturam autem preparationis proprie intellectui impossibile est demonstrari sine natura subiecti, cum preparatio propria unicuique subiecto currit cursu perfectionis et forme ex eo; sed oportet necessario per cognitionem nature preparationis scire naturam preparati. Et si intendebat per illos sermones demonstrare naturam preparationis simpliciter, tunc illud non est proprium intellectui, et omne hoc est perturbatio. Omnis enim preparatio, in eo quod est preparatio, vere dicitur nichil esse in actu ex eis que recipit, et quod est non passibile, et vere dicitur esse non corpus neque virtus in corpore".

35. Averroes, *LCDA* {397}; Taylor tr., 313: "[...] Impossibilia contingentia Alexandro, scilicet quod subiectum recipiens formas intellectas est corpus factum ab elementis, aut virtus in corpore [...]".

body, which the Philosopher refutes"[36]. Thus, both Aquinas and Averroes are in agreement that the possible or material intellect must be an immaterial apprehensive power which is not a body nor in a body nor an epiphenomenon consequent upon a mixture of the elements[37].

Averroes was the sole source of knowledge of the epistemology of Ibn Bājja (Avempace) for Thirteen Century Latins and Aquinas draws his critique from the *Long Commentary* by Averroes. For Ibn Bājja, writes Aquinas [F], "the possible intellect is nothing but the power of imagination, insofar as it is naturally constituted such that forms which come to be understood in act are [already] in it"[38]. This is only a paraphrasing of the remarks of Averroes that Ibn Bājja[39], "in the literal understanding of his discussion, seems to intend for the material intellect to be the imaginative power inasmuch as it is disposed so that the intentions which are in it may be intelligibles in act and [so] that there is no other power [which is] the subject for intelligibles other than that power"[40]. Aquinas finds this impossible for two reasons. First, since "the phantasms [...] move the possible intellect, as color moves vision", the identification of imagination with the possible intellect would impossibly require that the very same thing at the same time be both mover providing the phantasms or images

36. *Ib.* lines 146-47; 440-41; and 141-44, respectively.

37. As we shall see, Averroes asserts that the separate agent intellect and the separate material intellect must be "in" the soul as intrinsic to every intellectually understanding human soul but not in the body. In the response to the first objection in the present article, Aquinas writes that the intellect is a material form "since it gives being to matter as substantial form with reference to first being", though it has second being or act which an immaterial operation. Later in the *Summa theologiae* (Ottawa, 1953), Iª, q. 76, a. 1, resp., Aquinas asserts that the intellect is the form of the human body, but he qualifies this statement in his response to the fourth objection where he writes that "the human soul is not a form immersed in corporeal matter or totally comprehended by [matter], owing to its perfection. For this reason nothing prevents one of its powers from not being the act of a body, although the soul according to its essence is the form of a body". "Ad quartum dicendum quod humana anima non est forma in materia corporali immersa, vel ab ea totaliter comprehensa, propter suam perfectionem. Et ideo nihil prohibet aliquam eius virtutem non esse corporis actum; quamvis anima secundum suam essentiam sit corporis forma".

38. AQUINAS, *In 2 Sent.* d. 17, q. 2, a. 1, sol.

39. The Latin translation has Abubacher (Abū Bakr) here which Aquinas readily understood to refer to Ibn Bājja.

40. AVERROES, *LCDA* {397}; Taylor tr., 313: "Abubacher autem videtur intendere in manifesto sui sermonis quod intellectus materialis est virtus ymaginativa secundum quod est preparata ad hoc quod intentiones que sunt in ea sint intellecte in actu, et quod non est alia virtus subiecta intellectis preter istam virtutem".

qua imagination and moved qua receptive possible intellect[41]. In this he again follows Averroes who writes,

> But it is evident that what occurs to him is impossible. For the imagined intentions are what move the intellect, not what are moved. For it is explained that they are such that their relation to the discerning rational power is just as the relation of what is sensed to what senses, not as of what senses to the positive disposition which is sensation. If it were what receives the intelligibles, then the thing would receive itself and the mover would be the moved[42].

Second, for Aquinas, insofar as this power is the imagination, it would be employing a determinate organ of the body, the brain, which is impossible since the intelligibles in act can only be received into an immaterial subject. That is, in the language of Averroes, the power of imagination would be a disposition of a power of the soul which is generable and corruptible just as is the individual[43]. The definition of the possible or material intellect requires that it be receptive of intelligibles in act abstracted from material things and so must itself be immaterial[44]. For

41. *Ibid.*, lines 155-62: "[...] Et ideo oportet quod fantasmata sint mouentia intellectum possibilem sicut color mouet uisum; et aptitudo que est in intellectu possibili ad intelligendum est similis aptitudini que est in patiente in potentia ut sit patiens actu, aptitudo autem que est in ymaginatiua est sicut aptitudo agentis in potentia ut sit agens in actu. Impossibile est autem idem esse mouens et motum et agens et patiens. Ergo impossibile est quod uirtus ymaginatiua sit intellectus possibilis".

42. AVERROES, *LCDA* {398}; Taylor tr., 314: "Sed quod accidit ei impossibile manifestum est. Intentiones enim ymaginate sunt moventes intellectum, non mote. Declaratur enim quod sunt illud cuius proportio ad virtutem distinctivam rationabilem est sicut proportio sensati ad sentiens, non sicut sentientis ad habitum qui est sensus. Et si esset recipiens intellecta, tunc res reciperet se, et movens esset motum". Averroes also remarks that Ibn Bājja was deceived regarding the active disposition of the imagination and the receptive disposition of the material intellect. AVERROES, *LCDA* {406}; Taylor tr., 321: "Et propter hanc similitudinem inter has duas preparationes existimavit Avempeche quod nulla est preparatio ad rem intellectam fiendam nisi preparatio existens in intentionibus ymaginatis. Et hee due preparationes differunt sicut terra a celo; una enim est preparatio in motore ut sit motor, alia autem est preparatio in moto ut sit motum et recipiens".

43. AVERROES, *LCDA* {405-6}; Taylor tr., 320-21: "Preparatio autem que est in virtute ymaginativa intellectorum similis est preparationibus que sunt in aliis virtutibus anime, scilicet perfectionibus primis aliarum virtutum anime, secundum hoc quod utraque preparatio generatur per generationem individui, et corrumpitur per corruptionem eius, et universaliter numeratur per numerationem eius. Et differunt in hoc quod illa est preparatio in motore ut sit motor, scilicet preparatio que est in intentionibus ymaginatis; secunda autem est preparatio in recipiente, et est preparatio que est in primis perfectionibus aliarum partium anime".

44. See above, n. 14. Ibn Bājja's views are more complex than can adequately be conveyed here. Suffice it to say, he tried to avoid the problems of the materialism of

Averroes the Material Intellect is a separately existing substance, while for Aquinas it is an immaterial power or disposition of the individual human soul.

Thus, Aquinas rejects the views of both Alexander and Ibn Bājja for their materialism which entails the perishing of the human possible intellect at death and for their notion of the unity of the agent intellect as one for all human beings. Given that all that would remain of human beings at death is the unique agent intellect in which all shared, he concludes that "this is heretical in the extreme because in this way reward of those deserving after death would be abolished" [45]. Averroes also rejected their views, but his concern was not at all eschatological. Rather, Averroes rejected both because their explanations could not provide an adequate account of the nature of intelligibles in act as immaterial and separate from the constrictive particularity of body [46]. Moreover, quite contrary to the view of Aquinas, Averroes, just as al-Fârâbî and Avicenna before him, held the notion common to the Classical Rationalist tradition in Arabic philosophy that there is just one Agent Intellect enabling intellectual understanding for all human beings, though the late Averroes of the *Long Commentary* distinguished himself in this tradition by asserting the existence of one shared Material Intellect for all human knowers.

Avicenna

In the *Solutio* Aquinas found much more to his liking the view of Avicenna [H] that the possible/material intellect belongs to each human being as an individual and immaterial power of the rational soul. This rational soul comes into existence with the body but does not perish with the death of the body. To this extent, Avicenna's view is in accord with the Catholic faith, while his view that there is one Agent Intellect for all human beings Aquinas rejected as erroneous [47]. From the two mentions of these in the *Solutio* of the article, the extent of the importance of Avicenna to the thought of Aquinas appears less readily evident than it really is.

His appreciation of Avicenna is more clear in the response to the third objection. That objection claims that, if there were a plurality of individual

Alexander by making the subject of received intelligibles the power of imagination which, while not a body, is nevertheless a power in a body. For a short account of the thought of Ibn Bājja, see PUIG MONTADA (2007).

45. AQUINAS, *In 2 Sent.* d. 17, q. 2, a. 1, sol, section [G].

46. On this see TAYLOR (2007), 111-140.

47. AQUINAS, *In 2 Sent.* d. 17, q. 2, a. 1, sol, section [H].

human intellects in accord with the number of human bodies, then the understood forms would also be individuated in each human possible intellect. That individuation would make the received form no longer an intelligible in act as an understood universal essence required for knowledge. Rather, it would be a particular form individuated by the particular human intellect receiving it. And in that case, knowledge of intelligibles would then require that there be another intelligible over that one, and so forth to infinity[48]. The individuation occurring in each individual human intellect would be the same as that occurring in the reception of a form by prime matter, with the result that the possible intellect will be no more of a knowing power than is prime matter which does not know forms. As the objector puts it, "in the case of both they are received as those are and not as are forms taken absolutely. Hence, just as prime matter does not know forms which it receives, so too neither [does] the possible intellect [understand forms which it receives], as it seems"[49]. That is, insofar as form is particularized and consequently not intelligible when received into matter, so too form received into a particular human possible/material intellect would also be particularized and not intelligible.

The chief source of these issues raised in this objection are the texts of Averroes who argues that the Material Intellect must be one immaterially separate and shared power since it receives universal forms into itself as subject of intelligibles. Were it to be a particular power, it would receive forms in accord with its particular nature as diverse particulars. Hence, in order to be receptive of intelligible forms without contracting them to the particularity which would take place were there many individual material intellects, Averroes holds for a single, shared incorporeal Material Intellect as satisfying his concern about particularization. Averroes writes regarding the reception of universals forms in the Material Intellect,

> The reason why that nature is something which discerns and knows while prime matter neither knows nor discerns, is because prime matter receives diverse forms, namely, individual and particular forms, while this [nature] receives universal forms. From this it is apparent that this nature is not a determinate particular nor a body nor a power in a body. For if it were so,

48. Averroes is the source of this critique. AVERROES, *LCDA* {411}; Taylor tr. 328: "Et si posuerimus eum esse multa, continget ut res intellecta apud me et apud te sit una in specie et due in individuo; et sic res intellecta habebit rem intellectam, et sic procedit in infinitum". "[...] Prima materia recipit formas diversas, scilicet individuales et istas, ista autem recipit formas universales". See the continuation of Averroes's account at *LCDA* {388}, Taylor tr. 304-5.

49. AQUINAS, *In 2 Sent.* d. 17, q. 2, a. 1, obj. 3.

> then it would receive forms inasmuch as they are diverse and particular; and if it were so, then the forms existing in it would be intelligibles in potency; and thus it would not discern the nature of the forms inasmuch as they are forms, as is the disposition in the case of individual forms, be they spiritual or corporeal. For this reason, if that nature which is called intellect receives forms, it must receive forms by a mode of reception other than that by which those matters receive the forms whose contraction by matter is the determination of prime matter in them [50].

Averroes was also motivated by his reflections on the *Paraphrase of the De Anima* by Themistius [51] to posit a single shared Material Intellect out of concern for the unity of scientific or intelligible discourse that makes intersubjective discourse and understanding possible. He writes,

> That way in which we posited the being of the material intellect solves all the questions resulting from our holding that the intellect is one and many. For if the thing understood in me and in you were one in every way, it would happen that when I would know some intelligible, you would also know it, and many other impossible things [would also follow]. If we assert it to be many, then it would happen that the thing understood in me and in you would be one in species and two in individual [number]. In this way the thing understood will have a thing understood and so it proceeds into infinity. Thus, it will be impossible for a student to learn from a teacher unless the knowledge which is in the teacher is a power generating and creating the knowledge which is in the student, in the way in which one fire generates another fire similar to it in species, which is impossible. That what is known is the same in the teacher and the student in this way caused Plato to believe that learning is recollection. Since, then, we asserted that the intelligible thing which is in me and in you is many in subject insofar as it is true, namely, the forms of the imagination, and one in the subject in

50. AVERROES, *LCDA*, 388; Taylor tr., 304-5: "Et causa propter quam ista natura est distinguens et cognoscens, prima autem materia neque cognoscens neque distinguens, est quia prima materia recipit formas diversas, scilicet individuales et istas, ista autem recipit formas universales. Et ex hoc apparet quod ista natura non est aliquid hoc, neque corpus neque virtus in corpore; quoniam, si ita esset, tunc reciperet formas secundum quod sunt diversa et ista, et si ita esset, tunc forme existentes in ipsa essent intellecte in potentia, et sic non distingueret naturam formarum secundum quod sunt forme, sicut est dispositio in formis individualibus, sive spiritualibus sive corporalibus. Et ideo necesse est, si ista natura que dicitur intellectus recipit formas, ut recipiat formas modo alio receptionis ab eo secundum quem iste materie recipiunt formas quarum conclusio materia est terminatio prime materie in eis".

51. The key role of Themistius in the development of Averroes's thought in the *Long Commentary* is discussed in *LCDA*, Taylor, trad., introduction, LXII ff.; and in TAYLOR (forthcoming).

virtue of which it is an existing intellect (namely, the material [intellect]), those questions are completely resolved[52].

In responding to the third objection, Aquinas refuses to accept the analysis of Averroes and follows Avicenna[53] in holding that the species or form as understood can be considered either with regard to the being it has of its own nature in a human intellect whereby it has "singular being", or insofar as it is a likeness of the thing understood whereby it "leads to knowledge of it, and on the basis of this part it has universality". That is, the understood form or intelligible species is a likeness not insofar as it is of a particular thing but "according to the nature in which it agrees with others of its species". For Aquinas, as a representation of the nature or kind of the thing experienced, the intelligible species is the foundation for the formation of the universal in the intellect. Contrary to the view of Averroes

52. AVERROES, *LCDA*, 411-12; Taylor tr., 328-29: "Et iste modus secundum quem posuimus essentiam intellectus materialis dissolvit omnes questiones contingentes huic quod ponimus quod intellectus est unus et multa. Quoniam, si res intellecta apud me et apud te fuerit una omnibus modis, continget quod, cum ego scirem aliquod intellectum, ut tu scires etiam ipsum, et alia multa impossibilia. Et si posuerimus eum esse multa, continget ut res intellecta apud me et apud te sit una in specie et due in individuo; et sic res intellecta habebit rem intellectam, et sic procedit in infinitum. Et sic erit impossibile ut discipulus addiscat a magistro, nisi scientia que est in magistro sit virtus generans et creans scientiam que est in discipulo, ad modum secundum quem iste ignis generat alium ignem sibi similem in specie; quod est impossibile. Et hoc quod scitum est idem in magistro et discipulo ex hoc modo fecit Platonem credere quod disciplina esset rememoratio. Cum igitur posuerimus rem intelligibilem que est apud me et apud te multam in subiecto secundum quod est vera, scilicet formas ymaginationis, et unam in subiecto per quod est intellectus ens (et est materialis), dissolvuntur iste questiones perfecte".

53. In his *Metaphysics* of the *Šifā'* Avicenna makes his famous distinction of the three ways quiddity can exist: in things, in the soul or absolutely. IBN SĪNĀ, *al-Šifā'. Al-Ilāhiyyāt*, vol. 1, ed. G. C. Anawati and Sa'id Zayed, 31; AVICENNA LATINUS, *Liber de Philosophia Prima sive Scientia Divine, I-IV*, ed. S. Van Riet, 35; AVICENNA, *The Metaphysics of The Healing*, tr. Michael E. Marmura, 24. In his *De Anima* he says that the formation of universal intelligible intentions altogether separate from matter is the most proper characteristic of human beings, at Latin 76, Arabic 206. (See note 58 for the text). He later at Latin 89, Arabic 214 argues that the receptive subject of intelligible forms must be an immaterial substance. At Latin 127-28, Arabic 235, he explains that the human rational power considers individuals in the imagination and next the light of the Agent Intellect strips these intelligibles in potency of materiality and emanates the immaterial intelligible in act upon the rational soul. "What are in the imagination are intelligibles in potency and they become intelligibles in act". For Avicenna, then, the being that an intelligible in act has in the human intellect of an individual is distinct from the being of the intelligible in potency in the imagination since the latter is the being of a particular or singular because of its relation to the particular or singular in the world which is the cause of the image in the imagination and because of its presence in a power of the body, the imagination broadly considered.

for whom particularity of subject necessarily involves the particularization of what is received into a particular subject and, consequently, the loss of intelligible being, Aquinas holds that the reception of the intelligible species as a likeness of the nature does not involve the contraction of the received intelligible species into particularity or singularity. This is simply because matter is the cause of this particularization in concrete things of the world, while in the case of human intellectual understanding the receiving subject is immaterial. The received intelligible form or species in a singular human intellect is indeed in a singular receptive subject. But insofar as the subject is immaterial, the received intelligible form or species as a likeness representing the nature of the thing understood is not contracted to particularity or transformed into an intelligible in potency, as Averroes holds. As is evident in the case of separate substances as immaterial intelligences, an intelligible form or species may be individuated insofar as it belongs to its immaterial subject, "but that species is individuated through the individuation of the intellect and, consequently, it does not lose intelligible being in act". That is, the intelligible species is in or belongs to the individual intellect, but that does not make it no longer an intelligible in act, because it is received immaterially into an immaterial subject. The concern with particularization is a false one for Aquinas, "because the mode of individuation through intellect is other than [the mode of individuation] through prime matter"[54]. The presence of intelligible species belonging individually to a plurality of human intellects does not multiply the nature of the thing understood by means of the intelligible species, since it is the nature in the thing which is the object of knowledge, not the intelligible species in the intellect.

For his argument here Aquinas is drawing on Avicenna's *Metaphysics*, book 5, chapters 1 and 2. There Avicenna argues for this plurality of individual human intellects. In the Latin version of the text at the end of chapter 1, we find,

> This form [...], although it is universal with respect to individuals, nevertheless, with respect to the singular soul in which it is impressed, it is individual, for it is one of the forms which are in the intellect. And because singular souls are many in number, then in the way in which they are particulars they themselves will have a different universal notion[55].

54. All the translations in this paragraph are drawn from AQUINAS, *In 2 Sent.* d. 17, q. 2, a. 1, ad 3.

55. AVICENNA, *Metaphysics* 5.1, Latin v. 2, 238; Arabic, v. 2, 205-6: "Haec autem forma, quamvis respectu individuorum sit universalis, tamen, respectu animae singularis in qua

That is, the intelligible notion exists in the intellects of a plurality of individual human beings without losing its intelligibility. For Avicenna the intelligible comes to be in the soul's apprehension and its universality is due to its relation to a plurality of individuals [56]. The understood intelligible or species, then, has according to Avicenna precisely the two modes of consideration of which Aquinas speaks in the response to the third objection, consideration insofar as it is an understood intelligible possessed by an individual human intellect and consideration insofar as it is a universal intelligible in relation to the many particulars of the world. What is more, we can see in book 5, chapter 2, of Avicenna's *Metaphysics* the foundations for the teaching of Aquinas that intelligible species are representative of and derived from the natures of particular things. The Latin version of Avicenna has

> Therefore, when we say that the universal nature has being in these sensibles, we do not understand that from the fact that it is universal, namely, according to this mode of universality, but rather we understand that the nature to which universality accrues has being in these determinate particulars [57].

Still, just as Aquinas could not accept the views of Averroes on the separation of possible/material intellect, he likewise could not accept the notion common to Avicenna and the Arabic tradition of one separate Agent Intellect shared by all human beings. Avicenna held that what is most characteristic of human beings is to form universal intelligible intentions altogether separate from matter [58]. But he was acutely aware of the problem

imprimitur, est individua; ipsa enim est una ex formis quae sunt in intellectu, et quia singulae animae sunt multae numero, tunc eo modo quo sunt particulares habebunt ipsae aliud intellectum universale". MARMURA (2005), 157, translates the Arabic as follows: "This form, although a universal in relation to individuals, is an individual in relation to the particular soul in which it is imprinted, being one of the forms of the mind. And, because individual souls are numerically many, it is possible for this universal form to be numerically many from the aspect that it is individual". As Van Riet notes, the Latin suffers from an omission here. Still, Aquinas is able to take from this passage the view of Avicenna that the universal is received in a plurality of individual human souls or intellects without losing its nature as an intelligible.

56. See AVICENNA, *Metaphysics* 5.2, Latin v. 2, 241, Arabic, v. 2, 209; Marmura tr., 159.

57. AVICENNA, *Metaphysics* 5.2, Latin v. 2, 244, Arabic, v. 2, 211; Marmura tr., 161: "Cum ergo dicimus quod natura universalis habet esse in his sensibilibus, non intelligimus quod ex hoc quod est universalis, scilicet secundum hunc modum universalitatis, sed intelligimus quod natura cui accidit universalitas habet esse in istis signatis".

58. AVICENNA, *De Anima*, Latin 5.1, v. 2, 76.5-6: "Quae autem est magis proprie ex proprietatibus hominis, haec est scilicet formare intentiones universales intelligibiles omnino

of a suitable subject for intelligibles in act and asserted that it is inappropriate for the subject to be a body or something dependent upon a body. Properly speaking, intelligibles in act themselves should not be thought to have place; rather, they have place only insofar as they are in some way conjoined with a body [59]. For, were intelligibles literally to exist in a body having place, they could not then be intelligible [60]. While human formation of images in the imagination subsequent to sense perception is necessary, the formation of immaterial intelligibles in the soul can come about only thanks to a conjoining with the Agent Intellect [61]. This Agent Intellect in a way gives intelligibles to the soul, not by a changing, transforming or transferring of imagined forms in the imagination into intelligible forms in the human intellect, but rather by emanating (*emanet, yufīḍa*) the immaterial intelligible forms to the soul when the soul has been suitably prepared for reception through sense perception and the workings of the internal sense powers [62]. Human learning of intelligibles, then, is seeking after complete conjoining with the Agent Intellect to obtain this emanation of forms to the soul. These intelligibles, however, do not remain in the soul but rather the soul comes to possess the acquired intellect whereby it can at will conjoin again with the Agent Intellect and again receive the emanation of the intelligible [63]. For Avicenna the intelligibles

abstractas a materia". Arabic, 206: "*wa-akhaṣṣu akhaṣāṣi bi-l-insāni taṣawwuru al-maʿānà al-kullīyati al-mujarradati ʿan al-mādati*".

59. In his *Letter on the Intellect*, al-Fārābī writes regarding intelligibles in act, AL-FĀRĀBĪ, *Risalah fī al-ʿaql*, 17.7-8; tr. Hyman, 216: "[T]he meanings of these categories or many of them must be understood in some other senses, different from those senses, for example, place when it is considered in regard to the intelligible in actuality. For if you consider the meaning of place in regard to it, either you will not find in it any of the meanings of place at all, or, if you should apply the term 'place' it must be understood by you in regard to it in a different meaning, and this meaning according to a different sense". For a discussion of intelligibles and abstract in al-Fārābī, see TAYLOR (2006), 151-168.

60. AVICENNA, *De Anima* V 6, Latin v. 2, p. 146; Arabic, 245: "Iam autem diximus quod corpus earum et quod pendet ex corpore earum non est dignum ad hoc, nec est dignum ut sit subiectum intelligibilium, quia non est dignum ut formae intellectae sint habentes situm, sed coniunctio earum cum corpore faciet eas habere situm; si autem essent in corpore habentes situm, non essent intelligibiles".

61. At *De Anima* I. 5, Latin v. 1, 98-99, Arabic 50, Avicenna states that this comes about through a conjoining (*aliquo modo coniunctionis, nawʿan min ittiṣāl*) with an external intellect which is in act, that is, the Agent Intellect.

62. AVICENNA, Latin, *De Anima* V. 5, Latin v. 2, 126-27; Arabic, 234-35. At Latin, *De Anima* V. 6, v. 2, 147, Arabic 245, the metaphor of emanation is again used to describe this. For a short account of the importance of internal senses in the Arabic/Islamic tradition, including Avicenna, see IVRY (2008).

63. AVICENNA, Latin, *De Anima* V. 6, v. 2, 149-50; Arabic, 247-48.

are present to individual human intellects only when human rational souls are conjoined with the Agent Intellect.

To the concerns of Averroes for whom the intelligibles in act play a role in necessitating the existence of a single shared Material Intellect Aquinas responds in the response to the third objection, as indicated above. Again, for Aquinas there is a likeness in each individual human intellect by means of which the nature of the particular thing understood is known, the nature in which other particular things of that species share [64]. This, however, is a very different teaching from those of Avicenna and Averroes. For Aquinas the objects of knowledge are the natures of things of the world and not properly the unity of forms in the separate Agent Intellect (Avicenna) or the unity of abstracted forms in the separate Material Intellect (Averroes). In this way Aquinas accepts the doctrine of Averroes on the abstraction of intelligibles from sensory experience, while rejecting Avicenna's notion that intelligibles emanate from the transcendent Agent Intellect; and Aquinas accepts the assertion by Avicenna that intelligibles can be apprehended and understood in individual human possible or material intellects, while rejecting the assertion by Averroes of a single shared Material Intellect.

In responding to the second concern of the objection, that singularity or particularity is the key stumbling block to intelligibility, Aquinas responds again by rejecting the notion in Averroes that knowledge requires immediate reference to one common thesaurus of forms in the Material Intellect as objects of knowledge. He does so by appealing to the nature of self-knowledge in immaterial separate intelligences. These entities are purely intellectual beings which are both intelligible as immaterial forms and intelligent as forms existing in act separate from matter. Yet the singularity of each of these does not entail that each exists only as intelligible in potency. Hence, in these or in human intellects an understood "species is individuated through the individuation of the intellect" [65]

64. In his later *Disputed Questions on Soul* Aquinas describes this as follows: AQUINAS, *Quaestiones disputatae De anima*, Q. 5, A. 3, ad 7: "[L]icet species intelligibilis qua intellectus formaliter intelligit sit in intellectu possibili istius uel illius hominis, ex quo intellectus possibiles sunt plures, id tamen quod intelligitur per huiusmodi species est unum, si consideremus habito respectu ad rem intellectam, quia uniuersale quod intelligitur ab utroque est idem in omnibus. Et quod per species multiplicatas in diuersis id quod est unum in omnibus possit intelligi, contingit ex immaterialitate specierum, que representant rem absque materialibus conditionibus indiuiduantibus, ex quibus una natura secundum speciem multiplicatur numero in diuersis".

65. AQUINAS, *In 2 Sent.* d. 17, q. 2, a. 1, ad 3.

without the loss of being as an intelligible. Similarly then, argues Aquinas, the same is the case with my own intellectual understanding insofar "as I understand that I understand, although my understanding is a certain singular operation". He then concludes that "it is also evident in itself that the second unacceptable consequence does not follow, because the mode of individuation through intellect is other than [the mode of individuation] through prime matter"[66]. That is, individuation through prime matter involves the contraction of the form in a genuine hylomorphism with the entailed individuation of any received form as a determinate particular thing; individuation through intellect, however, involves a reception of intelligible species which remain intelligible in the particular human intellect which is their subject. The intelligible species of Aquinas, then, are neither the unique intelligibles in act themselves of Avicenna ontologically located in the unique Agent Intellect nor the abstracted intelligibles in act themselves of Averroes ontologically located in the unique Material Intellect. Rather, for Aquinas the intelligible species is a likeness representative of the nature of a thing as that by which the nature is understood.

Theophastus and Themistius

Theophrastus and Themistius, according to Aquinas [I], held for the unity of all intelligibles in a possible intellect which is one for all human beings[67]. Here Aquinas follows Averroes closely in recounting the teachings of these Greek thinkers and sets out portions of Averroes's critique of their views.

In defining the intellect in a positive disposition or intellect *in habitu* at the beginning of his *Solutio* in this article, Aquinas characterizes it as the "formal" intellect which comes to be "when the possible intellect already has been perfected by the intelligible species so that it is able to operate [in its own right]"[68]. That is, the intellect in a positive disposition, in the actualized state of knowing also called the theoretical intellect, is realized in a human being as intellectual understanding when the actualizing agent intellect and the receptive possible intellect are conjoined with the human knower. A sign that these intellects are conjoined to us is "that the action of

66. AQUINAS, *In 2 Sent.* d. 17, q. 2, a. 1, ad 3.

67. Averroes develops his view of the separate material intellect in critical engagement with Themistius, as I have shown in my introduction to *LCDA* Taylor tr. For a more detailed account, see TAYLOR (forthcoming).

68. AQUINAS, *In 2 Sent.* d. 17, q. 2, a. 1, sol, section [I].

the intellect which is in our power pertains to the intellect in a positive disposition. Therefore, since to abstract species from phantasms is in our power, it is necessary that the agent intellect belong to the intellect in a positive disposition as its form"[69]. They are motivated to present this account, writes Aquinas, by the fact that the possible intellect "is not a determinate particular (*hoc aliquid*) nor a power in a body, and consequently it is eternal"[70]. That is, the possible intellect has to be an immaterial nature which is receptive of all intelligibles without particularizing or individualizing them as it must if it were a determinate particular or a power in a body. As such, the possible intellect on this account can only be one and must constitute a unique species of entity in itself since it must contain all the intelligibles in act which have been abstracted and which constitute a single collection of intelligibles shared by all human knowers. Further, as noted above, insofar as it is immaterial the possible intellect on this account must be eternal, as also is the agent intellect, and so too must be the intellect in a positive disposition or theoretical intelligibles as effect of the eternal agent intellect and possible intellect[71]. From this it follows that "the understood species are eternal". Though on this account the objects of understanding are eternal, the natural human experience of intermittent understanding is to be explained as a consequence of intermittent conjoining of the agent and possible intellects[72].

Themistius held that there is a single Productive or Agent Intellect which comes to be present in human soul and to organize the possible intellect and human experiences through an abstraction of intelligibles from worldly experience as preserved in the human imaginative power. Themistius himself says,

> There is no need to be puzzled if we who are combined from the potential and the actual [intellects] are referred back to one productive intellect, and that what it is to be each of us is derived from that single [intellect]. Where otherwise do the notions that are shared (*koinai ennoiai*) come from?

69. AQUINAS, *In 2 Sent.* d. 17, q. 2, a. 1, sol, section [I].

70. AQUINAS, *In 2 Sent.* d. 17, q. 2, a. 1, sol. Averroes writes, AVERROES, *LCDA* {388}; Taylor tr., 304-5: "Et ex hoc apparet quod ista natura non est aliquid hoc, neque corpus neque virtus in corpore; quoniam, si ita esset, tunc reciperet formas secundum quod sunt diversa et ista, et si ita esset, tunc forme existentes in ipsa essent intellecte in potentia, et sic non distingueret naturam formarum secundum quod sunt forme, sicut est dispositio in formis individualibus, sive spiritualibus sive corporalibus".

71. AVERROES, *LCDA* {389}.

72. AQUINAS, *In 2 Sent.* d. 17, q. 2, a. 1, sol, section [I].

> Where is the untaught and identical understanding of the primary definitions and primary axioms derived from? For we would not understand one another unless there were a single intellect that we all shared [73].

That shared intellect is the Productive or Agent intellect which is eternal and which realizes intelligibles in act by sharing its abstractive power with the individual human intellect (called "actual intellect" by Themistius) which comes to have understanding, that is, comes to be the intellect in a positive disposition, through its role in and connection with the receptive possible or material intellect where all abstracted intelligibles are shared [74].

Averroes, however, refutes this view, writes Aquinas [J], "because it would follow that the forms of natural things which are understood would exist from eternity without matter and outside the soul", a form of Platonism [75]. Further, on this account the forms or species of natural things are not related to the possible intellect as what is responsible for its information; rather, the form of the possible or material intellect is the Agent Intellect. Such a view allows too little a role for the abstraction of intelligibles from experience and reveals itself as a forming of the possible intellect directly by the Agent Intellect. Moreover, there would be no difference between one human being and another here, since each soul has the same initial disposition of receptivity of the possible intellect and each soul has the same ultimate realization in the intellect in a positive disposition, that is, in the attainment of the theoretical intellect. As a consequence, writes Aquinas, "there would be one being and one operation

73. THEMISTIUS, *In Libros Aristotelis De Anima Paraphrasis*, R. Heinze, ed., 1899, p. 103.36-104.3; THEMISTIUS, *On Aristotle's On the Soul*, 129. The corresponding Arabic text THEMISTIUS, *An Arabic Translation of Themistius' Commentary on Aristotle's De Anima*, 188-189, tr. Taylor: "There need be no wonder that we all are as a group composites of what is in potency and of what is in act. All of us whose existence is by virtue of this one are referred back to a one which is the Agent Intellect. For if not this, then whence is it that we possess known sciences in a shared way? And whence is it that the understanding of the primary definitions and primary propositions is alike [for us all] without learning? For it is right that, if we do not have one intellect in which we all share, then we also do not have understanding of one another".

74. For a discussion, see TAYLOR (forthcoming).

75. AQUINAS, *In 2 Sent.* d. 17, q. 2, a. 1, sol, section [J]. *Cf.* AVERROES, *LCDA* {391}; Taylor tr., 307: "Si enim formare per intellectum esset eternum, oporteret ut formatum per intellectum esset eternum, quapropter necesse esset ut forme sensibiles essent intellecte in actu extra animam, et non materiales omnino [...]". Also see *LCDA* {452}.

for all human beings, which is impossible"[76]. All of these remarks by Aquinas are drawn from the texts of Averroes.

Averroes

Aquinas accurately describes the view of Averroes saying that "the agent intellect as well as the possible [intellect] is eternal and one in all [human beings], but the intelligible species are not eternal"[77], if we understand by "intelligible species" the perishable forms in the mortal theoretical intellect belonging to the particular human being. Aquinas then adds: "He also holds that the agent intellect is not related to the possible [intellect] as its form but as a craftsman to matter and [that] the understood species abstracted from phantasms are as form of the possible intellect [and that] from both of these there comes to be the intellect in a positive disposition"[78]. Aquinas correctly recounts the teaching of Averroes that

76. AQUINAS, *In 2 Sent.* d. 17, q. 2, a. 1, sol. *Cf.* AVERROES, *LCDA* {392}; Taylor tr., 308-9: "[S]i intellectus materialis est prima perfectio hominis, ut declaratur de diffinitione anime, et intellectus speculativus est postrema perfectio, homo autem est generabilis et corruptibilis et unus in numero per suam postremam perfectionem ab intellectu, necesse est ut ita sit per suam primam perfectionem, scilicet quod per primam perfectionem de intellectis sim alius a te, et tu alius a me (et si non, tu esses per esse mei, et ego per esse tui [...])".

77. AQUINAS, *In 2 Sent.* d. 17, q. 2, a. 1, sol. *Cf.* AVERROES, *LCDA* {406}; Taylor tr., 321: "Et ideo opinatus est Themistius quod nos sumus intellectus agens, et quod intellectus speculativus nichil est aliud nisi continuatio intellectus agentis cum intellectu materiali tantum. Et non est sicut existimavit, sed opinandum est quod in anima sunt tres partes intellectus, quarum una est intellectus recipiens, secunda autem est efficiens, tertia autem factum. Et due istarum trium sunt eterne, scilicet agens et recipiens; tertia autem est generabilis et corruptibilis uno modo, eterna alio modo".

78. AQUINAS, *In 2 Sent.* d. 17, q. 2, a. 1, sol. *Cf.* AVERROES, *LCDA* {438-39}; Taylor tr., 350: "Modo dat modum ex quo oportuit ponere in anima intelligentiam agentem. Non enim possumus dicere quod proportio intellectus agentis in anima ad intellectum generatum est sicut proportio artificii ad artificiatum omnibus modis. Ars enim imponit formam in tota materia absque eo quod in materia sit aliquid existens de intentione forme antequam artificium fecerit eam. Et non est ita in intellectu; quoniam, si ita esset in intellectu, tunc homo non indigeret, in comprehendendo intelligibilia, sensu neque ymaginatione; immo intellecta pervenirent in intellectum materialem ab intellectu agenti, absque eo quod intellectus materialis indigeret aspicere formas sensibiles. Neque etiam possumus dicere quod intentiones ymaginate sunt sole moventes intellectum materialem et extrahentes eum de potentia in actum; quoniam, si ita esset, tunc nulla differentia esset inter universale et individuum, et tunc intellectus esset de genere virtutis ymaginative. Unde necesse est, cum hoc quod posuimus quod proportio intentionum ymaginatarum ad intellectum materialem est sicut proportio sensibilium ad sensus (ut Aristoteles post dicet), imponere alium motorem esse, qui facit eas movere in actu intellectum materialem (et hoc nichil est aliud quam facere eas intellectas in actu, abstrahendo eas a materia)".

the Agent Intellect is not related to the Material Intellect in such a way that the Agent Intellect provides out of itself alone the intelligibles received by the Material Intellect. Rather, for Averroes the intelligible content of intellectual understanding comes from sensation and interior processing by imagination, cogitation and memory[79]. This is a teaching which Aquinas takes over as his own from Averroes. However, here Aquinas misreads the text of Averroes and the meaning of his metaphor. Instead of characterizing the agent intellect as craftsman or artist, Averroes speaks of art and artistry and denies that the metaphor properly obtains. This is because

> art imposes the form on the whole matter without it being the case that there was something of the intention of the form existing in the matter before the artistry has made it. It is not so in the case of the intellect, for if it were so in the case of the intellect, then a human being would not need sense or imagination for apprehending intelligible[80].

For Averroes sense and imagination are needed to supply imagined intentions or intelligibles in potency which the Agent Intellect separates from matter, abstracting and transferring the intention from the mode of being of an imagined intention to the mode of being of an intention intelligible in act now received into the Material Intellect[81]. As Averroes puts it,

> to abstract is nothing other than to make imagined intentions intelligible in act after they were [intelligible] in potency. But to understand is nothing other than to receive these intentions[82].

Hence, on this much Averroes and Aquinas are in agreement: the content of human intellectual understanding arises not from the agent intellect itself but rather through separating abstractive processes of sense

79. See AVERROES, *LCDA* {225-26}; {384-85}; {476-77}. *Cf.* TAYLOR (1999), 217-255; (2000), 111-146; and *LCDA* Taylor, tr., introduction, LIII-LXVI; LXIX-LXXVI.

80. AVERROES, *LCDA* {438}; Taylor, tr., 350: "Ars enim imponit formam in tota materia absque eo quod in materia sit aliquid existens de intentione forme antequam artificium fecerit eam. Et non est ita in intellectu; quoniam, si ita esset in intellectu, tunc homo non indigeret, in comprehendendo intelligibilia, sensu neque ymaginatione".

81. The doctrine of abstraction of intelligibles from imagined intentions is found in al-Fārābī, embraced by Averroes, and passed on to Aquinas, as I explain in TAYLOR (2006), 151-168.

82. AVERROES, *LCDA* {439}; Taylor, tr., 351: "Abstrahere enim nichil est aliud quam facere intentiones ymaginatas intellectas in actu postquam erant in potentia; intelligere autem nichil aliud est quam recipere has intentiones".

perception, imagination, cogitation, and intellection founded in experience of things of the world and initiated by living human beings who are existing composites of soul and body [83]. As we shall see, however, they disagree on two notions which have decisive ramifications for their teachings: (i) the manner in which the possible/material intellect and the agent intellect are *in* the soul [84] and (ii) the nature of the intelligibles in act [85].

To escape the problems of the account of Themistius, writes Aquinas [L], Averroes proposed that the intelligibles be understood as having a twofold subject,

> one in which it has material being, namely the very phantasms which are in the imagination, and according to this being those species are not eternal; and another [subject] in which it has immaterial being, namely the possible intellect, and according to this subject they do not have the characteristic of being generable and corruptible [86].

83. In contrast, for Avicenna the traditional understanding is that the abstractive powers of the soul function to prepare the rational soul for the reception of an emanation of intelligible forms or for a conjoining with the forms in the separate agent intellect. That commonly held view has been challenged recently by Dimitri Gutas and Dag Hasse with a more abstractionist account in GUTAS (2001), 1-38; and HASSE (2001), 39-72. More recently Jon McGinnis has proffered an altogether novel understanding of the issues which deserves careful consideration. See MCGINNIS (2007), 169-183. McGinnis explicates his novel account in his paper in the present volume. My own view, however, is that Avicenna's explanation may well be in accord with late Neoplatonic accounts which involve both abstraction in relation to perceptual experience and a conjoining with a transcendent intellect containing the intelligible forms. See D'ANCONA (2008), 45-71; and (2008), 57-89. Avicenna knew the *Paraphrase of the De Anima* by Themistius so it may well be that Themistius played an important role in the very different doctrines developed by Avicenna and Averroes. See GUTAS (1988), 313; 289; 291.

84. For a detailed discussion of how these intellects must be intrinsic to the soul, see TAYLOR (2009), 187-220.

85. On this see TAYLOR (2007).

86. AQUINAS, *In 2 Sent.* d. 17, q. 2, a. 1, sol. The complete text of Averroes from which Aquinas extracts his account is as follows. *Cf.* AVERROES, *LCDA* {400-01}; Taylor tr., 316-17: "Et hoc subiectum intellectus quod est motor illius quoquo modo est illud quod reputavit Avempeche esse recipiens, quia invenit ipsum quandoque intellectum in potentia et quandoque intellectum in actu, et ista est dispositio subiecti recipientis, et existimavit conversionem. Et ista proportionalitas magis invenitur perfecta inter subiectum visus quod movet ipsum et inter subiectum intellectus quod movet ipsum. Quemadmodum enim subiectum visus movens ipsum, quod est color, non movet ipsum nisi quando per presentiam lucis efficitur color in actu postquam erat in potentia, ita intentiones ymaginate non movent intellectum materialem nisi quando efficiuntur intellecte in actu postquam erant in potentia. Et propter hoc fuit necesse Aristoteli imponere intellectum agentem, ut videbitur post; et est extrahens has intentiones de potentia in actum. Quemadmodum igitur color qui est in potentia

Aquinas, however, finds this without value and charges that, since the species or form in a particular human being's imagination is not the same in number as the species or form existing in the possible intellect, the result is that the intelligible in act can exist only in the eternal separate possible intellect (scil., the Material Intellect of Averroes) apart from the perishable particular human being whose imagination provides the image or intelligible in potency for abstraction. This would then entail that particular human beings would not have intellectual understanding. Alternatively, it could be argued that the intelligibles in act are eternal in their own right but that would disconnect the intelligibles in act from the images or phantasms apprehended through sense perception by human beings and would be "contrary to the intention and words of the Philosopher" [87]. For the agent intellect and possible intellect were asserted to exist to account for the knowledge of intelligibles in act evident *in* human knowers subsequent to experience of the world. Intellectual understanding cannot properly be separated from human beings whose evident knowledge prompted the discussion of these issues in the first place.

Aquinas then [M] outlines the explanation of Averroes as to how there can be a plurality of distinct human knowers when there is one possible/material intellect. He rightly reports that according to Averroes,

> the understood species is related to the possible intellect in some way as form to matter and because of that somehow one complete thing is made from them. [Consequently, in this the possible intellect's] conjunction with us is through that which is formal in the mentioned conjunction, namely, through the understood species, which he says is the phantasm in us as one subject and the possible intellect itself as the other [subject] [88].

That is, insofar as human beings by way of the imagined intentions provide the formal content to the receptive possible intellect, the possible intellect can be said to be informed with the forms or natures of things of the world thanks to the abstractive power of the agent intellect. Here the

non est prima perfectio coloris qui est intentio comprehensa, sed subiectum quod perficitur per istum colorem est visus, ita etiam subiectum quod perficitur per rem intellectam non est intentiones ymaginate que sunt intellecte in potentia, sed intellectus materialis est qui perficitur per intellecta; et est + cuius proportio ad ea + est sicut proportio intentionis coloris ad virtutem visibilem. Et cum omnia ista sint sicut narravimus, non contingit ut ista intellecta que sunt in actu, scilicet speculativa, ut sint generabilia et corruptibilia nisi propter subiectum per quod sunt vera, non propter subiectum per quod sunt unum entium, scilicet intellectum materialem".

87. AQUINAS, *In 2 Sent.* d. 17, q. 2, a. 1, sol.

88. AQUINAS, *In 2 Sent.* d. 17, q. 2, a. 1, sol.

imagined intention or phantasm is the subject of truth or cause of the formal reality of the abstracted intelligible, an intention or phantasm provided by a particular human being. To this extent the truth of the intelligible in act is grounded in the imagination of the human being. When this abstraction takes place, recounts Aquinas, Averroes asserts the human being also to be conjoined in intellectual understanding to the possible intellect where the intelligibles in act have the Material/possible Intellect as the subject in which they are existent as intelligibles in act. In this way, since different human beings have different experiences and different intentions or phantasms in their imaginations, the possible intellect's conjunction to each is unique in that it takes place only through particular human imaginative powers. This then allows that intellect in human beings is in one way corruptible and in another incorruptible. Intellect in human beings is corruptible through the intentions or phantasms existing in the corruptible bodily power of imagination; but it is incorruptible insofar as the abstracted intelligible in act has as its subject the Material/possible Intellect which is incorruptible as immaterial. Although Averroes makes no mention of it in the context of these discussions, the consequence for him is that there is no personal human immortality since the only things persisting of particular human existence at the death of the human body are intelligibles in act formed in the eternal Material/possible Intellect thanks to the contributions of imagined intentions or phantasms [89]. There are no human souls existing in an afterlife or unearthly existence. However, it is not at all surprising that this point is stressed by Aquinas when he writes, "Hence, it follows also from this that there would remain no diversity of souls after the corruption of bodies" [90]. This explication by Aquinas is a reasonably accurate account of the views of Averroes on perishable human nature and the imperishable possible or Material Intellect.

Aquinas, however, describes [N] this account as frivolous with three arguments.

> First, [it is frivolous] because, as was said, the species which is the form of the possible intellect is not the same in number in the phantasm as in the subject, but rather, it is a likeness of that. Hence, it follows that the possible intellect is in no way conjoined with us, and so we will not understand through it [91].

89. For an extended discussion, see TAYLOR (1998), 87-110.
90. AQUINAS, *In 2 Sent.* d. 17, q. 2, a. 1, sol.
91. AQUINAS, *In 2 Sent.* d. 17, q. 2, a. 1, sol.

That is, insofar as it is not the same form in number in the possible intellect and in the imagined intention or phantasm in the human being but instead in the intellect it is only a likeness of that form now as intelligible in act, then the individual human being is not conjoined to the possible intellect through the imagined intention or phantasm and, consequently, the human being is not understanding the intelligible in act. From this remark it is clear that the only way this concern can be met satisfactorily for Aquinas is if the material/possible intellect is intrinsically present in the individual human being.

It is also frivolous, according to Aquinas, because human beings could not be located in a determinate species as rational animals according to substance if human beings were to have intellect only through conjunction with the separate possible intellect that takes place some interval of time after birth. If human beings are essentially rational animals, then the power of intellect be must intrinsically present in each from childhood and cannot be something that acrues to the animal by a conjunction with separate intellect at some significantly later time in life. Intellectuality must be in the "first perfection and substantial being" of a human being and not merely a "second perfection". Were the latter the case, human beings would have the power of intellectual understanding only as an accident subsequent to substantial being, not as an intrinsic specific difference. If human beings are to be essentially rational and intellectual, again, intellect must in some fashion be essentially present in the soul per se and not something separate and merely accidentally associated with the animal called human. Averroes holds that the particular human being's apprehended form in the imagination or cogitative power called intention or species functions as a medium linking the particular human knower with the Material Intellect in that those intentions or species have two subjects, one the human imaginative power and the other the possible/Material Intellect. But this would at best mean that the intellectual understanding taking place in the separate intellect is somehow accidentally associated with the particular human being's imaginative power, for Aquinas. And that is insufficient for supporting the view that human beings are essentially rational animals who understand intelligibles in act[92]. On the view of Aquinas what is required here is that the power called possible or material intellect be intrinsically present in each human being, not

92. AQUINAS, *In 2 Sent.* d. 17, q. 2, a. 1, sol, section [N].

separately existent outside the human soul as Averroes has it with his view that the Material Intellect is a substance in its own right[93].

The third reason for the frivolousness of the account of Averroes according to Aquinas is based on the notion that an operation of soul must arise from a potency or power in the soul. No operation belonging to the soul takes place solely on the basis of an extrinsic object. For a human being to see a stone, for example, that human being must possess the power of vision. The actuality of vision cannot be given to the human being from the stone, the object. Similarly, the power of intellectual understanding must be a power essentially intrinsic to a human being if that human being is to understand. The object of understanding alone cannot be a cause of the actuality of understanding unless there is a preexisting power of understanding in the soul intrinsically. Hence, Aquinas writes,

> If [...] the intellect is conjoined with us only through the fact that the understood species in some way has a subject in us, it follows that this human being, namely Socrates, does not understand but rather that the separate intellect understands these things which [a human being] imagines[94].

That is, the fact that human beings themselves provide forms or intentions in the imagination which prompt conjunction and intellectual understanding does not indicate intellectual understanding on the part of human beings but rather only understanding on the part of the separate intellect. Unless the power of intellect is intrinsic to human beings, human beings cannot properly be essentially rational or have intellectual understanding. What is required is that the separate Material Intellect and Agent Intellect posited by Averroes be intrinsically present in the human soul.

For clarity sake, the problems which Aquinas raises can be listed as four:

1. If the intelligible in act can exist only in the separate possible intellect apart from human beings, then the result will be that human beings will not have intellectual understanding.

93. It should be noted that Averroes was well aware that his interpretation of Aristotle was novel in the tradition, though he thought it the most reasonable understanding of Aristotle. He calls the Material Intellect a "fourth kind of being" since it is not matter, not form and not the composite of these but rather something altogether distinct and unique: an intellect which is essentially receptivity for intelligibles in act while also being a separate and immaterial substance. AVERROES, *LCDA* {409}: "Opinandum est enim quod iste est quartum genus esse".

94. AQUINAS, *In 2 Sent.* d. 17, q. 2, a. 1, sol, section [N].

2. If the intelligible in act is in the separate possible intellect alone and only a likeness of that intelligible is in the human being, the human individual is not conjoined with the intellect in intellectual understanding and instead only has an apprehension of a likeness.

3. If human beings are to be essentially intelligent, again, the possible intellect must in some fashion be present in the soul per se and not merely accidentally associated with the animal called human.

4. If human beings themselves provide forms or intentions in the imagination which prompt conjunction and intellectual understanding, this does not entail intellectual understanding on the part of human beings but rather only understanding on the part of the separate intellect.

Set forth in this way, it is clear that all four of these critical concerns can only be satisfied in one and the same way: intellectual understanding and intellect must be in human beings. As I explain elsewhere [95], this is precisely what can be found in the *Long Commentary* if one studies the text of Averroes with an eye to his use of the work of his predecessors in the Greek and Arabic traditions and to the the text and issues in the *De Anima* itself, without being prejudiced by the later reading of Averroes by Aquinas.

In four passages of the *Long Commentary* Averroes repeats precisely that the agent intellect and the material intellect should be understood to be "in the soul" [96] in accord with Aristotle's *De Anima* III 5, 430a13-14, which indicates that potential and actualizing powers of mind must be in the soul. Averroes also saw this teaching in Alexander and Themistius [97]. In the *Long Commentary* Averroes continues with even greater frequency and emphasis than he had in his *Short Commentary* and in the *Middle Commentary* to say that the agent intellect is "form for us" [98]. This is most

95. The view of AVERROES is discussed in *LCDA* Taylor tr., introduction, LXII-LXXV. Also see TAYLOR (forthcoming); and TAYLOR (2006), 151-168.

96. This phraseology is used by AVERROES at *LCDA* {390}, {406}, {437} and {438}.

97. Averroes understood another alternative to be the view of al-Fārābī that the Agent Intellect is only a cause acting on the human soul, not as "form for us". Regarding al-Fārābī, see TAYLOR (2006), 151-168. Also see VALLAT (2004); GEOFFROY (2002), 191-231. Also see TAYLOR (2005).

98. *ṣūrah la-nā*/*forma in nobis*; see AVERROES, *Talkhīṣ Kitāb al-Nafs*, 89.3-6: "[I]t is clear that its intellect can belong to us ultimately. I mean insofar as it is form for us and it is such that it has generated for us as necessary an eternal intelligible. Since it is itself an intellect whether or not we have intellectual understanding of it, it is not the case that its existence as intellect is from our activity as is the case in regard to material intelligibles". *Epitome de Anima*, S. Gómez Nogales, ed., (1985), 127.7-10; *La psicología de Averroes. Comentario al*

evident in a passage in which he stresses that the agent intellect is necessarily "form in us" and that intellectual understanding is a proper activity for human beings as intellectual. As such, the agent intellect is necessarily intrinsic and essential to the nature of human beings as rational and intellectually understanding entities.

> For, because that in virtue of which something carries out its proper activity is the form, while we carry out our proper activity in virtue of the agent intellect, it is necessary that the agent intellect be *form in us* [...].[I]t is necessary that a human being understand all the intelligibles through the intellect proper to him and that he carry out the activity proper to him in regard to all beings, just as he understands by his proper intellection all the beings through the intellect in a positive disposition (*intellectus in habitu*), when it has been conjoined with forms of the imagination [99].

libro sobre el alma de Aristóteles, S. Gómez Nogales, trans., (1987) 212. Regarding this notion of the Agent Intellect as "form for us", see GEOFFROY (2007), 77-110. Also see TAYLOR (2005) and (2007). "It is clear that, in one respect, this intellect is an agent and, in another, it is a form for us (*ṣūrah la-nā*), since the generation of intelligibles is a product of our will. When we want to think something, we do so, our thinking it being nothing other than, first, bringing the intelligible forth and, second, receiving it. The individual intentions in the imaginative faculty are they that stand in relation to the intellect as potential colors do to light. That is, this intellect renders them actual intelligibles after their having been intelligible in potentiality. It is clear, from the nature of this intellect – which, in one respect, is a form for us (*ṣūrah la-nā*) and, in another, is the agent for the intelligible – that it is separable and neither generable nor corruptible, for that which acts is always superior to that which is acted upon, and the principle is superior to the matter. The intelligent and intelligible aspects of this intellect are essentially the same thing, since it does not think anything external to its essence. There must be an Agent Intellect here, since that which actualizes the intellect has to be an intellect, the agent endowing only that which resembles what is in its substance". IBN RUSHD, *Averroes. Middle Commentary on Aristotle's De Anima*, ed and tr. A. L. Ivry, (2002), 116.

99. AVERROES, *LCDA* {499-500}; Taylor tr., 399: "Quoniam, quia *illud per quod agit aliquid suam propriam actionem est forma, nos autem agimus per intellectum agentem nostram actionem propriam, necesse est ut intellectus agens sit forma in nobis.* Et nullus modus est secundum quem generetur forma in nobis nisi iste. Quoniam, cum intellecta speculativa copulantur nobiscum per formas ymaginabiles, et intellectus agens copulatur cum intellectis speculativis (illud enim quod comprehendit ea est idem, scilicet intellectus materialis), necesse est ut intellectus agens copuletur nobiscum per continuationem intellect-torum speculativorum. Et manifestum est quod, cum omnia intellecta speculativa fuerint existentia in nobis in potentia, quod ipse erit copulatus nobiscum in potentia. Et cum omnia intellecta speculativa fuerint existentia in nobis in actu, erit ipse tunc copulatus nobis in actu. Et cum quedam fuerint potentia et quedam actu, tunc erit ipse copulatus secundum partem et secundum partem non; et tunc dicimur moveri ad continuationem. Et manifestum est quod, cum iste motus complebitur, quod statim iste intellectus copulabitur nobiscum omnibus modis. Et tunc manifestum est quod proportio eius ad nos in illa dispositione est sicut proportio intellectus qui est in habitu ad nos. Et cum ita sit, *necesse est ut homo intelligat per*

Averroes also stresses that the activities of abstraction and intellectual understanding take place by our will and so properly belong to willing human beings. He writes,

> The intellect existing in us has two activities insofar as it is ascribed to us, one of the genus of affection, namely, understanding, and the other of the genus of activity, namely, to extract forms and denude them of matters, which is nothing but making them intelligible in act after they were such in potency. [Hence] it is evident that, after we have possessed the intellect which is in a positive disposition (*intellectus in habitu*), it is in our will to understand any intelligible we wish and to extract any form we wish [100].

The notion of agent intellect as transcendent and yet also necessarily intrinsic Averroes found in Alexander, Themistius and Aristotle. The notion that the intellect is ours, because we employ it when we wish or will to do so, he found in Themistius and Aristotle [101]. This conception of intellect as both substantially transcendent and yet necessarily present "in the soul" as an intrinsic formal cause I have elsewhere termed "Aristotelian participation", since the separate intellects themselves on this account are reasoned to be intrinsically present in human beings for their voluntary use while also being substantially distinct and transcendent [102]. It is not Platonic since it does not involve a likeness or diminished and imperfect

intellectum sibi proprium omnia entia, et ut agat actionem sibi propriam in omnibus entibus, sicut intelligit per intellectum qui est in habitu, quando fuerit continuatus cum formis ymaginabilibus, omnia entia intellectione propria". Emphasis added.

100. AVERROES, *LCDA* {495}; Taylor tr., 395: "[…] Intellectus existens in nobis habet duas actiones secundum quod attribuitur nobis, quarum una est de genere passionis (et est intelligere), et alia de genere actionis (et est extrahere formas et denudare eas a materiis, quod nichil est aliud nisi facere eas intellectas in actu postquam erant in potentia), manifestum est quoniam in voluntate nostra est, cum habuerimus intellectum qui est in habitu, intelligere quodcunque intellectum voluerimus et extrahere quancunque formam voluerimus". AVERROES, *LCDA* {439-440}; Taylor tr., 352: "Et cum invenimus nos agere per has duas virtutes intellectus cum voluerimus, et nichil agit nisi per suam formam, ideo fuit necesse attribuere nobis has duas virtutes intellectus".

101. ARISTOTLE, *De Anima* 417a27: *boulētheis*. In his comments on *De Anima* III 5, 430a14-17, Averroes writes, AVERROES, *LCDA* {437-8}; Taylor tr., 350: "Deinde dixit: *et intellectus secundum quod facit ipsum intelligere omne*. Et intendit per istum illud quod fit, quod est in habitu. Et hoc pronomen *ipsum* potest referri ad intellectum materialem, sicut diximus; et potest referri ad hominem intelligentem. Et oportet addere in sermone: secundum quod facit ipsum intelligere omne ex se et quando voluerit. Hec enim est diffinitio habitus, scilicet ut habens habitum intelligat per ipsum illud quod est sibi proprium ex se et quando voluerit, absque eo quod indigeat in hoc aliquo extrinseco".

102. This is discussed in AVERROES, *LCDA* Taylor tr., intro., LXXIII; in TAYLOR (forthcoming); and TAYLOR (2006).

representation of the separate intellects to be in the soul but rather, again, the agent intellect and the possible/material intellect themselves must be "in the soul" as Aristotle himself writes at *De Anima* III 5, 430a13-14. That such a view is perhaps not far from contemporary understandings of Aristotle's *De Anima* can be seen in Miles Burnyeat's 2008 Aquinas lecture entitled, "Aristotle's Divine Mind", where Burnyeat insists that in Aristotle our human intellect cannot do without the presence of agent intellect which he also identifies with God following Alexander. Burnyeat writes, "Our mortal intellect needs an immortal intellect to achieve its goal of understanding" [103]. Nevertheless, this notion which in the special case of human intellectual understanding allows for the curious notion that one substance can be intrinsically present in another substance was not at all recognized by Aquinas who himself uses Averroes's own argument for the intrinsic presence of intellect to the soul to insist that possible intellect and agent intellect must be powers intrinsic to every human soul, not transcendent [104].

Averroes believed that he was compelled to this account by multiple philosophical issues such as key concerns about the nature of intellectual understanding, the nature of intelligibles in act, the reality of shared common human discourse and scientific understanding, and many more. The final account he provides in his *Long Commentary* goes far in dealing with the four problems arised by Aquinas which I listed above. The first of these is resolved precisely by his locating the Material Intellect "in the soul". The second is resolved with the same doctrine of participation which holds for the joining of the human soul with the Material Intellect in the apprehension of genuine intelligibles in act existing in the Material Intellect subsequent to abstraction and transference from the mode of being of particular intentions or what Aquinas calls phantasms. To this extent the doctrine of Averroes has rightly been understood to entail a certain kind of realism of intelligibles in act [105]. The third is also resolved by the presence

103. BURNYEAT (2008), 40. Burnyeat, in contrast to what we see in Averroes, finds the agent intellect or God to be present to the soul by final causality alone. I will address the details of this problematic account elsewhere.

104. On intrinsic formal cause in Aquinas and Averroes, see TAYLOR (2009).

105. In his *De unitate intellectus* Aquinas rightly notes that the key difficulty is in the conception of the nature of the intelligible in act. He writes in AQUINAS, *De unitate intellectus* V, ll. 164-70: "Sed inquirendum restat quid sit ipsum intellectum. Si enim dicant quod intellectum est una species immaterialis existens in intellectu, latet ipsos quod quodammodo transeunt in dogma Platonis, qui posuit quod de rebus sensibilibus nulla scientia potest haberi, sed omnis scientia habetur de forma una separata". On this issue in Averroes, see TAYLOR (2007).

of the intellect in the soul insofar as the human soul has in it primary propositions of understanding, e.g., that a thing both cannot be and not be in the same respect and other such general propositions of thought, from the Agent Intellect which it can use as tools for bringing about the actuality of the presence of the separate intellects in the soul. Averroes himself raises the issue of whether we "are called human beings equivocally" [106], if we do not ourselves have intellectual understanding. But he finds the issue sufficiently resolved by asserting that human beings have a natural disposition and affiliation, a potency, for the presence of the separate intellects to be in the soul, together with the primary propositions from the Agent Intellect. The development of intellect in a particular human being depends on the voluntary effort of individuals at understanding [107]. The fourth problem is also resolved by the presence of separate intellect "in the soul". For if the soul has a natural disposition and potency for linking with the separate intellects, then understanding of intelligibles in act takes place during that linking with the Material Intellect, not unlike the account of Avicenna regarding the Agent Intellect [108].

II. AQUINAS'S OWN DOCTRINE OF INTELLECT IN *IN 2 SENT* D. 17, Q. 2, A. 1

Aquinas himself [109] chose to follow Avicenna [O] in the view that the possible intellect comes into being in each individual with the body, is multiplied in different human beings as individual for each, and does not perish with the death of the body. However, he declines to follow Avicenna's conception of the separate Agent Intellect and instead adds that it is not improbable that the agent intellect must also be intrinsically present individually in each human being since that is required for the natural operation of intellectual understanding belonging to the human soul. His following remark indicating that this "follows if there is held to be one agent intellect, be it called God or intelligence" is surely meant as a criticism of those who would hold that God is the agent intellect, though he couches it in more general terms [110]. The unstated implication is that those who hold for one agent intellect will also have to hold that the transcendent agent intellect or God will have to be intrinsically present in the human soul

106. AVERROES, *LCDA* {495}; Taylor tr., 395: "Dicimur homines equivoce".
107. This is discussed at length in AVERROES, *LCDA* {394-400}.
108. See the discussion above and also note 84.
109. AQUINAS, *In 2 Sent.* d. 17, q. 2, a. 1, sol.
110. *Cf.* notes 25 and 26 above.

as a natural operation, something unthinkable in doctrine of natural knowing for Aquinas [111]. In this last section of his *Solutio* in this article Aquinas also argues that the agent intellect and the possible intellect, though powers of the soul constituting what together make up the general human intellectual power, must be understood as two diverse powers of the soul. For this distinction of powers in the soul Aquinas draws directly on Averroes's distinction of the separate intellects. Averroes writes,

> Hence, in view of our having asserted that the relation of the imagined intentions to the material intellect is just as the relation of the sensibles to the senses (as Aristotle will say later), it is necessary to suppose that there is another mover which makes [the intentions] move the material intellect in act, and this is nothing but to make [the intentions] intelligible in act by separating them from matter. Because this intention, which forces the assertion of an agent intellect different from the material intellect and different from the forms of things which the material intellect apprehends, is similar to the intention on account of which sight needs light, in view of the fact that the agent and the recipient are different from light [...] [112].

Nevertheless, in spite of his arguments, Aquinas [P] makes it clear that he is well aware that "how [the possible intellect and the agent intellect] could be rooted in one substance is difficult to see" since the receptivity of the possible intellect and the actuality of the agent intellect would mean that contrary powers related to the same object would exist in the soul [113]. His response to this is that these are distinct powers though they are related in their separate roles in the soul. For the power of soul called agent intellect as "an intellectual light in act" is "a power by which [the soul] makes sensible species to be intelligible [species] in act" by separation or abstraction of the intelligible, while the power of soul called possible intellect is "a power by which it is in potency for being made in the act of

111. Aquinas addresses this issue more fully at *In 4 Sent.*, d. 49, q. 2, a. 1 in the context of the notion of ultimate human happiness by the blessed *in patria* being found in seeing God face to face. This is discussed briefly in TAYLOR (2006), 217-219, but requires a more substantial study which I intend to provide in another publication.

112. AVERROES, *LCDA* {438-9}; Taylor tr., 351: "Unde necesse est, cum hoc quod posuimus quod proportio intentionum ymaginatarum ad intellectum materialem est sicut proportio sensibilium ad sensus (ut Aristoteles post dicet), imponere alium motorem esse, qui facit eas movere in actu intellectum materialem (et hoc nichil est aliud quam facere eas intellectas in actu, abstrahendo eas a materia). Et quia hec intentio cogens ad ponendum intellectum agentem alium a materiali et a formis rerum quas intellectus materialis comprehendit est similis intentioni propter quam visus indiget luce, cum hoc quod agens et recipiens alia sunt a luce [...]."

113. AQUINAS, *In 2 Sent.* d. 17, q. 2, a. 1, sol, section [O].

determinate knowing brought about by a sensible thing's species made intelligible in act" [114].

Here Aquinas displays his famous doctrine of intelligible species as what he will later call *representationes* and *rationes* of the natures of things, wherein the object of human intellectual understanding of things of the natural world is the nature as specific difference in the things [115]. In this the views of Aquinas and Averroes differ substantially. For Averroes, although intelligibles in act are derived by way of abstraction and transference from imagined intentions or phantasms in the human imagination, he regards the separated intelligibles in act ontologically present in the Material Intellect to be the proper object of human scientific understanding. This is a view he only came to express fully in his *Long Commentary* with the establishment of his conception of the Material Intellect as a shared source of intelligibles for all human knowers. In his *Short* and *Middle Commentaries* Averroes held for a plurality of individual human material or possible intellects and a very different conception of itelligibles in act [116]. In the *Long Commentary*, however, he chose to follow Themistius for several reasons which I have discussed elsewhere [117]. The most important motivating considerations Averroes discovered in Themistius were (1) the need for a shared and unique set of intelligibles for the unity of human discourse and for the unity of intellectual understanding, since these presuppose common referents, and (2) the need that intelligibles in act be immaterially existing realities in an immaterial subject. However, in his late treatise *On the unity of the intellect against the Averroists,* Aquinas recognized this and remarked that Averroes had somehow inadvertantly fallen into a form of Platonism in his doctrine of

114. AQUINAS, *In 2 Sent.* d. 17, q. 2, a. 1, sol, section [O].

115. Later he writes, AQUINAS, *Quaestiones Disputatae De Anima,* B.-C. Bazán, ed., Q.5, A.3, ad 7: "[L]icet species intelligibilis qua intellectus formaliter intelligit sit in intellectu possibili istius uel illius hominis, ex quo intellectus possibiles sunt plures, id tamen quod intelligitur per huiusmodi species est unum, si consideremus habito respectu ad rem intellectam, quia uniuersale quod intelligitur ab utroque est idem in omnibus. Et quod per species multiplicatas in diuersis id quod est unum in omnibus possit intelligi, contingit ex immaterialitate specierum, que representant rem absque materialibus conditionibus indiuiduantibus, ex quibus una natura secundum speciem multiplicatur numero in diuersis". For Aquinas these intelligible species as representations and also *rationes* or intelligible contents are the means by which human beings apprehend the natures of things of the world and not the direct object of human intellectual understanding.

116. For a discusssion of this, see AVERROES, *LCDA* Taylor, tr., introduction, XIX-XLII. Also see TAYLOR (2007), 117 ff.

117. See TAYLOR (forthcoming).

the intellect [118]. For Avicenna, as we have seen, intelligibles are described as coming to be in a plurality of human receptive intellects by emanation (*fayḍ*) from the separate Agent Intellect or by a conjoining (*ittiṣāl*) with the separate Agent Intellect. Aquinas rejected this role for a transcendent Agent Intellect and embraced with the abstractionist account of Averroes, while holding firmly that agent intellect and material/possible intellect are powers of the human soul. And, we have seen, Avicenna appears to have provided some valuable inspiration for Aquinas's doctrine of intelligible species with texts affirming the natures of things are the bases for universals in the soul [119].

III. Conclusion

In publication in 1994, the late Edward P. Mahoney remarked that in this article of the *Commentary on the Sentences*, "Aquinas [...] presents the basic analysis of Averroes that he will consistently maintain in his subsequent writings" [120]. That statement does prove to be correct, for the way in which Averroes is understood and misunderstood by Aquinas continues to be reflected in later works in which Aquinas deals with issues

118. See note 105.

119. Aquinas in this article of the *Commentary on the Sentences* confronts the teachings and texts of Averroes and Avicenna on the precise points he viewed as most important for the epistemological questions addressed. However, the foundations of the epistemology of Aquinas developed here can be found worked out in detail by Albert the Great about 1245 when he spelled out in even greater detail and more explicitly how he formed his epistemology out of the teachings of Avicenna and Averroes. The key texts in which Albert displays his dependence on and development of sources from the Arabic tradition are in his *De homine*, *Alberti Magni Opera Omnia* 27.2 (Cologne: Aschendorff, 2008) at various points in 402-457. Most important for the crafting of his epistemology is Albert's systematic misunderstanding of Averroes in which Albert asserts that the material intellect and the agent intellect are powers belonging individually and intrinsically to each human soul and are not separate intellectual substances. At 411.46-53 he cites Averroes regarding this: "Item, Averroes: 'Omnis intellectus in nobis existens habet duas actiones. Quarum una est de genere passionis, et est intelligere; alia de genere actionis, et est abstrahere eas a materia, quod nihil aliud est quam facere eas intellectas in actu postquam erant intellectae in potentia'. Cum igitur unum horum sit intellectus agens et alterum possibilis, uterque istorum intellectuum erit in nobis existens et non separata substantia". Aquinas, however, always held that Averroes taught a doctrine of two separate intellects, the Agent Intellect and the Material Intellect. Albert later changed his understanding to one similar to that of Aquinas. I will provide a detailed study of the epistemology of Albert in the *De homine* and its development out of sources from the Arabic tradition in another publication.

120. Mahoney (1994), 83-106; see 85.

of intellect and the meaning of the arguments and statements of Averroes. What has been seen here is that Averroes had found grounds for his understanding of the extrinsic transcendence and the formal immanence of intellect with respect to the human soul in works by Alexander and Themistius and also in Aristotle's *De Anima* itself. However, it is noteworthy that there is some evidence that Aquinas was aware of the proper understanding of this teaching on the part of Averroes. This is clear in his analysis of ultimate human happiness and beatitude in seeing God face-to-face in the afterlife found later in Book IV of his *Commentary on the Sentences* where he accepts the model of Averroes, which I have called "Aristotelian participation" above, as suitable for explicating this theological teaching central to Christian faith [121]. At *In 4 Sent.*, d. 49, q. 2, a. 1 Aquinas reasons that a proper model of understanding how God can be seen *per essentiam* or face-to-face is that of Alexander (as explicated by Averroes) and Averroes. He writes regarding the mode by which this takes place that on their account

> it is the separate substance itself which is conjoined to our intellect as form, so that it is what is understood and that by which it is understood. And whatever is the case for other separate substances, nevertheless, we must accept that mode in the vision of God in his essence, because, by whatever other form our intellect is informed, it cannot be brought through that to the divine essence [122].

In the context of the discussion of whether angels see God in his essence in his *De Veritate* Aquinas repeats this interpretation of the position of Averroes and Alexander found in Book IV of the *Commentary on the Sentences* but only ascribes it to Averroes. He writes,

> How a separate essence can be joined to the intellect as form the Commentator shows as follows in Book 3 of his commentary on the *De Anima*: whenever two things one of which is more perfect than the other are received into something able to receive [them], the proportion of the more perfect to the less perfect is as the proportion of form to what it is able to perfect, as light is the perfection of color when both are received in a transparent [medium]. For this reason since the created intellect which is

121. Regarding this, see TORRELL (1997), 43-68; reprinted in TORRELL (2000), 177-197. Also see BRENET (2006), 329. Also see ERMATINGER (1973), 91-115. I intend to provide a detailed study of *In 4 Sent.,* d. 49, q. 2, a. 1 and Aquinas's confrontation and use of sourses from the Arabic tradition in another publication.

122. AQUINAS, *In 4 Sent* d. 49, q. 2, a. 1, sol. This version is taken from a provisional text provided to me by Dr. Adriano Oliva, O.P., of the *Commissio Leonina*.

> present in a created substance is more imperfect than the divine essence existing in it, the divine essence is compared in a certain way as form in relation to that which is understood [123].

This is in the context of the supernatural epistemology of beatitude. As we find it here in *In 2 Sent. d. 17, q. 2, a. 1*, Aquinas is dealing with natural epistemology. In later works Aquinas consistently rejects the teachings of Averroes as well as those of Theophrastus, Themistius, Alexander, Avicenna, and Ibn Bâjjah, and crafts his own philosophical doctrine of intellectual understanding of the human soul. For that doctrine Aquinas holds for agent and material/possible intellect to be intrinsic powers of each human soul. And what are apprehended by the rational soul by means of these powers are not separate intelligibles in act in the separate Agent Intellect or in the separate Material Intellect but rather intelligible species which are themselves representations and *rationes* of the natures of things in the world. What we have seen here is that in Book 2 of his *Commentary on the Sentences* Aquinas first establishes his own teachings on intellect and intelligibles in critical dialogue with philosophers of the Arabic/Islamic and Greek traditions in ways that would continue to inform the development of all his later thinking on human soul and intellect [124].

123. AQUINAS, *Quaestiones disputatae de veritate*, q. 8, a. 1, 218.208-234: "Qualiter autem essentia separata possit coniungi intellectui ut forma, sic ostendit Commentator in III De anima: quandocumque in aliquo receptibili recipiuntur duo quorum unum est altero perfectius, proportio perfectioris ad minus perfectum est sicut proportio formae ad suum perfectibile, sicut lux est perfectio coloris cum ambo recipiuntur in diaphano; et ideo cum intellectus creatus, qui inest substantiae creatae, sit imperfectior divina essentia in eo existente, comparabitur divina essentia ad illum intellectum quodam modo ut forma. Et huius exemplum aliquale in naturalibus inveniri potest: res enim per se subsistens non potest esse alicuius materiae forrna si in ea aliquid de materia inveniatur, sicut lapis non potest esse alicuius materiae forma; sed res per se subsistens quae materia caret, potest esse forma materiae sicut de anima patet. Et similiter quodam modo essentia divina, quae est actus purus, quamvis habeat –esse omnino distinctum ab intellectu, efficitur tamen ei ut forma in intelligendo; et ideo dicit Magister in II dist. II Sententiarum quod unio corporis ad animam rationalem est quoddam exemplum beatae unionis rationalis spiritus ad Deum". As J.-B. Brenet points out in an article forthcoming in *Arabic Sciences and Philosophy*, reference to Averroes regarding this teaching disappears with the *Summa contra gentiles* where in an early autograph version Aquinas mentioned Averroes but in the final distributed text omitted mention of Averroes.

124. I would like to extend my sincere thanks to the conference participants for their valuable comments and discussion of the issues presented in this paper.

Bibliography

Sources

ALEXANDER OF APHRODISIAS (1887), *De Anima Liber Cum Mantissa*, Commentaria in Aristotelem Graeca, Suppl. II, pt. 1, ed. Ivo Bruns, Typis et Impensis Georgii Reimer, Berlin, 84.24-85.5.

AL-FĀRĀBĪ (1929), *De Intellectu,* in Etienne Gilson, "Les sources greco-arabes de l'augustinisme avicennisant", in *Archive d'histoire doctrinale et litteraire du moyen age* 4, 4-149.

ALFARABI (1983), *Risalah fī al-ʿaql*, ed. Maurice Bouyges, S.J., Dar el-Machreq Sarl, Beyrouth.

ANSELM (2000), *Cur Deus Homo*, in *Complete Philosophical and Theological Treatises*, J. Hopkins and H. Richardson, tr., Minneapolis.

AQUINO, S. Thomae (1929), *Scriptum super libros Sententiarum magistri Petri Lombardi episcopi Parisiensis*, vol. 1, ed. P. Mandonnet, P. Lethielleux, Parisiis.

– (1953), *Summa theologiae,* Commissio Piana, Ottawa.

– (1996), *Quaestiones Disputatae De Anima,* ed. B.-C. Bazán, Commissio Leonina / Éditions du Cerf, Rome / Paris.

AQUINO, Sancti Thomae de (1976), *De unitate intellectus*, in *Opera omnia* 43, Editori de San Tommaso, Rome.

– (1984), *Sententia de anima,* in *Opera omnia* XLV, 1, ed. R. A. Gauthier, Commissio Leonina / Librairie philosophique J. Vrin, Rome/Paris, 230-31.

AVERROES (1950), *Talkhīṣ Kitāb al-Nafs,* A. F. El-Ahwani, ed., Cairo.

– (1953), *De Anima: Averrois Cordubensis Commentarium Magnum in Aristotelis De Anima Libros*, ed. F. S. Crawford Cambridge.

– (1985), *Epitome de Anima*, S. Gómez, Nogales, ed., Consejo Superior de Investigaciones Científicas, Madrid, 1985.

– (1987), *La psicología de Averroes. Comentario al libro sobre el alma de Aristóteles,* S. Gómez, Nogales, trans., Universidad Nacional de Educación a Distancia, Madrid, 1987.

– (2000 sqq), *Scriptum super Sententiis.* Ed. R. Busa, E. Alarcón (Corpus Thomisticum: ad Universitatis Studiorum Navarrensis aedes, Pompaelone <http://www.corpusthomisticum.org/snp0000.html and ff.>

– (2002), *Middle Commentary on Aristotle's De Anima. A Critical Edition of the Arabic Text with English Translation, Notes and Introduction*, ed. and tr. A. L. Ivry, Provo, Utah.

– (2009) *Averroes of Cordoba's Long Commentary on the De anima of Aristotle,* tr. and intro. Richard C. Taylor, Thérèse-Anne Druart, subeditor, Yale University Press, New Haven.

AVICENNA (1959), *Kitâb al-Šifā', al-Nafs*, Part 5, in *Avicenna's De Anima (Arabic Text) Being the Psychological Part of the Kitâb al-Shifâ'*, ed. F. Rahman Oxford University Press, London.

–(1968), *Avicenna Latinus. Liber De Anima seu Sextus de Naturalibus IV-V*, ed. S. Van Riet, ed. (Louvain: Editions Orientalistes and Brill, Louvain/Leiden, vol. 2.
–(1972), *Avicenna Latinus. Liber De Anima seu Sextus de Naturalibus I-II-III*, ed. S. Van Riet, Peeters and Brill, Louvain/Leiden.
–(1977), *Avicenna Latinus. Liber de Philosophia Prima sive Scientia Divine, I-IV*, ed. S. Van Riet, Peeters/Brill, Louvain/Leiden.
–(2005), *The Metaphysics of The Healing*, tr. Michael E. Marmura, Brigham Young University Press, Provo, Utah.
IBN SĪNĀ (1960), *al-Šifā'. Al-Ilāhiyyāt*, vol. 1, eds. G. C. Anawati and Sa'id Zayed, Organisation Générale des Imprimeries Gouvernementales, Cairo.
THEMISTIUS (1899), *In Libros Aristotelis De Anima Paraphrasis*, ed. R. Heinze, Berlin, G. Reimeri, Commentaria in Aristotelem Graeca, 5.3.
–(1973), *An Arabic Translation of Themistius' Commentary on Aristotle's De Anima*, ed. M. C. Lyons, Columbia, South Carolina and Oxford, England.
–(1996), *On Aristotle's On the Soul*, tr. Robert B. Todd, Cornell University Press, Ithaca, N.Y.

Studies

BRENET, J.-B. (2006), "Vision béatifique et séparation de l'intellect au début du XIVe siècle. Pour Averroès ou contre Thomas d'Aquin ?" in *Les sectatores Averrois. Noétique et cosmologie aux XIIIe–XIVe siècles*, eds. Dragos Calma and Emanuele Coccia, *Freiburger Zeitschrift für Philosophie und Theologie*, 531/2, 310-342.
BURNYEAT, Miles (2008), *Aristotle's Divine Intellect*, Marquette University Press, Milwaukee.
D'ANCONA, Cristina (2008), "Degrees of Abstraction in Avicenna. How to Combine Aristotle's *De Anima* and the *Enneads*", in *Theories of Perception in Medieval and Early Modern Philosophy*, eds. Simo Knuuttila and Pekka Kärkkäinen, Springer, Dordrecht, 45-71.
–(2008), "Man's Conjunction with Intellect: A Neoplatonic Source of Western Muslim Philosophy", in *Proceedings of the Israel Academy of Sciences and Humanities* VIII 4, 57-89.
DAVIDSON, Herbert A. (1992), *Alfarabi, Avicenna, and Averroes, on Intellect. Their Cosmologies, Theories of the Active Intellect, and Theories of Human Intellect*, Oxford University Press, Oxford.
ERMATINGER, Charles J. (1973), "Giles of Rome and Anthony of Parma in an Anonymous Question on the Intellect", in *Manuscripta* 17, 91-115.
GEOFFROY, M. (2007), "Averroès sur l'intellect comme cause agent et cause formelle et la question de la 'jonction'-1", in *Averroès et les averroïsmes juif et latin. Actes du colloque tenu à Paris, 16-18 juin 2005*, éd. J.-B-Brenet, Brepols, Turnhout, 77-110.

– (2002), "La tradition arabe du d'Alexandre d'Aphrodise et les origines de la théorie farabienne des quatre degrés de l'intellect" in *Aristotele e Alessandro di Afrodisia nella Tradizione Araba*, eds. C. D'Ancona and G. Serra, Subsidia Mediaevalia Patavina 3, Padova, 191-231.

GILSON, Étienne (1926-7), "Pourquoi Saint Thomas a critiqué Saint Augustin", in *Archives D'Histoire Doctrinale et Littéraire du Moyen Age* 1, 5-127.

GUTAS, Dimitri (1988), "Avicenna and the Aristotelian Tradition", Brill, Leiden.

– (2001), "Intuition and Thinking: The Evolving Structure of Avicenna's Epistemology", in Robert Wisnovsky (ed.), *Aspects of Avicenna*, Markus Wiener Publishers, Princeton (reprinted from *Princeton Papers: Interdisciplinary Journal of Middle Eastern Studies*, Vol. IX), 1-38.

HASSE, Dag Nikolaus (2001), "Avicenna on Abstraction", in Wisnovsky (ed.), *Aspects of Avicenna*, Markus Wiener Publishers, Princeton (reprinted from *Princeton Papers: Interdisciplinary Journal of Middle Eastern Studies*, Vol. IX), 39-72.

HYMAN, Arthur tr. (1973), *Philosophy in the Middle Ages*, 2nd ed., ed. Arthur Hyman and James J. Walsh, Hackett Publishing Co., Indianapolis.

IVRY, Alfred L. (2008), "Arabic and Islamic Psychology and Philosophy of Mind", in *The Stanford Encyclopedia of Philosophy*, ed. Edward N. Zalta, URL = http://plato.stanford.edu/entries/arabic-islamic-mind/. First published April 18.

LIBERA, Alain de (2004), *L'Unité de l'intellect. Commentaire du* De unitate intellectus contra averroistas *de Thomas d'Aquin,* Librairie Philosophique J. Vrin, Paris, 497-8.

MAHONEY, Edward P. (1994), "Aquinas's Critique of Averroes's Doctrine of the Unity of the Intellect", in *Thomas Aquinas and His Legacy*, ed. David M. Gallagher, The Catholic University of America Press, Washington, D.C., 83-106.

MCGINNIS, Jon (2007), "Making Abstraction Less Abstract: The Logical, Psychological, and Metaphysical Dimensions of Avicenna's Theory of Abstraction", in *Proceedings of the American Catholic Philosophical Association* 80, 169-183.

PUIG MONTADA, Josep (2007), "Ibn Bajja", in *The Stanford Encyclopedia of Philosophy*, ed. Edward N. Zalta, URL = http://plato.stanford.edu/entries/ibn-bajja/. First published September 28.

REISMAN, David C. (2005), "Al- Fārābī and the philosophical curriculum", in *The Cambridge Companion to Arabic Philosophy*, eds. Peter Adamson and Richard C. Taylor, Cambridge University Press, Cambridge, 52-71.

TARRANT, Harold (1993), *Thrasyllan Platonism*, Cornell University Press, Ithaca and London, 108-147.

TAYLOR, Richard C. (1998), "Personal Immortality in Averroes' Mature Philosophical Psychology", *Documenti e Studi sulla Traduzione Filosofica Medievale* 9 (1998), 87-110.

– (1999), "Remarks on Cogitatio in Averroes' *Commentarium Magnum in Aristotelis De Anima Libros*", in *Averroes and the Aristotelian Tradition: Sources, Constitution and Reception of the Philosophy of Ibn Rushd (1126-1198)*, eds. Jan A. Aertsen and Gerhard Endress, Brill, Leiden, 217-255.

– (2000), "Cogitatio, Cogitativus and Cogitare: Remarks on the Cogitative Power in Averroes", in *L'élaboration du vocabulaire philosophique au Moyen Âge*, éd. J. Hamesse et C. Steel, Brepols, Turnhout, 111-146.

– (2005), "The Agent Intellect as 'form for us' and Averroes' Critique of al-Fārābī" in *Topicos* 29, 29-51. Reprint with corrections in *Proceedings of the Society for Medieval Logic and Metaphysics* 5, 18-32: http://www.fordham.edu/gsas/phil/klima/SMLM/PSMLM5/PSMLM5.pdf.

– (2006), "Abstraction in al-Fārābī", in *Proceedings of the American Catholic Philosophical Association* 80, 151-168.

– (2007), "Intelligibles in act in Averroes", in *Averroès et les averroïsmes juif et latin. Actes du colloque tenu à Paris, 16-18 juin 2005*, éd. J.-B. Brenet, Turnhout, Brepols, 111-140.

– (2009), "Intellect as Intrinsic Formal Cause in the Soul according to Aquinas and Averroes", in *The Afterlife of the Platonic Soul: Reflection on Platonic Psychology in the Monotheistic Religions*, eds. John Dillon and Maha El-Kaisy Friemuth, Brill, Leiden, 187-220.

– (forthcoming), "Themistius and the Development of Averroes' Noetics", in *Soul and Mind. Medieval Perspectives on Aristotle's De Anima,* (Philosophes Médiévaux LII), eds. J.-M. Counet and R. Friedman, Peeters Publisher, Leuven.

THERY, G. (1926), *De intellectu* in "Autour du décret de 1210: II. Alexandre d'Aphrodise. Aperçu sur l'influence de sa noétique", in *Bibliothèque thomiste* 7, Kain, Belgium, 3-120.

THIJSSEN, J.M.H.H. (1996), "Master Amalric and the Amalricians: Inquisitorial Procedure and the Suppression of Heresy at the University of Paris", *Speculum* 71, 43-65.

TORRELL, J,-P., O.P. (1997), "La vision de Dieu 'per essentiam' selon Saint Thomas d'Aquin", in *View and Vision in the Middle Ages – Micrologus. Nature. Science and Medieval Soceties*, V, Edizioni SISMEL-Il Galluzzo, Florence, 43-68; reprinted in *Recherches Thomasiennes. Études revues et augmentées*, Vrin, Paris, 2000, 177-197.

VALLAT, Ph. (2004), Farabi et l'École d'Alexandrie. Des prémisses de la connaissance à la philosophie politique, Paris, Vrin.

WISNOVSKY, Robert (2003), *Avicenna's Metaphysics in Context*, Cornell University Press, Ithaca, NY.

– (2005), "Avicenna and the Avicennian Tradition", in *The Cambridge Companion to Arabic Philosophy*, eds. Peter Adamson and Richard C. Taylor, Cambridge University Press, Cambridge, 92-136.

AVICENNA'S METAPHYSICS AND DUNS SCOTUS' *QUAESTIONES SUPER SECUNDUM ET TERTIUM DE ANIMA*

Thérèse-Anne DRUART
(The Catholic University of America)

That Avicenna influenced Duns Scotus is well-known, but this general statement needs some qualifications and precisions [1]. First, the *Avicenna Latinus*, that is to say the text Duns Scotus used, and the Arabic text of Ibn Sīnā cannot simply be equated: at times there are philosophically important discrepancies between the Arabic text and its medieval Latin translation. I am, therefore, deliberately speaking of Avicenna's influence on Duns Scotus rather than Ibn Sīnā's influence on the Subtle Doctor, reserving the name Ibn Sīnā for the author of the Arabic text [2]. Second, a serious study of Avicenna's influence on specific texts of Duns Scotus requires critical editions of both Avicenna's and Duns Scotus' texts. Already in 1926 Etienne Gilson had pleaded for a critical edition of the *Avicenna Latinus*, but the first volume only came out in 1968 and the last one in 2006 [3]. As for Duns Scotus's works the edition is still in progress, but many now are available, including the text I am interested in, the *Quaestiones super secundum et tertium De anima*, which was recently edited by my colleague Timothy B. Noone and his team [4]. The *Metaphysics* of the *Avicenna Latinus* plays an important philosophical role in *quaestio* 16, whether we

1. For a listing of some studies on this topic, see DRUART (2010), 13-28.

2. For an instance of a major textual and philosophical discrepancy between Ibn Sīnā's text and the *Avicenna Latinus*, see DRUART (2010).

3. GILSON (1927), 596; for the *Metaphysics*, see AVICENNA LATINUS, *Liber De philosophia prima*, ed. S. Van Riet.

4. DUNS SCOTI, *Quaestiones super secundum et tertium De anima*, ed. C. Bazán, K. Emery, R. Green, T. Noone, R. Plevano & A. Traver.

understand the more universal prior to the less universal, and *quaestio*, 21, whether being is the first object of our intellect [5]. Both these texts take very seriously Avicenna's doctrine of the primary notions developed mainly in *Metaphysics* I, 5 and I, 2, as well as his conception of metaphysics in I, 3 [6]. Recently Jan A. Aertsen published an interesting paper on Avicenna's doctrine of primary notions as presented in the *Avicenna Latinus* and its impact on medieval philosophy in which he argues that medieval authors and their doctrine of the transcendentals did transform Avicenna's views. Among the medieval authors he includes Duns Scotus but does not refer to the *Quaestiones super secundum et tertium De anima* [7]. In other texts, such as *Ordinatio* I, dist. 3 and dist. 8 and *Collatio* 24, Duns Scotus discusses the issue of the primary notions imprinted in the mind, determining in which sense such notions, which are the most universal, are prior to less universal ones and linking his claim that being is the first primary notion to his own famous doctrine of the univocity of being [8]. It is clear that Duns Scotus is not interested in presenting an exegesis of Avicenna's texts or even in commenting on them. His approach is much more selective and creative. As the text of the *Quaestiones super secundum et tertium De anima* has been little studied and also was not considered by Aertsen, I shall focus on it. We will begin with *quaestio* 21 as it presents the bulk of Duns Scotus' appropriation of Avicenna's doctrine of the primary notions to ground his own univocity of being and then move to *quaestio* 16, which gives further precision about the meaning of this primacy.

I. *Quaestio* 21: Whether being is the first object of our intellect

Of course, we all know the claim *primum in intellectu cadit ens* and we all also know that Duns Scotus argues that being is the first object of our

5. Duns Scoti, *Quaestiones super secundum et tertium De anima*, 145-55: "Utrum magis universale prius intelligatur a nobis quam minus universale", and 207-225: "Utrum ens sit objectum primum intellectus nostri".

6. For a translation of Ibn Sīnā's Arabic text see Avicenna, *The Metaphysics of The Healing*, trans. M. E. Marmura, or Avicenna, *Libro della guarigione*, trans. A. Bertolacci. For a commentary on the Arabic text of I, 5, see Marmura (2005), 149-69.

7. Aertsen (2008), 21-42.

8. A French translation with commentary of most of these texts can be found in Duns Scot, *Sur la connaissance de Dieu et l'univocité de l'étant*, trans., notes & commentaire O. Boulnois (Épiméthée).

intellect but we may wonder how much Duns Scotus makes use of this famous Avicennan thesis and how he transforms it for his own purpose.

1. Whether the first object is God – as Averroes contends – or being

Scotus twice raises this issue in this question. First, at the very beginning of the question he presents the following third and last objection based on Averroes's position:

> As some [things] are to being, so are they to being understood and known, following Aristotle's *Metaphysics* II. Therefore, that which is the first being, is the first intelligible, but God is the first being, as He is his own essence, whereas other beings are by participation, and as He is the cause of existence for the other beings, therefore, He and not common being is the first intelligible for our intellect [9].

Notice that Duns Scotus has substituted the typical scholastic language of "ens commune" or "common being" to Avicenna's "ens" or "being". After stating this objection to the Averroean position the Subtle Doctor then moves to the *contra* and immediately refers to Avicenna who maintains that "one" and "being" are first impressed on *our* intellect and, therefore, are its first object. Notice that here "one" precedes "being". Avicenna, on the other hand, in the famous passage of the *Metaphysics* of the *Ŝifā* I, 5, focuses on "being" and "res" or "thing". As Thomas clearly understood in his deduction of the transcendentals in *De veritate*, q. 1, a. 1 [10], and as Wisnovsky and I argued, Avicenna's careful presentation of how "being" and "thing" are concomitant, i.e. distinct but with the same extension, and, therefore, necessarily implying each other, grounds the real distinction between essence and existence [11]. This distinction combined with the disjunctive modal concepts of "possible", "necessary", and "impossible", underpins his proof for the existence of God. Duns Scotus,

9. DUNS SCOTI, *Quaestiones super secundum et tertium De anima*, 208, 3: "Item, sicut aliqua se habent ad esse, sic ad intelligi vel cognosci, ex II *Metaphysicae*. Quod igitur est primum ens, est primum intelligibile; sed Deus est primum ens, quia est per suam essentiam – alia per participationem – et est aliis causa essendi; igitur est primum intelligibile intellectus nostri, non igitur ens commune". For the *Quaestiones* we indicate first the page and then the paragraph number).

10. AERTSEN (2002), 149, points that in its second deduction of the transcendentals in q. 21, a. 1 of this text Thomas ignores "res".

11. WISNOVSKY (2000), 181-221 and DRUART (2001), 125-42. On the history of "res" among the scholastics, see AERTSEN (2002), 139-56.

on the other hand, is not interested in the real distinction but rather in the univocity of "being" and in fact, though he explores various meanings of "res" in *Quodlibet* 3, he never mentions it in any systematic account of the doctrine of the transcendentals, despites its importance for his conception of metaphysics [12]. So we are not surprised to see that in the passage we are discussing the Subtle Doctor drops "res" or "thing", whereas he makes use of the disjunctive modal concepts in his various versions of his proof for the existence of God, even if this topic is not dealt within the texts we are considering. I would like to argue that this dropping of "res" is deliberate, as Aertsen, I think, would contend, since in *Lectura* I, dist. 3, pars 1, q. 1-2, he refers more accurately to the text "being and thing are first imprinted in the soul by a first impression" [13].

Let us now return to our *contra* in which Scotus tells us that the primary concepts are "unum" and "ens", which are presented as on the same level, though later on we will see that for both Avicenna and Scotus "being" has a primacy over "one", as "one" will turn up to be simply one of the proper accidents or passions of being, the so-called scholastic transcendentals. Though the first *contra* directly referred to Avicenna as an authority, the second does not and simply uses reason. Reason, says, Scotus, can show that the first object that grounds our understanding of other beings is "common being", as it is essentially predicated of all that is *per se* understood, whereas, pace Averroes, God cannot be so predicated [14].

But let us move on and rush to the end of the *quaestio* where we find the reply to our original objection.

> *Per se* cognoscibility follows *entitas*, but not in respect to each intellect or whatever state, but only in respect to this intellect, which can know being according to its total community and such an intellect is God. From this truly follows that the divine essence is the first object of God's intellect as

12. DUNS SCOTUS, *The Quodlibetal Questions*, eds. F. Alluntis & A. B. Wolter, 3, 10-11, 62.

13. AVICENNA LATINUS, *Liber de philosophia prima sive scientia divina*, 31, 2-3: "Ens et res sunt quae primo imprimuntur in anima prima impressione", DUNS SCOTI, *Quaestiones super secundum et tertium De anima*, 255, 81: "Res et ens et necesse talia sunt quod statim imprimuntur in anima prima impressione", I am most grateful to my colleague Timothy B. Noone for this reference.

14. DUNS SCOTI, *Quaestiones super secundum et tertium De anima*, 208, 5: "Illud est primum obiectum intellectus nostri sub cuius ratione alia intelliguntur; sed ens in communi est huiusmodi, quia predicatur essentialiter de omnibus per se intellectis, non autem Deus".

He is the first being, but it is not necessary that God be the first object of *our* intellect [15].

Duns Scotus systematically distinguishes the first object of *our* intellect, while we are "on the way" or wayfarers from that of God or of those who already enjoy the beatific vision. To my knowledge Avicenna never made such a distinction.

The second passage, in which the Subtle Doctor raises the question of whether the first object of *our* intellect, at least as long as we are wayfarers, is being or God, presents indirect proofs of the adequation of being to the intellect under the two modes of adequation, i.e., virtually (*secundum virtutem*) or according to predication. This indirect argumentation involves a process of elimination of three of the four possible candidates for primary concept, that is, "true", "God", "substance", and "being".

True is another accident or passion of being and is eliminated by reference to the preceding *quaestio*, i.e., 20, which argued that "true" cannot be the first object of our intellect.

Scotus also eliminates God as adequate according to predication since the first *contra*, as we have seen, has already shown that God cannot be predicated of all intelligibles in a *per se* predication. God is also not adequate *secundum virtutem*, which is defined as "that which *per se* itself alone can move the intellect to know itself and others" [16]. God cannot be such an adequate object for *our* intellect as "God" does not move the intellect to first know Him and from Him all other beings. God cannot do so according to his simple and quidditative concept because such concept would immediately beatify and beatification cannot be attained by those who still are wayfarers. Neither can an abstractive concept of God do the job, since such concept would be abstracted from creatures and so would not be primary. The concept of God, therefore, gets eliminated as inadequate both according to predication and *secundum virtutem*.

15. DUNS SCOTI, *Quaestiones super secundum et tertium De anima*, 225, 40: "Ad aliud dicendum quod cognoscibilitas secundum se sequitur entitatem, non autem respectu cuiuscumque intellectus vel pro quocumque statu, sed tantum respectu illius intellectus qui potest cognoscere ens secundum suam totam communitatem, et hoc est Deus. Unde bene sequitur quod essentia divina est primum obiectum intellectus sui, cum sit primum ens; non autem oportet quod sit primum obiectum intellectus nostri".

16. DUNS SCOTI, *Quaestiones super secundum et tertium De anima*, 209, 6: "Illud autem dicitur obiectum adaequatum potentiae adaequatione secundum virtutem, quod per se ipsum solum potest movere intellectum ad notitiam sui et aliorum".

Finally, Scotus eliminates substance, the main predicament – we will return to this – and concludes that in this life natural knowing must rest on "common being".

Though in *Metaphysics* I, 2 Avicenna rejects the view that God is the subject of first philosophy as metaphysics proves the existence of God and no discipline proves the existence of its own subject matter, he never raises the question whether God could be a primary concept. Consideration of Avicenna's influence taking into account *Metaphysics* I, 5, which treats of the primary concepts, has yielded rather negative results. Yes, Scotus adopts Avicenna's basic thesis that being is the primary notion but abandons *res* as concomitant of being and eliminates three possible candidates Avicenna had not considered: 1. God, rejected on grounds that are not Avicennan; 2. True, cursorily dismissed, even if it is a passion or property of being – we shall return to this notion of passion or proper accident; and 3. substance, the main predicament, eliminated as predicaments are "quasi species of being" and, therefore, subordinated to being. We need now to turn to this Avicennan distinction between the "quasi species" and "quasi properties" of being as Scotus makes ample use of this distinction and its terminology.

2. Being and its quasi species and quasi properties

In his detailed analysis of Avicenna's reception of Aristotle's *Metaphysics* Amos Bertolacci focuses part II, ch. 5, on metaphysics as the science of being and its species and properties, a theme explored by Avicenna in I, 2 [17]. And on this topic the *Avicenna Latinus* faithfully follows Ibn Sīnā. The species of being are none other than the ten predicaments or categories, which only comprise created beings. As being is no genus, they are called "quasi" species as they are not derived by means of some addition to being that could be likened to a specific difference. As for the "quasi" proper accidents, properties, or passions of being, they are the attributes of being, such as one and multiple, potency and act, universal and particular, possible and necessary [18]. All the

17. BERTOLACCI (2006), 149-211: Avicenna's Reworking of the Structure of the *Metaphysics*: Metaphysics as the Discipline Dealing with the Species, the Properties and the Principles of "Existent".

18. AVICENNA LATINUS, *Liber de philosophia prima sive scientia divina*, 12, 30-31 & 13, 36-39 & 42-44: "Igitur ostensum est tibi ex his omnibus quod ens, inquantum est ens, est commune omnibus his […] Ideo primum subiectum huius scientiae est ens, inquantum est ens; et ea quae inquirit sunt consequentia ens, in quantum est ens, sine condicione. Quorum quaedam sunt ei quasi species, ut substantia, quantitas et qualitas […]. Et ex his quaedam sunt

examples Avicenna gives here for these "quasi proper accidents" are disjunctives rather than Aristotle's convertible attributes such as one or true.

Duns Scotus uses this "division" of being in quasi proper accidents and quasi species as well as its terminology as soon as he moves from the indirect to the direct proofs for the primacy of being. He begins with an examination of quasi accidents, i.e., "true" and "good".

> That which is first by adequation *secundum virtutem* in relation to a power is its first object; but being in comparison to true and good is first by adequation *secundum virtutem* in relation to *our* intellect [19].

The Subtle Doctor proves the minor in the following way: "being is subject in relation to true and good, which are passions of being, according to Avicenna and the philosopher in *Metaphysics*, 4" [20]. Notice that Duns Scotus without further ado equates the views of Avicenna and Aristotle, while Bertolacci carefully distinguishes between the views of Ibn Sīnā and those of Aristotle. Notice too that in I, 2 Avicenna's examples for quasi accidents of being are disjunctive ones, such as one and multiple, but that, while adhering to the terminology of quasi properties, Duns Scotus has moved to proper accidents that singly have the same extension as being and, therefore, are not disjunctive. So he has substituted some of the first concepts talked about in I, 5, to the disjunctive ones enumerated in I, 2. Such non-disjunctive accidents gave rise to the scholastic doctrine of the transcendentals and can more easily be equated to Aristotle's attributes of being, which are convertible in as far as they have the same extension.

Duns Scotus adds to the terminology as he also calls the quasi properties "passions" of being, a term present in the *Auctoritates Aristotelis*, but not found in the *Avicenna Latinus* [21]. Yet, later on he shows he is aware of this change in terminology, while explaining that there is no conversion in predications *per se*. So though two terms refer to the same thing or subject and have the same extension, one is not predicated *per se* of

ei quasi accidentalia propria, sicut unum et multum, potentia et effectus, universale et particulare, possibile et necesse".

19. DUNS SCOTI, *Quaestiones super secundum et tertium De anima*, 12, 14: "Illud quod est primum adaequatione secundum virtutem respectu potentiae est primum obiectum eius; sed ens in comparatione ad verum et bonum est primum adaequatione secundum virtutem respectu intellectus nostri".

20. DUNS SCOTI, *Quaestiones super secundum et tertium De anima*, 212, 14: "Ens est subiectum respectu veri et boni, quae sunt passiones entis, secundum Avicennam et Philosophum IV *Metaphysicae*".

21. See, n. 9 by the editors of the *Quaestiones*.

the other[22]. "This – says Duns Scotus – fits my view, that is to say, that 'one' as distinct from being expresses some accident through a passion of being – taking the term accident in a broad sense as Avicenna does for all that is outside of the essential *ratio* of something"[23]. Avicenna's use of a broad sense of accident explains why these passions of being are "quasi" accidents. He even goes so far as to defend Avicenna's usage against some criticism by Averroes in his Commentary on the *Metaphysics*, IV, com. 3. He then concludes that, therefore, "it is clear that being in relation to one, true, and good, which are its passions, is the first object of *our* intellect by a primacy of adequation *secundum virtutem* as subject in relation to its proper passions"[24].

Having taken care of the adequation *secundum virtutem*, we need to deal with the adequation of being according to predication in relation to its passions. True and good can be predicated of being and share the same extension, but not the converse, as a subject cannot be predicated of its passions and we can now understand why in the indirect proofs proceeding by elimination "true" a passion of being was so easily dismissed.

Further examining the primacy of being according to predication, Duns Scotus comes closer to argue for the univocity of being:

> That [being] be also the first object in relation to its inferiors, that is to say God and creatures, by a primacy of predication I shall show. It requires, as was said, that such an object be predicated essentially and *per se* of all intelligibles and, therefore, univocally by some univocity. But being is of this sort[25].

22. Duns Scotus contrary to Aristotle and Avicenna distinguishes two types of convertibility: 1. an extensional convertibility and in this sense being and its quasi passions are convertible since they enjoy the same maximal extension; and 2. an essential convertibility that requires essential identity and in that sense being and its quasi passions are not convertible. On these two types of convertibility, see AERTSEN (2008), 39. Notice that this distinction is foreign to Avicenna.

23. DUNS SCOTI, *Quaestiones super secundum et tertium De anima*, 214, 20: "Et hoc concordat proposito nostro, scilicet quod unum prout distinguitur ab ente dicit aliquod accidens per passionem entis – accipiendo large accidens cum Avicenna pro omni eo quod est extra rationem essentialem alicuius".

24. DUNS SCOTI, *Quaestiones super secundum et tertium De anima*, 214, 20: "Sic igitur patet quod ens respectu unius, veri et boni, quae sunt eius passiones, est primum obiectum intellectus primitate adaequationis secundum virtutem sicut subiectum respectu suae propriae passionis".

25. DUNS SCOTI, *Quaestiones super secundum et tertium De anima*, 214-15, 21: "Sed quod sit etiam obiectum respectu suorum inferiorum, scilicet Dei et creaturae, primitate praedicationis, ostendo: quia ad hoc requiritur, ut dictum est, quod tale obiectum praedicetur

According to Scotus, Aristotle's intention in *Metaphysics* II, is to claim that "fire is the hottest [thing], because it is the univocal cause of heat in other things" [26]. And so he asserts:

> Therefore, since God is the cause of created being and is said to be most being, it must be the case that being be said univocally of God and creature. This is what Avicenna says in his *Metaphysics*, i.e., that the concept of being is common to all the predicaments, which are its quasi species [27].

If the concept of being is said univocally of God and creatures, the more so will it be said univocally of substance and accidents, since the predicaments apply only to creatures.

But let us look now at Avicenna's own wording: "Therefore, we have shown to you from all these that being, in so far as it is being, is common to all these" [28]. Avicenna does not explain what he means by "common" and never hints that this commonality implies univocity, but Duns Scotus reads univocity in commonality and, therefore, we know why substance, the main predicament, had to be eliminated from the candidates for primary concept. Later on, he will indeed argue that common being is said univocally of both substance and accident and we will return to this topic.

Now Duns Scotus wishes to show by reason, what he had just accepted on the authority of Avicenna, at least as he reads him, i.e., the claim that common being, being predicated of the ten predicaments in common, implies that it is univocal. Those wishing to maintain that common being is equivocal or analogical hold that the concept of being pertains to God essentially but to others only by participation. So Duns Scotus denies that being pertains to God essentially for, if it were the case that this concept be proper to God, then by this very concept God could be distinguished from everything else, and so by means of such a concept of God we would be able to distinguish Him from creatures, but this is false. By means of "common being" we know God but only in a confused manner, i.e., only in

essentialiteer et per se de omnibus intelligibilibus, et per consequens univoce aliqua univocatione; sed ens est huius modi".

26. DUNS SCOTI, *Quaestiones super secundum et tertium De anima*, 215, 21: "Unumquodque est maxime tale inter alia quod est causa quod alia sunt talia univoce, ut ignis est calidissimus, quia est causa univoca caloris in aliis".

27. DUNS SCOTI, *Quaestiones super secundum et tertium De anima*, 215-16, 21: "Cum igitur Deus sit causa entitatis creaturae et dicatur maxime ens, oportet quod ens dicatur de Deo et creatura univoce; et hoc est quod dicit Avicenna in *Metaphysica* sua, quod conceptus entis est communis omnibus praedicamentis, quae sunt quasi eius species".

28. AVICENNA LATINUS, *Liber de philosophia prima sive scientia divina*, 12, 30-31: "Igitur ostensum est [...] quod ens, in quantum est ens, est commune omnibus his [...]".

so far as He and others share in this concept, which subsequently divides into finite and infinite[29]. *Quaestio* 16 will give us more information about how "common being" considered solely in itself and without addition of any specification yields knowledge of other beings only in a confused manner, since as such it is more universal than any of them.

Avicenna's project of a study of being qua being and its quasi properties or passions and its quasi species allows Duns Scotus to articulate the primacy of being both *secundum virtutem* and according to predication over its quasi proper accidents, such as one, true, and good, and over its quasi species or ten predicaments. Avicenna's consideration of the ten predicaments as quasi species opens for Duns Scotus a way to the univocity of being first at the level of the predicaments and beyond this at the level of infinite and finite being. Such univocity of being that Duns Scotus so generously and creatively attributes to Avicenna implies also that common being yields only a confused knowledge of God, even though it is a very important concept since it grounds the whole metaphysical enterprise.

Avicenna focuses his metaphysics on being and its quasi accidents and quasi species but rests much of it, except for his distinction between essence and existence and its use of one or unity, on the disjunctive accidents. Duns Scotus uses this approach but gives it a twist, or should I say, "colors" it, as his adoption of these quasi species or predicaments and his emphasis on the non-disjunctive quasi accidents of being leads him to his own emphasis on the univocity of being. As Scotus insists on natural knowledge for the wayfarers, he introduces the theme of univocity in claiming that it was somehow discovered by Avicenna himself through his reflections on the quasi species of being. Whether or not Avicenna would favor the univocity of being may be dubious since he never tackles this issue, but we need to examine how Duns Scotus overtly defends the univocity of being, which follows his defense of its primacy. Common being may be a concept that alone yields only confused knowledge of other beings but one thing is clear about it, at least for Duns Scotus, and that is its univocity. But exactly what is meant by this univocity will be explained further on.

3. The Univocity of Being

Duns Scotus first argues for the univocity of being among the predicaments and particularly between substance and accidents and then

29. DUNS SCOTI, *Quaestiones super secundum et tertium De anima*, 216, 22.

will clarify further what exactly is meant by the univocity of being. For him being is univocal logically speaking, though it is not so naturally or metaphysically speaking[30]. Recall that substance was one of the four original candidates for primary concepts. If there were no univocity of being for substance and accidents, we would not even have a concept of substance as we would have neither a quidditative nor an abstractive concept of substance. We do not have a proper, quidditative, intuitive concept of substance as substance as such is not accessible to the senses, except indirectly through its accidents, and, if substance were a primary notion, we also could not have such a concept by abstraction since then it would not be primary. Therefore, there must be a concept of substance by abstraction that is common to both substance and accidents and there is no such concept other than the concept of being. It follows that wayfarers do not know substance intuitively as they have no direct sensory access to it and must first discover common being that can be divided into what exist *per se* and what exists in another[31]. Notice here that the disjunctive attributes come back on the scene. This argument reminds us of one of those used to show that the concept of God is not adequate *secundum virtutem*, since we must first discover being and then see that it can be divided into finite and infinite. In the same way we first abstract the concept of being and only later on inquire whether it is such as to inhere in another and so be an accident or whether it is subsisting, and, therefore, a substance. Duns Scotus concludes that we know substance only confusedly.

Duns Scotus also offers another argument of the same type, which contrasts a sure concept with a dubious one. We can be sure that something is a being but doubt whether that something is a substance or an accident. Therefore, the concepts of substance and accident are distinct from one another and from the concept of being. Yet common being is common to substance and accidents and so we are back to Avicenna's quasi species of being[32].

Duns Scotus then presents four objections to his own position that are variations on a common theme. Someone may object that being is no genus and so can only be said equivocally or analogically of substance and

30. See the last line of the conclusion of this section: DUNS SCOTI, *Quaestiones super secundum et tertium De anima*, 224, 37: "Tamen, hoc non obstante, potest ab omnibus istis entibus abstrahi unus communis conceptus significatus nomine entis, qui est univocus logice loquendo, licet non naturaliter vel metaphysice loquendo".

31. DUNS SCOTI, *Quaestiones super secundum et tertium De anima*, 218, 25.

32. DUNS SCOTI, *Quaestiones super secundum et tertium De anima*, 219-20, 26.

accident. Rejecting the Avicennan notion of quasi species for the predicaments, this objector argues that, if common being were univocal and, therefore, undetermined, one could not explain how it gets "specified", so to speak, into substance and accident[33]. To which Scotus replies that Aristotle was not speaking determinately when claiming that being is no genus. He then asserts that common being is predicated univocally only logically speaking, though it is predicated metaphysically or naturally of the ten predicaments and so some being, substance, is more important than some others, the accidents[34].

Duns Scotus needs, therefore, to make of being a "quasi genus" and he does so, resting his case on the authority of Avicenna and Averroes[35]. Notice that to my knowledge Avicenna does not use the expression quasi genus. In order to explain the quasi specifications of this quasi genus, the Subtle Doctor distinguishes the way genera are specified from the way species fall into individuals. Genera are specified by addition and such addition must be either being or non-being, both impossible in the case of common being, which, therefore, can only be a quasi genus, which divides, so to speak, in quasi individuals, as species divides into individuals, which all agree in species but differ in number. They share the same concept but differ in number only and so nothing is added to the concept of the species and the specification or determination is by number rather than by addition[36]. In the same way the quasi genus being divides immediately in finite and infinite, a set of disjunctive properties.

33. DUNS SCOTI, *Quaestiones super secundum et tertium De anima*, 220-21, 29-32.

34. DUNS SCOTI, *Quaestiones super secundum et tertium De anima*, 222, 33: "Ad dictum autem Porphyrii dicendum quod, licet fuerit logicus, multa tamen dixit non logice, specialiter illud quod pertinet ad praedicamenta; ens enim, prout praedicatur de decem praedicamentis metaphysice vel naturaliter, non dicit unum conceptum – nec genus est naturale eorum nec metaphysicum; est tamen univocum, logice loquendo".

35. DUNS SCOTI, *Quaestiones super secundum et tertium De anima*, 223, 36: "Vel potest dici, sustinendo, quod sit genus, vel quasi genus secundum Avicennam et Averroëm".

36. DUNS SCOTI, *Quaestiones super secundum et tertium De anima*, 223, 35: "Ad aliud de descensu indeterminati in inferiora, dicendum quod duplex est indeterminatum. Unum quod descendit in inferiora per aliquid additum, et tale dicit totum quod inferius, tamen per modum partis determinabilis ut genus, vel per modum partis determinantis ut differentia – et tale non est ipsum ens. Aliud est commune indeterminatum, quod dicit totum illud quod inferiora per modum totius nec expectat terminari per aliud – ut species respectu individuorum, duo enim individua se totis in specie conveniunt et numero differunt –, et tale commune non descendit in inferiora per aliquid additum. Sic autem ens est commune ad Deum et decem praedicamenta, ad substantiam et accidens; nihil enim est in substantia et accidente quod non sit ens, et ideo statim seipso sine addito est substantia vel accidens".

Duns Scotus now can happily reach his conclusion grounded in the adoption of Avicenna's view of the predicaments as quasi species of beings and of being as a quasi genus, as well as of the quasi proper accidents of being:

> Therefore, all beings have an attribution to the first being, who is God, or the created beings to substance. Yet, despite this attribution, one can from all these beings abstract one common concept signified by the name being, which is univocal, when speaking as a logician, but not so, when speaking as a natural philosopher or a metaphysician [37].

So the logical or conceptual univocity of being does not prevent an ordered ontological dependence of all beings from God and of accidents from substance.

II. *QUAESTIO* 16: WHETHER WE UNDERSTAND THE MORE UNIVERSAL PRIOR TO THE LESS UNIVERSAL

In order to explain how the primacy of being, the most universal concept, must be understood, Duns Scotus examines whether a more universal concept is understood prior to a less universal. Here once again, as one would expect, he calls on Avicenna who holds that being is a primary notion and most universal. Yet, at first glance the text is confusing as Duns Scotus uses the Persian's text both in the objections and in defense of his own views. Such confusion dissipates once we realize that "whether we understand the more universal prior to the less universal" is a very ambiguous statement. First, there are no less than three kinds of priority: 1. in time, i.e., in the order of discovery (*generatione*); 2. in adequation (*adaequatione*); and 3. in perfection (*perfectione*) [38]. Only these first two types of priority are relevant to the examination of the primary notions [39].

37. DUNS SCOTI, *Quaestiones super secundum et tertium De anima*, 224, 37: "Omnia entia habent attributionem ad ens primum, quod est Deus, vel entia creata ad substantiam; tamen, hoc non obstante, potest ab omnibus istis entibus abstrahi unus communis conceptus significatus nomine entis, qui est univocus logice loquendo, licet non naturaliter vel metaphysice loquendo".

38. DUNS SCOTI, *Quaestiones super secundum et tertium De anima*, 147, 8: "Dicendum quod aliquid dicitur prius alio tripliciter, scilicet generatione, perfectione et adaequatione".

39. The priority of perfection is subdivided into absolute priority, for which the prior is the concept of God (152-3, 20-22), which we saw cannot be a primary notion, and into perfection according to proportion to its object and that is what more strongly moves the

Second, we need to make a distinction about cognition as what does apply to its object may not apply to the way one knows it. So a distinct object of cognition, such as human being, may be known confusedly or indistinctly, if we only know it generically, i.e., simply under the unspecified genus animal or if we only know of it that it is an animal, or if we only know it by its name. In the same way, what is confused as undetermined in relation to its species, such as animal in relation to human being, may be distinctly known in itself, if we know its genus and specific difference and so understand that it is a living being endowed with sensory perception.

Once the various senses of priority are distinguished and the distinction between the status of a cognitive object and its apprehension is established, Duns Scotus can determine which kind of priority the most universal notions enjoy. In the temporal order of discovery, the most universal is last to be known rather than prior, but in the order of distinct cognition the most universal, though last discovered, is first and by means of this distinctive cognition the metaphysician acquires the ability to know more distinctly than their practitioners the principles of other sciences, which are less universal. So let us examine how the Subtle Doctor uses Avicenna in his objections.

1. How Avicenna is used in the objections

If we assume that the priority of the more universal is merely temporal, as all the objections do, one can understand why Duns Scotus, who rejects this type of priority, opposes Avicenna who is cited as authority in two of them, i.e., the second and the fourth, which is the last one. The first states that "what is first imprinted in the intellect is first understood; but according to Avicenna 'being and one, which are most universal, are imprinted in the intellect prior' to the other intelligible objects" [40]. For us now it is clear that Avicenna is not referring to a temporal priority of the most universal, as some may have wrongly thought, but rather to a priority in distinct cognition, which in fact is temporally posterior in the order of discovery. Duns Scotus' reply to this objection emphasizes this view in

sense, since this is what more strongly moves the intellect, whereas primary notions do not move the senses (153-54, 23-24).

40. DUNS SCOTI, *Quaestiones super secundum et tertium De anima*, 145, 2: "Quod primo intellectui imprimitur, prius intelligitur; sed secundum Avicennam 'ens et unum, quae sunt maxime universalia, prius intellectui imprimuntur' quam obiecta alia intelligibilia".

clarifying Avicenna's statement [41]. The primary notions are more distinctly known as they cannot be grasped confusedly through their genus only as they have no genus and being is the quasi ultimate genus. Notice that once again both in the objection and the reply Duns Scotus drops "res" from Avicenna's famous list of primary notions at the beginning of I, 5.

The second objection in a subtle way prepares the reader for Duns Scotus's solution to the issue by means of the proper distinctions, even if the reference to Avicenna is somewhat puzzling. It maintains that:

> according to Avicenna in his *Metaphysics* and Aristotle's *Physics*, I, what is first understood is that of which a singular was first object of sense perception but a singular of what is more universal was object of sense perception prior to a less universal [42].

To identify which specific line in Avicenna Duns Scotus has in mind is difficult since no such claim can be found in the *Metaphysics*, though it might refer to the first book of *Natural philosophy* [43]. Besides, the statement itself is rather obscure, but kindly the Subtle Doctor gives us two examples, the first being taken from Aristotle's *Physics*, I, 1: children first call "father" all male human beings. The second given by Duns Scotus himself explains that "from a distance we perceive that something is material before perceiving that it is something alive and we perceive that it is something alive before perceiving that it is a human being" [44]. Notice that this example is one of progressive distinctness in sense perception. Just as to sense perception a sensory object perceived from a great distance may appeared very indistinct but becomes more and more distinct the closer the perceiver comes to it, so to intellection an unspecified genus or more extensive universal in relation to its remote species can progressively lead to more distinctness in relation to its species, if more and more specific differences are added. Distinct cognition of being leads to distinct cognition of Porphyry's tree.

41. DUNS SCOTI, *Quaestiones super secundum et tertium De anima*, 154, 26: "Ad aliud dicendum quod ens et unum prius imprimuntur intellectui quoad eorum cognitionem distinctam qua alia; et ideo illa cognitione sunt nobis prius nota, quia non possunt notificari priora; et hoc concede".

42. DUNS SCOTI, *Quaestiones super secundum et tertium De anima*, 146, 4: "Illud prius intelligitur cuius singulare prius sentitur; sed singulare magis universalis prius sentitur quam minus universalis, secundum Avicennam in *Metaphysica* sua, et secundum Philosophum I *Physicorum* [...]".

43. See the kind note of the editors of the text, n. 6, p. 146.

44. DUNS SCOTI, *Quaestiones super secundum et tertium De anima*, 146, 4: "Prius a remotis sentitur aliquid esse corpus quam animatum et prius animatum quam homo".

The reply emphasizes this parallel between sensory perception and intellectual cognition. A singular, i.e., an object of perception, adequate to the sense, grants to the intellect apprehension of its "species specialissima" and, therefore, distinct cognition. But, when there is no proper adequation to the sense, then, the intellect does not know it distinctly, as it only knows it by a species of greater extension and, therefore, more universal [45].

In the first of these two objections and its reply Duns Scotus does not so much opposes Avicenna's view on the priority of the primary notions than a misinterpretation of this priority. The second does call on Avicenna, maybe by mistake, but relies heavily on Aristotle and gives occasion to Duns Scotus to highlight his own conception while protecting it by means of a well-known authority.

2. The less universal is prior in the order of discovery, but is known less distinctly

The Subtle Doctor offers as one of his arguments that both Avicenna (I, 3) and Averroes (*Metaphysics* VI, com. 3) claim that "metaphysics is the ultimate science in the order of study", since we know and conceive of the principles of the other sciences before those of metaphysics and the principles of these other sciences are less universal than those of metaphysics, which treats of the most universal notions [46]. This statement, of course, contradicts the false interpretation of the beginning of I, 5, offered in the first of the two objections invoking Avicenna and Duns Scotus will tackle the apparent contradiction in the next section which deals with the order of distinct cognition.

45. DUNS SCOTI, *Quaestiones super secundum et tertium De anima*, 155, 28: "Ad ultimum dicendum quod quando aliquod singulare est praesens sensui secundum debitam proportionem, tunc intellectus primo apprehendit speciem specialissimam eius; sed quando non est proportionatum sensui, ita quod non possit ipsum distincte cognoscere, tunc intellectus primo apprehendit speciem eius proximiorem quam potest".

46. DUNS SCOTI, *Quaestiones super secundum et tertium De anima*, 148-49, 12: "Secundum Avicennam et Commentatorem VI *Metaphysicae*, 'metaphysica est ultima scientia in ordine doctrinae'; igitur principia aliarum scientiarum prius tempore a nobis cognoscuntur et concipiuntur quam metaphysicae; principia autem aliarum scientiarum sunt minus universalia, quia metaphysica est de universalissimis".

3. The more universal is prior in the order of distinct cognition

Duns Scotus first spells out what distinct cognition means:

> That is more distinctly known that enters the definition of something else [and] by means of which this other is distinctly known. Being, which is the most universal, enters the definition of anything since the concept of being is included in any concept. Being itself has only a distinct concept as it does not have anything in which it could be confusedly and indistinctly known [47].

In this last sentence Scotus does not express himself precisely. For him the content of the concept of being is confused or undetermined as maximally extended, but such content once grasped is distinctly known. Here Scotus speaking loosely applies to the content of the concept what in fact pertains to its mode of being known. As being is ultimate and a quasi genus, as we saw earlier, it does not itself have a genus in which it could be confusedly known.

Having presented his own view, Duns Scotus looks for support in Avicenna I, 3, which he reads in the following manner: "metaphysics is prior in the order of distinct cognition, though it is more universal" [48]. Such reading is a notable elaboration of what Avicenna says: "Just as this science [metaphysics] is principle of existence for those sciences, so it is principle of certitude in cognition for those sciences" [49]. Duns Scotus has not hesitated to equate Avicenna's "certitude" with being distinctly known as he has carefully defined it. Such interpretation reads much more than the text warrants but provides an authority – the only one he invokes – for his own understanding of "distinct cognition" that he has just spelled out.

Having called once again on Avicenna's authority, Duns Scotus now argues that his exegesis of Avicenna does not contradict the Persian philosopher's position explained in the previous section that metaphysics is posterior in the order of study. The order of study or discovery proceeds

47. DUNS SCOTI, *Quaestiones super secundum et tertium De anima*, 150-51, 18: "Prius distincte illud cognoscitur quod intrat definitionem alterius, per quod aliud distincte cognoscitur; sed ens quod est universalissimum intrat definitionem omnium, cum conceptus entis includatur in conceptu cuiuslibet – ipsum autem non habet conceptum nisi distinctum, quia non habet in quo possit confuse et indistincte cognosci".

48. DUNS SCOTI, *Quaestiones super secundum et tertium De anima*, 151, 19: "Metaphysica est prior secundum ordinem cognoscendi distincte, quae tamen est universalius".

49. AVICENNA LATINUS, *Liber de philosophia prima sive scientia divina*, 20, ll. 74-76: "Sicut enim haec scientia est principium essendi illas, sic scientia huius est principium certitudinis sciendi illas".

from confused to distinct cognition. The principles of the other sciences are known before those of metaphysics but only by means of a confused concept of their terms. They need metaphysics to reach proper definition of their own principles and their properties (*passiones*) [50]. So metaphysics of which the principles are distinctly known is posterior in the order of study. Yet, once we have acquired the science of metaphysics and return to an examination of the other sciences, we more distinctly know their principles thanks to our metaphysical knowledge. So any species is first indistinctly known – if we only know what its name refers to or know it in its undetermined universal. Once this universal is distinctly known and we add to it the specific difference, then, we can return to an examination of this species and distinctly know it [51].

These last two sections of *quaestio* 16 make much use of some general statements of Avicenna to allow Duns Scotus to find some authority for his own specific view on the utmost priority of metaphysics over all other sciences in the order of distinct knowledge, while affirming its utmost posteriority in the order of study and discovery. The *quaestio* itself was worded in very general terms so that it apply to whatever is more universal in relation to anything less universal, but Duns Scotus characteristically focuses his attention on an understanding of metaphysics and its relation to the other sciences and its necessity for their proper understanding. It is only at the end of the second section that Duns Scotus, the metaphysician, remembers that the question was more general and applies his answer to the priority of any universal over anything less universal.

50. DUNS SCOTI, *Quaestiones super secundum et tertium De anima*, 151, 19: "Nec tamen contradicit sibi Avicenna dicens quod est postrema ordine doctrinae, quia ordine doctrinae procedimus a cognitione confusa ad distinctam. Modo ita est quod principia aliarum scientiarum prius ordine doctrinae sunt nobis nota ex confuso conceptu terminorum, sicut geometer ex confuso conceptu lineae et puncti procedit ad cognoscendum eius definitionem et passionem".

51. DUNS SCOTI, *Quaestiones super secundum et tertium De anima*, 151-52, 19: "Et ideo metaphysica est posterior ordine doctrinae, cuius tamen principia sunt distincte cognita. Sed scientia metaphysicae acquisita, revertendo ad alias scientias, magis distincte cognoscuntur earum principia, scientia metaphysicae prius distincte cognita; et sic est prius ordine distinctae cognitionis. Sic in proposito: species prius cognoscitur indistinct – scilicet in cognoscendo quid dicitur per nomen vel in suo universali; sed cognito universali distincte, tunc per eius divisionem et contractionem – per additionem differentiae – fit reditus ad cognoscendum speciem distincte".

CONCLUSION

For Duns Scotus Avicenna is the great authority for his own new conception of metaphysics[52] and for the univocity of being, but Avicenna pays a price for this honor. The beginning of his *Metaphysics* is overtly much referred to, but quotations are truncated so that the primary notion "res" so important in Avicenna is discretely dropped out, as we saw in both questions. Some statements are elaborated and creatively read: in question 21 Duns Scotus goes as far as to attribute to Avicenna his doctrine of the univocity of being and in question 16 his conception of being as distinctly known. Undoubtedly the Subtle Doctor adopted some of Avicenna's positions and even some of the terminology of the *Avicenna Latinus*, such as the division of being into quasi properties and quasi species, but reworked them for his own purposes in "coloring" them. At times this coloring is no simple delicate retouching, but rather a serious remodeling.

BIBLIOGRAPHY

Sources

AVICENNA (2005), *The Metaphysics of* The Healing, A parallel English-Arabic text, trans., intro. & notes M.E. Marmura, ed. 2 (Islamic Translation Series), Provo, Utah.

– (2007), *Libro della guarigione. Le cose divine*, trans. intro. & notes A. Bertolacci, Turin.

AVICENNALATINUS (1977-1983), *Liber de philosophia prima sive scientia divina*, 3 vols, ed. S. Van Riet, Louvain/Louvain-la-Neuve.

DUNS SCOTI, Ioannis (2006), *Quaestiones super secundum et tertium De anima*, ed. C. Bazán, K. Emery, R. Green, T. Noone, R. Plevano & A. Traver, Washington, D.C., 2006.

DUNS SCOT, Jean (1988), *Sur la connaissance de Dieu et l'univocité de l'étant*, trans. notes & commentary O. Boulnois (Épiméthée), Paris.

DUNS SCOTUS, John (1975), *God and Creatures: The Quodlibetal Questions*, trans., intro., notes & glossary F. Alluntis & A.B. Wolter, Princeton.

Studies

AERTSEN, J. A. (2008), "Avicenna's Doctrine of the Primary Notions and its Impact on Medieval Philosophy", in A. Akasoy & W. Raven (ed.), *Islamic Thought in*

52. On this see for instance, HONNEFELDER (2007).

the Middle Ages: Studies in Text, Transmission and Translation, in Honour of Hans Daiber (Islamic Philosophy, Theology and Science 75), Leiden, 21-42.

– (2002), " 'Res' as Transcendental: Its Introduction and Significance", in G. Federici Vescovini (ed.), *Le Problème des Transcendentaux du* XIV*e au* XVII*e siècle*, Paris, 139-56.

BERTOLACCI, A. (2006) *The Reception of Aristotle's* Metaphysics *in Avicenna's* Kitâb al-Shifâ'*: A Millestone of Western Metaphysical Thought* (Islamic Philosophy, Theology and Science 63), Leiden.

DRUART, Th.-A. (2010), "Ibn Sīnā (Avicenna) and Duns Scotus", in M. B. Ingham and O. Bychkov (eds.), *John Duns Scotus, Philosopher*, Münster, 13-28.

– (2001), "*Shay'* or *Res* as Concomitant of 'Being' in Avicenna", in *Documenti e Studi* 12, 125-42.

GILSON, E. (1927), "L'étude des philosophies arabes et son rôle dans l'interprétation de la scolastique", in E. S. Brightman (ed.), *Proceedings of the Sixth International Congress of Philosophy, Harvard University Cambridge, Massachussetts, United States of America, September 13-17, 1926*, Toronto, 592-96.

HONNEFELDER, L. (2007), "Metaphysik als *scientia transcendens*: Johannes Duns Scotus und der zweite Aufgang der Metaphysik", in R.H. Pich (ed.), *New Essays on Metaphysics as* Scientia transcendens, Louvain-la-Neuve, 1-19.

MARMURA, M. E. (2005), "Avicenna on Primary Concepts in the *Metaphysics* of his *al-Shifâ'*", in *Probing in Islamic Philosophy: Studies in the Philosophies of Ibn Sina, al-Ghazali and Other Major Muslim Thinkers*, Binghamton, N. Y., 149-69.

WISNOVSKY, R. (2000), "Notes on Avicenna's Concept of Thingness (*shay'iyyat*)", in *Arabic Sciences and Philosophy* 10, 181-221.

ALBERT THE GREAT ON PERCEPTION AND NON-CONCEPTUAL CONTENT

Jörg Alejandro TELLKAMP
(Universidad Autónoma Metropolitana, Mexico City)

I. INTRODUCTION

13th century accounts of perception seem to be a plain issue. Their purported moderate realism holds that the content of perception is, due to a causal link between material thing and perceiving subject, a reliable copy of the object perceived so that if an object *X* causes sensory stimuli in the organs, the experience of *X* is the consequence. Although the aim of this article is not to deny this claim, there is, however, much more to perception – even in medieval accounts – than this simple picture. In fact, when focusing not so much on the epistemological conditions of perception, e.g. what realism amounts to as opposed to skepticism, as on its psychology and physiological underpinnings, it becomes pretty obvious that authors like Albert the Great thought that not only human beings are able to perceive the material world in a complex and non-trivial, i.e. intentional way, but also higher animals [1].

Yet, while humans tend to categorize conceptually their perceptual access to the world, animals do not, despite the fact that their sensitive grasp of the external world is based on the same physiological and

1. KÖHLER (2001), 440-441 thinks that the comparison of animals and human beings constitutes, in particular in Albert the Great, a "key paradigm" for the explanation of what is properly human insofar as the human being is the noblest of animals (*homo animal nobilissimum*). For an historic account of animals in philosophical debates see SORABJI (1993).

psychological principles [2]. If those principles are fundamentally the same across different animal species and if they explain the occurrence of intentional knowledge of particular objects, the question can be raised as to whether the properly human prerogative of language must indeed be seen as a necessary condition for perception [3]. When examining different works of Albert the Great regarding the link between intentionality, perception and language it seems that language and the use of concepts is a necessary condition at best, but not a sufficient one. Hence, in Avicenna's famous example, the sheep grasps the wolf's dangerousness without the ability to express a thought about it; its reaction is based on instinct alone. However, Albert insists that this kind of intentional knowledge (seeing the wolf as dangerous) entails the object to be perceived from a certain cognitive point of view. In order to approach this topic, there are significant passages in his *Commentary on De anima* that help to understand that perception is not essentially conceptual and yet one has to recur to the language of logic in order to explain perceptual experience:

> An intention is called what signifies a thing individually or universally according to various degrees of abstraction. It does not give being neither to the sense power, when it is in it, nor to the intellect, when it is in it, but it produces a sign (*signum*) and knowledge (*notitia*) of the thing. Therefore the intention is not a part of the thing like the form, but it is the species of the knowledge of the whole thing, whence the intention, because it is abstracted from the whole and because it is a signification of the whole, is predicated of a thing (*de re praedicatur*). The intention of a colored thing, which is in the eye, yields knowledge of the whole thing in the same way as the intention, which resides in the imagination of a particular thing, which is not present [4].

In this passage the emphasis lies upon a distinction, Avicennian in origin, that in sensory processes we have to distinguish the mere stimulus, i.e. the apprehension of a form, from the sensory experience, namely the apprehension of an intention. What properly makes an experience the experience of a particular object is that it signifies the object. In putting sensory experience in terms of predication, it would seem obvious that only human beings qualify as subjects of such an experience. Yet Albert

2. SEARLE (2002), 64 maintains that the "neurobiological continuity" between animal species, including human beings, is a strong argument in favor of intentionality across species. If human beings already have perceptual intentionality, there would be no compelling reason to say that mice, dogs etc. do not display any intentionality at all.

3. See also SEARLE (2002), 65.

4. ALBERTUS MAGNUS, *De anima* II 3, 4 (Ed. Colon. 7, 1), 102, 28-42.

argues that also animals not only have a grasp of what an object means, they also can distinguish whether the experience is true or false:

> We say that [fantasy] is a power that composes images with intentions and intentions with images and intentions with intentions regarding a twofold purpose to be found in particular objects. The first purpose consists in a better (*maior*) knowledge of particular things, which can be had in the sensible soul. Its purpose is a thought that this is this and the other is other. This is the same regarding everything of which a thought can be expressed by the way of an affirmation or negation. The second purpose is an action (*opus*), which is intended on the basis of those particular objects; e.g., the action of rational beings is the purpose of an art. And since such knowledge overtly shows itself in many animals, given that we see that they choose things and almost reject others – the prerequisite for choice and rejection is a thought and judgment (*sententia et decretum*) – therefore many held that fantasy belongs to reason [5].

As fascinating as this quote is, it contains many problems. What does it mean to grasp the meaning of something without the mediation of language, given that Albert acknowledges that animals arrive at practical conclusions through thought and judgment? How is it possible to discern truth and falsehood without concepts? Is perceptual experience dependent on having concepts? When I see a chair, do I have to be in possession of the concept "chair" in order to have an experience of it? What happens with animal cognition? Does a dog have to have the concept of a bone in order to actually perceptually grasp and desire it? What does this mean for the human ability to express experiences? The question is, then, if the content of perception can be construed as having non-conceptual content, so that language becomes non-essential for having intentional experiences.

This article will consist of three parts. In the first, and in a dogmatic fashion, I will advance what non-conceptual content is. In a second step I will shortly outline the essential aspects of Albert's psychology and physiology of perception. In the final third part I will look into what it means for animals to perceive intentions. Here I wish to discuss two test cases: animal learning and inferential, desire-driven perception of animals. I will argue that Albert develops a theory of intentional knowledge that displays some of the features that commonly are ascribed to language possession, and yet he shows that it cannot be an essential part of such an experience.

5. ALBERTUS MAGNUS, *De anima* III 1, 3 (Ed. Colon. 7, 1), 168, 27-44.

II. WHAT IS NON-CONCEPTUAL CONTENT?

Before discussing Albert the Great's theory regarding concepts, intentionality and perception, it should be helpful to draw an outline of what non-conceptual content is, at least insofar as it helps explaining his stance on the nature of perception. By limiting non-conceptual content to perceptual experiences, I will exclude other forms of non-conceptual content, such as sub-personal content, certain states of consciousness, etc.

In contrast to non-conceptual content the meaning of *conceptual content* is that its semantic value can be determined [6]. Content can thus be conceptual in a metaphysical sense of knowing its essence. It can also be conceptual when someone is able recognize it in terms of its semantic value. It might also be conceptual, when it is descriptive in the sense of being able to locate or identify the content. These are some good reasons to think that perceptual content is conceptual, also because perceiving appears to involve beliefs or thoughts about something. Thus, seeing the cat on the mat involves believing that this is the case, which can best be understood in conceptual terms [7].

At first sight non-conceptual content seems just to be the negation of conceptual content, but the question is as to what that amounts to. There are, in fact, different ways to conceive of non-conceptual content [8]. For instance, content can be non-conceptual if it *cannot* be represented conceptually. An example for this would be having diffuse feelings. Content can also be non-conceptual if the subject does not grasp the concepts involved or if it does not or cannot exercise the concepts involved [9]. When talking about non-conceptual content, I will be concerned with what has been called "intentional psychology" [10]. In opposition to a conceptual account of content, which points at what something is or whether the content is true or false, perceptual states seem

6. GUNTHER (2003), 12.

7. MCDOWELL (2003), 75: "Experiences are impressions made by the world on our senses, products of receptivity; but those impressions themselves already have conceptual content". On a similar note see HAMLYN (1994), 139-153 and PEACOCKE (2001), 239-264.

8. See GUNTHER (2003), 14-17.

9. BERMÚDEZ (2003), 31 distinguishes four dimensions that have to be taken into account when talking about non-conceptual content: a metaphysical one (how it is possible and what is its vehicle), a semantic one (what is the semantics of nonlinguistic thought), an epistemological one (how can we identify such content) and an explanatory one. This last dimension is the one that helps elucidating how nonlinguistic creatures plan, make decisions and come to infer.

10. GUNTHER (2003), 15ff.

to encompass content that is not about "knowing what" it represents, but rather "knowing how" it applies to practical aspects involved in the representation. This means that the nonpropositional representation might include some form of reasoning on the basis of images, emotions, bodily skills, etc. [11]. It comprises "abilities and skills that allow one to modify and adjust oneself to the environment – as opposed to bodies of information that one acquires about the environment" [12].

Therefore the content of perception can be said to be true or false in the sense that it is successful or unsuccessful, but not that it is necessarily true or false in the sense of containing true or false propositions. Again, Avicenna's example of the sheep and the wolf helps to illustrate the point. While the sheep's grasp of the wolf leads to a certain action, since it is instinctively seen as dangerous, it does not require to have an opinion about the wolf so that it comes the entertain a thought like: "Wolves are dangerous and since this particular thing is a wolf, it is dangerous. Therefore I have to run".

If sheep and other animals are able to acquire knowledge of complex, intentional states of affairs without entertaining concepts about them, it is important to analyze what the grounds for such a claim are. The foundation for intentionality in Albert the Great's psychology is his theory of the inner senses, mainly fantasy, imagination and estimation.

III. FANTASY AND IMAGINATION

At the beginning of any account of the inner senses, which includes an elaborate psychology of faculties, we probably will find Avicenna, who is, of course, the main source for Albert. Since the question about non-conceptual content is psychological in nature, it would seem necessary to expand on his psychology of perception, which is to be found in his theory of the inner senses. For Albert the Great a description of the function of the inner senses has the purpose of explaining how sensible forms are acquired and how mental representations, i.e. intentions, of particular objects are formed. Those intentions, however, are not properly sensed, so that they do not directly belong to the causal explanation of perception.

11. BERMÚDEZ (2003), 36ss creatively uses this famous distinction of "knowing that" and "knowing how" introduced in 1949 in G. Ryle's *The Concept of Mind*.

12. *Ibid*.

It is in his theory of abstraction, of Avicennian inspiration, that we find the clues as to what it means to grasp something that is not properly sensed by the outer senses. That what is being perceived in such a way is represented either under a general aspect (e.g. to see the son of Dion requires to have a grasp of what "son" means) or from a practical point of view (e.g. to grasp that this animal is friendly or not). Albert declares that "this degree [of abstraction] comes closest to knowledge (*cognitio*) and it never is without estimation and gathering"[13]. The result is an *intentio*, which has a cognitive value as well as a practical one. *Intentio*, as opposed to *forma*, not only refers to different activities of the inner senses – fantasy and estimation conceive *intentiones*, while the imagination grasps *formae* – but it also emphasizes the increasing degrees of cognitive and practical complexity.

The difference between forms apprehended and intentions elicited is crucial[14]. Although Albert identifies forms basically with their ontological role in constituting composite substances, it would be mistaken to think that forms are inert from the cognitive point of view, because they constitute the precondition for the formation of intentions. Thus, the difference between apprehending sensible forms, which Albert calls *imagines*, and eliciting intentions accounts for the difference between imagination on the one side and fantasy and the estimative power on the other. This means that the inner senses are representational powers in that they lead to a comprehension of particular objects under different degrees of complexity (temporal, non-temporal, cognitive, practical, etc.).

At the level of basic impressions grasped by the imagination, Albert thinks that there is a causal link between the accidental forms of the material object and the sensible forms (*imagines*), which the imagination retains. This causal relationship is one reason why form and intention differ in cognitive complexity. Albert himself gives the most telling indication: intentions signify the material thing as a whole, while forms do not. Another hint as to the difference between form and intention has to do with Albert's recurrent affirmation that intentions are produced by fantasy and estimation, while a form *qua imago* is some sort of crude impression. This difference shows, from a cognitive point of view, that the active involvement of fantasy and estimation leads to a meaningful knowledge of those aspects of a thing that are not "visible", as opposed to those features

13. ALBERTUS MAGNUS, *De anima* II 3, 5 (Ed. Colon. 7, 1), 102, 8-10.
14. See note 4.

of a material object that cause an impression in the imagination. In all of this the influence of Avicenna cannot be overlooked.

Again, the distinction between form and intention is of capital importance, because the mere retention of forms or images hardly constitutes knowledge in the sense of having and reacting in a meaningful way to events and objects of the physical world. By distinguishing inner senses that operate based on forms or images and those that operate based on intentions, Albert echoes Avicenna's distinction that apprehension *ab intus* relates to forms as well as to intentions [15]. While the object of the imagination is an image or form of an object that not necessarily has to be present, he considers that the key faculty regarding intentions is fantasy and not, as in Avicenna, the estimative faculty. The core function of fantasy consists in composing and dividing forms by which true or false intentions are produced [16].

For Albert the estimative power is subordinate to the role of fantasy, and although it is a distinct faculty, it shares with fantasy the same organic localization [17]. Its function is, however, different in that it reaches out to the harmful or convenient aspects of desirable objects. Its activity is, in fact, the flip-side of fantasy's action, which grasps intentions under the aspect of truth or falsehood [18]. Like fantasy, the estimative faculty elicits intentions, which are not grasped by the external senses, but which point at an action regarding a material object. This action is the result of a judgment made by an animal or human being regarding the practical signification of the object grasped [19].

When taken in its narrow meaning, the estimative faculty follows fantasy [20]. Albert says: "The estimative faculty is nothing but the extension of fantasy into the practical" [21]. Hence the specific difference between

15. AVICENNA, *De anima* I 5, (Ed. van Riet, 85), 88-90.

16. ALBERTUS MAGNUS, *De homine* II 2, 3 (Ed. Colon. 27, 2), 291, 19-26: "Ad aliud dicendum quod maior subtili[t]atio spiritus animalis exigitur ad comparandum imagines apprehensas, ut ex eis eliciatur verum vel falsum, quam ad recipiendum imagines tantum. Et ideo quia phantasia talem facit comparationem, oportet quod ipsa habeat spiritum similem illi spiritui qui est in media cellula, qui subtilissimus est, et quoad hoc dicit Algazel quod sit in media cellula".

17. ALBERTUS MAGNUS, *De homine* II 3, 3 (Ed. Colon. 27, 2), 295, 70-71: "Dicendum quod aestimativa et phantasia operantur in eodem organo [...]".

18. ALBERTUS MAGNUS, *De homine* II 3, 2 (Ed. Colon. 27, 2), 295, 18-28.

19. AVICENNA, *De anima* I 5, ed. van Riet, 89, 49-53.

20. ALBERTUS MAGNUS, *De homine* II 3, 1 (Ed. Colon. 27, 2), 294, 8-15.

21. ALBERTUS MAGNUS, *De homine* II 3, 3 (Ed. Colon. 27, 2), 295, 71-72: "[...] Aestimativa enim nihil aliud est quam extensio phantasiae in praxim [...]".

fantasy and the estimative faculty consists in that the latter is not a cognitive power, but a predominantly practical one[22]. Its activity of composing and discerning or judging has to do with the fact that every animal by nature seeks at least to satisfy basics needs, such as providing for food and shelter[23]. This might also be the reason why Albert says that the estimative faculty "through movement imitates nature to a greater extent than the science or the art of the practical intellect"[24]. The sheep fleeing from the wolf does not require the ability to reflect upon the means and the end of its action; it just acts uniformly whenever it sees a wolf, because instinctively it knows how to react to the stimulus of something grey, fast etc.[25].

According to Albert, intentions not only signify the whole of a material thing under an aspect that is not sensed by the outer senses, they also are depicted as being either true or false. Importantly he thinks that this is what animal perception has in common with that of human beings. But by saying that animals have *intentiones* that are either true or false, Albert seems to endorse the view that they have thoughts or beliefs to which truth or falsehood apply. Yet this promising idea of perception understood as a thought or belief that can be true or false is not fully examined in Albert's *Commentary on De anima* or in his *De homine*. For this reason I will draw on his *De animalibus*, where he explores the relation animals have with structured stimuli, like verbal utterances; there he also reflects upon the ability that certain animals have to perform incomplete syllogisms, similar to enthymemes.

IV. Do animals think?

As we have seen, there is a rather complex faculty psychology behind the generation of perceptual content; this psychology is rooted in a speculative physiology of the brain. Yet the most important lesson to be drawn so far is that human beings and higher animals share not only the same organic

22. ALBERTUS MAGNUS, *De homine* II 3, 2 (Ed. Colon. 27, 2), 295, 26s.

23. ALBERTUS MAGNUS, *De anima* III 1, 2 (Ed. Colon. 7, 1), 167, 78-86.

24. ALBERTUS MAGNUS, *De homine* II 3, 2 (Ed. Colon. 27, 2), 295, 41-43: "[...] Aestimativa magis imitatur naturam in movendo quam scientiam et artem intellectus practici [...]".

25. ALBERTUS MAGNUS, *De homine* II 3, 2 (Ed. Colon. 27, 2), 295, 43-46: "Unde licet uno modo ovis accipiat inimicum in omni lupo, tamen non utitur inquisitione et consilio in modo fugiendi quemadmodum homo; sed omnis ovis fugit uno modo omnem lupum".

structure of their cognitive functions, they also form the same kind of intentional perceptions, which differ only in degrees of complexity, but not in essence. Having sense organs and having a brain that houses the inner senses is, for Albert, a fact of nature that can be found in a wide range of different species of animals, and in this respect there are several points that should be reminded:

1) Perception is organic in nature.

2) Perceptual content resembles belief in the sense that seeing something leads to a non-trivial, intentional relation with a sense object.

3) Perception is not linguistic, evidence for which lies in the fact that animal do perceive and behave coherently without having the capacity to utter verbally their desires.

The first point has already been established. The last two will be at the center of what remains of this article. Albert, in order to examine whether an animal's cognitive structure is sufficiently complex as to produce and grasp intentional content, asks himself if it is able to learn. This is a question that arises in the context of the distinction of what the criteria are to distinguish more perfect animals from those that are less perfect. An animal is more perfect than others, when it can learn something in a more or less structured way; it has to be *disciplinabile*. As referred to animals it seems that the notion of *disciplina* is slightly problematic, since this concept uses to refer mainly to the ability of acquiring the basics of theoretical science (*scientia contemplativa*), of productive skills (*artes mechanicas*) and of moral virtues (*virtutes morales*)[26]. An animal, however, can learn neither discipline. But then what does it mean that an animal is *disciplinabile*?

In the first place, it requires the participation of sight and hearing and also the presence of some sort of dispositional cognitive and appetitive

26. ALBERTUS MAGNUS, *De animalibus* XXI 1, 3, (Ed. Stadler, 1330s): "Sed cum homo habeat sensus disciplinales duos, visum videlicet et auditum sicut determinatum est in libro de Sensu et sensato, visus deservit inventioni disciplinae: et cum huius inventio non fiat nisi ratione conferente memorias et sensata, non est aliquod animal disciplinabile visu quia non habet facúltateme inventivae ex collatione sensibilium. Auditus autem sensus est disciplinabilis ex signis rerum et ex alio et ideo animalia quaedam possunt disciplinari per auditum et nulla per solum visum. Et ex hoc cognoscitur symia maioris esse facultatis Quam aliud animal quoniam disciplinam recipit per auditum et imitationem representativam operum per visum: quod non facit aliud animal nisi homo et pigmeus et symia. Et ideo patet quod ista tria animalia continuis descendunt gradibus".

background. At least primates – but Albert also includes pigmies – have to rely to a greater extent on the power of hearing than the power of sight, because it is through articulate sounds (*voces*) that they can distinguish and even compose meaningful utterances[27]. The same is true of quadrupeds, like dogs, because they too can grasp the meaning of an utterance insofar as it makes known a practical aspect (*forma operabilis*)[28]. I will expand on this topic below.

The difficulties to ascribe the acquisition of *disciplina* to animals from a conceptual point of view, however, seem to vanish considering the practical dimension of sensible knowledge. Although animal sensory experience has certain cognitive restrictions – animals know particulars only insofar as they are relevant in a practical context – they nevertheless are able to learn in a structured manner. Here Albert distinguishes two aspects of animal perception. (1) The first consists in the fact that some animals are able to at least passively react to verbal stimuli, such as orders; (2) secondly, and beyond this basic grasp of *voces*, there are a few animal species, like primates, with the capacity of inferential knowledge by means of the active use of quasi-rational capacities. I hope to show that, combining these two issues, it will become clear how Albert conceives of perceptual non-conceptual content. One way of doing so is by looking at what Albert thinks about the way some animals handle language.

Voces

A dog listens to its master's voice, but what does it in fact understand? When asked to fetch a stick or detect drugs, does it (1) understand the meaning of the words and (2) does it know what those objects are? It seems that both questions have to be answered negatively, but the general account of intentions and the physiological and psychological functioning of animal perception indicates that their grasp of the material world is non-trivial and that it resembles human perception in more than one respect. If animals do not have knowledge about *what* the objects known are, it seems that we have to ask whether their knowledge consists in *knowing how* to apply it.

According to Albert there are three ways of learning, which relate respectively to hearing, estimation and memory. (1) In the first place every animal can discern sounds (*sonorum iudicium*), insofar as it has the inner

27. See ALBERTUS MAGNUS, *De anima* II 3, 22 (Ed. Colon. 7, 1), 131, 8 ss. On primates, pigmies and humans see KÖHLER (2008), 419ss. *Cf.* also KÖHLER (2007), 146 ss.

28. ALBERTUS MAGNUS, *De animalibus* XXI 1, 4, (Ed. Stadler, 1333).

sensory faculty of the *sensus communis*. (2) Human beings hear and acquire *disciplina* "to the extent that by hearing voices are grasped, insofar as they are signs of concepts or passions (*signa conceptuum et passionum*) that exist in the soul of the one who expresses them" [29]. In this sense, says Albert, no irrational creature can express or understand voices. (3) Such an understanding would only be possible, "insofar as they [the names] refer to a thing signified by words" [30], and only if we take the names to signify properly in one of the two following ways: (a) names can signify the essence of theoretical things (*quiditates rerum contemplativae*) or (b) they can lead to the knowledge of a practical form (*forma operabile*) to which human or animal desire leads [31]. The fact that Albert mentions the *formae operabiles* is significant, because, as already shown, from forms we can reach intentions. That seems to be reason why a dog can move toward the deer, when hearing the sounds it makes. Thus:

> It is proper of sense perception, insofar as it is a faculty, that it denotes escape or desire or action conjoined with what belongs to fantasy and estimation. Therefore there are certain animals, quadrupeds as well as bipeds that perceive sounds as well as voices in this way. Most animals perceive voices insofar as they are an indication of the one who utters them (*indicia vocantis*), and they chase to or flee from it, like the sheep fleeing from the wolf, when it hears it, and following the shepherd, when it hears him [32].

Again, the distinction between hearing forms and grasping intentions is significant, because it enlightens what an animal is able to grasp when listening, even though it does not understand its conceptual content. This apparently means that animals only are able to understand words, insofar they, being signs, express a certain emotional state of the one who utters them. If this picture is accurate, Albert would seem to consider three ways in which an utterance can be a sign: it can be (i) a natural sign, (ii) a sign by convention and (iii) something in between. According to the first meaning, an utterance that signifies naturally would be like the barking of a dog, in the sense that it expresses anger [33]. Secondly, an utterance that signifies by convention refers to natural languages. But animals, such as dogs or

29. ALBERTUS MAGNUS, *De animalibus* XXI 1, 3, (Ed. Stadler, 1333).

30. ALBERTUS MAGNUS, *De animalibus* XXI 1, 3, (Ed. Stadler, 1333).

31. ALBERTUS MAGNUS, *De animalibus* XXI 1, 4, (Ed. Stadler, 1333): "[…] Alio modo prout in nominibus innotescit forma operabilis circa quam est aut effectus proferentis, aut res in quam est appetitus animalis, sicut canes ad voces vel sonos moventur cervorum".

32. ALBERTUS MAGNUS, *De animalibus* XXI 1, 4, (Ed. Stadler, 1333).

33. On the notion of *signus* and its relation to animals see ECO *et al.* (1989), 3-41.

primates, do not grasp the conceptual meaning of a linguistic expression and their comprehension of the natural meaning of a sound does not seem to be enough as to explain the complex cognitive contents they arrive at. The notion of *intentio* becomes unavoidable in order to explain precisely those cognitive states [34], and it accounts for an alternative way to explain how animals are able to understand linguistic utterances, despite the fact that they do not understand them conceptually. I hope to at least insinuate that this in-between way, i.e. between the conventionality of the sign and its natural dimension, would explain why animals do have a comprehension of complex state of affairs and of utterances, even though they do not, obviously, speak. Here the ability to learn (*disciplinabilitas*) is again pivotal. Says Albert:

> The manner by which the voices that lead to the knowledge of an emotion and of the will of the one who expresses the voice can be understood in two ways; one in a distinct (*distincte*), and another in an undetermined (*confuse*) manner. Some animals that judge distinctly the object of the will of the one who utters the voice are able to acquire *disciplina*. Those are many animals, and they reach it only through instruction and not by nature. Others, however, do not perceive what is willed, but they grasp a certain anger or joy about the will, and they flee from the one who calls or approaches them. But they are not able to acquire *disciplina*, unless in a very diminished way. This is how we see that dogs and other animals learn a lot [35].

In this respect, there is a close relationship between the psychological description of what happens when an utterance is heard and the physiological disposition the animal has to have.

> In animals the estimation is composed of the grasp of fantasy and the inclination of a desire, and it relates to it in the same way as *prohairesis* does in rational beings. And when this is done in a pure fashion and with good organs, then good judgments about the intentions of things are produced [36].

34. Recall the text quoted above; *cf.* ALBERTUS MAGNUS, *De anima* II 3, 4 (Ed. Colon. 7, 1), 102, 31-38: "Intentio autem vocatur id per quod significatur res individualiter vel universaliter secundum diversos gradus abstractionis; et haec non dat esse alicui nec sensui, quando est in ipso, nec etiam intellectui, quando est in illo, sed signum facit de re et notitiam. Et ideo intentio non est pars rei sicut forma, sed potius est species totius notitiae rei [...]".

35. ALBERTUS MAGNUS, *De animalibus* XXI 1, 4, (Ed. Stadler, 1333).

36. ALBERTUS MAGNUS, *De animalibus* XXI 1, 4, (Ed. Stadler, 1333).

It is central to emphasize that, according to Albert, the ability to acquire a structured set of contents falls into the realm of practical considerations. The dog learns to fear a stick, because it learns to relate the occurrence of a stick to an associated state of fear [37]. But in this case there does not seem to exist a necessary or natural relationship between the occurrence of a given object, the stick, and the cognitive and appetitive reaction to it. The stick is not a natural sign; and even less does it seem to be a conventional sign. The in-between meaning of "sign", neither natural nor by convention, suddenly becomes relevant again. And, again, the key concept that allows to untangle this issue is the concept of *intentio*. As we have seen, Albert thinks of *intentiones* as pointing at a complete, or almost complete sensitive knowledge of a particular thing, which he characterizes as a thought (*sententia*) or judgment (*decretum*). The content of such a thought is primarily practical in nature, since it resembles choice, such as when birds build nests or provide for food. This complex practical knowledge, however, is only to be found in animals that have a complete set of sensory faculties and dispositions [38].

37. ALBERTUS MAGNUS, *De animalibus* XXI 1, 4, (Ed. Stadler, 1334s): "Disciplinabilitas tamen animalium magis attenditur in recordatione quam in memoria, et praecipue secundum eam partem quae est recordativa intentionum. Cuius signum est quod animalia disciplinata ad ludos, ad nutus et sermons magistrorum suorum, percipient voluntatem eorum et faciunt ea quae sibi imperantur ad intentionem suorum magistrorum. Quod autem in auditu et recordatione potius apprehendat voluntatem et affectum quam conceptum magistrorum suorum, ex hoc significatur quod aliquando non faciunt ea ad quae disciplinata sunt nisi cum minis et blanditiis vel aliquod signo terroris aut blanditiei: propter quod operantur ad effectum proferentis significatum in voce, et non ad conceptum: et ideo articulationem vocis non apprehendunt et tamen recte perficiunt sibi imperata et moventur ex disciplina potius modo quo movet natura, quam modo quo movet apprehensa et concepta intentione rerum aliquarum: quia moveri ex huiusmodi concepto est rationis: moveri autem ex habitu in modum naturae movente est etiam cuiuslibet in artibus bruti sensibilis".

38. ALBERTUS MAGNUS, *De anima* III 1, 3 (Ed. Colon. 7, 1), 168, 27-55: "De phantasia post hoc determinantes dicimus ipsam esse potentiam componentem imagines cum intentionibus et intentiones cum imaginibus et imagines cum imaginibus et intentiones cum intentionibus ad duplicem finem, qui est in particularibus. Unus autem finis est cognitio particularium maior, quae in sensibili anima haberi potest, et illius finis est sententia de hoc, quod sit illud, et de alio, quod sit aliud; et sic de omni eo de quo sententia profertur per modum affirmationis vel negationis. Secundus autem finis est opus, quod intenditur ex huiusmodi particularibus, sicut opus in habentibus rationem est finis artis. Et quia talis cognitio in pluribus animalibus expresse apparet, eo quod videmus ea quaedam eligere et alia quaedam quasi refutare, ad electionem autem et refutationem praeexigitur sententiam et decretum, et ideo multi dixerunt, quod phantasia est aliquid rationis. Non autem est intentio nostra veram electionem esse animae sensibilis, sed aliquid simile electioni expresse videmus in quibusdam brutis, et in uno plus et in altero minus; nos etiam videmus ea per modum artis

Such animals have the inner sense of fantasy, which, as I have already mentioned, is the pivotal sensory faculty, because its function is to combine images and intentions in various ways. By doing so it merges what is characteristic of the imagination, that is, the retention of images, and the production of intentions, which is attributed to the estimative faculty.

This shift from imagination toward fantasy and estimation puts a strong emphasis on the thought-like structure of the knowledge of intentions. While Albert stresses in his early *De homine* that fantasy operates by composing and dividing images regarding truth and falsehood, he does not explain it terms of thoughts that can be true or false. Also, while in the earlier text he tends to reduce the explanation of fantasy's activity to the force of animal spirits [39], which are in constant flow, in the *Commentary on De anima* he explores quite extensively truth and falsehood associated with the knowledge of intentions. But what could it mean that an animal is able to grasp intentions that represent state of affaires truthfully or not? In a very basic sense, it seems that Albert thinks of true or false *intentiones* in such a way that they are either accurate or inaccurate from a practical point of view. By this token, speaking of truth or falsehood of perceptual content becomes meaningful when the content represents the conditions under which a desire or its opposite can be fulfilled: the sheep's perception of the wolf and the corresponding movement is true or accurate, when it actually flees from the wolf: it instinctively knows what to do when seeing a grey, wolf-shaped object.

Inferential capacities

At the center of Albert's elucidation of non-conceptual content in perception is the idea that we can account for its existence if the animal in question is able to display a practical competence regarding the object it perceives, be it through learning or through instinct. In this respect Albert insinuates that animal perception can be construed as some sort of belief or thought and that it can be either true or false. Although this belief does not essentially depend on language, Albert reflects upon the capacity certain

facere casas et providere cibum in longum tempus, cuiusmodi operum oportet esse principium potentiam aliquam animae sensibilis. Hoc autem esse non potest nisi illa virtus quae componit et dividit imagines et intentiones modo supra dicto. Haec etiam opera non in omnibus videmus in quibus est imaginatio et aestimatio, sed in quibusdam quae perfectiora sunt".

39. ALBERTUS MAGNUS, *De homine* II 2, 3 (Ed. Colon. 27, 2), 290, 68ss.

higher animals like primates have to execute quasi-logical processes. A very enlightening text regarding this aspect of animal cognition is Albert's *De animalibus* XXI 1, 4. In this particular passage he is mainly concerned with establishing the criteria that would allow to distinguish more perfect animals from those that are less perfect. In virtue of his rational powers the most perfect animal obviously is the human being. Less perfect are pigmies, then monkeys, afterwards quadrupeds, etc.

This hierarchy depends upon different criteria. The first consists in having or not having rational capacities. The second points at the ability of a non-linguistic creature to represent the material world in a meaningful, i.e., intentional way. This criterion, in turn, has ramifications. On the one hand, thinks Albert, can we ask whether an animal is able to grasp something in a meaningful way, on the other hand, whether it can actually produce meaningful content. As we have seen, the important point is that higher animals, primates as well as dogs or horses, see their world in terms of its practical meaning. Hence, if an animal can acquire knowledge, it will have to do so because it apprehends the end of a particular action[40]. Primates, however, seem to be able to go beyond this limitation grasping not only the complex, intentional content of an utterance, but they also reach their own conclusions given a certain amount of information.

> It seems that monkeys with their senses, imagination and memory, can above all other animals judge what is becoming and unbecoming. [...] In all this it is known that monkeys have a better estimation than other animals. But in all this it only moves through phantasms. Therefore, like other animals, it frequently errs, because [...] when fantasy is not conjoined with the intellect, error is frequent. Such animals do not perform a practical syllogism, but an incomplete argumentation. And just as in theoretical issues enthymeme and example are incomplete argumentations – its incompleteness is removed by reducing it to a syllogism – so do those animals generate an impulse toward an activity due to the fantasy and estimation of something practical and desirable and desire[41].

According to Albert not even higher animals can think in the sense of using abstract notions and concepts. But maybe this might not be necessary, since it would be futile to reject the idea of animals having

40. ALBERTUS MAGNUS, *De animalibus* XXI 1, 3, (Ed. Stadler, 1331): "Et ideo ad ambulandum vel standum vel quaerendum aliquid disciplinantur animalia et non ad artem vel scientiam. Et ideo nullum omnino animalium disciplinatur nisi motivum et per appetitum operabilibus: eo quod haec sunt particularia etiam in particularibus accepta quorum perceptive sunt animalia huiusmodi".

41. ALBERTUS MAGNUS, *De animalibus* XXI 1, 3, (Ed. Stadler, 1331).

intentional perception just on the basis that they cannot reach formally valid, universal arguments. But even so they are able to reason based on imperfect argumentations, i.e., arguments that resemble enthymemes. Apparently this means that a primate is able to make sense of a situation and understand how to reach for something. The conclusion of this incomplete form of practical reasoning is an action.

A tentative conclusion

If we ought to make sense of the fact that animals possess non-conceptual perceptual content, it is, at least from the medieval perceptive, unavoidable to see it in a teleological, goal-driven framework, in the sense that an animal's perception and ensuing behavior can be understood as if it acted rationally, even though it is not actually rational [42]. Albert's account of animal cognition as being essentially the same as human perception stands in a stark contrast with the Cartesian tradition. In this respect his effort to reconcile animal and human cognitive processes based on psychological and physiological considerations stands out as an important early attempt to explore the sensitive mind from a point of view that tends to question the centrality of human intentional experience.

BIBLIOGRAPHY

Sources

ALBERTUS MAGNUS (1916-1920), *De amimalibus libri XXVI*, 2 vols., ed. H. Stadler, Münster.

– (1968), *De anima*, in Alberti Magni Opera Omnia *VII, 1*, ed. C. Stroick, Münster.

42. BERMÚDEZ (2003), 116-128 distinguishes three different levels of rationality. *Level 0 rationality* explains basic behaviors in which there is "no process of decision-making" (117) and it only explains how an animal is instinctively disposed to react given a certain type of stimulus. *Level 1 rationality*, however, displays "the location of contrast space of alternative possible courses of action" (121). In this case there is room for some type choice regarding particular courses of action and it represents "the minimalist conception of nonlinguistic thought" (122). *Level 2 rationality* goes beyond this basic sense by denoting high-level thoughts regarding the means and the outcome of an action, such as building tools to fabricate something. This capacity seems to presuppose to ability to "represent contingencies". Only level 1 and level 2 rationality qualifies as psychological explanations of behavior. When comparing this account with Albert's own, it seems that level 0 rationality has also to be included as a form of psychological explanation.

– (2008), *De homine*, ed. H. Anzulewicz and J. Söder, in Alberti Magni Opera Omnia XXVII, 2, Münster.
AVICENNA (1968-1972), *Liber De Anima seu Sextus De Naturalibus*, 2 vols., ed. S. van Riet, Leuven/Leiden.

Secondary Literature

BERMÚDEZ, J.-L. (2003), *Thinking Without Words*, Oxford / New York.
ECO, Umberto et al. (1989), "On animal language in the medieval classification of signs", in Eco, Umberto and Marmo, Costantino (eds.), *On the Medieval Theory of Signs*, Amsterdam / Philadelphia, 3-41.
GUNTHER, York (ed.) (2003), *Essays on Nonconceptual Content*, Cambridge (Mass.) / London.
HAMLYN, D. W. (1994), "Perception, Sensation and Non-Conceptual Content", in *The Philosophical Quarterly* 44, 139-153.
KÖHLER, Th. (2001), "Der Tiervergleich als philosophisch-anthropologisches Schlüsselparadigma – der Beitrag Alberts des Großen", in ed. W. Senner, *Albertus Magnus. Zum Gedenken nach 800 Jahren: Neue Zugänge, Aspekte und Perspektiven*, Berlin, 437-454.
– (2007), "Sachverhaltsbeobachtung und axiomatische Vorgaben. Zur Struktur wissenschaftlicher Erfassung konkreter Äußerungsweisen des Menschlichen im 13. Jahrhundert", in eds. A. Fidora and M. Lutz-Bachmann, *Erfahrung und Beweis. Die Wissenschaften von der Natur im 13. und 14. Jahrhundert*, Berlin, 125-150.
– (2008), *Homo animal nobilissimum. Konturen des spezifisch Menschlichen in der naturphilosophischen Aristoteleskommentierung des dreizehnten Jahrhunderts*, vol. 1, Leiden.
MCDOWELL, J. (2003), "Nonconceptual Content", in ed. Y. Gunther, *Essays on Nonconceptual Content*, Cambridge (Mass).
– (1994), "The Content of Perceptual Experience", in *The Philosophical Quarterly* 44, 190-205.
MICHON, C. (2001), "Intentionality and Proto-Thoughts", ed. D. Perler, D., *Ancient and Medieval Theories of Intentionality*, Leiden / Boston / Köln, 342-325.
PEACOCKE, C. (2001), "Does Perception Have a Nonconceptual Content?", in *The Journal of Philosophy* 98, 239-264.
SEARLE, J. (2002), "Animal Minds", in Searle, John, *Consciousness and Language*, Cambridge, 61-76.
SORABJI, R. (1993), *Animal Minds and Human Morals: The Origins of the Western Debate*, London.

ANIMAL AND HUMAN KNOWLEDGE IN THE *PERSPECTIVA*: (*OPUS MAIUS,* PART FIVE) OF ROGER BACON [1]

Jeremiah HACKETT
(University of South Carolina)

What kind of knowledge do animals possess? How is this kind of knowledge related to human knowledge? Roger Bacon does not devote a treatise to this topic yet he does refer to the topic in his works c. 1266-71. The most important of these references is found in his *Opus maius*, part five, the *Perspectiva*. The account of animal knowledge in this paper will deal mainly with this latter work, while brief reference will also be made to the account of the sensitive soul in the *Communia naturalium.*

Why did Roger Bacon write the *Perspectiva*? The esteemed editor of this work, David C. Lindberg, sees it as a progression of Bacon's application of the Laws of Physics (multiplication of species) to organic nature and to the human organic being [2]. A. Mark Smith has claimed that Bacon wrote the *Perspectiva* as an effort to solve some problems in philosophy of mind/psychology [3]. He holds that Bacon's fundamental concern was not with "Optics", in the modern mathematical sense of that word but with an understanding of the psychological problem of *Vision and Perception.* There is good evidence for both approaches in Bacon's above-mentioned text.

1. Further accounts of the connection of animal knowledge to experimental knowledge in Roger Bacon have been published in the time since this paper was delivered as a lecture. See HACKETT (2008-2009), 123-46; *idem.* (2011), 145-73. For an account of corporeal species in Bacon's account of knowledge, see RAIZMAN-KEDAR (2009), 131-57. For a comparison of Bacon and his opponent Richard Rufus of Cornwall, see WOOD (2007), 35-57.

2. BACON, *Perspectiva,* ed. Lindberg, Introduction, XVII-C.

3. SMITH (1992).

Bacon addressed himself to the issue of his own motivation in writing the *Perspectiva.* His remarks are found in a *Tractatus de anima* found in *Communia naturalium*[4]. Even in part six of the *Opus maius, de scientia experimentali,* one must be aware that although Bacon is providing a sketch of a structure of experimental science, he is also concerned with the epistemological role of experience in science and technology, common sense, critical thought (philosophy), moral/religious belief, and Statecraft.

Roger Bacon drew on many sources for his *Perspectiva.* Avicenna, Ibn al-Haytham and Aristotle stand out as primary in regard to issues of psychology and epistemology. Yet, there is a hidden presence in the background. This person, namely, Augustine, does not figure prominently in the text but his valorization of vision among the senses influenced Bacon.

AUGUSTINE ON VISION AND PERCEPTION

The only explicit mention in the text of the *Perspectiva* is to *De musica* with reference to the role of species in knowledge, and to *De trinitate* in reference to image formation[5]. One sees the influence of Augustine in the absolute primacy of vision among the senses and indeed the *De anima* of Aristotle is also influential here. Augustine is firm about this. What is discovered about vision can be generalized to the other senses, and vision as the primary sense can be given as the most basic example of sense-knowledge. Still, Augustine's language about sensation in the *Confessions* is interesting. The word *percipere* is used only once and then in Bk XIII. The main vision words are *sentire, intueor* and *censeri.* When we turn to Roger Bacon, we find that the words *visio, intuitio, sentire* and *percipere* are the key to his explanation of animal and human knowledge. We can speak of *percipere* by means of both sense and mind. This indicates the sustained use of the word *percipere* long before the word perception gained new meaning and common currency in early modern philosophy.

Bacon following Ibn al-Haytham divides sense knowledge as follows: First, there is *visio* by sense alone as in the case of the impact of light and color. Second, there is a comparison of things by means of a "generic" universal (vague singular). Third, there is knowledge *per syllogismum* (Ibn

4. BACON, *Communia naturalium*, ed. Steele, I, Part 4, *distinction tercia de anima*, Ch. 6, 297: "Partes vero sensitive virtutis ego posui omni diligencia in principio *Perspective*, quod capitulum est unum in quo totum vulgus errat medicorum naturalium et theologorum, et est unum de dignioribus capitulis que misi continens sapiencie potestatem".

5. BACON, *Perspectiva*, ed. Lindberg, 101, 189.

al-Haytham)[6]. The crux of the matter, however, is that the word 'syllogism' is being used here in a context quite distinct from that of Aristotle and specifically in relation to animal knowledge. Again, Bacon notes that we experience "things on earth *per visum*, and also by means of vision we *inquire* into things in the heavens. For the celestial objects are studied (*considerantur*) by means of visual instruments, as Ptolemy and other astronomers teach"[7]. For Bacon, light and color have special beauty beyond other sense objects, and with these greater utility and necessity present themselves. Bacon's next remark presents his strong neo-Augustinian emphasis on the primacy of vision."Through vision we also experience things here on earth, for concerning this world *the blind person* can have no *experience* worthy of the name"[8]. Again, he remarks, "Now hearing causes us to believe, [as is apparent] since we *believe* our teachers; but we cannot *experientially test* (*experiri*) what we learn in belief except through vision (*nisi per visum*)[9].

Bacon is adamant. If we take taste, touch and smell as counter-examples, we are guilty of adopting a conception of wisdom applicable to animals alone. For brutes are occupied with things that can be tasted and touched; and they cultivate smell, which is closely associated with taste and touch. However, the things concerning which these senses offer certification are unworthy, few in number, and common to brutes, and consequently they do not attain the dignity of human reason. Thus, for Bacon, there is, at one level, a radical division between *Animal* and *Human Knowledge*.But evidently human knowledge presupposes a strong element of animal knowledge which in the human knower has been subsumed into intellectual and spiritual vision.

Following Aristotle, Bacon argues that we only create a science and art of nature for matters that are difficult, good and useful. Some subjects are so difficult that an effort to construct a *science* would not be helpful. "But concerning sight alone and not the other senses, have philosophers created a separate science, *Perspectiva*. It follows that even wisdom gained through vision must have a special utility not found in the other senses"[10].

One would expect Bacon at this stage to proceed with his account of the geometry of *Perspectiva*. Instead, he postpones the technical account of the

6. BACON, *Perspectiva,* ed. Lindberg, 154-59; SMITH, *Alhacen's Theory of Visual Perception*, vol. 1, Introduction.

7. BACON, *Perspectiva*, ed. Lindberg, 3.

8. BACON, *Perspectiva*, ed. Lindberg, 3.

9. BACON, *Perspectiva*, ed. Lindberg, 5.

10. BACON, *Perspectiva*, ed. Lindberg, 4-5.

geometry of physical optics to the later parts of the work. As a way of placing the geometrical optics in the context of the psychology of vision, he provides the reader with a summary of the structure of perception as he finds it in his ancient and medieval sources. In brief, he presents his own account of vision, perception and knowledge based on ancient and medieval *auctoritates*, thus providing a synthetic account of the sensitive faculties of the soul, the common sense and imagination, the estimative and cogitative faculties.Bacon speaks of the deficiencies of the Latins in regard to this science, and acknowledges the obscurity of Aristotle's texts concerning the internal senses and the cogitative faculty. The solution is to be found in Ibn Sina (Avicenna). "Avicenna was the perfect imitator and expositor of Aristotle and the commander and prince of philosophy after him, as the *Commentator* says in his chapter on the rainbow. Therefore, the opinion of Avicenna, which is clear and perfect in this subject, is to be followed" [11]. Bacon presents an account of Avicenna's views on the inner senses and proceeds to explain them with the aid of Ibn al-Haytham's *Optics* and his own doctrine of the multiplication of species [12].

BACON'S SUMMARY OF AVICENNA ON COGNITION

There are three distinct faculties corresponding to the three cells in the brain. And a distinction between external and internal perception can be shown or inferred from the different objects of perception. These are two very different kinds of sense:

> Now there are two kinds of sensible: one external, such as the twenty-nine aforementioned sensibles; the other internal, concealed from the external senses, such as the quality of a harmful or useful complexion, or even a useful or harmful substantial nature itself. It follows the common sense, and the imagination, all of which are acted upon by the first genus of sensible, and another that includes the estimation and memory, which are associated with the second genus of sensible.But the cogitative faculty is distinguished from the others by the nobility of its operation [13].

11. BACON, *Perspectiva*, ed. Lindberg, 16-17. See KEMP (1990), Ch. 2-4; *idem* (1996), Ch. 4, 45-64 on the inner senses, for a summary of Avicenna's account of the body, soul, mind. See McGinnis chapter above.

12. On Avicenna's psychology see, MCGINNIS (2010). One could argue that in using Ibn al-Haytham's *Optics*, Bacon provides a stronger scientific explanation support for Avicenna's account, while providing a more naturalistic explanation.

13. BACON, *Perspectiva*, ed. Lindberg, 18-19.

Bacon claims that one could put it better by stating that "the sensitive soul has a twofold instrument or subject". The root is found in the heart but the place where the sensible species of the object and the operations of the senses are encoded and differentiated is the brain. Bacon explains the latter by focusing on the issue of a "judgment of vision" [14].

What makes for a judgment of vision and how is this related to the cogitative sense?

The visual power and sense of light and color resides in the glacial humor, but is not completed until it reaches the optic nerve. Yet, judgments of vision involving the particular senses are the task of the *common sense*. Yet, in the grand scheme of Mind, it is the "discriminative faculty" (the cogitative faculty) that by the mediation of sight (vision) makes judgments concerning the twenty-nine species of visible things. Thus, one needs to examine the brain to see if there is a distinctive place for the cogitative faculty. In Bacon's view, no one author is sufficient on this point, and so he proposes a synthesis of the medical and philosophical sources. Bacon claims that

> the cognition or cogitative sense is mistress of the sensitive faculties and takes the place of *reason* in brute animals. Therefore, it is called the *administrative faculty*, not because it manifests the use of reason, but because it represents the ultimate perfection in brute animals, as reason does in humans, and because in humans alone, the rational soul is immediately united with it. And through its use of this power the spider constructs a geometric web, the bee a hexagonal hive thus choosing one of the figures capable of totally filling space, the swallow its nest and similarly for other works of brute animals that resemble human artifice. Those who sleep see marvels by means of this power. And all the faculties of the sensitive soul, posterior as well as anterior, serve and obey it, since they exist for its sake. For the species that are in the imagination multiply themselves in the cogitative faculty, although they exist (according to primary being) in the imagination for the sake of fantasy, which makes use of these species; but the cogitative faculty possesses these species in a nobler way, and the species of the estimative faculty and the memory exist in the cogitative faculty according to a nobler mode of being than in the estimative faculty and memory. And therefore, the cogitative faculty uses all these other powers as its instruments. And in humans a rational soul is added from without by an act of creation, and the rational soul is united primarily and immediately with the cogitative faculty, which it puts to use

14. For an account of the influence of the topic of "judgments of vision" on late Medieval and Renaissance aesthetics, see SUMMERS (1990); see also TACHAU (1993), 653-70.

> mainly as its own special instrument, and species are produced in the rational soul by the cogitative faculty. Consequently, when the cogitative faculty is injured, the judgment of reason is thoroughly corrupted; and when it is healthy, the intellect functions well and rationally [15].

The section which follows here is a summary treatise on the structure of the eye, and in the following section, Bacon presents a summary of teaching on the process of vision and perception [16].

VISION: THE PROCESS OF ASSIMILATION BETWEEN OBJECT AND KNOWER

According to Bacon,

> The first thing to be considered is that vision requires the species of a visible object; for without this species there will be no sight, according to Aristotle, who says in *On the Soul*, book 2, that sense universally receives the species of sensible things so that the act of perception can occur. Moreover, a recipient must be assimilated to its agent, but vision is a passive power, as Aristotle shows in *On the Soul*, book 2, and therefore it must be assimilated to a visible agent [17].

Each object sends out species in all directions "along all diameters". Vision occurs by means of a species "but principally by means of a species of light and color" [18].

For example, one can look in a garden and see various shades of green in the color of the vegetation. And thus we can say that color is also an agent that influences sight. Other variations in the direct influence of light can be seen when the same color changes appearance as can be found in the dove and the peacock. Clearly, without sight one has limited knowledge of the external world.

How then is vision completed? The authors on P*erspectiva* hold that "vision is not completed in the eye". Since there are two species, one from each eye, the eye does not certify knowledge of one object.

> It is necessary, therefore, that the [ultimate] sentient power in which vision is completed be something other than the eyes; and the eyes, which pass the species of the visible object on to it, are its instruments. And this [ultimate

15. BACON, *Perspectiva*, ed. Lindberg, 14-17. See also *Communia naturalium* I, Part 4, *distinction tercia de anima*, Ch. 2, 284-86.

16. BACON, *Perspectiva*, ed. Lindberg, 21-61; 61-93.

17. BACON, *Perspectiva*, ed. Lindberg, 60-61.

18. BACON, *Perspectiva*, ed. Lindberg, 60-61.

> sentient organ] is the common nerve at the surface of the brain [...]. And since this faculty is unified at its source, and the [visual] powers of the eyes are continuous with it owning to the mediation of the optic nerves, therefore, in so far as this is the cause [of a single or double vision], a single thing can appear single [19].

Further, the species from both eyes converge in the optic nerve and the forms of the same species mix in the same place and thus they become one. "And since the faculty of judgment is one, and the species is one, a single judgment is formed of a single object". In this manner, one overcomes problems arising from double-vision. One reaches a single judgment in regard to a single object. Further, experience teaches (*experientia docet*) that injury to the common nerve leads to loss of vision, while healing of the common nerve leads to improved vision.

Alhazen, however, holds that the ultimate sentient power is in the front part of the brain and so "it would seem to some that it is [identical with] the common sense and imagination or fantasy, which are in the front part of the brain, as was stated above, especially since it was claimed that no judgment concerning any sensible is completed until the species reaches the common sense" [20].

At this juncture, Bacon makes a shift away from the common interpretations of his contemporaries, and bases his analysis entirely on Ibn al-Haytham. He remarks:

> However, it must be stated that the ultimate sentient power can be [defined as] the origin of all the senses (and this is the common sense in the anterior part of the brain); but in this chapter we do not speak of the ultimate sentient power *with this meaning*. The ultimate sentient power can be defined otherwise in relation to one particular sense, such as sight, hearing, the sense of smell and the like. And in these terms, the ultimate sentient power in binocular vision is the common nerve, the eyes being the instruments that are first altered by the visible object [...] [21].

By the first part of the brain, Alhazen means not the common sense or the first cell but rather

> the aperture in the skull where the nerves intersect [...]. It is equally clear that the eyes do perceive, and not only the common nerve [...]. Therefore the visual act is one and undivided, carried out by the eyes and the common nerve [...]. Thus, one can say that the sensitive power is extended through

19. BACON, *Perspectiva*, ed. Lindberg, 62-65.
20. BACON, *Perspectiva*, ed. Lindberg, 64-67.
21. BACON, *Perspectiva*, ed. Lindberg, 66-67.

> the whole optic nerve from the common nerve to the eyes as Alhacen says, therefore, the visual act is one and undivided, carried out by the eyes and the common nerve. And although Alhacen says that the eye is the instrument of the ultimate sentient power and the intermediary between it and the visible object, nevertheless the eye [itself] necessarily makes judgements and has the power of sight, although incompletely [22].

Bacon in what follows seeks to examine that geometry of vision and the arrangements of the visible object as it appears on the [anterior glacial humor].

The physics of the reception of the species of objects to vision are presented in the doctrine of the multiplication of species. These species are strictly corporeal and obey the universal physical laws of nature. In no sense can they be said to be purely 'spiritual.'

ROGER BACON'S CRITIQUE OF 'SPIRITUAL'/INTENTIONAL SPECIES

To grasp the epistemological dimensions of Bacon's treatment of experience, it is important to note that both in the *De multiplicatio specierum* and in the *Opus maius*, Part v, *Perspectiva*, Bacon makes it very clear that he rejects the majority opinion of his time concerning the nature of the assimilation process of sense knowledge [23]. Following Averroes's reading of Aristotle, many of the 13th century Latin philosophers claimed that species *in medio et in senso* were *spiritual or* intentional. These words are ambiguous due to the fact that in a strict sense only God, Angels or the human Soul were regarded as strictly *spiritual*. Nevertheless, by using the terms 'spiritual or intentional,' these authors were indicating the fact that nothing of the 'matter' of the object was multiplied in nature to the percipient. That is, only the form or intentional structure of the object independent of the matter of the object was communicated from the object to the five senses of the knower. Yes, there was the natural contact of light and color, but in addition something of the form of the object was communicated. Hence, one has a basis for the objectivity of knowing and one can avoid any skeptical doubts that might arise from a strict 'internalist' understanding of knowledge. This isomorphism of form was

22. BACON, *Perspectiva*, ed. Lindberg, 66-67.

23. BACON, *Perpsectiva*, ed. Lindberg, 81-83; 87-91; *De multiplication specierum*, ed., Lindberg, Part III, Ch. 2-3, 186-195.

again replicated in the case of intellectual knowledge of the *nature* of the object.

In the *De multiplicatione specierum*, Bacon offers a series of devastating physical arguments for the incoherence of "spiritual species" in the context of natural change. He distinguishes carefully between corporeal and spiritual being, and notes that he will later address the manner in which the spiritual soul receives corporeal species. He believes that the difficulties arise on the basis of the confusion of the words "spiritual" and "insensible". In Bacon's view corporeal species are multiplied according to determinate physical laws alone.

In the *Perspectiva,* he notes that the *multitudo philosophantium* oppose the doctrine of the mixing of corporeal species in the air. They maintain that the species have "spiritual being in the medium and in sensation" *(esse spirituale in medio et in sensu.)* Hence, whatever '*spirituale'* means, it is something non-material if still not quite spiritual in the religious/philosophical sense of that word.

> And they (the majority of the Philosophers at Paris) impute this opinion to Aristotle and to Averroes in [their respective] *Books on the Soul,* book 2. And since [according to them] species have spiritual rather than material being, *species do not obey the laws of material forms and consequently do not mix,* since it is on account of their material being that forms mix. Therefore, these philosophers posit that different species of light (even an infinity of lights) in a medium are reckoned to be at the same point of the air and [yet] remain distinct, and likewise the species of color and the like; and this explains how vision can discriminate among the things it sees. *This is a very serious error, for it contains many elements that are false and absurd.* And it originates in the belief that one must preserve [the power of] discrimination in vision, which they do not judge possible unless the species are altogether distinct [from one another] in the air. Therefore, I will first explain the ability of sight to discriminate [among the various parts or points in the visual field], so that it will be clear that it is unnecessary to err in the manner indicated. Then I will destroy the error and explain the authors who seem to hold it. Therefore, I say that species have material and natural existence in the medium and in sense [...] [24].

Thus, Bacon posits that "species have material and natural existence in the medium and in sense" in terms of the laws of straight, reflected and refracted vision. "And so the whole pyramid is mixed everywhere, but no

24. BACON, *Perspectiva*, ed. Lindberg, 80-83. See TACHAU, (1983), 394-443.

mixture involving the principal multiplication reaches the eye" [25]. Moreover, according to Bacon,

> when they [i.e. philosophers] say that species have spiritual being in the medium, this usage does not accord with the primary and proper meaning of the term "spiritual", from "spirit", according to which we say God, Angels and the Soul are spiritual beings; for it is clear that the species of corporeal beings are not spiritual in that sense. Therefore, of necessity such species have corporeal being, since body and spirit are opposites, without intermediary [26].

In other words, corporeal beings are strictly material beings and obey the laws of physics and optics. After all, the species are a representation or similitude of a corporeal thing, and must therefore have corporeal and not spiritual being. Bacon produces arguments from geometry, the equivocity of the language of body and spirit and the proof that corporeal species alone are material, including arguments from Ptolemy and Ibn al-Haytham.

The significance of this doctrine-Bacon's clearly stated univocal influence of physical impact due to the multiplication of species- becomes very clear when he comes to talk about the nature of syllogistic argument as part of the knowledge process [27]. It raises the issue: if animals have corporeal existence alone, and not pure spiritual existence such as one finds in God, Angels and Souls, can animals think, that is, can they argue (syllogize)? Further, what kind of experimental knowledge do animals have and how does it compare with human experimental knowledge?

First, let us take human experimental knowledge. Since vision is for Bacon the primary paradigm of knowledge, one can recall Bacon's three-partite interpretation of vision mentioned above. There are three kinds of "Visual Comprehension", (1) the perception of light and color, only by the intuition of sensation (*cognoscantur solo intuitu sensus*); (2) Comprehension of the vague singular or the recognition of a universal but in relation to many particulars. This happens due to a comparison of kinds of things; (3) A perception that is distinct from sense alone (*solo sensu*) and even by comparison with things previously seen. This kind of cognition,

25. BACON, *Perspectiva*, ed. Lindberg, 84-85. For a new recognition of the importance of Bacon's doctrine of the multiplication of species and Bacon's *Perspectiva* and the "perspectivist" tradition beginning with Bacon for the development of Linear Perspective in the Renaissance, see EDGERTON (2009), 15-16, 19-20. 28, 36-38.

26. BACON, *Perspectiva*, ed. Lindberg, 86-87.

27. For a comprehensive account of Bacon's doctrine of agency and species, see RAIZMAN-KEDAR (2009).

which resembles a kind of reasoning, considers the object at hand in an absolute manner. This visual intuitive cognition is far removed from the first kind of visual sensation mentioned, that is, (1). It is called *cognitio per syllogismum* and "*intuimur* hic cognitio subito, et non percipimus nos arguere cum tamen arguamus. Et iam in metaphysicis et logicalibus confirmavi hanc sententiam Alhacen"[28]. It is a form of syllogistic reasoning but it happens so fast that we do not see it. The normal treatises on Logic do not deal with this. But Alhazen does. He shows that the twenty common sensibles are grasped in this manner because they cannot be confirmed except by the third mode of visual cognition, namely, *visual intuitive cognition*. Further,"and the third mode of [cognition] is further removed from sense alone, since in it more things are considered than in the second mode, and its method of argumentation brings it closer to a work of reason (*opus rationis*)[29].

Bacon further remarks that the nomenclature here is unsuitable. The faculties of the sensitive soul have these cognitions without the need of either pure formal knowledge or formal syllogisms. The key to explaining this kind of knowledge is the study of *Perspectiva*, especially the scientific study of Direct, Reflected and Refracted Vision as outlined in the ancient authors on Optics, Euclid, Ptolemy, Al-Kindi, Ibn al-Haytham and others. And since vision and the study of vision is the key to any explanation of knowledge in this world of experience, what kind of knowledge, then, does the animal have and how is it both similar to and different from human experimental knowledge[30] ?

28. BACON, *Perspectiva*, ed. Lindberg, 156-59.

29. BACON, *Perspectiva*, ed. Lindberg, 158-59.

30. Care needs to be taken with respect to the place of corporeal species in intellectual knowledge in Bacon. Since we do not have a fully worked out *De anima* from Bacon, the necessary distinctions between animal experiential knowledge, human experiential knowledge and pure intellectual knowledge may not be obvious. Yet, it is clear from *Opus maius VI* that for Bacon, while 'human and philosophical knowledge' is necessary for full human intellectual knowledge, it is not sufficient. In fact, it is inadequate not only for spiritual matters but also for scientific experience. Hence, Bacon makes it a requirement that spiritual illumination is also required for a complete grasp of experiential scientific knowledge and especially for moral consciousness. One would not go wrong by taking John Peckham's *De anima* as an example of the broader context for Bacon's account of pure intellectual knowledge. In the latter knowledge, corporeal species as explained through *Perspectiva* is taken up and transformed by means of intellectual/spiritual illumination.

ROGER BACON ON ANIMAL KNOWLEDGE

Latratus canis– Thus the dog not only barks, indeed, it knows or in a manner, according to Bacon, it reasons [31]. My dog, Maximus Magnus, truly does know what I think (well up to a certain level, of course).But a great tradition of "the philosophers", medieval as well as modern, including the "first" Modern Philosopher, Descartes, hold that animals do not think, that is they do not know in any strict sense of the word. How does Bacon fit into this tradition?

In his account of the sensitive and intellectual souls in *Communia naturalium*, Bacon shows that he is very sensitive to the importance of animal knowledge. He recognizes that knowledge originating from the organic nature of the animal is adequate in itself. It does not require that in addition to organic nature, one must posit a specially created sensitive soul. Further, animals see and hear just as well as humans and it is similar with respect to the other sensitive powers. He adds:

> And many animals have better sense knowledge than humans as the linx which can see through a wall. And as Aristotle teaches, the human has a more deficient sense of smell than all other animals, and the latter have more certain and acute hearing than humans. Therefore it is obvious that the sensitive soul which is naturally induced is sufficient for the actions of the sensitive soul in both humans and brute animals. If therefore the actions of the sensitive soul are so much better in animals than in humans, then that natural sensitive soul present in humans is sufficient [32]. (That is, one does not require a separately created sensitive soul in the human being in addition to the sensitive soul induced by nature).

At the end of his discussion of the three kinds of perceptual knowledge in the *Perspectiva*, Bacon remarks:

> [...] It is appropriate to inquire which faculty of the soul is responsible, in knowledge and syllogism, for things seen by means of the sense of sight. And if we employ the terms "knowledge" and "syllogism as they are used by the common run of philosophers (*vulgi philosophantium*) in logic, natural philosophy, and metaphysics, this must be the rational soul, since

31. U. ECO et al. (1989), 3-42.

32. BACON, *Communia naturalium* I, Part 4, Ch. 1, 283-4: "[...] Et multa animalia melius senciunt quam homo, ut linx qui videt per medium parietem. Et homo habet olafactum pejorem omnibus animalibus, ut Aristoteles docet, et multa cercius et acucius audiunt. Ergo manifestum est quod illa sensitive que per naturam inducitur sufficit ad operaciones anime sensitive tam in homine quam in brutis. Si enim ita bene et melius quam in hominibus fiant opera sensitive, tunc illa sensitivva que naturalis est in homine sufficit".

> syllogism and knowledge, as understood in the sciences, pertain to it alone. And Alhacen calls this part of the soul "the discriminative faculty", and according to him it reasons and understands. Sometimes these and similar terms are employed in such a way as to imply, literally interpreted, that it is the intellective and rational soul [33].

But Bacon demurs and presents the reader with the following unexpected remark:

> Now it is apparent, when a dog sees a man whom it has seen before, that it recognizes him, and monkeys and many [other] animals [also] do this. And they distinguish between things they have seen of which they have memory; they know one universal from another, as man from dog or wood; and they distinguish individuals of the same species. Therefore, that cognition of which the perspectivists call "cognition through knowledge" *properly belongs to animals as well as to humans; consequently, it must occur by a power of the sensitive soul* [...] It is clear that the cognition called "cognition by syllogism" is similar, since motion is grasped through it [...]. Thus the animal perceives *motion, rest and distance* [34].

He adds:

> It must be conceded that animals have some cognitions of this kind by a certain natural industry and instinct of nature, without deliberation; and the faculty by means of which this occurs is the cogitative faculty, which is the mistress of the faculties and which makes use of the other faculties of the soul [35].

He proceeds to note that animals have knowledge of past events and kinds due to imagination and memory. Indeed, the animal sees the wolf and flees, and this exercise of the aestimative sense leads to a cognitive dimension. And here we have recognition of insensible (but not spiritual) intentions in the object by the animal (fear, etc.). But it is an insensible intention in regard to sensible matter. An equivocation occurs here and the term "syllogism" must be narrowed for present purposes. In fact, no argument can overcome the fact that animals perceive or know distance of objects, motion and rest.

Naturally, the arrangement of arguments in proper form is a function of formal logic and hence of the rational soul. "But a certain gathering of several things into one by natural industry and instinct of nature (the

33. BACON, *Perspectiva*, ed. Lindberg, 246-47.
34. BACON, *Perspectiva*, ed. Lindberg, 246-47.
35. BACON, *Perspectiva*, ed. Lindberg, 246-47.

several things resembling premises and the one resembling a conclusion, since it is gathered from several things) can easily be discovered in animals"[36]. He provides the following examples; monkeys giving out punishment to humans; spiders constructing geometrical webs. Wolves eat earth to be heavy when attacking other animals, and he continues:

> Also, I have observed a cat that coveted some fish swimming in a large stone container, and when it could not catch them because of the water, it pulled the stopper and allowed the water to run out until the container was dry, so that, with the water gone, it could catch them; thus the cat conceived of several actions in order to achieve its intended purpose[37].

The bee makes hexagonal cells, a figure that fills all space. Again, there is a kind of syllogistic gathering leading to a conclusion.Bacon concludes that, while animals do not organize their deliberation in terms of syllogistic mode and figure or distinguish beginning and end explicitly, nor do they perceive themselves as producing such patterning of behavior, "since their cognition is by natural instinct alone",

> Yet, this pattern is similar to argument and syllogism, and therefore the authors of [works on] *perspective* speak of "argument" and "syllogism". And certainly, it is the more appropriate for them to call this cognition "syllogistic" than to call the distinguishing of universals and particulars that have been previously seen "cognition through knowledge"[38].

We have now seen the high estimate that Bacon gives to animal knowledge, and when we come to knowledge *per experientiam* in the *scientia experimentalis*, we must bear in mind that it goes much further than some of the medieval followers of Aristotle in that he rejects 'spiritual being' in the medium and in sense, and instead follows Alhazen in attempting to give a corporeal and material account of the being of sense knowledge according to the geometrical laws of physics[39].

The *Perspectiva* itself is intimately linked to the *De scientia experimentalis* and scholars have wondered about Bacon's motivation in writing the *Perspectiva.*

In the *Communia naturalium*, as we saw above, he states that he needed to do a criticism of the common natural philosophy in order to give an adequate theory of vision and perception. It is important therefore to keep

36. BACON, *Perspectiva*, ed. Lindberg, 248-49.
37. BACON, *Perspectiva*, ed. Lindberg, 248-49.
38. BACON, *Perspectiva*, ed. Lindberg, 250-51.
39. See the studies of RAIZMAN-KEDAR cited above, notes 1 & 27 for this topic.

Bacon's views on Animal Knowledge in mind when we now to a discussion of *Opus maius,* Part Six and related works. Since Bacon does not provide us with a full treatise on *De anima*, we will need to draw on his remarks on the smaller account of *De anima* in the *Communia naturalium.* One thing would seem clear. There is a sense in which Bacon makes a strong distinction between the realm of the spiritual and that of the corporeal, not allowing for intermediaries. This is a form of substance dualism. And yet he allows for a union between the cogitative sense and the spiritual soul created from the outside. It would be easy but superficial to accuse Bacon of being a dualist on the assumption that Thomas Aquinas is not a dualist. The latter is less obviously a dualist on the basis of his teaching of the soul as form of an organic body and as a substance. I believe that most medieval thinkers distinguished firmly between the corporeal and the spiritual. Neither Bacon nor Aquinas for that matter were non-dualist in the modern sense of cognitive monism.

SCIENTIA EXPERIMENTALIS, ANIMAL KNOWLEDGE AND SCIENCE

When Bacon turns to the issues of epistemology in science (*Opus maius,* Part VI), he distinguishes between *argumentum* and *experientia/experimentum*[40]. For him, experience is raised to a level equal to if not above that of argument. Further, many of his examples of experiential confirmation are taken from the animal world. Naturally, Bacon distinguishes strictly between the world of the "pure spiritual experience" and the "corporeal experience". The latter is subject to "human and philosophical analysis", the former transcends such an analysis and is the result of an illumination. One might call it a dualism of regions. But in terms of his explanation of natural knowledge of things in the world, he clearly appreciates the role of animal knowledge. One can argue that Bacon sees experimental knowledge as something distinct from formal logic. That is, experimental science is *practical knowledge, or rather, a practical method.* The object of the method is to separate the true from the false in the realm of science, that is to separate an art and science of nature from magic, similar to the way formal logic separates the true from the false at a theoretical rational level. Indeed, the second main prerogatives of the *scientia experimentalis* involve the uses of instruments (manual knowledge) as in the astrolabe & armillary sphere, the collection of

40. BACON, *Opus maius*, part six, ed. Bridges, Vol. 2, 166.

medical and chemical cures from the animal world, and the study of the impact of the heavens on change on earth in animals and humans (astrology).

One can clearly see here (as indeed one can see in the researches of Albertus Magnus on the natural world) a greater emphasis on the role of *experientia/experiment* than one finds among the common run of philosophers in the Middle Ages[41]. The latter tend to deal with book-knowledge and reason without reference to the need to distinguish real from both fictional and from deceptive experiences. They were more concerned with the strict demands of formal logic in the determination of valid reasoning. While Bacon and Albertus are not alone in this new valorization of external experience of things in the world, they did set out an exemplary account of the role of certified experience in animal and human knowledge.

Conclusion

Roger Bacon in the *Perspectiva* provides us with an account of common sense and scientific knowledge that is a mode of knowing *per experientiam*. Following Augustine's emphasis on vision as a primary sense, Bacon collects the teachings of the experts on *Perspectiva* (Ibn al-Haytham, Ptolemy and others), Natural Philosophy and Philosophy of Mind (Aristotle, Avicenna, Averroes) and the Medical Thinkers (Constantine, Avicenna). He presents a synthesis of teaching on vision and perception. The latter is based entirely on a model of vision. Even hearing a teaching must ultimately be verified on the basis of vision. I have outlined the teaching on perceptual vision providing special emphasis to the importance of a distinction between 'spiritual' and 'corporeal' species. The emphasis on 'corporeal species' enables Bacon to lay the groundwork for a true scientific account of vision and perception free from 'spiritual or supernatural' concerns. This does not mean that Bacon in other places ignores the role of intellectual knowledge or that he dismisses the 'spiritual' realm. No, it simply means that he focuses in on the scientific basis for a theory of perception based on a scientific theory of vision based on the *ancient auctores*. This does not mean that he himself did not work with lens or that he ignored his own personal and scientific practice and experiences.But it does mean that he has moved from a purely logical

41. On this topic, see DRAELANTS (2011), 89-122.

"Scholastic Method" to a different kind of logical-experiential method. It might not have the new elements of the experimental science of early modernity but it certainly did proceed in a scientific manner as distinct from the procedures of "Formal Logic" alone.

By examining Bacon's account in the *Perspectiva*, we came to see that he had much to say about Animal Knowledge both in animals and in humans. It is often the case that experts in Medieval Philosophy move too quickly to the realm of "pure intellectual and mystical knowledge". In the process, they overlook the very important contribution that thinkers like Albertus Magnus, Roger Bacon and others made to our understanding of animal knowing and to an understanding of its connections to human knowledge. Descartes and his modern followers continued some of the bad habits of the more 'rationalistic' of the medieval philosophers. They might not approve, but I persist in my firm belief that my dog, Max, really does know my thoughts and really does think at least in the sense in which Bacon claims that his cat though about the fish or the monkey does work on a means to ends basis. Further, Bacon in his *scientia experimentais* illustrates the manner in which animal knowledge enters into the actual practice of experimental science, and he shows how we humans can learn and have learned much from animals for our own well being. And yet, Roger Bacon regards the senses of smell, taste and touch as belonging only to the world of brute beasts [42]. He sees the human form of knowledge to be beyond all that in the realm of intellectual light and vision. Today, after greater understanding of animal knowledge, the invention of Braile and the greater appreciation of the body in knowledge, we would not relegate smell, taste and touch as does Bacon in the *Perspectiva* to a merely brutish form of knowledge. The form a whole structure with vision in animal and human knowledge. Some philosophers still do, but then perhaps, they have a tendency to over-rationalize, over-ocularize, and have not noticed the re-contextualization of vision in terms of a less-dualistic philosophy of mind.

42. For a claim for the primacy of taste and smell as the most significant senses for experimental study in medicine even having primacy over vision, see BURNETT (2011), 337-58.

Bibliography

Sources

BACON, Roger (1905--), *Communia naturalium*, ed. Steele, (Fasc. III), Oxford.

– (1978), "An Unedited Part of Roger Bacon's 'Opus Maius': *De Signis"*, ed. K. M. FREDBORG, Lauge NIELSEN, and Jan PINBORG, in *Traditio* 34, 75-136.

– (1983), *De multiplication specierum*, ed., David C. Lindberg, Oxford.

– (1996), *Perspectiva*, ed. David C. Lindberg, Oxford.

Studies

BURNETT, Charles (2011), "Experimentum and Ratio in the Salernitan *Summa de saporibus et odoribus*", in Thomas BÉNATOUÏL and Isabelle DRAELANTS, eds., *Expertus Sum. L'expérience par les sens dans la philosophie naturelle médiévale (Actes du colloque international de Pont-à-Mousson-5-7 février 2009)*, Firenze: SISMEL-Edizioni Del Galluzzo, 337-58 (Micrologus Library 40).

DRAELANTS, Isabel (2011), "Expérience et autorités dans la philosophie naturelle d'Albert le Grand", in Thomas BENATOUÏL and Isabelle DRAELANTS, eds., *Expertus Sum. L'expérience par les sens dans la philosophie naturelle médiévale (Actes du colloque international de Pont-à-Mousson-5-7 février 2009)*, Firenze: SISMEL-Edizioni Del Galluzzo, 89-122 (Micrologus Library 40).

ECO, Umberto & MARMO, Constantine (1989), *On the Medieval Theory of Signs*, Amserdam / Philadelphia.

EDGERTON, Samuel Y. (2009), *The Mirror, the Window, and the Telescope: How Renaissance Linear Perspective Changes our Vision of the Universe*, Ithaca & London: Cornell University Press.

HACKETT, Jeremiah (2008/2009), "Roger Bacon's Concept of Experience: A New Beginning in Medieval Philosophy?", in *The Modern Schoolman*, LXXXVI, 123-46.

–(2011), "*Ego Expertus Sum*: Roger Bacon's Science and the Origins of Empiricism", in Thomas BÉNATOUÏL and Isabelle DRAELANTS, eds., *Expertus Sum. L'expérience par les sens dans la philosophie naturelle médiévale (Actes du colloque international de Pont-à-Mousson-5-7 février 2009)*, Firenze: SISMEL-Edizioni Del Galluzzo, 145-73 (Micrologus Library 40).

KEMP, Simon (1990), *Medieval Psychology*, Westport, CT., Greenwood Press, 1990.

–(1996), *Cognitive Psychology in the Middle Ages*, Westport, Ct. & London, Greenwood Press.

MCGINNIS, Jon (2010), *Avicenna*, Oxford University Press, (Great Medieval Thinkers).

RAIZMAN-KEDAR, Yael (2009), "The Intellect Naturalized: Roger Bacon and the Existence of Corporeal Species within the Intellect", in *Early Science and Medicine,* 14, nos. 1-3, 131-57.

– (2009), *Species as Signs: Roger Bacon (1220-1292) on Perspectiva and Grammatica*, University of Haifa PHD.

SMITH, A. Mark (2001), *Alhacen's Theory of Vision*, Transactions of the American Philosophical Society, Vol. 91, 4 & 5, Philadelphia.

– (2002) "Picturing the Mind: The Representation of Thought in the Middle Ages and Renaissance", in *Philosophical Topics* 20/2, 149-70.

SUMMERS, David (1990), *The Judgment of Sense: Renaissance Naturalism and the Rise of Aesthetics*, Cambridge University Press.

TACHAU, Katherine (1983), "The Problem of *Species in Medio* at Oxford in the Generation after Ockham", *Mediaeval Studies* 44, 394-443.

– (1993) "What Senses and Intellect Do: Argument and Judgment in Late Medieval Theories of Knowledge", in *Argumentationstheorie: Scholastische Forschungen zu den logischen und semantischen Regeln korrekten Folgerns,* ed., Klaus Jacobi, Leiden-New York-Köln, 653-70 (Studien und Texte zur Geistesgeschichte des Mittelalters, 38).

WOOD, Rega (2007), "Imagination and Experience in the Sensory Soul and Beyond: Richard Rufus, Roger Bacon and Their Contemporaries", in *Forming the Mind: Essays on the Internal Senses and the Mind/Body Problem from Avicenna to the Medical Enlightenment,* ed. H. LAGERLUND, Dordrecht, 35-57 (Studies in the History of Philosophy of Mind, 5).

A BODY FOR THE HUMAN SOUL

Bernardo Carlos BAZÁN
(Ottawa)

Thomas Aquinas examines the question concerning the kind of body that the human soul deserves in the following texts: *Commentary on the Book of Sentences* II, d. 1, q. 2, a. 5; *Summa contra Gentiles* II, ch. 90; *Disputed Questions on the Soul*, q. 8; *Summa Theologiae* I, q. 76, a. 5 and q. 91, a. 1 and a. 3; *Commentary on Aristotle's Treatise on the Soul* I, 8, and *Disputed Questions on Evil*, q. 5, a. 5. These texts and a few others that are partially related to them will be the focus of my attention. A modern reader might find that many of the theories and problems discussed by Thomas in them are completely *dépassé*, and that many of the arguments he makes – based on principles that we no longer share with the mediaeval thinker – are difficult to follow. That is why I will try to make sense of Thomas's doctrine about the human body by giving priority to the explanation of the principles of natural philosophy on which it is based and of the theological concerns that influenced its development. Particular aspects of that doctrine that are dependent on the 'scientific' knowledge of his time will be presented as needed, but will not be discussed in detail. While their analysis could raise curiosity, the explanation of the general principles that guided Thomas will help us better understand how the medieval mind understood the nature of the human body and determine whether the problems that Thomas tried to solve are similar to ours.

First we must understand that Thomas was a theologian, that a theologian considers human nature from the point of view of the soul, not of the body, and that the theologian studies the body and the operational faculties linked to the body only insofar as they are instrumental in the development of intellectual and moral virtues [1]. Then we must take into consideration that the mediaeval worldvision includes some ideas that inevitably condition the way in which medieval theologians and philosophers think about the body. There is, of course, the idea that the whole Universe, all the species of living creatures and the initial human beings were created by an intelligent, free and loving First Cause, who, by hypothesis, has done things in the best possible way. There is also the idea that the Universe was populated by purely spiritual and incorruptible substances (angels or intelligences), by corporeal but incorruptible beings (the celestial bodies) moved by some of the previous substances, and finally by corporeal and corruptible beings. Medieval thinkers never put into question the existence of spiritual substances. It was for them so obvious a fact that they made more philosophical efforts to demonstrate the existence of God than to demonstrate the existence of angels or separate substances. This is true to the point that some medieval thinkers doubted whether each individual human being has an intellect of his or her own, but never questioned the existence of separate Intelligences. Same thing can be said about the celestial bodies: they would discuss whether they were animated or not, but they would not put into question the idea that those bodies were incorruptible and moved by separate intelligences. Could the incorruptibility of spiritual substances and celestial bodies be matched somehow by human beings? The habit of dealing separately with the soul and the body, entrenched in Latin Theology by centuries of contact with Neoplatonic ideas, had considerable impact on the answers given to this question. With regard to the human soul, theologians would not hesitate to consider it as one of the incorruptible spiritual substances and consequently they would ask themselves whether the undeniably corruptible human body was indeed the most suitable companion for such a soul. Behind this kind of discussion was a dualistic conception of human nature whose main goal was to justify the natural incorruptibility of the soul. By the time Thomas was a young graduate student it was quite common among Masters of Theology and Masters of Arts alike to hold the doctrine

1. AQUINAS, *S.Th.* I *Pars*, q. 75, Introduction: "Naturam autem hominis considerare pertinet ad theologum ex parte animae, non autem ex parte corporis, nisi secundum habitudinem quam habet corpus ad animam"; q. 78, Introduction: "Ad considerationem autem Theologi pertinet inquirere specialiter solum de potentiis intellectivis et appetitivis, in quibus virtutes inveniuntur. Sed quia cognitio harum potentiarum quodammodo dependet ex aliis, ideo nostra consideratio de potentiis animae in speciali erit tripartita: primo namque considerandum est de his quae sunt *preambula* ad intellectum; secundo de potentiis intellectivis; tertio de potentiis appetitivis".

according to which the human soul is the last of the spiritual substances whose ontological weakness translates into a dependence on sensible images, from which it obtains the intelligible forms that actualize its thinking, and forces it to enter into a relation with matter as the form of the human body. This eclectic doctrine, to which Thomas subscribed at the early stages of his career [2], allowed Latin thinkers to believe that they could secure simultaneously the immortality of the soul and some kind of unity to the human being. This way of thinking, as eclectic as it may be, is a good point of departure for our presentation.

The idea that the soul is a spiritual substance can be traced back to Plato, but the idea that the soul relates to the body as the substantial form to matter comes from Aristotle's treatise *On the Soul*, where the hylomorphic theory developed in the *Physics* was used to explain the ontological status of all living beings, including humans. According to this theory – whose exact meaning was understood quite well by young Thomas even if initially he did not applied it properly to human beings – matter and form are correlative principles which do not exist by themselves, but only by their relation to each other within the structure of the composite substance which is the real subject of being [3], The structure and its principles were conceived by Aristotle to explain the generation and corruption of substances and should not be introduced except in corruptible substances.

2. AQUINAS, *II Sent.*, d. 19, q. 1. a. 1 ad 4m: "anima rationalis preter alias formas dicitur esse substantia et hoc aliquid secundum quod habet esse absolutum [...] anima potest dupliciter considerari secundum quod est forma et secundum quod est substantia [...] sed distinctio accipitur secundum diversam eius considerationem: non enim ex hoc quod est forma habet quod post corpus remaneat, sed ex hoc quod habet esse absolutum, ut substantia subsistens [...] *quamvis utrumque sit sibi essentiale*". *Cf.* also AQUINAS, *II Sent.*, d. 3, q. 1, a. 6: "*Ad hoc quod aliquid sit proprie in genere substantiae requiritur quod sit res quidditatem habens cui debeatur esse absolutum* [...] Anima autem rationalis habet esse absolutum, non dependens a materia, quod est aliud a sua quidditate sicut etiam de angelis dictum est, et ideo relinquitur quod sit *in genere substantiae sicut species, et etiam sicut principium* inquantum est forma hujus corporis. Et inde venit ista distinctio, quod formarum quaedam sunt formae materiales, quae non sunt species substantiae, quaedam vero sunt *formae et substantiae*, sicut animae rationales"; AQUINAS, *II Sent.* d. 17, q. 2 a. 2 ad 5m: "Anima et angelus in hoc conveniunt quod *utrumque est substantia subsistens, esse absolutum habens* [...] sed anima acquiritur esse inferius et minus nobile, in quo corpus sibi unitur ut unum sit animae esse et corporis, quod est esse coniuncti: et ideo est forma corporis et individuatio sua est ex unione ejus ad corpus".

3. AQUINAS, *De principiis naturae*, paragraphe 4 (Leon. Ed., t. XLIII, p. 44, v. 37-42): "Materia enim dicitur causa forme in quantum forma non est nisi in materia; et similiter forma est causa materie in quantum materia non habet esse in actu nisi per formam: *materia enim et forma dicuntur relative ad invicem*, ut dicitur in II Physicorum".

But he never thought of the components as things existing by themselves and put somehow together by an external agent. The point of departure of hylomorphism is the unity of the existent substance; its composite structure is recognized, however, as an explanation of its coming to be and its corruption. Thomas understood perfectly well this fundamental point: the substance is the subject of being, not its co-principles; neither matter nor form can be said "to be"; only the whole composite "is" [4]. If they are not the subject of being, matter and form are neither the subject of becoming or generation. (Aristotle clearly saw that if that were the case, matter and form would also be composite of matter and form, and so on *ad infinitum*) [5]. This in synthesis means that the form does not exist nor does it become without matter and viceversa. In this structured substance the form is the principle of actuality that grants all the essential determinations to the composite; matter is the potential subject that supports the forms that succeed each other throughout the natural process of generations and corruptions, giving individuation to the form and continuity to the process. Being correlative as act and potency, they are united by their very nature and need no intermediary to achieve unity. Conversely, the two principles are not separable, except logically speaking [6].

It is important also to outline the process by which matter acquires and loses substantial forms (generation and corruption). In book III of the *Physics* (201a 9-14) Aristotle describes this process as a "movement", a term whose meaning is difficult to grasp because movement is the act of what is in potency as long as it is in potency: a substance undergoes a movement when the agent (mover) modifies the dispositions suitable for the particular substantial form that the substance has and starts introducing dispositions appropriate for a new form. As long as the new form has not been acquired, there is movement; but as soon as the change of dispositions in matter is achieved, the composite of matter and old form corrupts, the composite of matter and the new form is generated and the movement ends.

4. AQUINAS, *De ente et essentia*, c. 2 v. 38-87; note: "Esse substantie composite non est tantum forme neque tantum materie, sed ipsius compositi;" *ScG* II, cap. 4: "esse non est proprium actus materiae, sed substantiae totius. Eius enim actus est esse de quo possumus dicere quod sit. Esse autem non dicitur de materia sed de toto [...]".

5. AQUINAS, *II Sent.*, d. 18, q. 2, a. 3: "*Esse formarum naturalium non est ipsarum absolute, sed ipsorum compositorum*: non enim per se possunt subsistere; et ideo ipsis formis per se loquendo non acquiritur esse, sed substantiis compositis. Unde *forma per se loquendo neque fit neque generatur, sed compositum* [...]"; *Q. de potentia*, q. 6, q. 3: "Id quod fit proprie est compositum, non forma vel materia; *compositum enim est quod proprie habet esse*".

6. ARISTOTLE, *Physics* II, 193b5: *kata ton logon*.

That is what is meant when it is said that the substantial form is the term of the generation: when the form actualizes matter, movement ends[7]. Two aspects of this account of generation must be underlined as particularly important for our subject. The first is that generation is conceived as the modification of dispositions in matter by an external agent. This is what I call the "artisan model" of generation. The second aspect is that the substantial form is the final cause of the process and the guiding principle of the action of the agent who works on matter until it has the appropriate disposition to be actualized by the form. In that sense, as Aristotle put it, the form is the end (final cause: *to ou eneka*) of movement and puts an end (term: *esjaton*) to movement[8].

It was necessary to offer this short synthesis of some basic principles of hylomorphism in order to understand why, when talking of matter, we cannot avoid talking of the form, because, as a potential principle related to form, matter receives all its determinations from the form, which is not only the formal but also the final cause of the composite. As Aristotle put it: "matter is relative: for if other is the form, other is the matter"[9]. When he decided in his treatise *On the soul* to extend the field of application of hylomorphism to all living beings, he opened a new chapter in the history of philosophical anthropology. Hereafter, body and soul in the Aristotelian tradition were to be thought of as matter and form and their perfect ontological unity was no longer a question: "so one need no more ask whether body and soul are one than whether the wax and the impression it receives are one"[10]. If we distinguish between body and soul, we should be aware that their distinction is a logical one. In reality they are co-principles

7. The Aristotelian notion of 'movement' was very well understood by Thomas. *Cf.* AQUINAS, *In octo libros Physicorum Aristotelis Expositio* III, 2 n. 285 (ed. Maggiòlo-Marietti): "Quod igitur est in potentia tantum, nondum movetur; *quod autem iam est in actu perfecto, non movetur*, sed iam motum est: illud igitur movetur quod medio modo se habet inter puram potentiam et actum, quod quidem partim est in potentia et partim in actu, ut patet in alteratione [...] Unde (motus) neque est potentia existentis in potentia, neque est actus existentis in actu, sed est *actus existentis in potentia*, ut per id quod dicitur 'actus' designetur ordo eius ad anteriorem potentiam, et per id quod dicitur 'in potentia existens' designetur ordo eius ad ulteriorem actum". In Book v Aristotle distinguished 'movement', 'generation' and 'corruption' as three different species of the common genus 'mutation', reserved 'movement' for accidental changes, and the other two for changes in substantial forms.

8. ARISTOTLE, *Physics* II, 194a 30.

9. ARISTOTLE, *Physics* II, 194b 9: *pros ti he yle, allô gar eidei alle yle* (my translation).

10. ARISTOTLE, *De anima*, II, 1, 412b 6-7; *cf.* AQUINAS, *Sentencia libri De anima* II, 1 v. 378-380: "Forma per se unitur materie sicut actus eius, et idem est materiam uniri forme quam materiam esse in actu".

of the same thing. My paper should be understood in the light of the principles that I have presented.

When in his *Summa contra Gentiles* Thomas rejected the conception of the soul as a complete intellectual substance and adopted Aristotelian hylomorphism as the best philosophical account of human nature, he also decided to follow the principles that we have just reviewed. His choice was made when he reached this fundamental conclusion: no composite has real ontological unity unless its components are related to each other as a substantial form and prime matter [11]. And it was strengthened by the realization that it is not merely the unity of the composite that is in question, but its very being, because, as he explained later, "a thing is a being according as it is one" [12]. It would not be correct to say that Thomas adopted hylomorphism passively. In some cases he, as many other commentators before him, was forced to interpret personally some aspects of the doctrine that Aristotle left undetermined (such as the nature of the possible and agent intellects). In other cases he incorporated elements of the long Aristotelian tradition (such as the number and functions of the internal senses). In some aspects he enriched hylomorphism (as when he insisted that the essence includes matter and form, and not only the form); in other cases he stretched hylomorphism to its limits (such as with the notion of subsistent substantial form). Let us then examine how the adoption of hylomorphism by Thomas affected his understanding of the nature of the human body.

First of all, he knows that if the soul is relative to matter as a substantial form, its intelligibility requires the body. It is impossible to define the soul without the body, because the soul does not have a complete essence by itself. Thomas follows Aristotle in his criticism of those who try to determine what the soul is without saying anything about the body that is its correlate, neglecting thus to take into account the basic truth that the soul is proportionate to its body and viceversa. This approach leads to absurdities, such as to think that the soul could be united to any kind of body, or that it can migrate to other bodies, and also to methodological errors, because the nature of the soul cannot be grasped without taking into consideration what kind of body is suitable for that particular kind of soul [13]. I cannot avoid thinking that this recognition could be used to show a

11. AQUINAS, *ScG* II, ch. 56: "Non fit aliquid ratione unum nisi sicut ex forma substantiali et materia".

12. AQUINAS, *S.Th. I Pars*, q. 76, a. 1: "Sic enim aliquid est ens, quomodo est unum".

13. AQUINAS, *Sentencia libri De anima*, I, 8 v. 320-363. Note: "Constat quod inter mouens et motum est aliqua proportio et inter agens et paciens et inter formam et materiam

serious flaw in the theological methodology mentioned at the beginning. Be that as it may, it is clear that for a natural philosopher, who considers the soul to be essentially the substantial form of the body, it is impossible to define the soul without the body or a particular kind of soul without its suitable kind of body [14]. Actuality cannot be defined without the receiving potentiality and the soul cannot be defined without its subject; this applies to the human soul as well, because no soul can be conceived by the intellect without the body that is its correlate [15]. I am not implying that the body is part of the essence of the soul (matter is essentially different from its form), but that it is part of its definition, because it is essential for the soul as substantial form to be united to the body, as it is essential to this soul to be united to this body [16]. Conversely the soul, as principle of actuality of the

similiter: non enim quelibet forma cuilibet corpori conuenit et unitur […]. Oportet quod sit inter ea aliqua communicatio et proportio […]. Non ergo sufficienter determinant de anima dum conantur dicere solum quale quid sit anima et negligunt ostendere quale quid sit corpus suscipiens ipsam, ex quo contingit eis illud quod in fabulis Pictagoricis habetur, quod quelibet anima in quodlibet corpus ingrediatur […]. Quamuis hoc non possit esse, cum unumquodque corporum et maxime animalium habeat propriam formam et propriam speciem […]. Sic ergo Plato et alii philosophi loquentes tantum de anime natura, insufficienter dixerunt, non determinantes quod corpus sit conueniens cuilibet anime et qualiter et quale existens uniatur sibi". *Cf.* also II, 4 v. 245-257.

14. The idea is expressed even in the early writings, when Thomas thought that the soul was a spiritual substance *and* a form. *Cf.* AQUINAS, *De ente*, c. 6: "Essentia est id quod per diffinitionem significatur […] nec forma substantialis completam essentiam habet nec materia, quia etiam in diffinitione forme substantialis oportet quod ponatur illud cuius est forma, et ita diffinitio eius est per additionem alicuius quod est extra genus eius […] unde et in diffinitione anime ponitur corpus a naturali qui considerat animam solum in quantum est forma phisici corporis […] forma substantialis non habet per se esse absolutum sine eo cui aduenit, ita nec illud cui aduenit, scilicet materia; et ideo ex coniunctione utriusque relinquitur illud esse in quo res per se subsistit et ex eis efficitur unum per se: propter quod ex coniunctione eorum relinquitur essentia quedam. Vnde forma, quamuis in se considerata non habeat completam rationem essentie, tamen est pars essentie complete".

15. AQUINAS, *Sentencia libri de anima* II, c. 1, v. 65-83; note: "Cum anima sit forma, oportet quod in diffinitione ipsius ponatur materia siue subiectum eius"; *In Metaph.* VII, 9 (ed. Marietti n. 1477) "Licet enim materia non sit pars formae, tamen *materia sine qua non potest concipi intellectu forma oportet quod ponatur in definitione formae, sicut corpus organicum ponitur in definitione animae*"; *Q. de anima*, q. 7 ad 16: "Anima diffinitur corporis forma"; *S.Th. I Pars*, q. 77 a. 1: "Unde etiam in definitione animae dicitur quod est actus corporis potentia vitam habentis", *et passim*.

16. AQUINAS, *S.Th. I Pars*, q. 75 a. 7 ad 3m: "*Corpus non est de essentia animae,* sed anima ex natura suae essentiae habet quod sit corpori unibilis"; *Q. de spiritualibus creaturis*, a. 9 ad 4m: "Licet *corpus non sit de essentia anime,* tamen <anima> secundum suam essentiam habet habitudinem ad corpus in quantum hoc est ei essentiale quod sit corporis forma: et ideo in diffinitione anime ponitur corpus; sicut igitur de ratione anime est quod sit

composite, is naturally inherent in its correlative potentiality, i.e. in its appropriate body. The body is what it is because of the soul. Consequently we must think of the soul as part of the essence of the animated body, as something of the body, namely its actuality and vital energy [17]. Any principle of actuality is in its appropriate potentiality; consequently the soul is in the appropriate body, is something of the body and cannot be received except in this particular body that has the suitable disposition [18]. One might think that these ideas, expressed in Thomas's commentary on *De anima*, are just a paraphrase of Aristotle's (*De anima* II 414a 20 *sqq.*), but I have no doubt that Thomas is expressing his own thought because the same idea is found in his personal works [19]. The main goal of this paragraph is to underline one central idea of Thomas anthropology, namely that the soul cannot be *understood* without the body, or the body without the soul. And that is so because the soul cannot *be* without the body: for the soul, to be without the body is indeed *contra naturam* [20]. Only the composite is intelligible by itself, because only the composite is the real subject of being.

Secondly, Thomas contributed to the development of hylomorphism by his well known doctrine of the unicity of the substantial form. He argued that if the substantial form is the principle of being (*esse simpliciter*), there could only be one substantial form because the first substantial form that confers the act of being to prime matter would constitute with it a substantial composite and any subsequent form actualizing this composite would necessarily confer an accidental perfection. What is of interest and importance for our subject is that this unique substantial form is the *formal*

forma corporis, ita *de ratione huius anime in quantum est hec anima est quod habeat habitudinem ad hoc corpus*".

17. AQUINAS, *Sentencia libri De anima* II, 2, v. 37-38: "Anima dicitur forma substancialis quia est de essencia siue de quiditate corporis animati". Cf. *ibid.*, II, c. 4, v. 241-243: "(Anima) non enim est corpus, quia non est materia, sed *est aliquid corporis*, quia est actus corporis".

18. *Ibid.* II, 4 v. 255-257: "Quia unusquisque actus 'natus est fieri in propria' et determinata 'materia', unde et anima oportet quod in determinato corpore recipiatur".

19. AQUINAS, *Q. de anima*, q. 10 v. 146-161; note: "Oportet quod forma sit *aliquid eius cui dat esse*, nam forma et materia sunt principia intrinsecus constituentia essentiam rei. Vnde oportet quod si anima dat esse et speciem ut forma cuilibet parti corporis secundum sententiam Aristotilis, quod sit in qualibet parte corporis, nam et ea ratione dicimus animam esse in toto, quia est forma totius".

20. AQUINAS, *ScG* IV, ch. 79: "Anima corpori naturaliter unitur: est enim *secundum suam essentiam corporis forma*. Est igitur *contra naturam* animae absque corpore esse"; *S.Th. I Pars*, q. 118 a. 3: "Si enim animae naturale est corpori uniri, *esse sine corpore est sibi contra naturam* et sine corpore existens non habet suae naturae perfectionem".

cause of all the substantial determinations of the composite. It is interesting to note that Thomas reached this conclusion at the very beginning of his career, at a time when he was still thinking that the soul was a substance and a form [21]. Later, in the *Summa contra Gentiles*, he extended the argument to the human soul and argued that if the soul as substantial form is the principle of being, it is also the principle of unity; consequently, the hypothesis of a plurality of substantial forms would ruin the ontological unity of the human being [22]. Since the substantial form confers the first act, its correlate can only be pure potency (prime matter). And since a substance has many substantial attributes, it must be said that they are all caused by the single substantial form. In the case of the human being, it is by the rational soul that the composite is a man, an animal, a living being, a *body*, a substance and a being [23]. That is why, when the link between the soul and matter brakes, the body ceases to belong to the human species and, in spite of the appearences, it can only be called a human body by homonymy (*equivoce*) [24]. It is difficult for us to grasp the full meaning of this statement because after Descartes we are used to considering that the body as a substance is defined by extension, which for Thomas is an

21. AQUINAS, *II Sent.*, d. 12, q. un. a. 4: "Avicenna improbat (positionem libri Fontis vitae de pluralitate formarum), quia omnis forma substantialis dat esse completum in genere substantiae. Quidquid autem advenit postquam res est in actu est accidens: est enim in subjecto quod dicitur ens in se completum. Unde oporteret omnes alias formas naturales esse accidentia; et sic rediret antiquus error, quod generatio idem est quod alteratio. Unde ipse vult quod ab eadem forma per essentiam ignis sit ignis et corpus et substantia".

22. AQUINAS, *ScG* II, ch. 58: "Cum igitur *a forma* unaquaeque res habeat *esse*, a forma etiam habebit *unitatem*. Si igitur ponantur in homine plures animae sicut diversae formae, homo non erit unum ens, sed plura... Omne enim quod advenit alicui post esse completum, advenit ei accidentaliter: cum sit extra essentiam eius. Quaelibet autem forma substantialis facit ens completum in genere substantiae: facit enim ens actu et hoc aliquid. Quicquid igitur post primam formam substantialem advenit ei accidentaliter adveniet".

23. AQUINAS, *Q. de spiritualibus creaturis* a. 3 v. 393-396: "Sic ergo dicimus quod in hoc homine non est alia forma substantialis quam anima rationalis, et quod per eam homo non solum est homo, set animal et uiuum et corpus et substantia et ens". Cf. *ibid.*, a. 1 ad 24m, et a. 1 ad 9m v. 517-519.

24. AQUINAS, *Sentencia libri de anima*, II, 1 v. 265-288: "Oportet enim secundum premissa (namely, that the form gives being simpliciter) dicere quod una et eadem forma substancialis sit per quam hoc indiuiduum est hoc aliquid siue substancia et per quam est corpus et animatum corpus et sic de aliis [...] ab anima est et quod sit et quod corpus sit et quod sit corpus uiuum [...]. Et inde est quod recedente anima non remanet idem corpus specie; nam oculus et caro in mortuo non dicuntur nisi equiuoce, ut patet per Philosophum in VII Met."; cf. *S.Th. I Pars*, q. 76 a. 6 ad 1m: "Una et eadem forma est per essentiam per quam homo est ens actu, et per quam est corpus, et per quam est vivum, et per quam est animal et per quam est homo" et q. 76 a 4 ad 1m.

accident of the genus quantity, that the term "body" express a univocal genus, and that the soul is another substance, distinct from the body. For Thomas, instead, the human being is a corporeal *substance* that owes its substantiality, corporeality and life to its unique substantial form, namely by its soul. This central thesis leads to an astonishing statement: the corporeality of human beings, when considered as a substantial determination, is not granted to the composite by a substantial form of corporeality distinct from the soul and prior to the soul (*à la Pinnocchio*), but by the rational soul itself, the only substantial form of the human composite and the only cause of all its substantial determinations [25]. There is no opposition between 'corporeality' and 'rationality' when they are considered substantial determinations, because both perfections are granted by the same soul. And it is impossible to think of the *human* body as something having substantial existence independently of the soul. Following Aristotle (*De anima* II, 412b 25-26), Thomas explains that the "natural body potentially possessing life" of which the soul is the first actuality, as the famous Aristotelian definition of the soul puts it, is not a body which has no soul, but which possesses its soul. In fact, when it is said that it possesses life potentially, it is meant that, although it has a soul, principle of life and vital operations, it may not actually exercise those operations [26].

25. AQUINAS, *ScG* IV, ch. 81: "Corporeitas autem dupliciter accipi potest. Uno modo secundum quod est forma substantialis corporis, prout in genere substantiae collocatur. Et sic corporeitas cuiuscumque corporis nihil est aliud quam forma substantialis eius [...]. Non enim sunt diversae formae substantiales in uno et eodem, per quarum unam collocetur in genere supremo, puta substantiae; et per aliam in genere proximo, puta in genere corporis vel animalis; et per aliam in specie, puta hominis vel equi. Quia si prima forma faceret esse substantiam, sequentes formae iam advenirent ei quod est hoc aliquid in actu et subsistens in natura; et sic posteriores formae [...] essent formae accidentales. *Oportet igitur quod corporeitas, prout est forma substantialis in homine, non sit aliud quam anima rationalis*"; *Compendium Theologiae* I, c. 154: "Si per corporeitatem intelligatur forma substantialis per quam aliquid in genere substantie corporee ordinatur, cum non sit unius nisi una forma substantialis, talis corporeitas non est aliud quam anima [...] alioquin anima adueniret corpori existenti in actu, et sic esset forma accidentalis"; *Q. de spiritualibus creaturis* a. 3 ad 14m: "Corpus autem quod est in genere substantie habet formam substantialem que dicitur corporeitas, que non est tres dimensiones sed quecumque forma substantialis ex qua sequuntur in materia tres dimensiones; et hec forma in igne est igneitas, in animali anima sensitiua et in homine anima *intellectiua*".

26. AQUINAS, *Sentencia libri De anima*, II, 2 v. 108-114: "Dicitur enim aliquid esse in potencia dupliciter: uno modo cum non habeat principium operationis, alio modo cum habet quidem set non operatur secundum ipsum; corpus autem cuius actus est anima est habens uitam in potencia, non quidem primo modo set secundo".

Human body and human soul are two inseparable faces of one single reality.

I would like to underline one more aspect of the formal causality of the soul. What we have said up to now allows us to avoid thinking of the body and the soul as if they were two *things*. There is only one thing, and that is the living human body of which the soul is the principle of being and the vital energy. Thomas realized very early that if body and soul where conceived as two things, they would need intermediaries to be kept together and would never achieve ontological unity. The idea that the soul was a substance that uses a body, so dear to any kind of Platonism, including some forms of Christian theology and some aspects of Averroism, all of which require intermediaries to explain the union, was never accepted by Thomas[27]. When he embraced fully the conception of the soul as substantial form of the body he rejected the notion of intermediaries as simply superfluous: a substantial form and its matter join together by their very nature of act and potency. The soul does not need intermediaries to join the body because they are both parts of the same essence and the intrinsic components of the same being[28]. As substantial form *the soul is something of the body*, namely its actuality and energy, and must be immediately present in the whole body and each of its parts. Thomas stated very clearly that the soul is immediately present, by the totality of its essence in the whole body and in each of its parts[29]. How could it be otherwise if the soul is the actuality and energy of the body? This

27. *Cf.* in that respect, AQUINAS, *II Sent.*, d. 1, q 2, a. 4, ad 3.

28. AQUINAS, *ScG* II, ch. 71: "Anima unitur corpus ut forma eius. Forma autem unitur *materiae* absque omni medio: per se enim competit formae quod sit actus talis corporis et non per aliquid aliud. Unde nec est aliquid unum faciens ex materia et forma nisi agens [...] nam materia et forma habent se ut potentia et actus". *Q. de anima*, q. 10 v. 145-168: "Anima secundum quod est forma corporis non unitur toti corpori mediante aliqua parte, sed toti corpori immediate [...]. Vnde oportet quod quelibet pars hominis et animalis recipiat esse et speciem ab anima sicut a propria forma [...]. Non est autem possibile quod aliquid recipiat esse et speciem ab aliquo separato sicut forma [...] set oportet quod forma sit aliquid eius cui dat esse, nam forma et materia sunt principia *intrinsecus* constituentia essentiam rei".

29. AQUINAS, *ScG* IV, ch. 72: "Est igitur in toto corpore, et non in una parte tantum, secundum suam essentiam, secundum quam est forma corporis [...]. Si enim esset forma totius et non partium, non esset forma substantialis talis corporis"; *S.Th. I Pars*, q. 76 a. 8: "Substantialis autem forma non solum est perfectio totius, sed cuiuslibet partis [...]. Anima vero est forma substantialis, unde oportet quod sit forma et actus non solum totius, sed cuiuslibet partis"; Cf. *Q. de anima*, q. 10 ad 16m: "Anima autem est forma substantialis corporis dans esse et speciem toti et partibus; et totum ex partibus constitutum est unum simpliciter". *Cf.* also *In De sensu et sensato* I, ch 4 (Leon. ed.), t. XLV-2, 28 v. 82-87.

thesis has an enormous impact on Thomas's understanding of the human body. Let's see how.

Inspired by Aristotle, Thomas conceived the ensemble of natural forms as structured hierarchically according to the variety and richness of the perfections that they bestow on matter. All substantial forms confer the act of being, as well as the perfection of being a substance and a body, but they differ by the substantial perfections that they can add to the composite on top of those mentioned. As a result of their differences, the species of natural beings are established. However, the different perfections of one individual composite are not caused by different forms but by its single substantial form. This is so because when a substantial form is capable of bestowing on matter a higher specific perfection it is also capable of bestowing the specific perfections of inferior forms [30]. The theory obviously applies to souls, which are the substantial forms of living beings. Once again following Aristotle, Thomas distinguished three species of souls: the vegetative, proper to plants, the sensitive, proper to animals, and the intellectual soul, proper to human beings. These kinds of souls differ specifically by their vital power, which translates into the number and variety of operations that their respective subjects are capable of performing. A higher soul gives to its body all the substantial perfections that the inferior soul gives to its correlate, and adds a new one. What was the soul for living beings of an inferior species becomes a power of the soul for living beings of a higher species [31]. In the case of the human composite the vegetative, sensitive and intellectual operations should not be explained by the presence of three souls, but by the single rational soul,

30. AQUINAS, *Q de anima*, q. 9 v. 173-190: "[...] Cum forme rerum naturalium sint sicut numeri [...] ut dicitur VIII Metaphysice-, oportet intelligere diuersitatem formarum naturalium, secundum quas materia constituitur in diuersis speciebus, ex hoc quod una addit perfectionem super aliam. Vt puta quod una forma constituit in esse corporali tantum [...] alia perfectior forma constituit materiam in esse corporali et ulterius dat ei esse uitale; et ulterius alia forma dat ei esse corporale et esse uitale et super hoc addit esse sensitiuum; et sic est in aliis". *Cf.* q. 11 v. v. 231-258; note: "Nulla forma substantialis unitur materie mediante alia forma substantiali, set forma perfectior dat materie quicquid dabat forma inferior, et adhuc amplius".

31. AQUINAS, *Q. de anima*, q. 2 ad 8: "Sicut tetragonum habet quicquid habet trigonum et adhuc amplius, et pentagonum quicquid habet tetragonum, ita sensitiua anima habet quicquid habet nutritiua, et intellectiua quicquid habet sensitiua, et adhuc amplius". Cf. *Sentencia libri de anima* II, c. 5 v. 270-281; note: "Et quia dixerat quod 'eodem modo' se habeat 'ratio anime' sicut ratio 'figure', ostendit conuenienciam inter utrumque [...] manifestum est enim in figuris quod trigonum, quod est prius, est potencia in tegragono [...] et similiter in anima sensitiua 'uegetatiuum' est quasi quedam potencia eius et <non> quasi anima in se; et similiter est de aliis figuris et aliis partibus anime".

which contains and assumes in its own vital energy (*virtus*) the power of the inferior ones [32]. These ideas and their sources were clearly presented in the *Summa Theologiae*:

> we observe that the species and forms of things differ from one another as the perfect and the imperfect. As in the order of things, the animate are more perfect than the inanimate, and animals more perfect than plants, and man than brute animals. And in each of these genera are various degrees. For this reason Aristotle, *Metaphysica* VIII, compares the species of things to numbers, which differ in species by the addition or subtraction of unity. And in *De anima* II, 3 he compares the various souls to the species of figures, one of which contains another, as a pentagon contains and exceeds a tegragon. Thus the intellectual soul contains virtually (*virtute*) whatever belongs to the sensitive soul of brute animals and to the nutritive soul of plants. Therefore, as a surface which is of pentagonal shape is not tetragonal by one shape and pentagonal by another – since a tegragonal shape would be superfluous as contained in the pentagonal – so neither is Socrates a man by a soul, an animal by another, but by one and the same soul he is both animal and man [33].

This text makes us understand that, since there is only one soul in the human body, this soul *cannot be* just an intellectual soul; it is rather an essentially vegetative, sensitive and intellectual soul. The human soul is a total power or vital energy (*virtus, totum potentiale*) which includes a vegetative, a sensitive and an intellectual part [34]. We should be aware that it

32. AQUINAS, *Q. de spiritualibus creaturis*, a. 3 v. 406-429: "Perfectior forma facit per unum omnia que inferiores forme faciunt per plura, et adhuc amplius: puta si forma corporis inanimati dat materie esse et esse corpus, forma plante dabit ei et hoc et insuper uiuere, anima uero sensitiua et hoc <et> insuper sensibile esse, anima uero rationalis et hoc et insuper rationale esse. Sic enim inueniuntur differre forme rerum naturalium secundum perfectum et magis perfectum [...] propter quod species rerum comparantur numeris, ut dicitur in VIII Methaphisice [...]. Vnde etiam Aristotiles in II De anima dicit quod 'uegetatiuum est in sensitiuo' et sensitiuo in intellectiuo 'sicut trigonum in tetragono' [...]. Sic etiam anima intellectiua uirtute continet sensitiuam, quia habet hoc et adhuc amplius, non tamen ita quod sint due anime".

33. AQUINAS, *S.Th. I Pars*, q. 76, a. 3; *cf.* also *Compendium Theologiae* I, c. 92.

34. AQUINAS, *S.Th.. I Pars*, q. 79, a. 4: "Anima autem humana intellectiva dicitur per participationem intellectualis virtutis, cuius signum est quod *non tota est intellectiva, sed secundum aliquam sui partem*"; *S.Th. I Pars*, q. 76, a. 3: "Si igitur homo ab alia forma haberet quod sit vivum, scilicet ab anima vegetativa, et ab alia forma quod sit animal, scilicet ab anima sensitiva, et ab alia quod sit homo, scilicet ab anima rationali, sequeretur quod homo non esset unum simpliciter [...]. Sic ergo dicendum est quod eadem numero est anima in homine sensitiva et intellectiva et nutritiva".

is only by a synechdoque that we call it an "intellectual" soul [35]. This point is of great importance to decide the kind of body that is suitable for that kind of soul. The text of the *Summa* makes us understand also that, since the soul is united to the body without intermediaries and is the actuality of the whole body and of each the parts of the body by the totality of its essence of substantial form, the perfection of the body is dependant upon the perfection of the soul from which it receives being and vital energy. Concerning this point Thomas has always maintained that the definition of the soul is analogical because it applies to souls having different degrees of ontological perfection. The bodies that are the correlate of these different souls must also reflect this difference in perfection, which is defined by the range and quality of their modes of life. In this respect Thomas has been quite decisive: the vegetative and sensitive life of the human being is nobler than the vegetative and sensitive life of animals for the simple reason that in the case of human both aspects are inserted in a mode of life that is also intellectual. In fact human sensation is not the same as animal sensation because it takes place in the framework of a perception of the world that is simultaneously sensible and intellectual. And the same applies to vegetative operations. The reason is that the whole essence of the soul, with all its richness, is present in every operational power of the living being soul [36]. The vegetative and sensitive powers of human beings are nobler than those of animals because the source and the energy of human powers is the essence of an intellective soul. We can see then than just as the notion of soul is analogical, so the notions of body and of operational powers are also analogical. Only for the logician is the genus "body" univocal; for the natural philosopher, who considers the modes of being bestowed by different substantial forms, that notion is analogical [37].

The difference of nobility between the body of brute animals and the human body is nowhere more visible than at the level of the operational powers linked to bodily organs, particularly the sensitive powers. Thomas explains that, although from a logical point of view animal sensibility and human sensibility belong in the same genus, they are specifically different because their sources, namely the essence of the sensitive soul and the essence of an intellectual soul, are specifically different, and this difference

35. AQUINAS, Sententia libri De anima, II, 4 v. 134-138: "Quibuscunque autem inest unum solum predictorum, oportet quod illud in eis sit anima; in quibus uero insunt plura, quodlibet est pars anime, set illa denominatur a principaliori uel sensitiua uel intellectiua".

36. AQUINAS, *Q. de anima*, q. 10 ad 10m: "Potentia anime radicatur in essentia; et ideo ubicumque est aliqua potentia anime, ibi est essentia anime".

37. *Cf.* AQUINAS, I *Sent.* d. 19, q. 5 a. 2.

translates also in a different degree of nobility [38]. Vegetative and sensitive powers linked to bodily organs are more perfect in human beings than in animals by the fact that they are joint to higher operational powers (the intellectual powers) within a more complex and rich totality of vital energy (*toto potestativo*) where they are rooted [39]. Thomas has given a few examples of sensitive powers that are nobler and more perfect in rational animals than in brute animals. We have seen (*cf.* n. 34) that he mentions the case of the sense of touch and of the internal senses in the *Disputed Questions on the power of God*. The same examples had been previously given in his *Commentary on the Book of Sentences* [40]. Later, in the *Summa Theologiae*, after insisting once again on the nobility of the human sense of touch, he pointed out particularly to the case of two internal senses. First is the internal sense which deals with the *intentiones* or representations of sensible things that are not grasped by the external senses. This sense is generically the same in animals and in humans since the object is the same, but their nobility is not because animals perceive the intentions by natural instinct, while human beings by a sort of inference. That is why, in the view of Thomas, this internal sense is called "estimativa" in one case, and "cogitativa" in the other. Another case is the internal sense of memory, which in the exclusive case of human beings is reinforced by reminiscence. All these differences can only be explained by the greater richness of the vital context of the internal senses in human beings [41].

38. AQUINAS, *De potentia*, q. 3 a. 11 ad 1: "Licet anima sensibilis in hominibus et brutis sit eiusdem rationis secundum genus, non tamen est eiusdem rationis secundum speciem, sicut nec idem animal specie est homo et brutum; unde et operationes animae sensibilis sunt multo nobiliores in homine quam in brutis, ut patet in tactu et in apprehensivis interioribus". *Cf.* II *Sent.* d. 18, q. 2 a. 3 ad 4: "Homo et equus non sunt unum animal in specie; unde in homine anima sensibilis est multo nobilior quam in aliis animalibus quantum ad principales actus, ut patet in actibus interiorum sensuum et in operatione tactus".

39. AQUINAS, *II Sent.*, d. 18, q. 2, a. 3 ad 4: "In omni enim toto *potestativo* potentia inferior superiori conjuncta perfectior invenitur".

40. AQUINAS, *II Sent.* d. 18, q. 2 a. 3 ad 4: "Homo et equus non sunt unum animal in specie; unde in homine anima sensibilis est multo nobilior quam in aliis animalibus quantum ad principales actus, ut patet in actibus interiorum sensuum et in operatione tactus".

41. For the sense of touch, *cf.* AQUINAS, *S.Th. I Pars*, q, 75, a. 5; cf. *infra*, note 68; note: "Homo inter omnia animalia melioris est tactus"; for the estimative and rememorative powers, cf. *S.Th. I Pars*, q. 78, a. 4: "Alia animalia percipiunt huiusmodi intentiones solum naturali quodam instinctu, homo autem etiam per quandam collationem; et ideo quae in aliis animalibus dicitur aestimativa naturalis in homine dicitur cogitativa, quae per collationem quandam huiusmodi intentiones adinvenit. Unde etiam dicitur ratio particularis, cui medici assignant determinatum organum, scilicet mediam partem capitis [...]. Ex parte autem memorativa non solum habet memoriam, sicut cetera animalia, in subita recordatione

The formal causality of the human soul as the single substantial form of the human composite is the foundation of the complete ontological unity of body and soul and of the richer and nobler life of the human composite. It is now appropriate to examine how the final causality of the soul affects the human body. Thomas has indicated that the more perfect a substantial form is, the more numerous and diverse its operations are, and in turn this multitude and diversity of operations must be matched by a larger number of parts and organs in the body that is its correlate; consequently, since the human soul is the most perfect of natural forms, the human body must have the greatest diversity of bodily organs [42]. Thomas indicated also that the more perfect a substantial form is, the more it overcomes the limitations of bodily matter by its operational powers. This central doctrine in Thomas's vision of nature was already elaborated in his *Commentary on the Sentences* and he never ceased to invoke it in later writings. According to it, nature is animated by a process in which potentiality is constantly being surpassed by actuality and forms emerge progressively from their material substract until the process reaches the human soul, the highest of substantial forms, capable of performing an operation without even using a bodily organ [43]. The perfection of the human soul is correlative to the

praeteritorum, sed etiam reminiscentiam, quasi syllogistice inquirendo praeteritorum memoriam secundum individuales intentiones".

42. AQUINAS, *Q. de anima*, q. 9 v. 256-280. Note: "Forme perfectiores habent plures operationes et magis diuersas quam forme minus perfecte [...] in rebus autem magis perfectis requiritur ulterius diuersitas partium, et tanto magis quanto forma fuerit perfectior [...]. In corporibus uero animatis, que nobiliores formas habent, diuersis operationibus deputantur diuerse partes [...] cum anima sit perfectissima formarum materialium, in homine inuenitur maxima distinctio partium propter diuersas operationes; et anima singulis earum dat esse substantiale secundum illum modum qui competit operationi ipsarum". *Sentencia libri De anima* I, 14 v. 125-130: "Quanto anima est perfectior, tanto exercet operationes plures et diuersas, et ideo ad exercendum huiusmodi operationes, necessaria sunt ei plura et diuersa organa corporalia; quia uero anima rationalis est nobilior et perfectior, tanto maiorem exigit diuersitatem organorum". Conversely, "quia anima plante inperfecta est in ordine animarum, non requirit magnam diuersitatem in partibus" (II, 4, v. 57-59).

43. AQUINAS, *II Sent.*, d. 17, q. 2, a. 1 ad 2: "Cum ergo in conjunctione formae ad materiam forma inveniatur dominans, quanto forma est nobilior et magis vincens materiam, tanto magis poterit habere virtutem praeter conditionem materiae. Unde quaedam corpora mixta praeter virtutes qualitatum activarum et passivarum, quae tenent se ex parte materiae, habent quasdam virtutes quae consequuntur speciem, ut quod magnes attrahit ferrum; et magis hoc invenitur in plantis, ut patet in augmento [...]; et hoc adhuc invenitur plus in animalibus, quia sentire omnino est supra virtutem qualitatum elementarium; et perfectissime in anima rationali, quae est nobilissima formarum, et ideo ipsa habet quasdam virtutes in quibus nullo modo communicat corpus"; cf. *S.Th. I Pars*, q. 76, a. 1: "Quanto forma est nobilior, tanto magis dominatur materiae corporali et minus ei immergitur et magis sua

complexity and variety of organs in the human body and is finally expressed by the soul's power to go beyond the capacities of the body. The degree of organization of the body follows the perfection of the soul because the substantial form is the final cause of matter. Nature makes sure that matter develops the dispositions that are needed for the complete fulfillment of the form's operational richness. This means, according to Thomas, that the participation of matter in forms is not for the sake of matter, in order that matter might achieve its perfection, as the Platonists would want it, but for the benefit of the forms, in order that they might reach their perfection. And he adds: "it is not because matter has this particular disposition that a form of a particular kind is united to it, but rather because the form is of this particular kind that it becomes necessary that matter have this particular disposition. That is why the body of a human being has the particular disposition that is suitable to the kind of form that the human soul is"[44]. The idea reached a perfect expression in the *Summa Theologiae*: "since the form is not for the matter, but rather matter for the form, we must gather from the form the reason why the matter is such as it is, and not conversely"[45]. Thomas had explained the point to his dear friend Reginald de Piperno some time before: "forms do not diversify to respond to the diverse ways in which matter has been organized, but matter has been organized in diverse ways to respond to diverse forms"[46].

operatione vel *virtute* excedit eam. Unde videmus quod forma mixti corporis habet aliquam operationem quae non causatur ex qualitatibus elementaribus. Et quanto magis proceditur in nobilitate formarum, tanto magis invenitur *virtus* formae materiam elementarem excedere; sicut anima vegetabilis plus quam forma metalli, et anima sensibilis plus quam anima vegetabilis. Anima autem humana est ultima in nobilitate formarum. Unde in tantum sua *virtute* excedit materiam corporalem quod habet aliquam operationem et virtutem in qua nullo modo communicat materia corporalis. Et hec virtus dicitur intellectus".

44. Aquinas, *Q. de anima*, q. 8 ad 16: "Unio forme ad materiam non est propter materiam set propter formam. Non igitur quia materia est sic disposita, talis forma sibi datur; set ut forma sit talis, oportuit materiam sic disponi. Et sic supra dictum est quod corpus hominis dispositum est secundum quod competit tali forme" (see previous lines *infra*, n. 52).

45. AQUINAS, *S.Th. I Pars*, q. 76, a. 5: "Cum forma non sit propter materiam, sed potius materia propter formam, ex forma oportet rationem accipere quare materia sit talis, et non e converso".

46. AQUINAS, *Compendium Theologiae* I, ch. 71 v. 14-20: "Non autem habent esse forme propter materias, sed magis materie propter formas, nam actus melior est potentia, id autem propter quod aliquid est oportet melius esse. Neque igitur forme ideo sunt diuerse quia sunt materie diuerse, sed magis materie institute sunt diuerse ut competant formis diuersis". The idea was formulated in *ScG* II, ch. 40: "Formae igitur non consequuntur dispositionem materiae sicut primam causam, sed magis e converso materiae sic disponuntur ut sint tales formae".

From a teleological perspective, the order of things in nature is presided by the principle that matter is for the benefit of the form [47]. The source of the principle "materia est propter formam et non e converso" (matter if for the benefit of the form and not the reverse) is Aristotle's *Physics* II, 26, its axiomatic formula comes from Averroes, *In Phys.* II, 26 et *In De anima*, II, 36, p. 185, v. 26, and its most comprehensive formulation from Thomas, who stated that "the less perfect is always for the sake of the more perfect, and consequently as the matter if for the sake of the form, so the form, which is the first act, is for the sake of its operation, which is the second act; and thus operation is the end of the creature" [48]. The organization of matter responds to the ontological and operational perfection of the substantial form. Thomas however did not use this principle in either of his two first essays to answer to the question "is the human body a suitable correlate for the human soul"? He does not even mention it in the *Commentary on the Sentences*, and in the *Summa contra Gentiles*, where he is perfectly aware of the significance of the principle, he does not use it to determine what characteristics should possess the body to which the human soul is united. This is a revealing fact. It probably means that at the time he wrote the *Commentary on the Sentences* he had not yet discovered the principle in Aristotle or Averroes; or it could also mean that the principle is not relevant when the soul is considered to be a substance. But the fact that Thomas did not invoke the principle in the *ScG* requires another explanation. It is possible that Thomas did not realize immediately the impact that his recently adopted notion of the soul as substantial form had on the discussion of the human body's constitution. I will try to show however that the importance of the principle increases as Thomas realizes that the nature of human beings has to be explained in terms of Aristotelian hylomorphism.

The first time he dealt with the question of the kind of body that was suitable for the human soul was in Book II of the *Commentary on the Sentences* (d. 1, q. 2, a. 5). At that time, influenced by Avicenna, who asserted in true Neoplatonic spirit that the order of perfectible things should follow the order of perfected things, Thomas answered the question by drawing a parallel between human beings and celestial bodies: as the human soul should ressemble the perfection of the mover of the celestial

47. AQUINAS, *ScG* III, ch. 75: "In comparatione rerum ad finem talis ordo apparet quod [...] in substantiis vero materia est propter formam".

48. AQUINAS, *S.Th. I Pars*, q. 105, a. 5: "Semper enim imperfectum est propter perfectius; sicut igitur materia est propter formam, ita forma, quae est actus primus, est propter suam operationem, quae est actus secundum; et sic operatio est finis rei creatae".

bodies, so the human body should be similar to the perfection of the celestial body. The nobility of the latter consists in the fact that its constitution has no contrary, which ensures its incorruptibility, and consequently the perfection of any other body is determined by how far it is removed from contrariety. The bodies of corruptible things cannot however be totally free of contraries, such as hot and cold, wet and dry, but must achieve a medium in which none of the contraries is in act. The human body has achieved the most balanced mixture and has the best constitution (*complexio*) among all corruptible bodies. That is why it is the most similar to the celestial body and only to it should the human soul be united. That is also why human beings, among all animals, possess the best sense of touch, a sense whose subtlety requires a well balanced bodily constitution, and the quality of this sense infrastructure influences the quality of the intellectual faculties. The better is the sense of an individual, the better is his intellect[49]. In another question (d. 15, q. 2 a. 1) Thomas explained that the fact that the constitution of the human body is perfectly balanced is not incompatible with the existence of different temperaments in individual human beings, one of which can be a melancholic, another a choleric, because there can be degrees of balance according to the proximity of an individual body to one or the other limits of heat and humidity that are compatible with a balanced constitution in the human species; and that is fine provided that the limits of the balance are not exceeded (in which case death would occur). He clarified that the balance between the elements is not merely quantitative, but has to be also based on quality, because elements do not have the same active power and thus a merely quantitative balance will indeed be profound operational imbalance[50]. In another text (d. 17, q. 3 a. 1) Thomas shows again his allegiance to Avicenna and repeats the basic idea that the human body ressembles the celestial bodies by its perfectly balanced constitution. The most interesting contribution of this first attempt to define the qualities of the human body is the insistence on the balance of its

49. Aquinas, *II Sent.*, d. 1, q. 2, a. 5; note: "Illud corpus quod venit ad maximam aequalitatem mixtionis est simillimum caelo, et tale corpus debet esse corpus humanum".

50. AQUINAS, *II Sent.*, d. 15, q. 2 a. 1; note: "Complexio debita corpori humano est complexio temperatissima, et tamen sunt multi gradus temperamenti secundum quod quidam dicuntur melancholici, quidam cholerici, secundum propinquitatem ad terminus complexionis humanae speciei vel in calore vel in frigore, ita tamen quod est aliquis gradus caloris vel frigoris quem non transit humana complexion [...] oportet inferiora elementa, quae minus sunt activa eo quod habent plus de materia et minus de forma, secundum quantitatem excedere, ut virtutis defectum suppleat quantitatis excessus".

chemical and physical components and the influence of this chemical composition on the individual temperaments.

The discussion about the qualities of the human body in *Summa contra Gentiles* II, ch. 90 is quite disappointing for the modern reader because it is focused on a subject that is completely dépassé, namely whether the human soul could be united to a body made out of a single simple element. Thomas opens the chapter by recalling his previous thesis, i.e. that if the soul is united to a body made out of a mixture of elements, it could only be united to the one that has achieved the most balanced constitution and that consequently has the best sense of touch. We would not talk of progress here if it were not for the fact that the the quality of the body is no longer based on its ressemblance to the quality of the celestial bodies, a sign that Thomas has abandoned the Avicennan worldvision, but on the quality of the soul of which it is a correlate, a sign that Thomas has embraced Aristotelian hylomorphism as the valid explanation of human nature. But immediately after Thomas embarks on a discussion of an hypothesis which has no meaning for us, namely whether an intellectual substance as the soul could be united to a simple element, but which was probably inspired by the desire of ensuring the immortality of the soul. To the credit of Thomas it must be said that he sees not much sense in the hypothesis either. Consequently we'll consider the reasons he opposes to such a strange idea taking into consideration only their philosophical value for a more relevant discussion. One of them is interesting because it distinguishes between the human soul and the spiritual substances: spiritual substances are purely intellectual and have no reason to be united to the body, because the intellectual operation is not performed with the help of a bodily organ; the human soul, by its very essence, is not only intellectual, but also vegetative and sensitive, so it needs a body that has a diversity of organs; consequently it could not be united to a body made of a simple element. Another reason is that, although the totality of simple elements is incorruptible, their parts are however corruptible; by hypothesis the composite of intellectual substance and a part of a simple element would then be corruptible; but nature provides corruptible beings with a sense that can discriminate contraries and allow them to avoid danger and corruption; such is the sense of touch, which requires an organ made of a well balanced mixture of contraries; consequently it is impossible that any simple body be animated by the soul. Finally I call the attention to another reason that Thomas opposes to an alternative hypothesis, namely that even if the soul does not unite to a simple element as its form, it could unite to such a body as its mover. Thomas, who has often said that the soul is united to the body as the substantial form and as a mover, opposes to this new version of the hypothesis a reason that clarifies the meaning of his position. He argues that the power of a mover united to a simple element as its proper movable subject is limited to the body to which it is united because the movement it causes cannot excede its proper movable subject. But it would be "ridiculous" to say that the power of a spiritual substance cannot excede a part of a simple element *or of a body made of a mixture of elements*. The only way that a movable subject could limit the power of the mover is if the mover is a substantial form and the movable subject its material correlate. I underline this response because some might be tempted to think that, when Thomas says that the soul is united to the body as mover and form, he is saying that the soul is a substance and a form, and that he never went beyond his initial dualism. He clarifies here that the soul cannot be a mover unless it is essentially the form of the body.

A new approach was developped by Thomas during his sojourn in Italy (1265-1268), more particularly in Rome (1267-1268), at the convent of Saint Sabine. It was made possible by his detailed reading of the new translation of Aristotle's *De anima* and it was expressed in an impressive ensemble of writings dealing with psychology and anthropology. This ensemble includes the *Disputed Questions on the soul* (1266-1267), the *Commentary on Aristotle's De anima* (1267-1268), and Part I of the *Summa Theologiae* (1266-1268). Given that all these writings belong to the same period, express the same doctrinal position and clarified each other in questions of interpretation, allows to make a synthetic presentation of their doctrinal content. I'll take the *Questions on the soul* as the guiding text for two reasons: first, it is a text where Thomas is not forced to follow the order of ideas of another author, as it happens in the *Commentary on Aristotle's De anima*; second it has been the laboratory (chantier de travail) where he tested his ideas before writing the *Summa*. By comparing the two texts we will be able to see where Thomas felt the need to provide further elaboration.

The *Disputed questions on the soul* are the first text where Thomas discuss as the qualities of the human body in the light of the principle "matter is for the sake of the form". At the time of these disputes he had begun working on his commentary of the newly revised text of Aristotle's *De anima* and had reached a very deep understanding of the consequences of applying hylomorphism to human beings. As a result of this his exposé concerning the conditions that a body must meet to be suitable for the human soul is of a luminous clarity. Question 8 asks whether the human soul ought to be united to a body such as the human body. The text could be considered a very open criticism of Avicenna's (and young Thomas's) doctrine according to which the qualities of the human body should be those which make it as similar as possible to the celestial body, and a no less open discussion of some theological points of view which raise doubts about the suitability of a corruptible body for an incorruptible soul. Instead of embarking in an historical analysis of sources I prefer to start directly with Thomas's magisterial ruling about the subject. I will divide it in 8 points and the presentation of each of them will be enriched by the contributions of the parallel texts, namely the *Sentencia libri De anima*, the *I Pars*, and the *Q. de malo*.

1. The point of departure of Thomas's position is the principle "matter is for the benefit of the form". He is indicating that only by reflecting on the soul, which is the substantial form of the body, can we determine what kind of disposition our body must have, not by establishing comparisons with the celestial bodies. This is so because, according to Aristotle, the soul is not only the formal cause and mover of the body but also its final cause (*De anima*, II, 415b10-15). According to this finalistic interpretation of Nature, common to Aristotle and Thomas, the disposition of matter is not the cause of the specific form, but the specific form is the cause of the disposition of matter (cf. *supra*, n. 44 and 46). In the *Summa Theologiae* we find the same point of departure and the same appeal to the finalistic interpretation of Nature [51]. I have mentioned (cf. *supra*, n. 44) that for Thomas the opposite doctrine is not Alexander of Aphrodisias's materialism, as one would have expected, but Plato's theory of ideas. According to Thomas's interpretation, Plato asserts that the participation in the subsistent forms by portions of matter is for the benefit of these portions of matter, in order that they might achieve the fullness of their being, but that this participation is not for the benefit of the forms, which subsist by themselves. Consequently forms were granted to portions of matter in accordance to their merits (deserving qualities) [52]. If it is accepted, on the contrary, that the forms do not subsist by themselves, it must be said that matter is for the benefit of the

51. AQUINAS, *Q. de anima*, q. 8, v. 177-182: "Cum materia sit propter formam et non e conuerso, ex parte anime oportet accipere rationem quale debeat esse corpus cui unitur. Vnde in II De anima dicitur quod anima non solum est corporis forma et motor, set etiam finis"; *S.Th. I Pars*, q. 76, a. 5: "Cum forma non sit propter materiam, sed potius materia propter formam, ex forma oportet rationem accipere quare materia sit talis, et non e converso".

52. AQUINAS, *Q. de anima*, q. 8 ad 16: "Plato ponebat formas rerum per se subsistentes, et quod participatio formarum a materiis est propter materias ut perficiantur, non autem propter formas, que per se subsistunt. Et ideo consequebatur quod forme darentur materiis secundum merita earum" (I use J. Robb's translation, with some modifications).

forms (see the rest of the text in n. 44). This reference to Plato clarifies an aspect that risks being neglected in the interpretation of the principle *materia est propter formam*. We should not take it as meaning only that the matter *serves* the form, but also as meaning that the form *needs* the matter in order to be, and needs it to have a particular disposition in order to achieve the fullness of its being, which, as we said, takes place at the level of operations [53]. That is why in his *Commentary on De anima* Thomas explains that form and matter are mutually proportionate, in the sense that not every form suits or can be united to every body, but there must be a communion and proportion between them. Consequently every philosopher asserting that the soul is in the body must explain what disposition has this body, why the soul is united to this body, and what is the mutual relationship between this soul and this body. Any effort to understand the soul that neglects to consider the qualities that make its body an appropriate correlate of the soul is philosophically inadequate [54]. That of course is the risk of anyone who thinks that the soul is subsistent by itself and does not need the body to be and to operate in accordance with its own nature [55].

2. The next step in Thomas's argument is to state, in conformity with the general principle that is his point of departure, that the union between soul and body is necessitated by the fact that the soul is last in the order of realities of intellectual nature [56]. Far from having innate ideas, as the angels do, the soul is in potency to intelligible species ("as a wax tablet on which nothing has been written") and consequently it cannot perform the act of intellection, which is its proper operation, by itself. The soul must acquire the intelligible species (i.e. the forms representing the essence of things in

53. AQUINAS, *Q. de spiritualibus creaturis*, a. 6 v. 205-208 "Unio enim corporis et anime non est propter corpus, ut corpus scilicet nobilitetur, set propter animam, que indiget corpore ad sui perfectionem, sicut supra dictum est"; *cf.* also a. 3 ad 11.

54. AQUINAS, *Sentencia libri De anima*, I, 8 v. 320-363; cf. *supra* n. 13. Pythagoras, Plato, and his Neoplatonic followers have a lot of common with Carlo Collodi, author of The Adventures of Pinocchio.

55. AQUINAS, *S.Th. I Pars*, q. 89 a. 1: "Et ideo (anima) ad hoc unitur corpori, ut sit et operetur secundum naturam suam".

56. AQUINAS, *Q. de anima*, q. 8 v. 185: "Infima in ordine intelligibilium substantiarum". To avoid misinterpretations of Thomas's thought concerning the nature of the soul (which is not to be a 'substance' but a 'substantial form', I translate 'substantia' as 'essence' or 'nature', which can be predicated of substances, accidents and parts of substances. The translation is legitimate, taking into consideration the polysemy of the term 'substantia', which can mean 'first substance' and 'essence'"; cf. *I Sent.*, d. 9, q. 1, a. 1: "Sed substantia dicitur dupliciter: quandoque enim sumitur pro essentia, sicut est in usu Latinorum; quandoque pro supposito essentiae, vel pro re naturae primi predicamenti, quae dicitur hypostasis apud Graecos".

the mind) from the things outside itself through the mediation of sense powers. That is the reason why it is necessary for the human soul be united to the body [57]. The *Summa* follows the same order of ideas, but introduces two interesting changes. The first is to invoke Ps. Denys's authority, instead of Aristotle's, in support of the thesis that the soul has to gather the intelligible species from the sensible through the mediation of sense power. The second, of greater philosophical importance, is to underline that if to accomplish its intellectual operation the soul must acquire the intelligible species from sensible data, the soul must possess sense powers, because "nature never fails in necessary things". That implies that the essence of the human soul is not only intellectual but sensitive (and consequently vegetative as well, because the sensitive cannot exist without the vegetative). The point was notmade sufficiently clear in *Questions on the soul*, and that might have lead someone to think that the soul is an exclusively "intellectual" form that needs a "sensitive" body and that the union between the two is merely operational (à l'Averroès) [58]. This clarification allows understanding much better the following point.

3. In the *Questions on the soul* the argument goes on to explain that if the reason why the soul joins the body is because it needs to acquire the intelligible species from sensible things by means of sensation, it is necessary that the body to which the soul is united be very well equipped for the acquisition of sensible data from which intelligible species can be abstracted. Consequently, the human body must possess the best possible disposition for the operation of sensing [59]. The *Summa* echoes this conclusion, but does it from a better theoretical premise, as has been

57. AQUINAS, *Q. de anima*, q. 8 v. 183-198: "Naturale est anime humane corpori uniri quia, cum sit infima in ordine intelligibilium substantiarum [...] non habet anima humana intelligibiles species sibi naturaliter inditas quibus in operationem propriam exire [...]. Vnde oportet quod species intelligibiles a rebus exterioribus accipiat mediante potentiis sensitiuis, que sine corporeis organis operationes proprias habere non possunt. Vnde et animam humanam necesse est corpore uniri".

58. AQUINAS, *S.Th. I Pars*, q. 76, a. 5: "Natura autem nulli deest in necessariis; unde oportet quod anima intellectiva non solum haberet virtutem intelligendi, sed etiam virtutem sentiendi".

59. AQUINAS, *Q. de anima*, q. 8 v. 199-207; note: "Necessarium est quod corpus, cui anima rationalis unitur, tale sit ut possit esse aptissimum ad representandum species sensibiles ex quibus in intellectu species intelligibiles resultent. Sic igitur oportet corpus cui anima rationalis unitur esse optime dispositum ad sentiendum". *Cf.* ad 15: "Anima unitur corpori propter intelligere, quod est propria et principalis eius operatio. Et ideo requiritur quod corpus unitum anime rationalis sit optime dispositum ad seruiendum anime in hiis que sunt necessaria ad intelligendum".

explained: the soul needs a body with an excellent disposition for sensorial activity because the soul is essentially sensitive[60].

4. The next step is to determine the foundation of sense activity. Although there are a number of senses, one is "the foundation of all the others, namely the sense of touch, in which resides mainly (*principaliter consistit*) the totality of the sensitive nature". To prove his point Thomas gives three arguments. The first is of authority: it is said in book II of *De anima* II (413b2-5), continues Thomas, that it is on account of this sense that living things are first called "animal"[61]. The two others are of experience: when the sense of touch becomes inoperative, as when we fall asleep, all the other senses become inoperative; and all senses become inoperative not only by the excess of their own proper sensible objects (an excessive light, a sound too loud), but also by an excess in the sensibles that are proper to touch (an intense heat or cold). In the *Commentary on De anima* Thomas expands his arguments. He explains that the organ of the sense of touch pervades (*diffunditur*) the whole body so that the organ of each of the other senses is also an organ of touch, and thus the sense of touch is the reason why a living being is called sensitive[62]. In his exegesis of Book III he justifies the importance of the sense of touch by noting that, while excess in the object of other senses can destroy these senses while leaving the animal alive, excess in the object of the sense of touch can not only destroy the sense, but the whole animal as well. It is then on this sense of touch that the animal's life depends[63]. The *Summa* just gives the thesis

60. AQUINAS, *S.Th. I Pars*, q 76, a. 5: "Actio autem sensus (clearly identified as a power of the soul not of the body, *cf.* n. 57) non fit sine corporeo instrumento. Oportuit igitur animam intellectivam tali corpori uniri quod possit esse conveniens organum sensus". The power of the soul is the form of the organ, as the soul is the form of the body. Cf. *Sentencia libri De anima*, II, 2 v. 85-95: "si oculus esset animal, oportet quod uisus esset anima eius, quia uisus est substantialis forma oculis, et oculus est materia uisus, sicut corpus organicum materia anime"; *cf.* also v. 135-138. The finalistic principle also applies to the relationship between *potentia* and *organum*; cf. *S.Th. I Pars*, q. 78, a. 3: "Non enim potentiae sunt propter organa, sed organa propter potentias; unde non propter hoc sunt diversas potentias, quia sunt diversa organa, sed ideo natura instituit diversitatem in organis, ut congruerent diversitati potentiarum".

61. AQUINAS, *De anima*, II, 413b2-5. Aristotle indeed states in this passage that "the first characteristic of a animal is sensation" and that "the first essential factor of sensation, which we all share, is a sense of touch", but the formula 'tactus est fundamentum aliorum sensuum' comes from Albert the Great, as R.-A. Gauthier has shown in *Sentencia libri De anima*, II, 19 adn. 91-92.

62. AQUINAS, *Sentencia libri De anima*, II, 19 v. 91-96.

63. AQUINAS, *Sentencia libri De anima*, III, 12 v. 60-96.

according to which the sense of touch is the foundation of sensitive but does not offer arguments to prove it [64]. The conclusion of this step is that, since the body to which the human soul is united must possess the best disposition for a sensitive nature and the sense of touch is the foundation of all sense activity, it is necessary that the human body be the most suitable organ for the sense of touch [65]. Two corollaries complete this step: the human sense of touch is more exact (*certior*) than that of all other animals; and also on account of the excellence of this sense one human being is better prepared than another to perform intellectual operations [66]. In a personal passage of his *Commentary on De anima* Thomas gives an even stronger formulation of this corollary: "nobility of the soul follows up upon a well-balanced physical constitution, because forms are proportionate to their matter. It follows that those whose touch is good have a nobler soul and a better intelligence" [67]. The *Summa* provides similar statements: among animals, man has the best sense of touch, and among men, those who have the best sense of touch have the best intelligence [68].

5. In a fifth step Thomas focuses on the particular conditions that a body must meet to be the most suitable organ for the sense of touch. Sensation, like every cognitive operation, is a "passive" operation characterized by the reception of a form. In order to avoid altering the reception and secure the objectivity of the act of knowledge, the recipient must lack the thing received. In the case of sensitive powers using bodily organs this principle

64. AQUINAS, *S.Th. I Pars*, q. 76, a. 5: "Omnes autem alii sensus fundantur supra tactum".

65. AQUINAS, *Q. de anima*, q. 8 v. 219-223: "Cum igitur corpus cui anima rationalis unitur debeat esse optime dispositum ad naturam sensitive, necessarium est ut sit conuenientissimum organum sensus tactus".

66. *Ibid.*, v. 224-227: "Hunc sensum habemus certiorem inter omnia animalia [...] propter bonitatem huius sensus etiam unus homo alio est habilior ad intellectuales operationes".

67. *Cf.* AQUINAS, *Sentencia libri De anima* II, 19 v. 96-114: "Ex hoc quod aliquid habet meliorem tactum, sequitur quod simpliciter habeat meliorem sensitiuam naturam et per consequens quod sit melioris intellectus, nam bonitas sensus est dispositio ad bonitatem intellectus [...] ad bonam complexionem corporis sequitur nobilitas anime, quia omnis forma est proportionata sue materie. Vnde sequitur quod qui sunt boni tactus sunt nobilioris anime et perspicacioris mentis".

68. AQUINAS, *S.Th. I Pars*, q. 76, a. 5: "Homo inter alia animalia melioris est tactus, et inter ipsos homines, qui sunt melioris tactus sunt melioris intellectus"; *cf.* also q. 85, a. 7: "Quanto corpus est melius dispositum, tanto meliorem sortitur animam [...] cum etiam in hominibus quidam habeant corpus melius dispositum, sortiuntur animam maioris virtutis in intelligendo [...] illi enim in quibus virtus imaginativa et cogitativa et memorativa est melius disposita sunt melius dispositi ad intelligendum".

imposes that no organ of a sensitive power ought to possess the contrary qualities which that sense is capable of perceiving, but must be in potency to them so that it might receive them. This requirement applies differently to the sense of touch and to the other senses. For example, the organ of the sense of sight cannot have any kind of color in order to receive them all, and something similar happens in the case of the organs of the sense of hearing and smelling[69]. But the sense of touch is an exception to the rule. The reason is that the contrary qualities that are its objects are the same qualities of the elements of which the animal body is composed, i.e. the hot, the cold, the moist and the dry (*cf.* n. 65). Hence it is impossible that the organ of the sense of touch be totally deprived of any of the elements whose qualities are its objects. Instead of lacking these contraries, the organ of touch must have a disposition that is a kind of mean among them: that is the way in which the organ is in potency to those contraries. "Consequently the body to which the rational soul is united, since it must be extremely suitable for the sense of touch, must be brought to the highest possible degree of this median state through an equal blending of the four simple elements[70]. Same idea is presented in the *Commentary on De anima*[71] and in the *Summa*, where Thomas argues however from the point of view of the formal causality of the soul. From the point of view of matter, the more balanced is the blending of elements in a body, the more perceptive is the sense of touch. From the point of view of the formal causality of the soul, the higher is the soul, the more perfect are its operational powers. The human soul is the most perfect of the substantial forms, consequently its sensitive powers (*virtutes sensitivae*) are not only the most perfect among

69. The sense of taste (*gustus*) is a case apart because, as Aristotle says, "gustus est tactus quidam" (*De anima* II, 421a 19). Since human beings have the best sense of touch, they have also the best sense of taste. *Cf.* AQUINAS, *Sentencia libri De anima* II, 19 v. 63-77. The superiority of human sense of touch and taste makes human beings the 'wisest' (*prudentissimum*) of all animals because they have the most accurate discriminative powers concerning objects that are essential for survival. Cf. *ibidem* II, 5 v. 180-187: "Quia necessarium est omnibus animalibus uti alimento [...] ideo necessarium est quod habeant sensum tactus quo percipiant alimentum sibi conueniens. Et quod tactus sit sensus alimenti, manifestum est: sicuti enim corpora uiuencia constant ex calidis et humidis et frigidis et siccis, ita ex eis nutriuntur; tactus autem est sensus discretiuum horum".

70. AQUINAS, *Q. de anima*, q. 8 v. 245-248: "Corpus igitur cui anima rationalis unitur, cum debeat esse conuenientissimum ad sensus tactus, oportet quod sit maxime reductum ad medium per equalitatem complexionis".

71. AQUINAS, *Sentencia libri De anima*, II, 19 v. 105-110: "Cum enim instrumentum tactus non possit esse denudatum a genere tangibilium qualitatum eo quod est ex elementis compositum, oportet quod sit in potencia ad extrema saltem per hoc quod est medium inter ea".

animals because they are inserted in the context of a whole that includes an intellectual power (*cf.* n. 38 and 41), but require also the most perfect blending of elements. After saying this Thomas returns to material causality and concludes that this balanced constitution of the body is the reason why man has the better sense of touch [72]. It is an interesting text that shows the reciprocal causality of the two principles of a hylomorphic composite.

6. The reciprocity between matter and form allows Thomas to present, in the following step of his exposé, a fascinating picture of Nature proceeding gradually from simple elements, combining them until it achieves the the most perfect mode of blending, which is found in the human body, whose perfectly balanced constitution makes it the suitable correlate of the human soul [73]. This picture of the emergence of the perfect bodily constitution has its counterpart in the picture of the gradual emergence of forms in nature. According to Thomas, nature gradually gives rise to forms that progressively elevate themselves above the limitations of their material correlate until it reaches the human soul, which is capable of an operation performed without using a bodily organ [74]. Unfortunately none of these pictures express a dynamic view of nature, but a mere description of a static hierarchy of souls and their bodily correlates. Neither the Aristotelian doctrine of the eternity of the species, nor Thomas's doctrine of the creation of species, allow for a dynamic view of nature, because in both doctrines the species and their parts (matter and forms) have always been the same, ever since they existed. This might be inevitable in a finalistic conception of the world: if the organization of

72. AQUINAS, *S.Th. I Pars*, q. 76, a. 5: "Ad organum autem tactus requiritur quod sit medium inter contraria quae sunt calidum et frigidum, humidum et siccum, et similia quorum est tactus apprehensivus; sic enim est in potentia ad contraria et potest ea sentire. Unde quanto organum tactus fuerit magis reductum ad aequalitatem complexionis, tanto perceptibilior erit tactus. Anima autem intellectiva habet completissime virtutem sensitivam, quia quod est inferioris praexistit perfectius in superiori, ut dicit Dionysius in libro De div. nom. Unde oportuit corpus cui unitur anima intellectiva esse corpus mixtum inter omnia alia magis reductum ad aequalitatem complexionis. Et propter hoc homo inter omnia animalia melioris est tactus".

73. AQUINAS, *Q. de anima*, q. 8 v. 251-257: "Tota operatio nature inferioris terminatur ad hominem sicut ad perfectissimum. Videmus enim operationem nature procedere gradatim a simplicibus elementis, commiscendo ea quousque perueniatur ad perfectissimum commixtionis modum, qui est in corpore humano. Hanc igitur oportet esse dispositionem in communi corporis cui anima rationalis unitur, ut scilicet sit temperatissime complexionis".

74. For the emergence of forms, *cf.* AQUINAS, *Q. de anima*, q. 1 v. 291-326; *Q. de anima*, q. 7 v. 251-275; *Q. de potentia*, q. 3 a. 11; *S.Th. I Pars*, q. 76 a. 1.

matter is for the sake of the form and forms are not the result of the organization of matter, it is impossible to even think of a gradual emergence of form and useless to reflect on the gradual complexity of matter as the cause of the different forms of life. In Aristotle's eternal world as well as in Thomas's created world, form precedes matter as actuality precedes potentiality. But in Aristotle's system this only implies that an individual of a given species always precedes the generation of another individual of the same species. Thomas introduces a metaphysical cause to explain a physical problem: for him the first individuals of any given species, and consequently the species themselves, regardless whether they are eternal or had a beginning in time, are caused by the First Cause. It is not the purpose of this paper to analyse whether the appeal to metaphysical causality to explain a physical problem is legitimate.

What is interesting to add, however, is that for Thomas the human body has achieved not only the best chemical blending of elements in its general constitution, but also the best physical organization of its particular parts and organs so that the human being might sense most effectively. That is why the human brain is well disposed and is proportionally the largest among the animals, so it can be the effective organ for the internal senses like imagination and memory, which are essential for the performance of intellectual activities. That is also why the head in human beings is placed at the top of the body, so the human operations can be performed more freely. And that is why the human heart must possess a great deal of heat, so it can generate vital and animal spirits that keep the body in an upright position and facilitate the transmission of sense data. The highest degree of chemical balance of the human body, and the superior physical disposition of its parts, make of it the suitable correlate for the human soul [75].

7. Thomas then proceeds to the assessment of the chemical and physical dispositions of the human body. And he does so in the light of a principle that is worthwhile analysing, given its philosophical interest. In things which are constituted of matter we find some properties that explain why such kind of matter has been chosen by the agent for the benefit of such kind of form; and we find also some other properties that result from the necessary condition of matter and have nothing to do with the choice of the agent. For example, if an artisan wants to make a saw, he would choose

75. AQUINAS, *Q. de anima*, q. 8 v. 258-276. *Cf.* Apparatus fontium: notes 264 and 265 for the disposition and size of the human brain; note 267-268 for the placement of the head; note 270-271 for the heart; note 271 for the notion of 'spiritus;' note 272-273 for the importance of narural heat.

the iron for its hardness, because his goal is to make an instrument suitable for cutting, but he does not choose the fact that the iron can loose its sharpness or get rusted, conditions that result necessarily from the nature of the material. If it were possible to find a material that has the hardness of iron and none of its disadvantages, the artisan would certainly choose it. The same thing happens in the case of the human body. The maker of man chose this body because it is perfectly suitable for the operations of the sense power due to its well balanced mixture of elements and excellent disposition of organs. Unfortunately, a body which is constituted of contrary elements is subject to corruption, which is a necessary consequence of the kind of matter that the body is; but it is not for that reason that it was chosen as the correlate of the human soul. And nobody should argue that God could have done things differently, because concerning the creation of natural species we should not ask what God could do, but what the nature of the thing requires for it to be made[76]. Philosophically it must be said that the body suitable for our soul is a body composed of contrary elements, and that makes it necessarily corruptible.

8. Obviously this is a satisfactory approach to the problem of our finitude. But it still leaves unanswered questions about the compatibility of this corruptible body and the soul, especially for those who, like Thomas and many theologians, think that the human soul is immortal by nature. As Thomas himself admits it: "corruption that results necessarily from matter is specially incompatible with this substantial form that is the intellectual soul, because the other forms are corruptible at least per accidens, but the intellectual soul is neither corruptible by accident nor per se"[77]. In order to

76. AQUINAS, *Q. de anima*, q. 8 v. 277-303; note: "Quod enim (corpus humanum) taliter sit commixtum et secundum partes dispositum, ut sit conuenientissimum ad operationes sensitiuas, est electum in hac materia a factore hominis; set quod hoc corpus sit corruptibile, fatigabile et huiusmodi defectus habeat, consequitur ex necessitate materie"; *cf.* also *S.Th. I Pars*, q. 76, a. 5 ad 1, which repeat almost litterally the text of *Q. de anima*. A more elaborate account is given in *Q. de malo*, q. 5, a. 5 v. 174-218; note: "Cum enim anima humana sit intellectiua in potentia, unitur corpori ut per sensus accipiat species intelligibiles, quibus fit intelligens actu. Non enim unio anime et corpus est propter corpus set propter animam: non enim forma est propter materiam, set materia propter formam. Primus autem sensuum est tactus, qui quodammodo est fundamentum aliorum, organum autem tactus oportet esse medium inter contraria, ut probatur in II De anima. Vnde corpus congruens tali anime fuit corpus ex contrariis compositum; quod autem sequitur ex necessitate materie quod sit corruptibile" (perfect synthesis of what has been said up to now).

77. AQUINAS, *Q. de malo*, q. 5, a. 5 v. 232-237: "Set speciali modo corruptio proueniens ex necessitate materie est preter conuenientiam huius forme que est anima intellectiua. Nam

solve the problem Thomas has no other choice but to discuss it in theological terms. A historian of philosophy has to listen and to see whether there is some philosophical principle at work in the theological discourse and to check for inconsistencies. There is nothing more that he can do. Thomas's thesis is that, in order to remediate the incompatibility between the inmortal soul and the corruptible body, God by his grace granted to the first human beings at the very moment of their creation the assistance of the original justice (by which the inferior faculties are subject to reason and the conditions of the body to the soul; cf. *ScG* IV, ch. 52) whereby the body would be totally subject to the soul as long as the soul remains subject to God. That ensured that neither death nor sickness or defects would affect the original human beings unless the soul first separated from God. But due to the sin of the founders of the species, human beings lost this benefit of grace and are now subject to death and other defects resulting from the necessity of matter [78]. From a philosophical point of view it can be said that Thomas theological discourse does not affect his philosophical thesis that the body is a well balanced blend of elements subject naturally to corruption, because the body of the first human beings was not naturally but gratuitously incorruptible. That is precisely what Thomas clarified in the *Summa*, written after the *Questions on the soul*: "before the original sin the human body was incorruptible not by nature, but by a gift of divine grace" [79]. But in the *Q. de malo* the tension between an incorruptible soul and a corruptible body – a tension unconceivable if the soul is conceived as a substantial form and the body as its correlative matter, both of which exist only as long as they are mutually related – becomes quite apparent and force Thomas into using a language that is close to dualism and into appealing to a theological solution of a problem that his eclectic philosophical anthropology has created. Death and corruption are indeed natural to man, he explains, but only from the point of view of the necessity of matter; but from the point of view of his form, immortality is more appropriate for him. As we can see, matter and form no longer seem to be correlative principles of a single substance; they seem rather to have different ontological status and a different relationship with the act of being. Their transcendental relationship has been broken, and with it the unity of man. This is confirmed by the way Thomas

alie forme sunt corruptibiles saltem per accidens, set anima intellectiua non est corruptibilis nec per se nec per accidens".

78. AQUINAS, *Q. de anima*, q. 8 v. 304-313.

79. AQUINAS, *S.Th. I Pars*, q. 76, a. 5 ad 1: "Corpus hominis ante peccatum immortale fuit non per naturam sed per gratiae divinae donum".

continues his thoughts: man has a natural aptitude for immortality by reason of his soul (which is incorruptible *by nature*), but the incorruptibility of man cannot be ensured by the principles of nature, consequently the complement that will allow the realisation of the natural aptitude for immortality must come from the divine power, just like our natural aptitude for moral virtues is not realised without the complement that comes from the exercice of moral acts. The text appear to be inconsistent because it states at the same time that nature cannot grant immortality to man and that the immortality of the soul is a natural property. It establishes thus an ontological separation between man and his soul that only a divine intervention can overcome. The nature of man is presented as being contradictory: "insofar as immortality is natural for us (because of our soul), death and corruption (due to our material nature) are unnatural for us" [80].

The theological doctrine of the creation of the first human beings does not seem to lead to inconsistencies with respect to the constitution of the human body: as far as its natural constitution is concerned, the body of the founders of the species and the bodies of the rest of us seem to have the same natural characteristics (those properties that the body of the "founders" may have had by grace are not of our business). On the contrary, the doctrine of the natural immortality of the soul accentuates the incompatibility between the soul and the corruptible body and puts in crisis the hylomorphic conception of the human composite. Thomas knows that this problem of incompatibility cannot be solved by nature, because there are no natural means to bestow incorruptibility to a body composed of contrary elements. The situation is absurd from a philosophical point of view: nature has produced a substantial form that is incorruptible by nature and it has linked it to a naturally corruptible body; consequently the soul, after the corruption of its body, is condemned to be naturally incapable of fulfilling its nature of substantial form. That is where Thomas introduces

80. AQUINAS, *Q. de malo*, q. 5, a. 5 v. 258-270: "Mors et corruptio naturalis est homini secundum necessitatem materie, set secundum rationem forme esset ei conueniens immortalitas. Ad quam tamen prestandam nature principia non sufficiunt; set aptitudo quidem naturalis ad eam conuenit homini secundum animam, complementum autem eius est ex supernaturali uirtute. Sicut Philosophus dicit in II Ethicorum quod habemus aptitudinem ad uirtutes morales ex natura, set perficiuntur in nobis per consuetudinem. Et in quantum immortalitas est nobis naturalis, mors et corruptio est nobis contra naturam". The analogy between a supernatural intervention and the practice of moral acts that allows the development of virtues is frankly of very little theoretical value. Besides, the union of matter and form, which is supposed to guarantee the unity of human nature, ends up being viewed as a structure whose components are naturally opposed.

the theological thesis concerning the intervention of the divine power that resurrects the body and grants it once again incorruptibility, this time not by grace (as in Paradise), but by glory (in heaven)[81]. But all this discourse is developped after the transcendental link that unites soul and body in a hylomorphic conception of human nature has been broken. In heaven man is a composite of a soul that is incorruptible by nature and a body that is incorruptible by glory. They no longer seem correlative and neither the formal causality nor the final causality of the soul is taken into consideration to explain the properties of the body. That is why Thomas has contradictory statements concerning the status of the resurrected body. Sometimes he says that in accordance to the newly acquired incorruptibility its constitution is no longer that of a mixture of elements requiring food to subsist, but that of a spiritual body which has no need for animals and plants[82], a thesis that ressembles those *Pictagoricis fabulis* that Thomas used to criticize for thinking that the human soul could be united to any kind of body. In other occasions he is more consistent with his philosophical principles and states that the resurrected body will have the same properties as the body that we have now, because the human soul can only be united to its proper material correlate. Consequently the soul will be reunited to a human body, made of the same bones and flesh as now and equipped with the same organs. Only on that condition the body could still be for the benefit of the form and have some meaning[83]. All this is far beyond the reach of philosophy and might be even just theological fiction. What remains to be discussed as a legitimate philosophical problem is how the human body acquires, through the embryonic development, the

81. AQUINAS, *Q. de potentia*, q. 5, a. 3 ad 8: "Sed quod habeat incorruptibilitatem ex gratia vel gloria hoc non prohibetur, sicut corpus Adae fuit quodammodo incorruptibile per gratiam innocentiae et corpora resurgentium erunt incorruptibilia per gloriam".

82. AQUINAS, *Q. de potentia*, q. 5, a. 9: "In illa mundi innovatione (at the end of the world) nullum corpus mixtum remanebit praeter corpus humanum [...] plantae sunt propter animalia, praeparatae eis in cibum a natura; animalia vero propter hominem, necessaria ei ad cibum et ad alia auxilia. Ista autem necessitas est vita animalis hominis durante, quae quidem in illa rerum innovatione tolletur, quia *corpus resurget non animale sed spirituale* ut dicitur I *Corinth*, XV, 44, et ideo tunc etiam animalia et plantae cessabunt".

83. AQUINAS, *Compendium Theologiae* I, 152: "Cum autem anima corpori uniatur ut forma, unicuique autem forme propria materia respondeat, necesse est quod corpus cui iterato anima unietur sit eiusdem rationis et speciei cum corpore quod deponit per mortem. Non igitur resumet anima in resurrectione corpus celeste uel aereum, uel corpus alicuius alterius animalis, ut quidam fabulantur, sed *corpus humanum ex carnibus et ossibus compositum, organizatum eisdem organis ex quibus nunc consistit*". Cf. *Q. de anima*, q. 8 ad 12.

dispositions that make it suitable for the human soul. But that has to be left for another paper.

BIBLIOGRAPHY

ARISTOTLE (1952), *Physique*, texte établi et traduit par H. Carteron, Paris, Les Belles Lettres.

– (1957), *On the Soul*, with an English translation by W.S. Hett (The Loeb Classical Library), London-Cambridge (Mass.), W. Heinemann Ltd-Harvard University Press.

AVERROES (1562-1574), *Aristotelis Opera cum Averrois Commentariis*, Venetiis.

– (1953) *Commentarium Magnum in Aristotelis De anima libros*, recensuit S. Stuart Crawford (Corpus Commentariorum Averrois in Aristotelem), Cambridge (Mass.), The Mediaeval Academy of America.

THOMAS AQUINAS (1929), *Scriptum super libros Sententiarum*, Editio nova cura R.P. Mandonnet O.P., tomes I and II, Paris, P. Lethielleux Éd.

– (1934), *Summa contra Gentiles*, Editio Leonina Manualis, Roma, Apud Sedem Commisionis Leoninae, Desclée & c.- Herder.

– (1949), *Quaestiones disputatae de potentia*, in *Quaestiones disputatae vol. II*, Cura et studio P. Bazzi, M. Calcaterra et al., Romae-Taurini, Marietti, Editio IX revisa.

– (1954), *In octo libros Physicorum Aristotelis Expositio*, Cura et studio P.M. Maggiòlo O.P., Romae-Taurini, Marietti.

– (1957), *Summa Theologiae*, Texto latino de la Edición crítica Leonina, Madrid, Biblioteca de Autores Cristianos, segunda edición.

– (1964), *In duodecim libros Metaphysicorum Aristotelis Expositio*, Cura et studio M.R. Cathala O.P. - R.M. Spiazzi O.P., Romae-Taurini, Marietti.

– (1976), *De principiis naturae*, Editio Leonina, t. XLIII, Cura et studio Fratrum Praedicatorum, Roma, Editori di San Tommaso.

– (1979), *Compendium Theologiae*, Editio Leonina, t. XLII, Cura et studio Fratrum Praedicatorum, Roma, Editori di San Tommaso.

– (1979), *De ente et essentia*, Editio Leonina, t. XLIII, Cura et studio Fratrum Praedicatorum, Roma, Editori di San Tommaso.

– (1982), *Quaestiones disputatae de malo*, Editio Leonina, t. XXIII, Cura et studio Fratrum Praedicatorum, Roma-Paris, Commissio Leonina - Vrin.

– (1984), *Questions on the Soul (Q. de anima)*, translated with an introduction by J.H. Robb, Milwaukee (Wisc.), Marquette University Press.

– (1984), *Sentencia libri De anima*, Editio Leonina, t. XLV, 1, Cura et studio Fratrum Praedicatorum, Roma-Paris, Commissio Leonina - Vrin.

– (1985), *Sentencia libri De sensu et sensato, cuius secundus tractatus est De memoria et reminiscencia*, Editio Leonina, t. XLV, 2, Cura et studio Fratrum Praedicatorum, Roma-Paris, Commissio Leonina - Vrin.

– (1996), *Quaestiones disputatae de anima*, Editio Leonina, t. XXIV, 1, edidit B.-C. Bazán, Roma-Paris, Commissio Leonina - Les Éditions du Cerf.
– (2000), *Quaestio disputata de spiritualibus creaturis*, Editio Leonina, t. XXIV, 2, edidit J. Cos O.P., Roma-Paris, Commissio Leonina - Les Éditions du Cerf.

APPENDIX

COMMENTARY ON BOOK II OF THE *SENTENCES*, DISTINCTION 17, QUESTION 2, ARTICLE 1

Richard C. TAYLOR, tr.

WHETHER THERE IS ONE SOUL OR INTELLECT FOR ALL HUMAN BEINGS [1]

QUESTION 2

Third it is asked whether the soul was created outside the body. Regarding this two issues are raised. First, whether there is one soul or intellect for all human beings, as a certain separate substance flowing into all bodies. Second, if there are many [souls and intellects], whether they are created in the body or outside the body.

First Article

To the first we proceed as follows.

1. This translation is from a provisional Latin text prepared by the late P.-M. Gils, O.P., and provided by Dr. Adriano Oliva, O.P., president, *Commissio Leonina*. Where this text varies from that in the edition of Mandonnet (1929), the Latin of the provisional text is given together with the corresponding text in the edition of Mandonnet (M) in notes.

[Objections]

1. It seems that the rational soul or intellect is one in number in all human beings[a]. For no form except a material form is[b] multiplied in being with the division of matter. But the intellect, as is proven in *De Anima* 3[2] is not a material form since it is not the act of a given body. This is proven from its very act because it knows all material forms. This could not be the case if it were to have one of these in its own nature or [if] it were determined to [one] on the basis of the body for which it is the act, just as the visual power would not know all colors if the pupil which is its organ were to have a determinate color. Therefore, the intellect is not multiplied in being with the division of matter and so it remains one in all individuals of the human species who[c] are divided [into individuals] only in virtue of matter.

2. Furthermore, it is impossible that the principle be more material than what it is the principle of, because the principle must be more simple. But, as is conceded by all, there are some powers[d] of the rational soul which are not acts of a given body nor of an attached organ, the principle and root of which is the very essence of the soul. Therefore, it seems that neither is the rational soul[e] united to the body through its essence[f] as its act[g]. And so it follows, as it seems, that rational souls are not distinguished[h] with the division of bodies.

3. Furthermore, everything which is received in something is received in it in the mode of the recipient, not in its own mode, as is held by Dionysius and the *Book of Causes*[3]. If, therefore, the intellect were individuated with the division of body in order to be distinct[i] in diverse [individuals], it is necessary that intelligible[j] forms received in [the individual intellect] also be individuated. From that two unacceptable consequences seem to follow. One is that, since no particular is understood

(a) in omnibus hominibus; M: in omnibus (b) nisi sit; M: nisi (c) que; M: qui (d) potentie sunt; M: sunt potentiae (e) anima; M: ipsa anima (f) per essentiam suam corpori uniatur; M: corpori uniatur per essentiam suam (g) actus; M: actus ejus (h) anime rationales non distinguantur; M: anima rationalis non distinguatur (i) alius et alius; M: alius (j) intelligibiles; M: intellectuales

2. ARISTOTLE, *De Anima* 3.4, 429a24-28.

3. *Liber de causis*, prop. 23 (24). Aquinas often cites Pseudo-Dionysius as holding this Neoplatonic principle of participation but it is difficult to find in a precise formulation in the latter's works.

in act but rather [only] in potency, species[4] of this sort will not be intelligible in act but will require that they be understood through other species, and so forth into infinity. The other is that the mode of receiving forms in prime matter and in the possible intellect will be the same, because in the case of both they are received as those are and not as are forms taken absolutely. Hence, just as prime matter does not know forms which it receives, so too neither [does] the possible intellect [know forms which it receives], as it seems.

4. Furthermore, for any things distinguished from one another, it is necessary that there be something diverse in the nature of each. But since the intellect is none of the things which exist before [it is actually] understanding, it seems that there cannot be[k] something diverse found[l] in it unless according to[m] the diversity of understood[n] species. Therefore, the intellects of one individual[o] and another do not differ in essence but through understood species[p] alone.

5. Furthermore, for all substances existing per se and immaterial, diversity in number is due to diversity of species. [This is] because, if they have their own absolute subsisting being, they cannot be distinguished essentially through something which is outside their essence on which they are spread, as bodily forms are spread on matter. However, in the essence of these there is nothing but form, and the diversity of [form][q] brings about the diversity of species.But it cannot be said that the intellects of diverse human beings differ in species because human beings themselves differ in species by the diversity of their forms. Therefore, since the rational soul is a substance subsisting in itself–otherwise it would not remain[r] [in existence] after [the death of] the body–and is[s] immaterial, it seems that it also does not differ in number in diverse human beings.

(k) possit; M: sit (l) inveniri; M: invenire (m) apud; M: secundum (n) intellectarum; M: intellectivarum (o) huius; M: istius (p) species intellectas; M: species (q) nisi forma, cuius diuersitas; M: diversitas formae, quae (r) remaneret; M: maneret (s) et sit; M: et etiam sit

4. The Latin *species* can be employed denote a species of a genus in logic and it can also be used as here to denote an apprehended form. A sensible species is a form apprehended by sense, a species apprehended by imagination is a form in the imagination or a phantasm, and an intelligible species is a form apprehended by intellect.

[Contrary arguments]

1. The case for the contrary is that it is impossible for a form one in number to belong to many individuals.But the rational soul is the form of any given human being. For, if a human being were to have the being of a human [t] from the substance of the sensitive or nutritive soul, it could not be found in a human being in reference to his first being [5] which is the basis for [a human being] rising above other animals [u], and that is an unacceptable consequence. Therefore it is impossible for there to be one [v] rational soul belonging to all [human beings].

2. Furthermore, it is impossible for diversity in second being to be found in those things for which there is no diversity with respect to first being. [This is] because the diversity of secondary perfections and contrariety cannot exist at once [w] with the unity of first perfection because in this way contraries would exist in the same thing. But we find ultimate perfections in second being to be diverse and contrary in diverse human beings, for some of them are fools and some wise, some vicious and some virtuous. Therefore, it is necessary that the first perfection, namely the soul, be varied in diverse [human beings] in first being.

3. Furthermore, the soul is the form and mover of the body. But in celestial bodies, according to the position of the philosophers, diverse movers are assigned to diverse bodies. Therefore it seems that diverse souls are much more surely in diverse human beings.

[Solution]

[A] [6] Response. It should be said [x] that there are many opinions on the part of the philosophers regarding the unity and diversity of the rational soul, when we have set aside those who assert that the intellect is one for all

(t) esse hominis; M: esse (u) alia animalia; M: animalia (v) esse unam; M: unam esse (w) simul esse; M: esse simul (x) Responsio. Dicendum; M: Respondeo dicendum

5. In Aristotle, *De Anima* 2.1, the first perfection or actuality of a thing is its substantial being or first being, while second or later perfections or being (also called "second act" and "operation" by Aquinas in the response to the first objection) are actualizations of powers or activities on the part of the thing. *Cf.* the terminology used in the second contrary reason below.

6. These letters in brackets are divisions of the text corresponding to parts of my commentary.

intellectual nature or who hold that the intellect is the same as the divine essence[y][7].

[B] To understand these [sorts of views] it is necessary to understand that intellect is distinguished by the philosophers into three: the possible intellect[z][8], the agent intellect and the intellect in a positive disposition[9]. Possible intellect names what is in potency for receiving all understood forms[10], as vision[a] is in potency for receiving all colors. Agent intellect names what makes intelligibles in potency to be [intelligibles] in act, as light which makes colors visible in potency to be visible in act. Intellect in a positive disposition or formal [intellect] is so named by them when the possible intellect has already been perfected by the intelligible species so that it is able to operate [in its own right], for no passive power[b] has an operation unless perfected by the species of its object[c], as vision does not see before it has received the species of color.

[C] In light of these considerations, it should be known that nearly all the philosophers after Aristotle are in agreement that the agent intellect and the possible [intellect] differ[d] in substance and that the agent intellect is[e] a certain separate substance. It is both last among the separate intelligences and related to the possible intellect as[f] that by which we understand, as higher intelligences [are related] to the souls of the spheres. But this cannot

(y) essentia divina; M: divine essentia (z) intellectus possibilis; M: scilicet intellectus possibilis (a) visus; M: oculus (b) virtus; M: potentia (c) perfecta per speciem obiecti sui; M: per speciem objecti sui perfecta fuerit (d) differant; M: differunt (e) et est postrema; M: et postrema (f) et habet se ita; M: et ita se habet

7. Aquinas is likely referring to the view of Amalric of Bene. See J. M. H. H. THIJSSEN, "Master Amalric and the Amalricians: Inquisitorial Procedure and the Suppression of Heresy at the University of Paris", *Speculum* 71 (1996) 43-65, particularly 46-47.

8. The term "possible intellect" is based on Aristotle, *De Anima* 429a21-24. *Cf.* AVICENNA, *De Anima*, 5.1, 81.77, Arabic 209; and 76.5-6, Arabic 206. AVERROES, *Commentarium Magnum in Aristotelis De Anima Libros* (hereafter *LCDA*), 387.

9. *Intellectus in habitu* corresponds to the Arabic *al-ᶜaql bi-l-malakah*. This term denotes the intellect as having received actualization in knowledge and so as positively disposed with knowledge. As Aquinas notes below, this can also be called "formal intellect" insofar as it is in a disposition of having been actualized or perfected by the reception of intelligible forms or species. This is the human intellect subsequent to apprehension of intelligibles in act and as in a positive disposition for the reconsideration of intelligibles in act in intellectual understanding without an additional abstraction from sensible experience required. See AVICENNA, *De Anima*, 5.1, Latin 81.78-82, Arabic, 209; and AVERROES, *LCDA*, 438.

10. Averroes writes *LCDA*, 387; Taylor tr. 304: "non habet naturam secundum hoc nisi naturam possibilitatis ad recipiendum formas intellectas materiales".

be sustained[g] according to the faith. For if, as Anselm proves[11], God did not will that the salvation of humanity come about through an angel, lest the parity in glory of human beings and angels be abolished were an angel to come to be the cause of human salvation. Likewise, if our soul were held to depend on some intelligence or angel for a natural operation, it could not reasonably be sustained that the soul will be equal to the angel in glory[h]. [This is] because the ultimate perfection of any given substance is in the completion of its operation. For this reason the philosophers mentioned hold that the ultimate happiness of human beings is to be united with the agent intellect[12]. And for this reason some Catholic teachers, correcting and partially following this opinion, asserted in a probable enough way that God Himself is the agent intellect[13]. [This is] because by turning to Him our soul is made blessed, which they confirm in virtue of what[i] is written at *John* 1, 9: *He was the true light, etc.*

[D] Concerning the possible intellect there has likewise been great diversity among the philosophers following Aristotle. For some have said that the possible intellect is diverse in diverse [human beings], while others [have said that it] is one for all [human beings].

Among those who held it to be diverse[j] in diverse [human beings] there are three opinions.

[Alexander]

[E] For some say that the possible intellect is nothing other than a disposition which is in human nature for receiving the impressions of the agent intellect and that this is a bodily power consequent upon the human constitution. This was the opinion of Alexander [of Aphrodisias]. But this

(g) sustineri non potest; M: non potest sustineri (h) futura sit in gloria; M: sit in gloria futura (i) per id quod; M: per hoc quod (j) diversum; M: diversum esse

11. ANSELM, *Cur Deus Homo*, 1.5, in *Complete Philosophical and Theological Treatises*, J. Hopkins and H. Richardson, tr., Minneapolis, 2000, p. 305: "Don't you realize that man would rightly be deemed to be the servant of whatever other person would redeem him from eternal death? And if so, then man would not at all have been restored to the dignity which he would have had if he had not sinned. For man, who was meant to be the servant only of God and meant to be equal in every respect to the good angels, would become the servant of him who is not God and whom the angels do not serve".

12. This is discussed at length by AQUINAS in *In 4 Sent. D. 49, Q. 2, A. 1*, "Whether the blessed will see God in his essence".

13. Functions of the agent intellect were attributed to God by Roger Bacon, John Peckham, Roger Marston, and some others of the Latin tradition.

cannot stand up even according the intention of Aristotle who wants the possible intellect to be receptive of intelligible species. However, a disposition is not [itself] receptive but rather something which has been disposed[k] [is receptive][14]. But what has been disposed by this disposition is a body or a power in a body, and in that way what receives intelligible forms would be a body or a power in a body, which the Philosopher refutes[15]. Furthermore, it would follow that the possible intellect would not be a power for having knowledge. For no power caused by the commixture of elements is able to know, because in this way the quality belonging to the elements would act beyond [the limits of] its species[16], which is impossible[17].

[Ibn Bâjjah/Avempace]

[F] For this reason other [philosophers] said that the possible intellect is nothing but the power of imagination, insofar as it is naturally constituted such that forms which come to be[l] understood in act are [already] in it. This is the opinion of Ibn Bâjjah. But this is also impossible because, according to the Philosopher in Book 3 of the *De Anima*, phantasms which are in the imaginative [power] are related to the human intellect as colors to vision. For this reason it is necessary that the phantasms be what move the possible intellect, as color moves vision[18]. The ability[m] which is in the possible intellect for understanding is similar to the ability which is in the patient in potency so that it may be patient in act[n]. The ability which is in the imaginative [power] is as the ability of the agent in potency so that it may be agent in act. However, it is[o] impossible that the same thing be[p] mover and moved, agent and patient. Therefore, it is impossible that the

(k) preparatum; M: praeparativa (l) fiunt; M: fuerent (m) et aptitudo; M: unde aptitudo (n) actu; M: in actu (o) est autem; M: autem est quod (p) esse; M: sit

14. That is, a disposition is a state of something disposed in some way, not a substance or nature in its own right.

15. At *De Anima* 1.1, 403a10 Aristotle states that, if there is some activity of soul proper to it without body, then the soul may be separate from body. He determines just that and reasons that the reception of forms in knowledge requires that the intellect be unmixed with body at *De Anima* 3.4, 429a15 ff.

16. That is, beyond its nature.

17. The account of Alexander provided by Aquinas is based solely on Averroes. See *LCDA*, 395-97, 430-31, 443-44.

18. Aquinas's source is Averroes's *Long Commentary on the De Anima*, not Aristotle. See Averroes, *LCDA*, 410; Taylor tr., 316-317.

imaginative power be the possible intellect. Furthermore [q], to this extent it would follow that the power receiving the intelligibles in act which is called possible intellect would be employing a bodily organ, since the imaginative power would have a determinate organ [19].

[Conclusion re. Alexander and Ibn Bâjja/Avempace]

[G] It should also be known that, according to these opinions, the possible intellect is generated with the generated body and corrupted with the corrupted body and, since there is no difference of intellect in diverse human beings except the possible [intellect] [r] because the agent [intellect] is one, what [s] remains of the intellect from all human beings after death is [t] one in number, namely the agent intellect. And this is heretical in the extreme because in this way reward of those deserving after death would be abolished.

[Avicenna]

[H] For this reason there is the third opinion belonging to Avicenna, who holds the possible intellect to be diverse in diverse individuals, to be founded upon the essence of the rational soul and not to be a bodily power, to begin to exist with the body [u] but not to come to an end with the body [20]. Hence, with respect to the possible intellect, his opinion is what we hold according to the Catholic faith, although he errs with others concerning the agent intellect, as was said.

[Theophrastus and Themistius]

[I] Among those who hold the possible intellect to be one for all [human beings], there is a twofold opinion [v]. One is that of Themistius and Theophrastus, as the Commentator [Averroes] attributes to them in his *Commentary* on book 3 of the *De Anima*. For they say that even [w] the intellect in a positive disposition, which is the third, is one in all [human

(q) Et preterea; M: Praeterea (r) nisi possibilis in diversis hominbus; M: in diversis hominibus nisi intellectus possibilis (s) quod; M: sequeretur quod (t) est; M: esset (u) cum; M: et cum (v) est duplex; M: duplex est (w) quod etiam; M: quod

19. The account of Ibn Bajjah/Avempace provided by Aquinas is based solely on Averroes. See *LCDA*, 397, 404, 406, 412, 487.

20. AVICENNA, *De Anima* 5.3-4.

beings] and eternal and [that] it is, as it were, composed of the agent intellect and the possible [intellect] such that the agent intellect is as its form and, through the conjoining of the possible intellect, the agent intellect is also conjoined with us[x]. [This occurs] in such a way that the agent intellect is of the substance of the theoretical intellect which also is called the intellect in a positive disposition through which we understand. They indicate as a sign of this sort of thing that that action of the intellect which is in our power pertains to the intellect in a positive disposition. Therefore, since to abstract species from phantasms is in our power, it is necessary that the agent intellect belong to the intellect in a positive disposition as its form. They are led to this position because[y], since they wish[z] on the basis of the demonstration of Aristotle to hold the possible intellect to be one in all [human beings] because [the possible intellect] is not a determinate particular nor a power in a body and consequently[a] is eternal. And, further[b], the agent intellect is likewise eternal according to them[c], and it is impossible for the effect to be generable and corruptible if the agent and recipient are eternal. [Hence,] they asserted[d] that the understood species are[e] eternal. For this reason it does not happen[f] that, in virtue of the fact that new intelligible species which were not before come into being, sometimes the intellect understands and sometimes it does not. Rather [this intermittent understanding happens] from the conjunction of the agent intellect with the possible [intellect], according to which[g] it is conjoined to us[h] through its impression[21].

[Averroes Refutation of Theophrastus and Themistius]

[J] But the Commentator also refutes[i] this opinion[j]. [This is] because it would follow that the forms of natural things which are understood would exist from eternity without matter and outside the soul. Due to that those species are not placed in the possible intellect as its form because the form of the possible intellect is asserted by them to be the agent intellect. Since[k] the ultimate perfection of human beings is according to the intellect in a positive disposition and the first [perfection] according to possible

(x) nobiscum; M: in nobis (y) quia, cum; M: qui (z) velint; M: volunt (a) per consequens; M: per consequens quod (b) et iterum; M: et dicunt iterum quod (c) eternus secundum eos; M: aeternus (d) posuerunt; M: Unde posuerunt (e) sint; M: sunt (f) contingat; M: contingit (g) quem; M: quod (h) nobis; M: in nobis (i) reprobat; M: improbat ubi supra (j) opinionem etiam; M: opinionem (k) cum; M: quod cum

21. This account of Theophrastus and Themistius provided by Aquinas is based solely on Averroes. See *LCDA*, 389-92, 406, 432-33, 448, 487.

intellect, it would also follow that one human being would not differ from another human being, neither according to ultimate perfection nor according to first [perfection] [l]. Thus, there would be one being and one operation for all human beings, which is impossible.

[Averroes]

[K] For this reason he himself held another way, that the agent intellect as well as the possible [m] [intellect] is eternal and is one [n] in all [human beings], but the intelligible species are not eternal [22]. He also holds that the agent intellect is not related to the possible [intellect] as its form but as a craftsman to matter and [that] the understood species abstracted from phantasms are as form of the possible intellect [and that] from the two of these there comes to be the intellect in a positive disposition [23].

[Aquinas's Refutation of Averroes]

[L] In virtue of this position he tried to escape all the impossible things which occurred for Themistius. First because [o] he shows that, if the agent intellect [p] is eternal and the recipient eternal, namely the possible intellect, it is not necessary that they, namely the intelligible species, be made [q] eternal [24]. For the visible species has a twofold subject: one in which it has spiritual being, namely vision, and one in which it has material being, namely a colored body. Similarly, the intelligible species also has a twofold subject: one in which it has material being, namely the very phantasms which are in the imagination [r], and according to this being those species are not eternal; and another [s] [subject] in which it has immaterial being, namely the possible intellect, and according to this subject they do not have the characteristic of being generable and corruptible [25]. But that seems to be no response [at all]. For, as the species of color which is in the wall and which is in the eye is not the same in number, so too [t] the species

(l) neque primam perfectionem neque secundum ultimam; M: neque ultimam perfectionem, neque secundum primam (m) etiam possibilis; M: possibilis (n) est unus; M: unus (o) quia; M: quidem (p) si agens intellectus; M: quod si intellectus agens (q) facta sunt eterna; M: formae sint aeternae (r) ymaginatione; M: ymagine (s) aliud in; M: aliud est in (t) ita etiam non; M: ita non

22. AVERROES, *LCDA*, 406-7.
23. AVERROES, *LCDA*, 438-39. Aquinas misunderstands Averroes here.
24. AVERROES, *LCDA*, 497-501.
25. AVERROES, *LCDA*, 400-401, 500-502.

which is in the imagination and in the possible intellect are not the same in number. Hence, it still remains that that species which is in the possible intellect has one subject only which is eternal and in such a way that [that species] is itself eternal only [u] and what is generable and corruptible in the imagination is different in number. [This is so] unless perhaps he says [v] that [the species] are eternal absolutely but not by reference to a [particular human being] [w] in whom the phantasms – the likenesses of which are present in the possible intellect – do not exist from eternity. But nevertheless, since no phantasms are eternal, it still would follow that those species which are in the possible intellect from eternity would not have been abstracted from some phantasms, and this is contrary to the intention and words of the Philosopher.

[M] Secondly, however, he tries to show that from this position it does not follow that there is one being and one operation [x] belonging to all human beings, according to which all are equally wise [y]. For he says, the understood species is related to the possible intellect in some way as form to matter and because of that somehow one complete thing is made from them. [Consequently, in this the possible intellect's] conjunction with us is through that which is formal in the mentioned conjunction, namely, through the understood species, which he says is the phantasm in us as one subject and the possible intellect itself as the other [z] [subject]. Hence, since diverse phantasms are in diverse [human beings], the possible intellect is conjoined to diverse human beings with a diverse conjunction. On the basis of this human beings have diverse being [a]. Also on the basis of this one knows and another is ignorant. [This is] because [the possible intellect] is conjoined to one [human being] according to one understood species without being conjoined to another according to that [same species]. Still, there are certain understood [things] [b] such as the first conceptions of the intellect by which [c] it is conjoined to all human beings, [concepts] which the possible intellect is never deprived of, with [the understanding that] human beings exist from eternity, as he says. Hence, however much of the intellect that is in us he concludes is in a way corruptible and in a way incorruptible [d]. [This is] because for that part in virtue of which it is

(u) unum subiectum tantum quod est eternum, et ita quod ipsa sit eterna tantum; M: unum subjectum tantum (v) dicat; M: dicatur (w) hunc; M: eum (x) operatio una; M: una operatio (y) sapientes; M: facientes (z) et aliud ipsum; M: et ad ipsum (a) diversum esse; M: esse diversum (b) intellecta; M: intentiones intellectae (c) que; M: quas (d) incorruptibile; M: est incorruptibile

multiplied, namely[e] the phantasm, corruption occurs; but for the part in virtue of which it is a unity, namely on the part of the possible intellect[f], there is incorruptibility. Hence, it follows also from this that there would remain no diversity of souls after the corruption of bodies.

[N] But this response[g] is shown to be frivolous in many ways. First, [it is frivolous] because, as was said, the species which is the form of the possible intellect is not the same in number in the phantasm as[h] in the subject. Rather, it is a likeness of that. Hence, it follows that the possible intellect[i] is in no way conjoined with us, and so we will not understand through it. Second, [it is frivolous] because the conjunction of the possible intellect[j] with the understood species is through an operation of intellect pertaining to second perfection. Hence, it is impossible that his first perfection and substantial being be acquired by a human being through such a conjunction. In this way, since a human being has intellect from such a conjunction as they say, a human being would not be a human being in a determinate species insofar as [the human being] has intellect[26]. [This is] because[k] that medium, namely the understood species, is conjoined with both of the extremes by the mode of an accident to a subject, namely with the imaginative power and with the possible intellect. [But] this is also[l] contrary to [what] the Philosopher [writes] at *Metaphysics* 8[27], where he shows[m] that the soul is united to the body without anything intermediate and also without any mediating knowledge, as Lycophron said. That position seems to return to the one [of Lycrophon]. Third, [it is frivolous] because the operation does not come forth from the object but from potency, for the visible thing does not see but rather vision [does]. If, therefore, the intellect is conjoined with us only through the fact that the understood species in some way has a subject in us, it follows that this human being, namely Socrates, does not understand but rather that the separate intellect understands these things which [a human being]

(e) multiplicatur, scilicet fantasmatum; M: multiplicantur phantasmata (f) ex parte illa unde est unitas, scilicet ex parte intellectus possibilis; M: ex parte intellectus possibilis (g) responsio; M: ratio (h) ut; M: et (i) intellectus possibilis; M: intellectus (j) intellectus possibilis; M: intellectus (k) istud; M: illud (l) est etiam; M: est (m) ubi ostendit; M: ubi dicit

26. That is, if a human being only comes to have intellect after sense experience, image formation, and conjunction with separate intellect, then human beings are not essentially rational animals at birth and throughout early childhood and do not have the power of intellect per se but only acquire it later in life.

27. ARISTOTLE, *Metaphysics* 8, 1045a8-12.

imagines. And it is not difficult to adduce many other absurd things [from the position of Averroes].

[Aquinas]

[O] For this reason, when all the errors mentioned have been set aside, I say with Avicenna that the possible intellect begins to exist [n], but does not go out of existence with the body, that it is diverse in diverse [human beings], and that it is multiplied according to the division of matter in diverse individuals, just as other substantial forms. And I also add that the agent intellect [o] is diverse in diverse [human beings], for it does not seem likely that in the rational soul there does not exist some principle which [p] can fulfill a natural operation. That follows if there is held to be one agent intellect, be it called God or [q] intelligence. Nor again do I say these two [r], the agent intellect [s] and the possible [intellect], are one power named in diverse ways due to diverse operations. [This is] because [when] any given actions are reduced to contrary principles, it is impossible to reduce them to the same [t] power. On the basis of this memory is distinguished from sense because receiving species of sensibles which belongs to sense and retaining [them] which belongs to memory are reduced to contrary principles also in bodily things [u], namely dampness and dryness. Therefore, since receiving understood species which belongs to the possible intellect and making them intelligibles in act which belongs to the agent intellect cannot [both] come together in the same thing, but receiving belongs to some thing insofar as it is in potency and making [belongs to something] insofar as it is in act, then it is impossible that the agent [intellect] and the possible [intellect] not be diverse powers.

[P] But how [the possible intellect and the agent intellect] could be rooted in one substance is difficult to see. For it does not seem that it could belong to one substance both to be in potency with respect to all intelligible forms which is the possible intellect and to be in act [v] with respect to all those [intelligible forms] which is the agent intellect. [But were it] otherwise, it could not make all intelligible forms, since nothing acts except insofar as it is in act. But, nevertheless, it should be known that it is not unacceptable that there be some two things each of which is in potency with respect to the other in diverse ways, as fire is in potency cold which

(n) esse; M: esse in corpore (o) intellectum etiam agentem; M: etiam intellectum agentem (p) quod; M: quo (q) sive; M: vel (r) duo; M: duo, scilicet (s) intellectum; M: scilicet intellectum (t) eandem; M: eamdem (u) corporalibus; M: corporibus (v) esse in actu; M: esse actu

belongs to water in act, and water is in potency hot [w], which is in act in fire. Hence, [both] act and are acted upon with respect to one another. I say that the sensible thing is related to the intellective soul similarly. For the sensible thing is intelligible in potency and has a nature distinct in act. Yet there is in the soul an intellectual light in act. But the determination of knowing with respect to this or that nature is there [x] in potency, as the pupil is in potency with respect to this or that color [y]. For this reason the soul has a power [z] by which it makes sensible species to be intelligible [species] in act, and this power is the agent intellect. And [the soul] has a power by which it is in potency for being made in the act of determinate knowing brought about by a sensible thing's species made intelligible in act [a], and this power or potency is called possible intellect. Upon the operations of these two powers follows all our understanding, both of principles as well as of conclusions. Hence what some say appears to be false, [namely] that the agent intellect is a disposition of principles [28].

[Responses to objections:]

1. Therefore to the first it should be said that the intellect is not denied to be a material form, so that [b] it might be prevented from giving being to matter as substantial form with reference to first being. For this reason it is necessary that the multiplication of the intellect, that is, of the intellective soul, follow upon the division [c] of matter which causes diverse individuals. But this is said [d] with respect to its second act which is an operation. [This is] because understanding does not take place by means of a mediating bodily organ. This occurs because an operation proceeds from the essence of the soul only through its mediating power or potency. Hence, since it has certain powers which are not acts of certain [e] organs of the body, it is necessary that certain operations of the soul are not through a mediating body.

2. To the second it should be said that, whenever two things which are such that one is more powerful than another are joined and one draws the other to itself, one has some power beyond that which is subject to it.

(w) potentia calidum; M: in potentia calida (x) est ibi; M: est (y) huius coloris vel illius; M: hujus vel illius coloris (z) habet virtutem: M: virtutem habet (a) facta intelligibili in actu; M: factae intelligibilis actu (b) quin; M: cum (c) divisionem; M: ad divisionem (d) hoc dicitur; M: dicitur immaterialis (e) vires que non sunt actus quorundam; M: virtutes quae non sunt aliquorum

28. Here Aquinas is following AVERROES, *LCDA*, 496.

[This] is clear in regard to a flame, because fire, overcoming the vapor to which it is conjoined, has the power of illuminating and the action of the enflamed vapor can extend itself by making heat in addition to that [illuminating]. Since, therefore, in the conjunction of form to matter the form is found controlling, the more noble and the more controlling of the matter the form will be [f], the more it will be able have a power exceeding the condition of matter. Hence, beyond the active and passive qualities which they themselves hold on the basis of matter, certain mixed bodies have certain powers which follow upon the species, such as that the magnet attracts iron. This is even [evidently] more found in plants, as it is clear in growth which is controlled by the power of soul, which could not be through the power of fire, as is said in *De Anima* 2 [29]. This is found still [g] more to be the case in animals because sensing is in every way above the power of the elemental qualities and [is found] most perfectly in the rational soul which is the most noble of forms. For this reason [the soul] has certain powers in which it does not share with the body at all and certain [powers] which it does share [with the body].

3. To the third it should be said that, according to Avicenna, the understood species can be considered in two ways, either with respect to the being that it has in the intellect, and in this way it has singular being, or with respect to the fact that it is a likeness of such an understood thing, to the extent that it leads to the knowledge of it, and on the basis of this part it has universality [30]. [This is] because it is not a likeness of this thing insofar as it is this thing [h] but rather according to the nature in which it agrees with

(f) erit; M: est (g) adhuc; M: hoc adhuc (h) est hec res; M: haec res est

29. ARISTOTLE, *De Anima* 2.4, 416a10-19.

30. Here Aquinas follows AVICENNA, *Liber de Philosophia Prima* V, 1, ed. S. Van Riet, 238: "Haec autem forma, quamvis respectu individuorum sit universalis, tamen, respectu animae singularis in qua imprimitur, est individua; ipsa enim est una ex formis quae sunt in intellectu, et quia singulae animae sunt multae numero, tunc eo modo quo sunt particulares habebunt ipsae aliud intellectum universale". See also AVICENNA, *The Metaphysics of the Healing*, M. E. Marmura tr., Provo, 2005, 157: "This form, although a universal in relation to individuals, is an individual in relation to the particular soul in which it is imprinted, being one of the forms of the mind. And, because individual souls are numerically many, it is possible for this universal form to be numerically many from the aspect that it is individual." As Van Riet notes, the Latin suffers from an omission here. Still, Aquinas is able to take from this passage the view of Avicenna that the universal is received in a plurality of individual human souls or intellects without losing its nature as an intelligible.

others of its species[31]. Nor is it necessary that every singular being be intelligible in potency alone, as is clear concerning separate substances[32]. But [it is necessary] in regard to those which are individuated by matter, as are bodies. But that species is individuated[i] through the individuation of the intellect and, consequently, it does not lose[j] intelligible being in act. [This is] just as I understand that I understand, although my understanding is a certain singular operation. It is also evident in itself that the second unacceptable consequence does not follow, because the mode of

(i) illa individuatur; M: istae individuantur (j) perdit; M: perdunt

31. This is Aquinas's own novel teaching on intelligible species according to which the intellect apprehends the natures of things in the world. The source of this is surely Avicenna, though Avicenna himself holds the very different position that the source of intelligibles in act is the Agent Intellect. The Latin AVICENNA, *Philosophia Prima* V, 2, ed. S. Van Riet, 211, has: "Cum ergo dicimus quod natura universalis habet esse in his sensibilibus, non intelligimus quod ex hoc quod est universalis, scilicet secundum hunc modum universalitatis, sed intelligimus quod natura cui accidit universalitas habet esse in istis signatis". AVICENNA, *The Metaphysics of the Healing*, 5.2, M. E. Marmura tr., 161: "If we then say that the universal nature exists in external things, we do not mean in asmuch as it is universal in this mode of universality; rather, we mean that the nature to which universality occurs exists in things external [to the mind]".

32. Aquinas follows the reasoning of Avicenna regarding the knowledge existing in separate substances to establish the notion that intelligibles received into an immaterial substance are not contracted to particularity. The source for this is AVICENNA, *Philosophia Prima* V, 2, ed. S. Van Riet, 238: "Ergo haec forma est quae acquiritur de exspoliatione animalitatis a qualibet imaginatione individuali accepta de esse extrinseco, quamvis ipsa non habeat esse extrinseco, sed imaginatio abstrahit eam. Haec autem forma, quamvis respectu individuorum sit universalis, tamen, respectu animae singularis in qua imprimitur, est individua; ipsa enim est una ex formis quae sunt in intellectu, et quia singulae animae sunt multae numero, tunc eo modo quo sunt particulares habebunt ipsae aliud intellectum universale, quod in tali comparatione est ad ipsas in quali est ad extra, et discernitur in anima ab hac forma quae est universalis comparatione sui ad extra quae praedicatur de illis et de aliis". AVICENNA, *The Metaphysics of the Healing*, 5.1, M. E. Marmura tr., 156-157: "This form is what is realized as a result of abstracting animality from any particular image, taken either from an external existent or from something that plays the role of an external existent-even if it itself does not exist externally but [is something] the imagination invents. This form, although a universal in relation to individuals, is an individual in relation to the particular soul in which it is imprinted, being one of the forms in the mind. And, because individual souls are numerically many, it is possible for this universal form to be numerically many from the aspect that it is individual. There would be another universal intelligible for it, standing in relation to it, as it stands in relation to what is external. [The universal intelligible] differs in the soul from this form that is universal with reference to what is external in that it is predicable of [itself] and of another".

individuation through intellect is [k] other than [the mode of individuation] through prime matter [33].

4. To the fourth it should be said that, as the Commentator also says in his *Commentary* on book 3 of the *De Anima* [34], it is not necessary that what is receptive of some things be deprived of any determinate nature but that it be free of the nature of what are received, as the pupil [is free] of the nature of colors. For this reason it is necessary that the possible intellect have a determinate nature. But before the understanding which is through the reception of species it does not have in its nature any of these things which it receives from sensibles. This is because it is said that "it is none of these things which are", etc. [35].

5. To the fifth it should be said that, although the soul does not have matter as a part of itself by which it exists, nevertheless it has matter in which it exists as [the matter's] perfection. With the division [of matter] [l] [the soul] is multiplied in number and not in species. However, it is otherwise in the case of those immaterial substances which do not also have matter for which they are the forms. [This is] because in these there

(k) modus est individuationis per intellectum; M: individuationis modus est per intellectum (l) ad cuius divisionem; M: ad ejus enim divisionem

33. Note that Aquinas has changed the terms of the debate here. For Averroes the issue under consideration is the intellectual understanding of intelligibles in act which makes universal knowledge possible. Arguing on the basis of the intellectual understanding had by an immaterial intelligence or separate substance as pure form for whom intellectual understanding of its own essence is necessarily immediate (insofar as it is per se intelligible and intelligent), Aquinas asserts that a human being's awareness and understanding of one's own activity of understanding is of the same sort. However, that does not follow due to equivocation, as Aquinas later makes clear in a more sophisticated discussion of the issue in his *De Veritate* q. 10, a. 8. There he distinguishes under the influence of Augustine the immediate self-awareness of its essence and operations by the human soul from the understanding or knowledge gained through apprehension of intelligibles in act for knowledge of universals. Here in the *Commentary on the Sentences* Aquinas argues from the notion of individual separate intelligences having immediate self-understanding that the term 'understanding' need not be confined to intellectual understanding of the quiddities of things as universals but can also suitably be used of individual acts of awareness. If that use is not equivocal but univocal, then Aquinas can argue there are individual acts of intellectual understanding that take place in individual human intellects. This would then refute the notion that there can be only one intellect (agent intellect, possible intellect, or both) for all human beings.

34. AVERROES, *LCDA*, 410. Also see 385-86.

35. ARISTOTLE, *De Anima*, 3.4, 429a21-24.

can be no material multiplication [m] but only formal [multiplication] which brings about the diversity of species.

(m) multiplicatio materialis; M: materialis multiplicatio

BIOS

Bernardo Carlos BAZÁN, Ph.D. in Philosophy (1967); Ph.D. in Medieval Studies (1972), both granted by Université Catholique de Louvain; Fellow of the Royal Society of Canada (Académie des arts, des lettres et des sciences humaines). Field of expertise: 13th Century Psychology and Philosophical Anthropology.

Deborah BLACK is Professor of Philosophy and Medieval Studies at the University of Toronto. She works on Classical Arabic philosophy and on its impact on the West, with a focus on issues in epistemology and cognitive psychology, in particular medieval theories of the imagination and the internal senses.

Jean-Baptiste BRENET, Professeur à l'Université de Paris I-Panthéon Sorbonne (UMR 7219, Sphère) où il enseigne l'histoire des philosophies médiévales arabe et latine.

Thérèse-Anne DRUART is Ordinary Professor at The School of Philosophy, The Catholic University of America, Washington, DC. She specializes in Arabic Philosophy for which she prepares an annual bibliography. Currently she is the President of Société Internationale d'Histoire des Sciences et de la Philosophie Arabe et Islamique.

Alexander FIDORA holds a Research Professorship at the Institució Catalana de Recerca i Estudis Avançats (ICREA) in the Department of Ancient and Medieval Studies of the Universitat Autònoma de Barcelona and is Executive Director of the Institut d'Estudis Medievals of the UAB.

Jeremiah HACKETT is Professor of Philosophy at the University of South Carolina, Columbia. He continues to work on Roger Bacon and also on 14th century Mysticism in Germany.

Jon McGINNIS is Professor of classical and medieval philosophy at the University of Missouri, St. Louis. His general research interest is in the history of natural philosophy done within the Aristotelian tradition, with a particular focus on the medieval Arabic-speaking world.

Luis Xavier LÓPEZ-FARJEAT is Professor of Philosophy at Universidad Panamericana in Mexico City and has been resident member at the Center of Theological Inquiry at Princeton. He works on Classical Arabic Philosophy.

Richard C. TAYLOR is Professor of Philosophy at Marquette University, Milwaukee, and member of the De Wulf Mansion Centre for Ancient, Medieval and Renaissance Philosophy at the Katholieke Universiteit Leuven, Belgium.

Jörg Alejandro TELLKAMP is Professor of Philosophy at the Autonomous Metropolitan University in Mexico City being his fields of research 13th century theories of the soul and knowledge and also 16th century Spanish Scholasticism.

INDEX

ANCIENT AND MEDIEVAL

INDEX

CONTEMPORARY

Imprimé sur les presses de Jouve - Mayenne
2074653U - dépôt légal : mars 2013 - date d'impression : Mars 2013